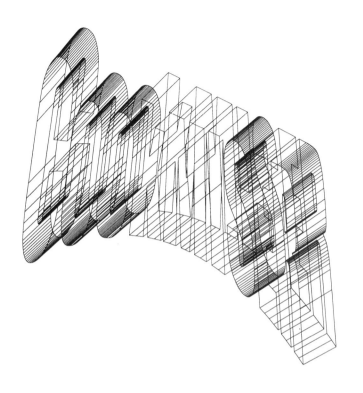

R.J. Lavigne

Scrypt Publishing

CookMISER
By R.J. Lavigne

Published by:

Scrypt Publishing
Post Office Box 624
Snowdon Station
Montreal, Quebec
(Canada) H3X 3X8

Canadian Cataloguing in Publication Data

Lavigne, Robert, 1956-
   Cookmiser

Includes index.
ISBN 0-9684112-0-7

   1. Low budget cookery. I. Title. II Title: Cookmiser

TX714.L38 1998   **641.5'22**   **C98-900894-0**

Copyright © 1998 by Robert Lavigne

First Printing, Spring of 2000

Editor: R.J. Lavigne
Photographs: «IMSI's MasterClips® and MasterPhotos™ Premium Image Collection » & «HEMERA Photo Objects Premium Image Collection»
Clipart: «IMSI's MasterClips® and MasterPhotos™ Premium Image Collection » & « (c) 1995 Softkey International Inc. »
Cover and book design by Geco Products
Special illustrations by R.J. Lavigne

This book is distributed to the book trade by Scrypt Publishing, Post Office Box 624, Snowdon Station, Montreal, Quebec (Canada) H3X 3X8. Individuals may order this book from bookstores or directly from Scrypt Publishing. Please include $3.00CAN/ $2.00US for postage and handling (in addition to the price of book(s) plus taxes) with mail orders.

Printed in Canada

Warning-Disclaimer

This book is intended as to provide information in regard to the subject matter covered. It is sold with the understanding that the publisher and author are not in any way engaged in rendering professional consulting services. Should culinary, nutritional, or other expert assistance be required, the services of competent professionals should be sought.

Every effort has been made to make this book as complete and accurate as is possible and practical. However, there *may be mistakes* both typographical and in content. Therefore, this text should be used only as a general guide and a step in the right direction. It should not be used or viewed as a perfect source of information.

The purpose of this book is to help, educate and entertain. The author and publisher shall have neither liability nor responsibility to any person or entity with respect to any loss or damage, or alleged to be cause, directly or indirectly by the information contained in this book.

If you do not wish to be bound by the above, you may return this book in its entirety with proof of purchase to the publisher for a full refund.

CONTENTS

CookMISER

"Preserve a good constitution of body and mind. To this a spare diet contributes much. Have wholesome, but no costly food."

William Penn
Some Fruits of Solitude, 1693

INTRODUCTION

CookMISER was conceived, researched and written with several goals in mind. The predominant ones were about acquiring optimal savings in money, time and effort when cooking. The resulting book came from taking an in-depth look at an activity we engage in three times a day. Cooking consumes a large portion of our savings and takes up tens of thousands of hours over a lifetime.

In this book, you will find a substantial collection of tasty everyday cooking style recipes that are based on classic and sometimes unusual combinations of vegetables, fruits, rice, pasta, grains, meat, poultry, fish, and legumes. The recipes were arranged, formulated and organized for the widest possible appeal in taste, eating habits and lifestyle. Moreover, that's true whether you consume meat, are vegetarian, or enjoy fast foods.

Many of the recipes in this book were inspired from various parts of the globe, despite being economical and time-saving, present a truly international flavor to its users. With over twenty chapters of recipes to choose from, your traveling taste bags will be enchanted. They offer choices ranging from exotic Middle Eastern cuisine to spicy Mexican or more traditional American favorites. They range from speedy main dishes to sensational desserts and pies. Whether the recipes are for New York style pizzas or bagels, French-style Bourbonnaise cabbage soup, or Moroccan tabouli or couscous grain dishes, they are sure to please.

CookMISER has close to 700 recipes, and if we include the sub-variations and suggestions, and this can amount to tens of thousands of recipe possibilities. Written in a condensed-style with step by step directions, this book was designed for the modern city dweller on the go and on a very strict budget for whatever reasons. No other book in this category goes this far and achieves such results. It doesn't ask of you that you, grow a vegetable garden, spend your days bargain hunting and saving coupons, or pick up road-kills on your way home from work. All we ask is that you shop for groceries in a specific way, at a particular kind of large supermarket, a few times a month. That you organize, prepare and cook your meals according to numerous yet simple guidelines. In addition, meals assembled from them along the sample menu guidelines can be quickly prepared for pennies instead of dollars.

This book is a must buy whether you're a young professional or professional couple on a strict budget for whatever reason(s). Whether you have a family of four or more struggling weekly to make ends meet...whether you're unemployed having a hard time making it through the month...whether you just like to cook and explore new culinary concepts. Moreover, this book can help you learn the basics of cooking. It can save up to 90% of your food bill. Allow you to discover new and interesting dishes and send your taste buys traveling around the world.

In the **CookMISER**, you will also find out how to make, for as little money possible and in as little time possible, many popular foods. Make a few varieties of cheesecakes complete with quick crust and a stretched fruit pie filling that can double as low-cost dessert topping. Bake mouth-watering yet very inexpensive pizza the professional way. Incidentally, the chapter on pizzas allows for hundreds of combinations. Bake bagels, dinner rolls and flat breads in 15 to 45 minutes using homemade refrigerated dough earlier thawed from freezer. This *always-ready* refrigerator dough allows you to turn your kitchen into an almost instant yet efficient bakery. Prepare countless meat-spreads, liver paté and sandwich fillings. Make yogurt, sour milk and buttermilk from bulk instant skim milk powder. Make your own cheeses for savoring or cook with, many of which are very expensive when purchased at supermarkets. Make your own tofu quickly from bulk soybeans. This tofu is very inexpensive, contains complete proteins and is used extensively throughout the book for those reasons. With your blender, make raw fruit or vegetable juices for less than one tenth the cost of a making it with a juicer. Your blender can also grate certain vegetables like cabbage in seconds. Make great tasting muffins, cookies, desserts, soups, salads, casseroles, stews cheaply and quickly too, and much, much more!

Some food technology and effort-saving techniques adapted from those used by mass food manufacturers were incorporated whenever applicable. This allows you to make cakes from scratch almost as easily as cake mixes. Make freshly baked bread within the hour. Bake cookies that are comparable to commercial ones, with a high yield and volume very quickly and cheaply. Whenever possible, the one-mixing bowl and one-pan cooking method*s were* used to save you dish washing labor.

In conclusion, the **CookMISER** utilizes certain concepts and food-stretching techniques to increase recipe yield, reduce the cost of cooking and save money. It includes hundreds of built-in money-saving ideas and cuts prices everywhere possible. Before applying these money-saving techniques, you must be able to buy your basic ingredients inexpensively. This is where the miserly grocery shopping information comes in. All these ideas and methods combined, allow you to quickly make these food products at home, from inexpensive ingredients, cuts prices fifty to ninety-percent. *No more food banks?*

Our recipes, range from fair to blue ribbon, most are definitely decent...you be the judge. Planning your meals from such an assortment of recipes will ensure that your family eats well-balanced and nutritious meals made with food elements that are basic, wholesome and fun to cook. Most importantly, literally made for pennies and often made in minutes.

HOW & WHY THIS BOOK WORKS

As mentioned in the introduction, the aim of this book is to provide its readers with information from which very inexpensive meals can be quickly prepared and yet supply a more than adequate nutrition. How these things are accomplished takes longer to explain. It might be easier to explain if the question is divided into three parts. Which is to saving money, time, and supply adequate nutrition.

First, how does the information in the **CookMISER** save you money? We're not talking about 10% savings, but closer to 90% savings when the **CookMISER** system is fully applied. Perhaps our first concern, when grocery shopping, should be total avoidance of readymade or prepared foods. In a way, store-bought readymade foods are nothing more than nicely packaged leftovers. They usually lack freshness, moisture and flavor. Because they are convenient and save you time, the **CookMISER** compensates for that lost as much as and in as many ways as possible.

Further substantial savings *(and added convenience)* are obtained by grocery shopping at very large supermarkets or even larger mega-size supermarkets. You usually get everything you need *(or almost)* at these supermarkets. Apart from having 99% of what you need with the possible exception(s) of soy flour, sausage casings, ascorbic acid, etc. They also carry the right formats for decent savings without going overboard on very large format sizes *(as purchased by restaurants at suppliers)*. We do not recommend the club-type warehouse stores that sell just about anything. The type of groceries they specialize in are mostly readymade and prepared foods sold in quantity packs.

This brings us to the next three money saving considerations. They are selective purchasing, brand and especially format discrimination. While it is obvious that selective purchasing would save us money, what we mean is that certain food items, leaving aside brands and formats for now, are just too expensive. The small caloric and nutritional value they offer does justify their high price by **CookMISER** standards. For example, most fruits and vegetables are off limits because they are seasonal and when out of season are just too pricey. That does not apply to year-round inexpensive staples like carrots, yellow onions, cabbage, celery, potatoes, and regional fruit(s). They are somewhat seasonal too but far more affordable and useful year-round. These staples when teamed with legumes, whole grains and sprouts supply a more than adequate nutrition. Peak season harvests become the exception when most of these unaffordable fresh produces become somewhat inexpensive. Selective purchasing applies to any food item, that according to our standards, don't even come close to being affordable.

By brand discrimination, it is meant, that any brand of acceptable quality may be purchased as long that it's the least expensive one. Whether it's the store's own brand, a generic brand, or a big name brand, you pick the lowest priced one(s) *(in the recommended formats)* and that's all there is to it.

By format discrimination, we mean, buy the largest format that's practical for you. Some of the great savings promised would not happen if you take a commonly used ingredient like flour and buy it in a small package instead of large sacs or bags. In other cases, like certain occasionally used legumes a couple of pounds (a kilo) will suffice. See the chapter entitled *Miserly Grocery Shopping* for more on selective purchasing and formats. Expensive food items such as mushrooms, milk powder, homemade cheese and yogurt, dried raisins are used throughout the book in recipes but in small quantities. They are utilized only to add or give flavor texture and quality to the various dish recipes. They should not be eaten alone as snacks, desserts, or with a dish. You would be amazed to know how far two or three average size mushrooms can go to adding flavor to an extra-large all-dressed pizza when very thinly sliced. On the other hand, how far 1 or 2 tablespoon(s)/15-30 ml of dried raisins will go in a typical muffin, cake or cookie recipe. The **CookMISER** also contains numerous booster and stretcher recipes. Boosters are mostly used with minced meat, in the form of patties or burgers, meatballs, meatloaves, meat spreads and sandwich fillings. As for stretcher recipes, they generally apply to expensive food items like cheese and pie fillings. It incorporates massive built-in recipe *(both ingredients and procedures)* manipulations and modifications *(as compared to standard recipes)*. This means traditional, classic and non-classic recipes usually have some of their ingredients and cooking technique changed *(or substituted)* and manipulated to bring it in the proper price range, which in the case of this book is very, very low. With the tasty and fun addition of sprouts make from dried legumes, whole grains and seeds, you get a year-round inexpensive vitamin and flavor boost.

CookMISER does not recommend or employ the use of costly canning, bottling, or fancy food processing and storage techniques. All recipes and techniques described therein require but only simple and basic kitchen appliances, equipment, utensils and hand tools. See chapter entitled *Before Starting* for more on that.

Secondly, lets address the question of how does the information in the **CookMISER** allow its user(s) to save time. An enormous amount of time is saved by periodically preparing certain long to cook ingredients ahead of time. Rice, potatoes and dried legumes are typically amongst those ingredients. They are precooked and placed in sealed plastic containers or bags, and stored in freezer or refrigerator until needed. See the chapters entitled *Preparation is the Key* and *Before Starting* for more elaborate explanations.

A lot of time can be saved when you freeze your cooked and baked recipes. If you don't mind that type of leftover and you have a microwave, speedy and very inexpensive frozen dinners might turn out advantageous for you. Many casseroles, stovetop, rice, and sides dishes freeze, thaw and reheat well. They retain most properties, like their texture, firmness and taste. Though a microwave is useful for re-heating meals, it is by no means necessary. When thawed, most frozen dishes *(homemade dinners)* reheat well in a frying pan with a little water.

Medium and large batch cooking or baking can be used with many of our recipes and is strongly recommended for families, parties or those with large freezers. Increased batch cooking simple means multiplying by a factor of lets say, 4 or 8 the quantities indicated for any given recipe. Larger mixing bowls and numerous (or larger) pans will be required and should be taken into consideration ahead of time. This technique is a natural for bread making and recipes that will be frozen.

This book uses a lot of applied physics and some chemistry, with its built-in *(concept-oriented)* structure that saves time. Valuable seconds and sometimes minutes are gained whenever possible. For example, filling large but shallow baking pans with thinner than usual batter reduces baking time considerably. The savings in minutes depend on the oven's temperature, how much water is in the batter, the thickness of the batter, the position of the pan in the oven, and to what capacity is the oven being used. The larger the number of cold *(or room temperature)* masses (by that is meant the pan and their contents) you place in a preheated oven, the longer they will take to bake, which is also relative to their respective positions in that oven. It is recommended that ovens be used to capacity, overcrowding must be avoided to maintain adequate ventilation. A good rule of thumb would be to keep a *two-inch clearance everywhere.* The pans should be two inches from each other, the walls on the sides of the oven and each other's top or bottom. Increasing the temperature of a pan or oven dish and its contents before placing it in the preheated oven will speed things up too. That's accomplished by using hot tap water instead of cold water in the batter. Hot tap water is recommended *only* in applications where its temperature will elevated to close to the boiling point during cooking. This is due to its higher bacterial count than cold tap water. For all other applications use cold tap water. *Please do not use hot tap water if you're not comfortable with it!*

In certain cases, this book saves you time by replacing time-consuming oven dish recipes with comparable much quicker stovetop ones. **CookMISER** *incorporates* numerous quick casserole techniques. Additional time is saved by utilizing a technique of continuous stir and fry in skillet on vegetables and meats. This is done a few minutes before placing them in final recipe. After that, the stir-fried ingredients can be placed in meatloaves or meatless loaves, casseroles, potpies, soups, etc.

Thirdly, we will show you how this book allows for a more than adequate nutrition. The fact is most fruits and vegetables in a particular group (or family) contain comparable amounts of vitamins, minerals, sugars, carbohydrates, proteins, and even enzymes. It is safe to state that if you consume one or two item(s) from each group that more that adequate nutrition will result. In addition, you will have cheap access to most of the remaining popular fruits and vegetables from though groups when they are inexpensively in their peak season. Not to be ignored, are the nutritional gains obtained from the consumption of various inexpensive whole grains and legumes. Grains such as brown rice, rolled oats, barley, and millet are some of the main ones used in recipes throughout the book which offer superior nutrition. The same applies to legumes from the three groups, beans, lentils, and peas. Wheat germ and bran are equally important and found in many recipes. They are automatically included if you use whole-wheat flour. The **CookMISER** regime *(of sorts)*, in addition, gets a potent year-round vitamin boost from sprouted seeds and dried legumes. And we get a friendly bacteria shot from homemade yogurt and buttermilk.

Concerning proteins, the **CookMISER** offer solutions for the replacement of unaffordable meat, poultry, fish and seafood protein. These animal proteins are nevertheless used in recipes but in somewhat smaller amounts than is customary. Although, the amount of protein supplied by the inclusion of these animal proteins is more than adequate for the average person, the **CookMISER** uses numerous other sources as protein supplement. These sources are vegetarian in nature and are rarely complete proteins. The only complete sources of vegetarian proteins are soybeans and nutritional yeast. Complimentary proteins that are incomplete are what the other vegetarian protein sources supply. Major sources are dried legumes, whole grains, seeds and their by-products. Dairy food and eggs contain complete proteins and are used throughout the book to compliment or complete most of the incomplete vegetarian proteins. Some nutritionists support the complete proteins per meal combination approach. Others support the theory that incomplete proteins from one meal can wait *(a few days or longer)* for a complimentary protein *(or missing amino acids)* to come along and combine into a complete and usable protein. The writer of this book supports the latter hypothesis. Billions of vegetarians or almost vegetarians across the globe that thrive on an almost vegetarian diet with a small portion of animal protein not more than once a week tend to prove our contention.

Incomplete protein combinations that yield complete proteins are as follows:

BEST COMBINATIONS		FAIR COMBINATIONS	
Whole grains_____	Legumes	Seeds_____	Milk products
Whole grains_____	Milk products	Legumes_____	Milk Products
Seeds_____	Legumes	Whole grains___	Seeds

Please Note *Whole grains also include corn meal, corn flour, couscous, and bulgar wheat which yield good amounts of incomplete proteins. Fresh vegetables yield incomplete proteins that are automatically complimented in the* **CookMISER** *recipes. Meat, poultry, eggs, fish and seafood are not included in the above combinations because they already yield complete and usable proteins.*

ALL DESIGN STRUCTURES AND CONSIDERATIONS THAT WERE POINTED OUT IN THIS CHAPTER ARE BUILT-IN AND INCORPORATED IN THIS BOOK. ALL YOU NEED TO DO IS FOLLOW DIRECTIONS AND RELAX...

MISERLY GROCERY SHOPPING

In this chapter, we are mostly concerned with grocery shopping because it is this aspect of the **CookMISER** system that account for more than half of the monetary savings. And that is the primary job of the **CookMISER**.

As mentioned in the previous chapter, we recommend that you shop at very large *(in some cases, warehouse-like)* or mega-size supermarkets. You must entirely avoid readymade or prepared foods and purchase *only* basic ingredients.

Buy your ingredients or food items in the right formats and packaging style. Be especially selective about what you purchase when it comes to fresh fruits and vegetables. That is so because they are relatively inexpensive *only* during the peak of there harvest season and sometimes its not the case. A large portion of the fresh produce is too expensive most of the year. You must rely on the inexpensive year-round staples like carrots, onions, cabbage, potatoes, regional fruits, and most of the time celery *(this may not apply in all regions of North America)*. As previously discussed, these fresh produce staples are supplemented with whole grains and dried legumes, and homegrown sprouts. Shopping for the remaining food items like meat, flour, rice, vegetable oil, spices, etc., is simpler since their prices are not or very little affected by the seasons. For the greatest savings, item and format style selection must strictly be adhered to. As for brands, always choose the least expensive, but it must be of decent quality.

Pages 18 and 19 feature the **CookMISER ESSENTIAL GROCERY SHOPPING LIST**. It's referred to on the back book cover as the **Super Economizer Grocery Shopping List** and is well deserving of the name. The list contains the ingredients from which most of the **CookMISER** recipes may be made from. The following two pages (20 and 21) feature the **CookMISER OPTIONAL GROCERY SHOPPING LIST**. Using the ingredients on the second list, most of the remaining recipes in the **CookMISER** can be made. The ingredients from that list tend to be slightly more expensive and many items are by no means necessary.

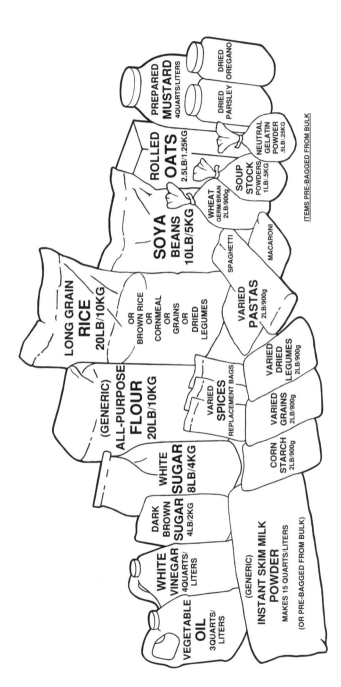

PREPARED MUSTARD 4QUARTS/LITERS

DRIED PARSLEY

DRIED OREGANO

ROLLED OATS 2.5LB/1.25KG

NEUTRAL GELATIN POWDER .5LB/.25KG

SOUP STOCK POWDERS 1LB/.5KG

WHEAT GERM/BRAN 2LB/900g

SOYA BEANS 10LB/5KG

SPAGHETTI

MACARONI

LONG GRAIN RICE 20LB/10KG

OR BROWN RICE OR CORNMEAL OR GRAINS OR DRIED LEGUMES

VARIED PASTAS 2LB/900g

(GENERIC) ALL-PURPOSE FLOUR 20LB/10KG

VARIED SPICES REPLACEMENT BAGS

VARIED DRIED LEGUMES 2LB/900g

VARIED GRAINS 2LB/900g

WHITE SUGAR 8LB/4KG

DARK BROWN SUGAR 4LB/2KG

CORN STARCH 2LB/900g

WHITE VINEGAR 4QUARTS/LITERS

(GENERIC) INSTANT SKIM MILK POWDER MAKES 15 QUARTS/LITERS

(OR PRE-BAGGED FROM BULK)

VEGETABLE OIL 3QUARTS/LITERS

ITEMS PRE-BAGGED FROM BULK

The formats & packaging styles for most of the pantry items from the SUPER ECONOMIZER GROCERY SHOPPING LIST should look a lot like this!

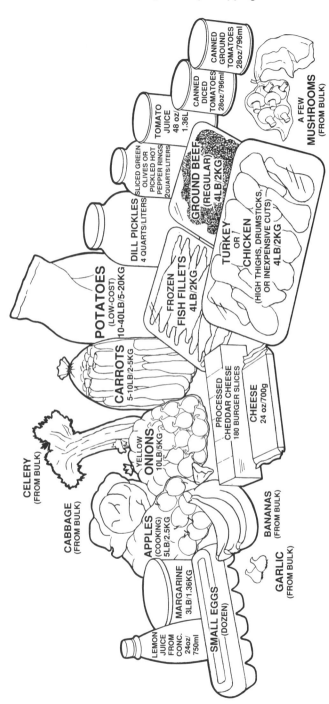

CANNED GROUND TOMATOES 28oz/796ml

CANNED DICED TOMATOES 28oz/796ml

A FEW MUSHROOMS (FROM BULK)

TOMATO JUICE 48 oz/ 1.36L

SLICED GREEN OLIVES OR PICKLED HOT PEPPER RINGS 2QUARTS/LITERS

GROUND BEEF (REGULAR) 4LB/2KG

DILL PICKLES 4 QUARTS/LITERS

TURKEY OR / CHICKEN (HIGH THIGHS, DRUMSTICKS, OR INEXPENSIVE CUTS) 4LB/2KG

POTATOES (LOW-COST) 10-40LB/5-20KG

FROZEN FISH FILLETS 4LB/2KG

CARROTS 5-10LB/2-5KG

CELERY (FROM BULK)

PROCESSED CHEDDAR CHEESE 180 BURGER SLICES

CHEESE 24 oz/700g

YELLOW ONIONS 10LB/5KG

CABBAGE (FROM BULK)

APPLES (COOKING) 5LB/2.5KG

BANANAS (FROM BULK)

GARLIC (FROM BULK)

MARGARINE 3LB/1.36KG

SMALL EGGS (DOZEN)

LEMON JUICE FROM CONC. 24oz/ 750ml

The formats & packaging styles for many of the fresh, frozen, refrigerated, and certain pantry items from the SUPER ECONOMIZER GROCERY SHOPPING LIST should look a lot like this!

ESSENTIAL GROCERY SHOPPING LIST
(Refered to as Super Economizer Grocery Shopping List on back cover)

✔	No	INGREDIENTS	SUGGESTED FORMAT
❑	1.	#All-purpose flour (bleached)	20 lb/10 kg SAC
❑	2.	#Long grain rice (parboiled)	20 lb/10 kg SAC
❑	3.	#Granulated sugar	8 lb/4 kg BAG
❑	4.	Dark brown sugar	4 lb/2kg BAG
❑	5.	Molasses	16 fl.oz./500ml CARTON
❑	6.	#Rolled oats ('1 Minute' & 'Quick')	2.5 lb/1.25 kg BOX
❑	7.	#Cornstarch	2 lb/1 kg BULK
❑	8.	Wheat germ	2 lb/1 kg BULK
❑	9.	Wheat bran	2 lb/1 kg BULK
❑	10.	Barley (pearl or pot)	2 lb/1 kg BULK
❑	11.	Couscous (medium)	2 lb/1 kg BAG
❑	12.	Bulgar wheat	2 lb/1 kg BAG
❑	13.	Yellow cornmeal (medium)	10 lb/5 kg SAC
❑	14.	Corn flour	2 lb/1 kg BAG
❑	15.	Peanuts (blanched & unsalted)	2 lb/1 kg BULK
❑	16.	#Dried soybeans	10 lb/5 kg SAC
❑	17.	Dried chick peas	2 lb/1 kg BAG
❑	18.	Dried red kidney beans	2 lb/1 kg BAG
❑	19.	Dried whole green peas	2 lb/1 kg BAG
❑	20.	Dried lima beans	2 lb/1 kg BAG
❑	21.	Dried mung beans	2 lb/1 kg BAG
❑	22.	Dried low-cost lentils	2 lb/1 kg BAG
❑	23.	Alfalfa seeds	6 oz/180 g BULK
❑	24.	Sesame seeds	.5 lb/.25 kg BULK
❑	25.	Sunflower seed kernels	1 lb/.5 kg BULK
❑	26.	#Active dry yeast	TINY JAR
❑	27.	Fresh baking yeast	2.2 lb/1 kg BLOCK
❑	28.	#Baking powder (generic)	1 lb/500g BULK
❑	29.	Baking soda (bulk)	16 oz/500g BULK
❑	30.	#Pasta(s) (varied)*	2 lb/1kg BAG
❑	31.	#Skim milk powder (instant)	(for 15 L/Q) SAC/BULK
❑	32.	#Semisweet chocolate chips	1 lb/500g BULK
❑	33.	#Chicken/beef soup stock powder	1 lb/500g BULK
❑	34.	#Sweetened flavored drink crystals	1 lb/500g BULK
❑	35.	#Table salt	2 lb/1 kg BOX
❑	36.	#White vinegar	4 quarts/liters PLASTIC CONTAINER
❑	37.	#Vegetable oil	3 quarts/liters PLASTIC CONTAINER
❑	38	Prepared mustard	4 quarts/liters PLASTIC JAR
❑	39.	Soy sauce	1 quart/liter PLASTIC BOTTLE
❑	40.	#Artificial vanilla extract	8 fl oz/240ml BOTTLE

ESSENTIAL GROCERY SHOPPING LIST *(continued)*

✔	No	INGREDIENTS	SUGGESTED FORMAT
❑	41.	#Potatoes (low-cost)_____	10-40 lb/5-20 kg BAG
❑	42.	#Carrots_____	5-10 lb/2-5 kg BAG
❑	43.	#Yellow onions_____	10 lb/5 kg BAG
❑	44.	#Green cabbage_____	AS NEEDED
❑	45.	#Garlic bulb(s)_____	AS NEEDED
❑	46.	#Celery_____	AS NEEDED
❑	47.	Mushrooms (few)_____	FROM BULK
❑	48.	#Apples (or regional fruit)_____	5 lb/2.5 kg BAG
❑	49.	#Seedless raisins_____	1 lb/.5 kg BAG
❑	50.	#Canned diced tomatoes_____	28 fl oz/796 ml CANNED
❑	51.	#Canned ground tomatoes___	28 fl oz/796 ml CANNED
❑	52.	Canned tomato juice_____	48 fl oz/1.36 L CANNED
❑	53.	Cinnamon powder_____	LARGE JAR
❑	54.	#Dried parsley_____	LARGE JAR
❑	55.	#Dried oregano_____	LARGE JAR
❑	56.	#Garlic powder_____	REPLACEMENT BAG
❑	57.	Onion powder_____	REPLACEMENT BAG
❑	58.	Paprika_____	REPLACEMENT BAG
❑	59.	#Ground black pepper_____	REPLACEMENT BAG
❑	60.	Dried fine herbs_____	REPLACEMENT BAG
❑	61.	Dried Italian herbs_____	REPLACEMENT BAG
❑	62.	#Chili powder_____	REPLACEMENT BAG
❑	63.	Red cayenne pepper_____	REPLACEMENT BAG
❑	64.	Ground cumin_____	REPLACEMENT BAG
❑	65.	Curry powder_____	REPLACEMENT BAG
❑	66.	Ground Turmeric_____	REPLACEMENT BAG
❑	67.	Crushed chilies_____	REPLACEMENT BAG
❑	68.	#Margarine (low-cost)_____	3 lb/ 1.36 kg PLASTIC TUB
❑	69.	#Yogurt 'Firm Style' (as starter)_____	6 oz/180 ml JAR
❑	70.	#Cheese (Mozzarella or old Cheddar)	24 oz/700g PACK
❑	71.	Processed cheese (180 burger slices)____	4.4 lb/2 kg
❑	72.	#Eggs (small or extra-large)_____	DOZEN
❑	73.	#Lemon juice from concentrate	24fl oz/750 ml BOTTLE
❑	74.	#Stewing beef or pork cubes_____	2 lb/1 kg PACK
❑	75.	#Ground beef (regular-grade)__	4 lb/2 kg STYRO-PACK
❑	76.	Chicken (inexpensive cuts)__	4 lb/2 kg STYRO-PACK
❑	77.	Turkey (inexpensive cuts)___	4 lb/2 kg STYRO-PACK
❑	78.	#Pepperoni (very thin slices)_____	2 lb/ 1 kg PACK
❑	79.	Frozen fish fillets (Turbot or Alaskan cod)_____	PACK
❑	80.	#Ice Cream (generic-brand)_____	2-4Q/L TUB

*   *Pastas: Spaghetti, readycut macaroni, penne rigate and soup pasta*

OPTIONAL GROCERY SHOPPING LIST

✔	No	INGREDIENTS	SUGGESTED FORMAT
❑	81.	Whole wheat flour_____	20 lb/10 kg SAC
❑	82.	Brown rice_____	10-20 lb/5-10 kg SAC
❑	83.	Flax seeds_____	1 lb/.5 kg BULK
❑	84.	Wild rice (buy very little)_____	1/4 lb/ 1/8 kg BULK
❑	85.	Millet_____	2 lb/1 kg BULK
❑	86.	Honey (flavorful liquid or solid)_____	16 oz/500 g JAR
❑	87.	Peanut butter_____	2 lb/1 kg JAR
❑	88.	Dried black beans_____	2 lb/1 kg BAG
❑	89.	Dried split peas (yellow or green)_____	2 lb/1 kg BAG
❑	90.	Dried blacked-eyed beans_____	2 lb/1 kg BAG
❑	91.	Dried navy (pinto) beans_____	2 lb/1 kg BAG
❑	92.	Tapioca seeds_____	1 lb/.5 kg BAG
❑	93.	Shredded coconut (unsweetened)___	.5 lb/.25 kg BAG
❑	94.	Sugar cones_____	24 pcs. PACK
❑	95.	Cones or cups for ice cream_____	36 pcs. PACK
❑	96.	Popping corn_____	2 lb/1 kg BULK
❑	97.	Pickled hot pepper rings_____	24 oz/750 ml JAR
❑	98.	Dill pickles_____	4 quarts/liters JAR
❑	99.	Sliced green or black olives_____	2 quarts/liters JAR
❑	100.	Dijon mustard_____	16 oz/500 g JAR
❑	101.	Ketchup & relish (generic)___	24 fl oz/750 ml BOTTLE
❑	102.	Grape vine leaves (about 100 leaves)__	1 lb/.5 kg JAR
❑	103.	Caramel or fudge spread_____	1 lb/400 g CONTAINER
❑	104.	Jams (raspberry, strawberry)_____	16 fl oz/500 ml JAR
❑	105.	Bell pepper (green or red) **_____	AS NEEDED
❑	106.	Lettuce (Iceberg) **_____	AS NEEDED
❑	107.	Fresh corn **_____	A DOZEN
❑	108.	Cucumber **_____	AS NEEDED
❑	109.	Tomatoes **_____	AS NEEDED
❑	110.	Spinach **_____	AS NEEDED
❑	111.	Broccoli **_____	AS NEEDED
❑	112.	Cauliflower **_____	AS NEEDED
❑	113.	Brussel sprouts **_____	AS NEEDED
❑	114.	Squash **_____	AS NEEDED
❑	115.	Eggplant **_____	AS NEEDED
❑	116.	Beets **_____	5 lb/2-3 kg BAG
❑	117.	Turnips **_____	AS NEEDED
❑	118.	Oranges **_____	AS NEEDED
❑	119.	Peaches **_____	AS NEEDED
❑	120.	Pears **_____	AS NEEDED

OPTIONAL GROCERY SHOPPING LIST *(Continued)*

✔	No	INGREDIENTS	SUGGESTED FORMAT
❑	121.	Bananas **	AS NEEDED
❑	122.	Grapes (blue or red) **	AS NEEDED
❑	123.	Pitted dates	16 oz/500 g BAG
❑	124.	Canned pineapple pieces	14 fl oz/398 ml CAN
❑	125.	Canned keta salmon	14.75 oz/418 g CAN
❑	126.	Canned Pacific Jack Macqueral	15 oz/425 g CAN
❑	127.	Canned tuna or crabmeat	6 oz/170 g CAN
❑	128.	Dried thyme leaves	REPLACEMENT BAG
❑	129.	Ground ginger	REPLACEMENT BAG
❑	130.	Dried basil	REPLACEMENT BAG
❑	131.	Nutmeg	REPLACEMENT BAG
❑	132.	Allspice	REPLACEMENT BAG
❑	133.	Dried tarragon	REPLACEMENT BAG
❑	134.	Ground sage/rosemary	REPLACEMENT BAG
❑	135.	Ground anise	REPLACEMENT BAG
❑	136.	Dried majoram	REPLACEMENT BAG
❑	137.	Dried mint leaves	REPLACEMENT BAG
❑	138.	Coriander/cardomon	REPLACEMENT BAG
❑	139.	Savory	REPLACEMENT BAG
❑	140.	Caraway/mustard seeds	AS NEEDED
❑	141.	Tea bags	100 tea bags SAC
❑	142.	Coffee regular grinds (generic-brand)	2 lb/1 kg CAN
❑	143.	Instant coffee (generic-brand)	7 oz/200 g JAR
❑	144.	Cocoa powder	AS NEEDED
❑	145.	Generic pop	2 quarts/liters BOTTLE
❑	146.	Neutral gelatin/pectin	.25 lb/.12 kg BULK
❑	147.	Vegetable shortening (generic)	1 lb/500 g PACK
❑	148.	Ground pork	2 lb/ 1 kg STYRO-PACK
❑	149.	Bacon (generic-brand)	1 lb/500 g PACK
❑	150.	Breakfast pork sausages (low-cost)	2 lb/1 kg PACK
❑	151.	Beef bone (for soup)	AS REQUIRED
❑	152.	Beef or chicken weiners (generic)	1 lb/454 g PACK
❑	153.	Baloney, salami, ham (thin slices)	AS REQUIRED
❑	154.	Pork liver	1 lb/.5 kg PACK
❑	155.	Processed cheese (80 sub slices)	4.4 lb/2 kg PACK
❑	156.	Dried grated cheese (Romano, Parmesan)	.25 lb/.5 kg
❑	157.	Beef/pork/veal sausage casings	about 30 ft/10 m EA.
❑	158.	Frozen whole fish (low-cost)	2 lb/1 kg STYRO-PACK
❑	159.	Frozen potato fries	2-4 lb/1-2 kg BAG
❑	160.	Frozen blanched vegetables	2-4 lb/1-2 kg BAG

** *Purchased inexpensively in peak harvest season only*

How do you know if you're shopping at the right supermarket?

A good large supermarket or even larger mega-supermarket should have or designate an area for pre-bagged items from bulk or ingredients like cornstarch, instant milk powder, soup stock powders, etc.! They will also hold generic and non-generic low-cost brands in large formats. They should have items like rice, dried legumes, flour, and sugar available in large sacs or bags. Prepared mustard, condiments, soy sauce, etc., should be available gallon or half-gallon (2 or 4 liters) containers or jars. Otherwise, it may be difficult to cook inexpensively!

Exceptions to not buying readymade foods!

- Generic-brand bargain ice cream
- Generic-brand hot dog wieners
- Economically packaged frozen or refrigerated pork breakfast sausages
- Generic-brand bargain hot dog or hamburger buns pack
- Generic-brand pop 2Q/L soft drinks
- Economically packaged frozen fish cakes
- Large bag generic-brand frozen French fries
- Mozzarella, old Cheddar, Cheddar, or Feta cheeses
- Generic-brand caramel spread and sugar cones
- Generic-brand pie fillings or jam (if stretched)
- Low-cost bologna, salami or pepperoni, and cooked ham
- Generic brand relish and ketchup
- Bulk nougat
- Generic-brand enriched white sandwich bread

Generic-brand refers to the supermarket's own brand or brands which compete with the big name brands but are noticeably less expensive and often of comparable quality though not always. Select the least expensive.

OTHER LISTS

WINE-MAKING SUPPLIES STORE LIST

Yeast nutrients	Cream of tartar (tartaric acid)
Citric acid (crystals, not liquid)	Ascorbic acid crystals

HEALTH FOOD STORE LIST

Bulk soybeans & soybean flour	Lecithin (from soya)
Rye & other whole grain flours	Alfalfa seeds

PHARMACY

Epsom salts	Oil of spruce
Saltpeter	Cheesecloth

BUTCHER SHOP
Sausage casings

SMALL LOCAL BAKERY
Fresh yeast

NOTE: The items marked with an # in first shopping list are the most essential ingredients from which most CookMISER recipes can be made. You may want to buy those items only to lower the initial cost!

PREPARATION IS THE KEY

This entire chapter is about being prepared with the necessary precooked ingredients before you actually need them. Ingredients must be prepared ahead of time in order to make many of the **CookMISER** recipes quickly. These precooked items are stored appropriately till needed. Preparation is about saving time not money, as opposed to previous chapter that was about saving money.

CookMISER uses 12 different methods of early or ahead of time preparation for convenience and saving time. The following list quickly describes each one:

1. **Presoaked, precooked, or pre-toasted ingredient preparation** where each ingredient is presoaked, precooked, pretoasted before being frozen, refrigerated, or stored. Or may be subjected to a combination of these.

2. **Precooked recipe preparation** where recipes are precooked and immediately refrigerated or frozen.

3. **Premixed dry ingredients or seasonings preparation** where dry ingredients often used for cake type batters, or main-course or side dish seasonings, etc., are mixed together ahead of time and stored in plastic bags or sealed containers.

4. **Blanched vegetable preparation** where mostly non-starchy vegetables quickly blanched in top water, properly placed in plastic bags and frozen until needed.

5. **Refrigerated or frozen dough preparation** where dough is ready for use whenever freshly baked bread is needed.

6. **Batch baking (or cooking) preparation** where items like bread is baked in certain quantities instead of one at time. Throughout the book, the batch cooking idea is merely suggested where it seems appropriate.

7. **Homemade yogurt, buttermilk, and sour cream preparation** where dairy products are cultured every 10 days or so for use in our recipes.

8. **Cheese & Tofu preparation** where soybeans are used in the making of a vegetarian cheese-like food for use in various recipes.

9. **Homegrown sprout(s) preparation** where dried legumes, seeds and whole grains are sprouted before they're needed for use in salads and other recipes.

10. **Special premixes preparation** where items such as Italian bread crumbs, premixed seasoning and other premixed ingredients are prepared ahead of time in case they're needed.

11. **Meat recipe preparation** where cooked or uncooked recipe items such as sausages, burger patties, etc. are prepared ahead of time in batch amounts to be stored, refrigerated, but usually frozen.

12. **Snack recipe preparation** where items like chocolate bar, ice cream bars, and even doughnuts are prepared ahead of time in batch amounts to be stored, refrigerated, but usually frozen.

Please Note *The first four preparation methods are covered in this chapter and the remaining eight are described, or included elsewhere in the book.*

PRECOOKED INGREDIENTS

These precooked ingredients are used all over the **CookMISER** and should probably be prepared at regular interval, weekly, bimonthly, monthly, or every 2-3 months. This depends on whether you cook for one or a large family. The right time to replace some of the precooked grains and legumes is when you notice a few varieties in the freezer have run out. Chicken and turkey are the only meat that is precooked. These precooked ingredients fall into four categories:

1. **Presoaked, precooked and frozen (or refrigerated).**
2. **Presoaked and frozen (or refrigerated).**
3. **Precooked and refrigerated (or frozen).**
4. **Blanched and frozen (or refrigerated).**

Presoaking Procedure: Place 1 or 2 cups/250-500mL of dried legumes (or grains) into a large bowl. Add three times that volume of cold tap water. Soak for about 12 hours, preferably in the refrigerator or cool spot. This should be done early morning or before retiring. Presoak the ingredients you think you'll need in the coming month.

Precooking Procedure: Pour several quarts (liters) of hot tap water in a medium-size or large pan. Bring to a boil over a high heat; add legumes, grains, vegetable, pasta, or poultry to be cooked *(one variety only)*. Lower heat, simmer until ingredient is cooked tender but not soft and mushy. Rinse in cold tap water *(except pasta)* and drain thoroughly. *When precooking poultry always make soup.*
*EXCEPTION FOR PASTA Add a little salt and vegetable oil to hot tap water before bringing to a boil and **do not rinse** before draining.*
EXCEPTION FOR RICE Precooked rice must not be over-cooked or precooked too quickly and must be well rinse in cold water or else will stick and clump up together while stored refrigerated.

Refrigerating Procedure: Place precooked ingredient(s) in a **plastic bowl** or **plastic container with lid** in refrigerator, preferably on the upper shelf where it's cooler, for up to 5 days.

Freezing Procedure: Place the presoaked or precooked legumes, grains, or starchy vegetables loosely on baking sheets and freeze a few hours. Place them in zipper or plastic bags with twist-ties and immediately freeze. This is called loose-pack freezing and is the most convenient freezer packaging method *(see page 31)*. Please make sure there is as little air as possible in bags before close them to avoid freezer burns, or the food will become dry and tough. Place ingredient in such a way that it will lie flat instead of a large lump inside the plastic bag. If a small amount of precooked legume is required for a recipe, it is then easy to take out the desired quantity, immediately close and return bag to freezer. *No hassles!*

PRECOOKING (& PRESOAKING) CHART

Quantities indicated below are dry or uncooked, before presoaking or precooking, and are per person. Presoaking, when applicable, is best-done overnight (8-10 hours) in cold water and preferably refrigerated.

INGREDIENT	QTY	PRESOAK	PRECOOK	FREEZE	REFRIGERATE
Long grain rice	2 cups (480 ml)	No	15-20 minutes	3 months	Up to 5 days
Brown rice	2 cups (480 ml)	No	30-40 minutes	3 months	Up to 3 days
Potatoes	2.2 lb (1 kg)	No	40-50 minutes	3 months	Up to 5 days
Beets	2.2 lb (1 kg)	No	30-40 minutes	3 months	Up to 7 days
Soybeans (tofu)	2 cups (480 ml)	Yes	No	3 months	Up to 5 days
Soybeans	2 cups (480 ml)	Yes	50-60 minutes	3 months	Up to 5 days
Whole green peas	2 cups (480 ml)	Yes	30-40 minutes	3 months	Up to 5 days
Liard Lentils	2 cups (480 ml)	No	15-20 minutes	3 months	Up to 5 days
Navy beans	2 cups (480 ml)	Yes	60-90 minutes	3 months	Up to 5 days
Chickpeas	1 cup (240 ml)	Yes	20-25 minutes	3 months	Up to 5 days
Red kidney beans	1 cup (240 ml)	Yes	30-40 minutes	3 months	Up to 5 days
Lima beans	1 cup (240 ml)	Yes	15-20 minutes	3 months	Up to 5 days
Split peas	1 cup (240 ml)	Yes	30-40 minutes	3 months	Up to 5 days
Lentils	1 cup (240 ml)	No	15-20 minutes	3 months	Up to 5 days
Other Legumes	1 cup (240 ml)	Yes	As is necessary	3 months	Up to 5 days
Wheat	1 cup (240 ml)	Yes	No	3 months	Up to 2 days
Bulgar wheat	1 cup (240 ml)	1/2 hr.	No	3 months	Up to 5 days
Barley	1 cup (240 ml)	Yes	No	3 months	Up to 7 days
Millet	1 cup (240 ml)	No	30-40 minutes	3 months	Up to 5 days
Dried raisins	1 cup (240 ml)	Yes	No	3 months	Up to 5 days
Chicken	To suit	No	50-60 minutes	3 months	Up to 2 days
Turkey	To suit	No	50-60 minutes	3 months	Up to 2 days

NOTE *If you precook (or try to) pulses using hard water, add 1/8 tsp (1/2 ml) baking soda per cup of dried legumes to the water. Year-round vegetable staples like carrots, green cabbage, celery, and those that are unaffordable except in their peak season vegetables like string beans, broccoli, cauliflower, etc., cannot successfully be frozen when uncooked or precooked and instead must be blanched. **See blanching procedure on pages 27 & 28.***

PRE-TOASTING CHART

Pre-toast the following ingredients in baking sheets using one or two oven rack(s). Bacon slices should be placed on wire rack, which are in turn placed on baking sheets for simultaneous draining. Immediately loose-pack freeze the bacon. Dried legumes are usually presoaked, then precooked and immediately loose-pack frozen. The presoaking only of dried legumes apply principally to tofu making. Pre-toasted ingredients are stored, either in pantry, refrigerator, or freezer in sealed containers or plastic bags. Bacon should be stored frozen only. In addition, because bacon is so thin it will thaw or reheat very quickly.

INGREDIENT	QTY	PRE-TOAST	TEMPERATURE	STORE	FREEZE
Wheat germ	1 cup (240 ml)	15 minutes	275°F/135°C	1 month	3 months
Sunflower seed kernels	1 cup (240 ml)	30 minutes	275°F/135°C	1 month	3 months
Sesame seeds *(Quick)*	.5 cup (120 ml)	30 minutes	275°F/135°C	1 month	3 months
Rolled oats *(One-Minute)*	2 cups (480 ml)	30 minutes	275°F/135°C	3 months	3 months
Rolled oats	2 cups (480 ml)	30 minutes	275°F/135°C	3 months	3 months
Chickpeas	1 cup (240 ml)	50 minutes	275°F/135°C	1 month	3 months
Soybeans	2 cups (480 ml)	50 minutes	275°F/135°C	1 month	3 months
Peanuts	1 cup (240 ml)	25 minutes			
Potatoes	1 lb (454 g)	40 minutes	375°F/190°C	refrigerated	3 months
Bacon slices	1 lb (454 g)	30 minutes	275°F/135°C	refrigerated	3 months

Please Note *Potatoes and bacon may be are referred to as pre-baked.*

About Pre-chopped Ingredients!

Blender chopped pre-toasted peanuts should be stored in plastic bags for later use as toppings on desserts, or for making chocolate and ice cream bars.

Precooked Recipes

This is about being prepared as in precooking you favorite dishes and freezing them afterward. You must package them for freezing as outlined in chapter four. Freeze them in one or two serving(s) format. They are usually thawed in the refrigerator 4 to 8 hours in advance and reheated in a skillet with a little water. Reheat on a medium heat until hot. The best categories of recipes to freeze are soups, main dishes, rice, breads, and desserts. Side dishes and pastas may be frozen but with reservations. Microwave ovens, if you have one, are handy to thaw and reheat, or rise dough, but are by no means necessary.

Premixed Dry Ingredients or Seasoning

Premixing the ingredients that are common to many recipes, especially if there are four or more such ingredients, then premixing is well worth the effort. They will save you perhaps two minutes every time you make that recipe. Place the ingredients in large all-purpose plastic bags or airtight containers, and store in pantry. Premixed dry ingredients or seasoning must be thoroughly mixed before storage to be effective. Reference about when to use the premixed ingredients or seasoning and quantities required are given in all applicable recipes. Premixed ingredients and seasoning must be made from dry ingredients *only* and stored in a cool, dark, and dry place. *Shake premix before using!*

Premixed dry ingredients #1 (Use with cakes, muffins, and cookies)

10 cups (2.4 liters) all-purpose flour *(generic-brand & bleached)*
5 cups (1200 ml) granulated sugar

1/2 cup (120 ml) skim milk powder
2 1/2 tbsp (37 ml) baking powder
2 tsp (10ml) table salt

Premixed dry ingredients #2 (Use with doughnuts)

4 3/4 cups (1.14 liters) all-purpose flour *(generic-brand, bleached)*
1 cup (240 ml) granulated sugar
3/8 cup (90 ml) instant milk powder

1 1/2 tbsp (22 ml) baking powder
3/4 tsp (3-4 ml) table salt
1 tsp (5 ml) ground cinnamon
1/2 tsp (2 ml) nutmeg

Premixed dry ingredients #3   (Use with pancakes and waffles)

5 cups (1.2 liters) all-purpose flour
   (generic-brand & bleached)
1/3 cup (80 ml) granulated sugar

1 cup (240 ml) instant skim milk
   powder
2 1/2 tbsp (37 ml) baking powder
1 1/4 tsp (6 ml) table salt

Premixed dry seasoning #4   (Use with tomato pasta or pizza sauces)

2 1/2tbsp (37 ml) dried oregano
1 1/2 tbsp (22 ml) chili powder
2 tsp (10 ml) dried basil
2 tbsp (30 ml) dried parsley *(optional)*

1 tsp (5 ml) garlic powder
2 tsp (10 ml) onion powder
1 cup (240 ml) all-purpose flour
Salt and pepper *(optional)*

Premixed dry seasoning #5   (Use with salads)

3 tbsp (45 ml) dried parsley
2 tsp (10 ml) celery salt

2 tsp (10 ml) onion powder
1/2 tsp (2 ml) garlic powder

Premixed dry seasoning #6   (Use with rice dishes, etc.)

2 1/2 tbsp (37 ml) chicken *(or beef)*
   soup stock powder
2 tsp (10 ml) celery salt

2 tsp (10 ml) dried parsley
2 tsp (10 ml) onion powder
1/4 tsp (1 ml) garlic powder

All premixes can be multiplied by 2, 4, or 8 to suit your needs…
(You can use the dry premix idea with puddings, soups, quick breads, etc.)

BLANCHING VEGETABLES

Freezing is the easiest and most effective way to store vegetables for numerous months but they must first be blanched. *Freezing vegetables without blanching them first just doesn't work.* Blanching vegetables inactivates the enzymes that cause them to lose their properties and quality prior to freezing. Properties such as freshness, vitamin content, color, keeping quality and flavor are greatly enhanced through the blanching process. This is especially true for carrots which are relative inexpensive year-round, but it's also valid for many other vegetables bought inexpensively during late summer peak harvest season. In short, blanching is done by soaking fresh vegetables in boiling water for a couple of minutes and then soaking in cold, or iced water for about one minute. They are drained, packaged and frozen until needed.

BLANCHING PROCEDURE

STEP 1. Quickly clean the fresh vegetables. Cut them into small pieces. For carrots, slice them about 1/8-3/16-inch (3-5 mm) thick. For broccoli or cauliflower, cut them into flowerets or flowerets halves. For green beans, cut them in one-inch/2.5 cm lengths. If they are vegetable from the squash family, slice them in 1/4-inch (1/2 cm) slices. For greens like spinach, Swiss chard, or turnip leaves, course chop them.

STEP 2. Take 1 or 2 cups (250-500 ml) of clean/cut vegetables and place them in a sieve. Place the sieve in a large saucepan of boiling water, maintain them

plunged in the water the time indicated in the following table or until the
vegetables are pliable but crisp and color brightens. Drain.

STEP 3. Immediately plunge vegetables in cold running tap water or iced water
in a bowl to stop the cooking process at once. Cool thoroughly for at least one
minute. Drain thoroughly at least a few minutes.

STEP 4. Loose-pack *(see page 31)* them directly on large plastic zipper bags, or
plastic bags with twist-ties. Always rest the bag and its content flat, and not as a
ball or lump *(in the same fashion that the supermarket frozen blanched vegetables
are stored and sold).* Freeze at once. There is no real need to label the bags with
the vegetable names and dates. Will store well for at least 3 months.

GUIDELINE FOR BLANCHING VEGETABLES

Vegetable	Preparation	Blanching time
Beans, string	Cut into 1-inch (2.5 cm) lengths	Blanch for 3 minutes
Broccoli	Break or cut into flowerets	Blanch for 3-4 minutes
Brussels sprouts	Keep whole	Blanch for 4-5 minutes
Cabbage	Shred course or slice	Blanch for 2 minutes
Carrots	Slice	Blanch for 5-6 minutes
Cauliflower	Break or cut into flowerets	Blanch for 3-4 minutes
Celery	Slice	Blanch for 3 minutes
Corn (cob)	Slice off corn kernels	Blanch for 4 minutes
Greens	Keep leaves whole	Blanch for 2 minutes
Onions	Slice	Blanch for 1-2 minutes
Peas	Keep whole	Blanch for 1-2 minutes
Potatoes (new)	Keep whole	Blanch for 4 minutes
Squash	Slice	Blanch for 1-2 minutes
Turnips	Slice	Blanch for 2-3 minutes

EXCEPTIONS TO BLANCHING BEFORE FREEZING!

Beet root: Cook and skin. Slice, chop, or dice them. Bag and freeze.
Mushrooms: Wash and fry. Then bag and freeze.
Tomatoes: Purée. Bag or place in containers. Freeze.

BEFORE STARTING

This chapter covers everything that might be useful to know before using the **CookMISER** system. The major topics covered are:

1. **General Tips**
2. **Freezing (& packaging) Tips**
3. **Kitchen Equipment**
4. **Refrigerator Food Storage**
5. **Optimizing Oven Usage**
6. **Servings & Shallow Frying**
7. **Conversions & Abbreviations**

After reading this chapter about all the **CookMISER** basics and methods, cooking recipes the **CookMISER** way will become clear and simple.

GENERAL TIPS

The following tips, comments, and bits of information are very general in nature and do not apply to any chapter in particular. When tips do apply to a given chapter, they are included in that chapter as *TIPS & HINTS*. The following tips are not placed in any particular order.

- *All teaspoon, tablespoon, and cup measures are leveled and not heaping.*
- *Spices, herbs, and stock powders from recipes may be adjusted to taste.*
- *Spices & herbs should be kept in airtight containers & used within 2 years.*
- *When dicing carrots cut them length-wise, then slice them.*
- *When baking cakes and muffins never use soy flour with white flour, instead use whole-wheat flour to camouflage its bean taste.*
- *Always use oven and freezer close to maximum capacity to ensure efficiency and economy.*
- *Use the 2 inches everywhere rule when using oven to capacity at moderate or low temperatures.*
- *When not using oven to capacity use the mid-level rack.*
- *Test to see if your baking powder is still good by placxing a small amount in hot water, if mixture bubbles vigorously its still effective.*
- *When adding skim milk powder to a recipe place it directly with the other dry ingredients.*
- *To prevent food from sticking to any pan, always heat the pan first, then add oil or margarine to the hot skillet and finally the food to be sauteéd.*
- *Dash or pinch of an ingredient means a minute amount that's to taste.*

FREEZING TIPS

The freezing tips, comments and bits of information are all directly or indirection associated with freezing foods as used in the **CookMISER** book. Some tips might be the same as those seen in other cookbooks, while others are unique to this one. The freezer may allow you to take advantage of bargains or volume packs, and stock up on fresh vegetables inexpensively in peak season, their quality at its best. There will be more on freezing (and blanching) fresh vegetables further on in this chapter. Ideally, your  refrigerator should be of the two-door type and the freezer compartment should have shelves in it. Freezer temperature should be set to about medium or a little less cold. As a general rule, nothing should kept frozen for more than 3 months so exceedingly cold freezer temperatures are not necessary except when adding a new supply of meat, fish and poultry to it. Then, you must not forget to bring it back to its original setting. A temperature of about 5°F (-15°C) is perfect for most of the time and -10°F (-24°C) best for several hours of fast deep-freeze. We recommend you set a timer to remind to reset freezer to its original setting. Freezers that are almost full operate more efficiently and economically. There is less air pockets to keep chilled and the bulk of frozen food help maintain the low temperature. This is especially true during a power shortage. Try to keep your freezer at least 3/4 full. That allows space for more food when you restock or find a good buy. During the fresh vegetable harvesting period, allow more space for this purpose. Don't freeze large objects like potpies or large frozen turkeys unless you have huge freezer and family. Try to allocate sections of your freezer to different types of foods or ingredients like, blanched *(uncooked)* vegetables, precooked legumes, presoaked grains, raw meat, poultry or fish. Use the selves, dividers and boxes to separate the different foods. Keep things moving in the freezer, use the food and replace the food. Always place the new food at the bottom and rear of freezer compartment. Likewise, move the older food to the top and front. In order not to spoil food and economical operation, the food in your freezer should turn over about 4-5 times a year. This way, there's no need to keep tabs of dates since nothing should stay in there much longer than one to three months. Immediately after shopping, properly pack and freeze all foods that must be frozen. Do not chill meat, fish and poultry in refrigerator first. Adjust your freezer's dial to deep freeze. Food that is frozen quickly forms smaller ice crystals and retain better properties and quality. Cool hot recipes on counter and then in the refrigerator before packaging and freezing. Packaging foods for the freezer is very important, not only to preserve quality but must also allow for easy food removal in small amounts. Proper packaging provides a barrier that prevents the moisture in food from escaping. But if you need a quarter cup (60 ml) of precooked legumes, a patty, a fish fillet or quarter pound (.12 kg) of ground beef in the next 10 seconds, that's where proper packaging comes in.

Essentials for Freezer Packaging

We recommend the *loose-pack* freezer packaging technique for most items or the use of small plastic bags in a larger bag or container method. All you really need for proper freezer packaging are large storage or freezer bags, preferably zip-lock or zipper type. Useful too are small *sandwich or non-sandwich type* plastic bags, wax paper, and recycled plastic containers. Recycled plastic containers (from margarine, ice cream, etc.) are not as good as store-bought ones but cheap if not used to store food for much longer than two weeks.

Size of small plastic (fold-lock) sandwich bags: 5.5 x 5.5 inches (14 x 14 cm)
Size of large zipper or twist-tie all-purpose plastic bags: 10 x 14 inches (25 x 36 cm)
Width of wax paper: about 12 inches (30 cm)

What is loose-packed freezer packaging?

To loose-pack freezer packaged items, you must first freeze them or at the very least freeze their outer surface by scattering them on a metal baking sheet or tray placed in freezer. *Make sure that whatever you're freezing has cooled down to room temperature before placing in freezer, not to needlessly lower the freezer compartment temperature.* Once frozen they are then quickly placed in plastic bags or containers without worrying that they will stick together. This way when small amounts or portions are required, it can easily and quickly be retrieved without hassles. The bags or containers must immediately be returned to freezer after removal of small portion(s). Smaller bags in larger bags or containers are not required with this method. The loose-packed food is usually placed in plastic bags with zipper or twist-tie or recycled plastic container with lid. It is used when freezing presoaked or precooked legumes and grains, poultry sections, stewing beef or pork, and small round portions of ground beef or pork. When closing zipper or placing tie on bag exclude as much air as possible, do so even after

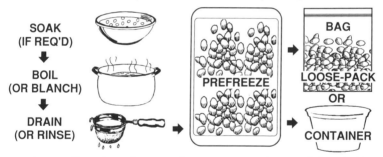

SOAK (IF REQ'D) → BOIL (OR BLANCH) → DRAIN (OR RINSE) → PREFREEZE → BAG LOOSE-PACK OR CONTAINER

removing small portions. *Loose-pack your meat, poultry, or fish only if you intend to use it within 2 or 3 weeks, or use an individual bag per portion.* For freezer storage of processed cheese slices, place in smaller portions in small bags.

Freezer packaging procedure for ground meat and poultry

For ground meat, make portions about half a cup (120 ml) shaped as patties or flat lump and either loose-pack or wrap them in separate small bags. If you loose-pack them, make sure you pre-freeze them first on the metal tray. Then place several into a large plastic storage bag or container

SMALL BAGS

LOOSE-PACK

while excluding as much air as possible on closure. Flattened ground meat will freeze and thaw faster then when shaped round. For poultry fresh pieces like drumsticks, and high-thigh, use the same packaging method as ground meat except there's no shaping. Rinse and let drain the chicken pieces before loose packing or bagging.

Freezer packaging procedure for frozen whole fish and fillets

For frozen fillets, loose-pack them in large plastic bags with zipper or twist-tie, or break them in two and place in small bags. Always remove as much of the air in large bag before closure. When packaging frozen whole fish for the freezer, loose-pack them in a large plastic storage bag with zipper or twist-tie. When needed take one out and thaw the fish in the refrigerator. Once thawed, prepare whole fish as you normally would for cooking.

Freezer packaging procedure for precooked recipes or meals

Many of your favorite recipes may be frozen after cooking and cooling to room temperature. They can be packaged for the freezer individually in serving size portions in small bags closed with zipper or a twist-tie. Small portions of these recipes may also be combined into groups of two or three and placed into recycled or airtight plastic containers to serve as a complete frozen meal. Due of ambient air, freeze recipes in recycled containers for no more than 3 weeks, or 3 months in airtight plastic containers. Thaw for a several hours in refrigerator before reheat. Alternately it may be thawed using microwave oven and then reheated in skillet with a little water. For desserts, cakes and cookies its better to package in plastic bags closed with zipper or twist-tie excluding as much air as possible.

Freezer packaging procedure for precooked ingredients

Follow *Freezing procedure* on pages 24-5.

Freezer packaging procedure for blanched vegetables

For proper blanching procedure, see pages 27-8. After blanching and draining, place vegetables in one or more large plastic bag(s). Place in the usual flat fashion to a thickness of not more than one and half inch. Close with a twist-tie excluding as much air as possible. Place flatly in freezer, do not bunch or lump contents.

KITCHEN EQUIPMENT

Remembering that the underlying **CookMISER** concept about doing the most for the least, more meals for less money, time, and effort. Proper minimal selection of kitchen equipment yields much towards that goal. Most recipes in this book utilize very little equipment apart from the standard 30" electric range and two-door freezer/refrigerator. The essential equipment is separated from the optional one. *Please note that all the recipes in this book were tested and were prepared and/or cooked with the least expensive small appliances, utensil, and pan available on the market today. The equipment proved to be satisfactory and durable in most cases!* The kitchen equipment is subdivided into four subsections:

a. *Small appliances*
b. *Kitchen Items*
c. *Pots & Pans*
d. *Ovenware & Baking Pans*

Small Appliances

Apart from the usual toaster, electric can-opener and electric kettle, you will need at least the first two of the following:

Essential Small Appliances

HAND MIXER

BLENDER

Optional Small Appliances

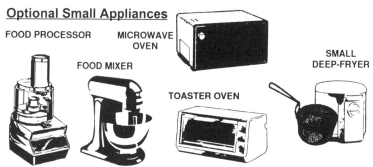

FOOD PROCESSOR

MICROWAVE OVEN

FOOD MIXER

SMALL DEEP-FRYER

TOASTER OVEN

Kitchen Items

Apart from the usual table utensils, assortment of dishes, pitchers, etc., you will need most of the following:

Essential Kitchen Items

(SERRATED) BREAD KNIFE

CHEF'S KNIFE

CARVING KNIFE

CUTTING BOARD

METAL SPATULA

FUNNEL

SIEVE

POTATO PEELER

MEASURING SPOON SET

MEASURING CUP

PLASTIC MIXING SPOON

ROLLING PIN

WHISK

GRATER

PLASTIC BOWLS & LIDS

MEASURING CUPS (DRY)

LADLE

Optional Kitchen Items

PERFORATED SPOON

GARLIC PRESS

COLANDER

PASTRY BRUSH

PLASTIC SPATULA

BULB BASTER

PIZZA CUTTER

CANDY OR FLOATING THERMOMETER

MEAT POUNDER

POTATO MASHER

RUBBER SPATULA

TIMER

KITCHEN FORK

SKIMMER

SIMMER PLATE

KEBOB SKEWERS

COOLING/DRAINING RACKS

TONGS

Pots and Pans

*Most of the following items should **not** be non-stick pots and pans, because they can not handle as well the slightly higher than normal temperatures* **CookMISER** *recommends. You will need some of the following:*

Essential Pots & Pans

LARGE FRYING PAN

LARGE SAUCEPAN

Optional Pots & Pans

SMALL SAUCEPAN

STOCKPOT

NON-STICK SKILLET

SMALL FRYING PAN

WOK

Pans should be made of aluminum with thick bottom for uniform heat distribution to avoid burning food. Non-stick skillets should be used for the LITE! version(s) of recipes and lower heat settings used to avoid damaging them and premature wear. To avoid cross-contamination of germs and bacteria all pans should be washed with soap and water instead of just being wiped clean after use. This also applies to cast-iron frying pans though foods will stick more afterwards.

Ovenware & Baking Pans

Non-stick baking sheets and pans are so convenient, that it's all we recommend.

Essential Ovenware & Baking pans

LARGE CASSEROLE DISHES

MUFFIN TRAYS

BAKING SHEETS

LOAF PANS

SQUARE
CAKE PANS

DULL METAL
PIE PANS OR
GLASS PLATES

Optional Ovenware & Baking Pans

PIZZA PANS

MEDIUM
CASSEROLE DISHES

LARGE CAKE PANS

ROUND
CAKE PAN(S)

The fore-mentioned ovenware and baking pan formats were carefully selected to fit conventional 30" oven racks (see pages 36-7). This goes well with the **CookMISER** concept of using oven to full capacity whenever possible. The numbers above which are underlined indicate the number of identical pans that will fill one rack yet allow enough hot air circulation in oven. For example, two medium cookie pans or six medium loaf pans would fit comfortably on one rack. This applies to all except the large pizza pan, which takes an entire rack by itself.

In Addition…

*You'll need **Miscellaneous Equipment** for bread, cheese, pop, and sausage making (see matching chapters). Plus sprouting trays, dispensers, etc., etc., etc.*

About Dispensers & Recycled Containers!

Smaller dispenser containers are essential when buying most food items in large formats and preparing other items like mayonnaise, fancy mustards and sauces from scratch. Most dispenser-type containers are reused or if you prefer recycled containers, which were originally store, bought. These usually include mayonnaise, soy sauce, vinegar, yogurt, cream cheese, margarine, etc. plastic or glass containers, bottles, tubs, and jars.

Special care should be taken to remove their labels by soaking them several hours in very hot water. Wash in hot water and soap as you would for dirty dishes. Other dispensers usually made of plastic must be purchased.

CURING PANS

To cure or season a pan means to treat it with heat and oil a few times at one sitting in order to render it stick-free. The use of cured pans though useful is not the most hygienic. Nonetheless, we include the technique for reference's sake.

This technique applies to aluminum or cast iron frying pans as well as steel Chinese woks but does not work with stainless steel pans. To cure or season a pan, whether new or used, it must first be washed with soap and water. This must be done using a cloth or sponge and never with steel wool pads. The pan is then rinse and dried. ***Never should it be washed with soap again!*** The pan is then heat on a medium-high heat until quite hot and 2 to 3 tablespoons (30-45 ml) of peanut oil poured in it. The pan is removed from heat as the oil is being swirled around to cover all surfaces. Afterward the pan must be allowed to cool. This process must be repeated two more times and the pan is ready for use. Should some food stick, do not resort to washing it with soap. Remove what's sticking to the pan using a green scouring cloth with a little oil and rub clean using a paper towel.

REFRIGERATOR FOOD STORAGE GUIDE

Cakes	5-7 days		Poultry-uncooked	1-2 day(s)
Cheese-hard	3-4 weeks		Precooked rice,	
Cheese-soft	7-10 days		potatoes, etc.	5-7 days
Cream or milk	10-15 days		Meat-cooked	3-4 days
Eggs	3-4 weeks		Meat-uncooked	2-3 days
Fish-uncooked	1-2 day(s)		Salad dressings	1 month
Margarine	8-12 weeks		Wheat germ/bran	6 months
Pies	4-5 days		Yogurt/sourcream	7-12 days

Please Note *This chart is based on an average refrigerator temperature of about 39 to 43°F (4 to 6°C) and that the food items are relatively fresh when placed in it. Many of the above items can be stored longer and in some cases less long than indicated. A quick eye, nose, and taste inspection should always prevail. Bulk wheat germ (even bran) should be refrigerated and **not** stored in pantry!*

OPTIMIZED OVEN USAGE

The following information is included as to allow you to use your oven to full capacity and turn your kitchen into a small bakery or food factory. It is recommended that you use your oven to its maximum capacity whenever possible. This way a lot of time and electrical energy is saved. You also utilize you oven to its maximum capacity when large batch cooking or baking. When there isn't much to bake or a small reheat is required, then better to use a toaster-oven or microwave oven. The illustrations were based on the standard 30-inch electric range, which has 4 or 5 level settings for the two oven racks.

OPTIMIZED OVEN USAGE GUIDELINES

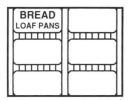

Bread loaf pans
2 racks of 6 each
5" x 9" (13 x 22 cm)
Moderate temperatures

Large pizza pan
Below top rack only
16-17" (40 cm)
High temperatures

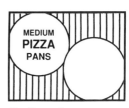

Medium pizza pans
Below top rack only
12" (30 cm)
High temperatures

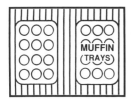

Muffin trays
2 racks of 2 each
Dozen medium-size
Moderate temperatures

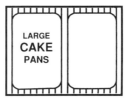

Large cake pans
2 racks of 2 each
9"x13" (23 x 33 cm)
Moderate temperatures

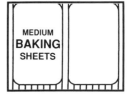

Medium cookie trays
Medium rack only
10"x15" (25 x 38 cm)
Med-high temperatures

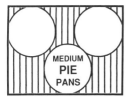

Medium pie pans
Medium rack only
8-9" (20-23 cm) round
Med-high temperates

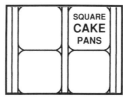

Medium cake pans
2 racks of 4 each
8" (20 cm) square
Moderate temperatures

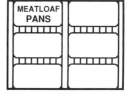

Meatloaf pans
Medium rack only
5" x 9" (13 x 22 cm)
Med-high temperatures

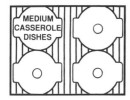

Med-small casseroles
2 racks of 4 each
8" (20 cm) round
Med-high temperatures

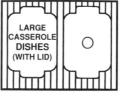

Large casseroles
2 racks of 2 each
10" x 12" (25 x 30 cm)
Med-high temperatures

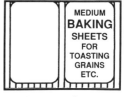

Medium toasting trays
2 racks of 2 each
10" x 15" (25 x 38 cm)
Low temperatures

TYPICAL SERVINGS
Small servings are about 1/2 cup (120 ml)
Medium servings are about 1 cup (240 ml)
Large servings are about 1 1/2 cups (360 ml)

SHALLOW FRYING

Shallow frying is the least expensive way to fry. It is best done in a large saucepan (because of its high wall) covered with a simmer plate, splash screen, or lid. A frying pan or skillet works well also but makes more of a mess. It has its place in this book because electric deep fryers and frying baskets (to be used with a saucepan) are expensive. Shallow frying must at least submerge half (plus some) with hot oil or fat. Keep in mind shallow frying takes a bit longer than deep-frying because the food is not completely submerged. It uses very little oil or fat, which can be stored refrigerated in a container and reused many times, making it inexpensive. The oil itself can be filtered using a funnel and a paper coffee filter. The ideal temperature of the oil or fat when frying is 365-375°F/185-190°C (use a candy thermometer). If the fat is not hot enough the food will absorb it and be greasy. Anything to be shallow fried (even deep-fried) must be dried first or the hot fat will spatter. Don't leave a pan used for shallow frying unattended because of the fire hazard potential.

CONVERSIONS & ABBREVIATIONS

Weights and Measures

1 tablespoon = 3 teaspoons = 1/16 cup = 1/2 fluid ounce = 15 milliliters

2 tablespoons = 6 teaspoons = 1/8 cup   = 1 fluid ounce = 30 milliliters

4 tablespoons = 12 teaspoons = 1/4 cup = 2 fluid ounces = 60 milliliters

16 tablespoons = 48 teaspoons = 1 cup   = 8 fluid ounces = 240 milliliters

1 quart   = 4 cups = 32 fluid ounces = .96 liter

4 quarts   = 16 cups = 128 fluid ounces = 3.84 liters

3 tablespoons = 1 jigger   = 1 1/2 fluid ounces = 45 milliliters

1 ounce   = 28 grams

1 pound   = 16 ounces   = 454 grams

2.2 pounds   = 1 kilograms   = 1000 grams

Temperature Conversions

Fahrenheit		Celsius
212F	=	100C
250F	=	120C
300F	=	150C
350F	=	180C
400F	=	200C
450F	=	230C

Legend of abbreviations

tbsp	=	tablespoon(s)
tsp	=	teaspoon(s)
ml	=	milliliter(s)
lb	=	pound(s)
kg	=	kilogram(s)
g	=	gram(s)
l	=	liter(s)

SAMPLE MENUS, LEGEND, & COOKING TERMS

This chapter is one of the most important because not only does it suggest recipe combinations but also offer a method to further reduce and minimize the cost of every single meal (see top of page 41).

BREAKFAST

LIGHT BREAKFAST
One serving or portion of instant oatmeal, or mueslix, or granolas, or other grain cereals *(with reconstituted milk)*, or cake, or muffin, or pancake, or waffle, or sweet pie, etc. *(all homemade of course)*
With...
One cup *(or glass)* of instant coffee, or tea, or milkshake, or raw vegetable juice, or fruit beverage, etc. *(all homemade again)*

FULL COURSE BREAKFAST
One serving of fried eggs, or other egg variations like scrambled or an omelet, or even quiche, etc.
With...
One serving of fried potatoes, or French fries or other potato variations.
With...
Two bread toasts or one sliced toasted bagel with margarine, or cream cheese, or with 1 tbsp (15 ml) jam stretcher. *(homemade too)*
With...
One cup *(or glass)* of instant coffee, or tea, or raw vegetable juice, or fruit beverage, etc.

LUNCH

One serving or portion of soup, or salad, with or without bread *(and margarine)*.

With...

One serving or portion of rice/pasta/potato/or side sish.

With...

One sandwich or slice of pizza, or one meat or meatless hamburger, or restaurant food selection like a small submarine or burritos, or one dish pie or pot pie portion.

With...

One portion or serving of dessert or cake.

With...

One cup *(or glass)* of instant coffee, or tea, or pitcher filtered water.

SUPPER

One serving or portion of soup, or salad with or without bread or a hot dinner roll *and margarine.*

With...

One cup *(or glass)* of instant coffee, or tea, or pitcher filtered water

With...

> One serving or portion of a rice/potato/pasta/or side-dish.
>
> **With...**
>
> One serving or portion of meat or meatless loaf, or fish or innards.
>
> **With...**
>
> One small serving of a white sauce variation.

Or...

> A large portion or serving of a main course dish like chicken pot pie, or ragout, or a meal in a pan or stove top dish. Alternately, a large serving of a rice/potato/pasta/or side dish converted to a main course dish by the addition of meat, poultry or fish.

Please Note *All the above dishes and items are homemade from the recipes in this book. This includes the cream cheese, salad dressings, bagel, cereals, etc.*

MINIMIZING THE COST OF MEALS

To lower the cost of meals even further, you must combine servings of recipes from the various groups in such a way as to lower the overall cost of that meal. For the purpose of this book, we came up with seven identifiable groups. The list may be sub-categorized as follows:

1. **Protein/carbohydrate group.**
2. **Mostly carbohydrates group.**
3. **Cook or uncooked vegetables group.**
4. **Sauce, dressing, and condiment group.**
5. **Soup and broth group.**
6. **Hot and cold beverage group.**
7. **Desserts, muffins and cakes group.**

Servings from the more expensive recipe containing ingredients like meat, poultry, fish, cheese, eggs, certain vegetables and fruits, canned tomatoes, milk powder, chocolate, honey, etc. must be counter balanced with servings from the much less expensive recipes. Recipes that are less expensive tend to contain ingredients like rice, grains, pasta, certain inexpensive vegetables and fruits, flour, potatoes (fries), and water (as in soups and beverages). Fast food vendors, frozen dinners, and meat helpers use the same idea!

> ***TIPS & HINTS:*** *A larger percentage of each meal should include much more of the much less expensive food items and recipes!*

SAMPLE MEAL COST

One bowl of Vegetable & Pasta Soup *(see page 49)*	*about 10¢*
One medium (3-4 oz/100 g) Italian-Style Fried Fillets *(see page 138)*	*about 30¢*
One tablespoon (15 ml) Chickpea Sauce *(see page 143)*	*about 5¢*
One average serving Buttery-Lemon Rice *(see page 88)*	*about 18¢*
One small serving of Mediterranean Carrot Salad *(see page 60)*	*about 10¢*
One piece of Buttermilk-Raisin Cake *(see page 198)*	*about 7¢*
One cup of Instant Coffee *(see page 229)*	*about 6¢*

Total......about 86¢ (Canadian)   Or about 58¢ U.S.

Apart from the above example and mentioning on the back cover that the recipes in this book actually yield 3 meals (not just one) for 1½ to 3 Canadian dollars (1 to 2 U.S. dollars), there will be no other exact references to cost. Any vague references to recipe cost later in this book are based on Canadian dollars. The **CookMISER** *book optimizes the concept of low-budget cookery and regardless what year you'll be using this book and how much food prices rise, you just can't cook for less!* ***Any further references as to recipe cost are in Canadian currency.***

LEGEND

Legend of Symbols

 The piggy bank symbol is always positioned beside the name of the least expensive CookMISER recipes. A piggy placed beside the *Basic* recipe usually means most variations are very low cost too. This <u>does not mean</u> that all other CookMISER recipes are expensive.

? minute(s) This gives the total time required to <u>prepare & cook</u> recipes and assumes all precooked or pre-toasted ingredients & dough are ready.

How are the recipes in this book written & structured?

Most recipes in this book were written in a condensed style and are linked to a basic recipe and are shown as one of its variations. They share the same basic instructions or procedure, and contain the phrase **<u>Basic XXXX recipe</u>** *as a reminder. A basic recipe in itself is a recipe but not always a definite one. All other recipes are not linked to any basic recipe and stand on their own.* **Please note** *in all 'Basic' recipes, that ingredients <u>not in italics</u> definitely belong to basic recipe and* **<u>all</u>** *its variations. Where as, the ingredients or references to ingredients that are in <u>italics</u> (but not in parenthesis) are not definite and you must rely on the recipe variations or pick your own.*

COOKING TERMS

AL DENTE *Pasta cooked till just firm to the bite.*
BASTE *To moisten food with the liquid in which it is cooking.*
BROIL *To cook on upper oven rack under intense direct heat.*
CARAMELIZE *To heat sugar or foods until their sugar turns brown.*
COMBINE (TO) *To place ingredients together in a container and mix.*
CREAM (TO) *To beat a mixture until it has the consistency of cream.*
CRIMP *To make a decorative seal or bond around a pie crust.*
CUT IN *To incorporate chilled fat into flour using fingers or two knives.*
DEEP FRYING *To cook food by completely submersion in hot oil or fat.*
DREDGE *To cover with flour or sugar by sprinkling or using a bag.*
DRIZZLE *To sprinkle drops of a liquid over food.*
FOLD *To combine by turning gently with a spatula or metal spoon.*
GARNISH *To decorate a dish to enhance its flavor and appearance.*
GREASE (TO) *To lightly coat the inside of a pan or dish with solid fat.*
INCUBATE *To place in a warm place for a certain amount of time.*
MINCE (TO) *To chop very fine.*
MIX *To uniformly combine ingredients by stirring.*
PARBOIL *To partially cook in boiling water.*
SCALD *To heat milk short of its boiling point or pour boiling water on.*
SHALLOW FRYING *To cook food by partial submersion in hot oil or fat.*
SIMMER *To simmer a liquid mixture so gently that it barely bubbles.*
STEEP *To pour liquid over herbs or ingredient(s) and let it sit a while.*
STIR *To mix ingredients with a spoon using circular motions.*
STIR-FRY *To cook (in a little oil) over high heat while continuously stirring.*

Breakfast Cereals

All our cereals cost but a small fraction of their store-bought equivalent.

INSTANT OATMEAL

Basic Instant Oatmeal   *5 minutes*

1/2 cup (120 ml) *'One Minute'* rolled oats   **1/8 tsp (1/2 ml) table salt**
3/4 cup (180 ml) boiling water   ***Flavoring to taste!***

Place about 2 cups (480 ml) of hot tap water into an **electric kettle** and get water boiling. Meanwhile, in a **small bowl**, add rolled oats, salt *plus ingredients for one of the instant oatmeal recipe variations.* Pour in the boiling water; stir a few seconds and serve hot. **Makes about 8 ounces (240 ml) or 1 average serving**

INSTANT OATMEAL VARIATIONS

Old-Fashioned Oatmeal   *5 minutes*

1 tbsp (15 ml) dark brown sugar   **1 tbsp (15 ml) table syrup** *(pg. 218)*
Add the above to *Basic Instant Oatmeal* recipe.

Apple & Cinnamon Oatmeal   *5 minutes*

1 tbsp (15 ml) *Quick Applesauce*   **1 tbsp (15 ml) dark brown sugar**
   (see page 217)   **1/8 tsp (1/2 ml) cinnamon**
Add the above to *Basic Instant Oatmeal* recipe.

Raisin-Bran Oatmeal   *5 minutes*

1/2 tbsp (7 ml) dried raisins   **1 tbsp (15 ml) dark brown sugar**
1 tsp (5 ml) *bulk* **wheat bran**
Add the above to *Basic Instant Oatmeal* recipe.

Molasses & Spice Oatmeal   5 minutes

1 tsp (5 ml) molasses   1/2 tbsp (7 ml) dark brown sugar
1/8 tsp (1/2 ml) cinnamon   Dash of allspice
Add the above to *Basic Instant Oatmeal* recipe.

Apple & Spice Oatmeal   6-7 minutes

Quarter apple, peeled and diced   1/8 tsp (1/2 ml) cinnamon
1 tbsp (15 ml) dark brown sugar   1/8 tsp (1/2 ml) nutmeg
Add the above to *Basic Instant Oatmeal* recipe.
SUB-VARIATIONS *Try a quarter banana, or other sweet or sub-acid fruit at peak harvest only!*

Honey-Raisin Oatmeal   5 minutes

1 tsp (5 ml) dark liquid honey   1/2 tbsp (7 ml) dried raisins
1 tsp (5 ml) granulated sugar
Add the above to *Basic Instant Oatmeal* recipe.

Date & Wheat Germ Oatmeal   5 minutes

1 tbsp (15 ml) *bulk* wheat germ   1 tbsp (15 ml) dark brown sugar
          1/2 tbsp (7 ml) finely chopped dates
Add the above to *Basic Instant Oatmeal* recipe.

MUESLIX

delicious
CEREAL

net weight 10.5 ounces

For the mueslix-style cereal recipes, some of the ingredients must be pre-toasted as a batch (see page 26). All ingredients required for the basic mueslix recipe must be premixed and placed in bags in advance. Quantities should be multiplied by a factor of four or more when premixing. Shake bag before serving.

Basic Mueslix   1-3 minutes

1/2 cup (120 ml) pre-toasted rolled oats   1 tbsp (15 ml) brown sugar
(use '1 minute' oats, see page 26)   2 tbsp (30 ml) skim milk powder
1 tbsp (15 ml) pre-toasted wheat germ   1/2 tbsp (7 ml) pre-toasted sun-
(see page 26)   flower seed kernels *(see page 26)*
Or about 3/4 cup (180 ml) of a premixed mueslix cereal recipe!
In a **small serving bowl**, place above ingredients *plus those for a recipe variation* or premixed mueslix; add 3/4 cup (180 ml) cold water, stir and serve. **Makes 3/4 cup (180 ml) or 1 serving**

MUESLIX VARIATIONS

Date-Peanut Mueslix   1-3 minutes

1/2 tbsp (7 ml) dried pitted dates,   1/2 tbsp (7 ml) roasted peanuts,
fine chopped   blender chopped
Add the above to *Basic Mueslix* recipe.

Sesame & Raisin Mueslix   *1-3 minutes*

1/2 tsp (2 ml) pre-toasted sesame seeds   1/2 tbsp (7 ml) dried raisins,
(see page 26)   chopped

Add the above to *Basic Mueslix* recipe.

Coconut-Date Mueslix   *1-3 minutes*

1/2 tsp (2 ml) grated dried coconut   1/2 tbsp (7 ml) dried pitted dates,
                                                    fine chopped

Add the above to *Basic Mueslix* recipe.

GRANOLA CEREALS

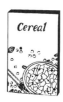

For these granola-style cereal recipes when premixing granola cereals in advance, batch quantities should be multiplied by a factor of four or more.

Basic Granola Cereal   *30 minutes*

DRY INGREDIENTS:
1 cup (240 ml) *'Quick'* rolled oats
1/3 cup (80 ml) *bulk* wheat germ
2 tbsp (30 ml) *bulk* wheat bran
1 tbsp (15 ml) *bulk* sunflower seeds
1 tsp (5 ml) *bulk* sesame seeds

LIQUID MIXTURE:
1/4 cup (60 ml) hot tap water
1/4 tsp (1 ml) artificial vanilla
    extract
1 1/2 tbsp (22 ml) vegetable oil
2 tbsp (30 ml) granulated sugar
2 tsp (10 ml) molasses

OR *1/4 cup (60 ml) dark brown sugar instead of molasses & granulated sugar*
Preheat oven to 400°F(200°C). Meanwhile, in **a large bowl**, place all of the liquid mixture ingredients and stir. Quickly add all of the dry ingredients *plus ingredients for any of the variations* and mix well. Using **baking sheets**, spread out the mixture evenly, bake about 20 minutes until golden. *There is no real need to turn the toasting cereal over unless you want perfection.* Let cool and store in an airtight plastic bag or container. Serve with chilled *Mock Whole Milk, Reconstituted Skim Milk,* or *Homemade Soymilk,* see pages 231 and 234.
Makes 1 1/2 cups (360 ml) or 2 good servings

GRANOLA CEREAL VARIATIONS

Harvest Munch Cereal   *30 minutes*

1 tsp (5 ml) peanut butter   1 tbsp (15 ml) blender chopped peanuts
Add the above to *Basic Granola Cereal* recipe. *Use dark brown sugar instead of molasses and granulated sugar.*

Raisin-Bran Cereal   *30 minutes*

1 tbsp (15 ml) dried raisins   2 tbsp (30 ml) *bulk* wheat bran
Add the above to *Basic Granola Cereal* recipe.

Apples & Cinnamon Cereal   *30 minutes*

2 tbsp (30 ml) chopped dried apples   **1/2 tsp (7 ml) cinnamon**
   (see page 26)
Add the above to *Basic Granola Cereal* recipe.
SUB-VARIATIONS *Try with same amount of dried sliced bananas, fresh chopped apples, or fresh sliced bananas!*

Coconut & Dates Cereal   *30 minutes*

1/2 tbsp (7 ml) dried shredded coconut   **1 or 2 pitted date(s), chopped**
Add the above to *Basic Granola Cereal* recipe.

OTHER CEREAL RECIPES

Breakfast Cornmeal   *8 minutes*

7/8 cups (210 ml) cornmeal (#250)   **1/4 tsp (1 ml) table salt**
2 cups (480 ml) hot tap water
In a **frying pan** or **heavy skillet**, bring water to a boil over the highest heat setting. Lower heat to medium and gradually add the cornmeal, stirring at the same time. Stir until the cornmeal *(polenta)* is smooth and thick, about 5 minutes. Serve immediately as a mushy cereal with milk *(powdered skim milk and cold water)* and dark brown sugar. **Makes about 2 cups (480 ml)**

Chewy Wheat Cereal   *5 minutes*

1 1/4 cups (300 ml) presoaked wheat   **3 cups (720 ml) hot tap water**
   berries

 In a **saucepan**, place wheat and bring to a boil; maintain up to a minute. Drain and rinse under cold tap water. Serve in cereal bowls with a little milk *(instant milk powder and cold tap water)* or *Mock Whole Milk (page 234)* and brown sugar. **Makes two servings**

Breakfast Rice   *5 minutes*

2/3 cup (160 ml) hot tap water   **2 tbsp (30 ml) dark brown sugar**
2 cups (480 ml) *refrigerated* precooked   **Dash of nutmeg**
   long grain rice   **2 tbsp (30 ml) dried pitted**
2 tbsp (30 ml) skim milk powder   **dates, chopped**
In a **frying pan** or **heavy skillet**, place all ingredients except dates and cinnamon; simmer and stir about 5 minutes until thickened. Pour in two bowls; stir in dates and cinnamon. Serve hot or cold. **Makes about 2 cups (480 ml)**

SOUPS

Soups are inherently low-cost and easy to make. Soup recipe instructions are always easy to follow with little preparation time. Using soup stock powders furthers this.

INSTANT SOUPS

Basic Instant Soup   *3-7 minutes*

1 1/2 cups (360 ml) hot tap water
1/2 tbsp (7 ml) chicken or beef soup
   stock powder

1 tsp (5 ml) cornstarch or
   all-purpose flour
Dash of Worcestershire sauce
Salt and pepper to taste

Using a **large heavy saucepan**, **skillet**, or even a **frying pan**, start heating the water on the highest heat setting. Immediately add stock powder and the starch or flourwhile stirring with a **whisk** *(then add ingredients for a recipe variation)*. As soon as mixture boils, lower heat to medium and simmer one to two minutes. Stir occasionally. Serve at once. *The Worcestershire sauce helps to give the soup the taste of a longer simmer period* .**Makes almost 12 ounces (360 ml) or one large serving**

INSTANT SOUP VARIATIONS

Chicken Noodle Soup   *6-7 minutes*

Use chicken soup stock powder!
1 tbsp (15 ml) instant soup noodles
1 tsp (5 ml) dried parsley

1 tbsp (15 ml) *refrigerated*
   precooked minced chicken
   (optional)

Add the above to *Basic Instant Soup* recipe.
SUB-VARIATIONS *Try with, or in combination of, any of the following: rice, pasta, finely diced potatoes, barley and numerous legumes... all precooked of course!*

Beef-Flavored Bean Soup   *7 minutes*

Use beef soup stock powder!
1/3 cup (80 ml) *frozen* precooked
   red kidney beans
2 tbsp (30 ml) canned ground
   tomatoes or tomato juice

1/8 tsp (1/2 ml) onion powder
1/8 tsp (1/2 ml) paprika
1/2 tsp (2 ml) dried parsley
1/4 tsp (1 ml) celery salt
Dash of garlic powder

Add the above to *Basic Instant Soup* recipe.
SUB-VARIATIONS *Try with, or in combination of, any of the following: rice, pasta, finely diced potatoes, barley and numerous legumes... all precooked of course!*

Savory Vegetable-Rice Soup   *6-7 minutes*

Use vegetable soup stock powder!
1/4 cup (60 ml) *refrigerated* precooked
   potatoes, peeled and diced
2 tbsp (30 ml) *refrigerated* precooked
   or blanched carrots, finely diced

1 tbsp (15 ml) canned ground
   tomatoes or paste
2 tbsp (30 ml) canned diced
   tomatoes, mashed with fork
1/2 tsp (2 ml) dried fine herbs
1/4 tsp (1 ml) onion powder

Add the above to *Basic Instant Soup* recipe.
SUB-VARIATIONS *Try with, or in combination of, any of the following: rice, pasta, barley and numerous legumes...all precooked of course!*

New Age Vegetable Soup   *7 minutes*

These new age soups may be made with any soup stock powder flavor. They may contain any pleasant combination of grated raw vegetables instead of precooked.

Use vegetable, chicken, or beef
   soup stock powder!
1/4 cup (60 ml) grated raw carrots
2 tbsp (30 ml) grated raw cabbage
Quarter celery stalk, finely chopped

1/4 cup (60 ml) *Mock Light Cream*
   (see page 232)
1/8 tsp (1/2 ml) dried basil
1/4 tsp (1 ml) celery salt

Add the above to *Basic Instant Soup* recipe but use grated or finely chopped vegetables instead of precooked items.
SUB-VARIATIONS *Try with or in combination of any of the following; grated or minced raw cucumbers, broccoli, spinach, etc., all in peak harvest season. Also great with other seasonings and ingredients like tomato juice, Worcestershire or soy sauce, salad dressing, etc.!*

Condense-Style Tomato Soup   *3-4 minutes*

Use chicken soup stock powder!
1/4 tsp (1 ml) onion powder
1 cup (240 ml) canned tomato juice
   OR 1/2 cup (120 ml) canned ground
   tomatoes *(replaces same amount water)*

1 1/2 tbsp (22 ml) cornstarch
   (instead of 1/2 tbsp (7 ml))

Add the above to *Basic Instant Soup* recipe. *Use half the amount of soup stock powder prescribed in the basic recipe.*

CHICKEN SOUPS

Basic Chicken Soup    *35-45 minutes*

1 tbsp (15 ml) vegetable oil
1 yellow onion, finely chopped
9 cups (2160 ml) cold tap water
1 *frozen* chicken neck *(optional)*
    OR cook a few *frozen* chicken
      or turkey pieces with the
      chicken soup for recipes

2 tbsp (30 ml) chicken stock powder
1 bay leaf
1 tsp (5 ml) dried parsley
1/2 tsp (2 ml) celery salt
1/2 tsp (2 ml) onion powder
1 tbsp (15 ml) all-purpose flour
Salt and pepper to taste

In a **large saucepan**, sauté onion in oil over a medium-high heat. Stir frequently and sauté a few minutes. Immediately, add water, optional chicken pieces, stock powder, and seasoning ingredients *(plus ingredients for a recipe variation).* Bring to a boil on highest setting. Save flour, salt and pepper for later. When boiling, lower heat to medium-low and add flour dissolved in a little water. Cover and simmer at least 30 minutes. Add salt and pepper to taste. Remove chicken parts before serving. Serve it hot or refrigerate. *Always make soup when precooking chicken or turkey sections for later use in various recipes.* **Makes about 8 average servings of 1 cup (240 ml) each or 2Q/L**

LITE! VERSION *Use only 1/4 tsp (1 ml) vegetable oil in a large non-stick saucepan and use only chicken bits omitting chicken section(s), and use low-fat chicken stock powder!*

CHICKEN SOUP VARIATIONS

Chicken & Rice Soup   *35-45 minutes*

1 cup (240 ml) precooked long grain
    rice

1/2 tsp (2 ml) lemon juice from
    concentrate...per serving
Half celery stalk, finely chopped

Using *Basic Chicken Soup* recipe, add celery immediately after water and add precooked rice at early simmer stage. *Add lemon juice to serving bowl only.*

Chicken & Pasta Soup   *35-45 minutes*

1/2 cup (120 ml) uncooked pasta, any
    kind *(break them up if too long)*

1 tsp (5 ml) oregano

Using *Basic Chicken Soup* recipe, add pasta when stock mixture is boiling. *Add oregano and/or replace thyme.*

Chicken & Barley Soup   *35-45 minutes*

1 garlic clove, finely minced
1/2 cup (120 ml) raw barley,
    presoaked overnight

1/2 tsp (2 ml) Dijon mustard
1/8 tsp (1/2 ml) garlic powder

Using *Basic Chicken Soup* recipe, sauté garlic too. Add soaked barley to boiling stock mixture, then add mustard and garlic powder to simmering stock.

Chicken & Potato Soup   *35-45 minutes*

1 large precooked potato,   Half celery stalk, finely chopped
  peeled and finely diced

Using *Basic Chicken Soup* recipe, add celery immediately after adding water and add precooked potato at early simmer stage.

Chicken & Bean Soup   *35-45 minutes*

1/3 cup (80 ml) *frozen* precooked   1/16 tsp (1/4 ml) garlic powder
  red kidney beans, thawed   1/4 tsp (1 ml) ground rosemary
1/2 cup (120 ml) carrot, grated   1/4 tsp (1 ml) ground sage
1 garlic clove, sliced

Using *Basic Chicken Soup* recipe, sauté carrot and garlic. Add beans to boiling stock mixture, then garlic powder and additional seasoning at early simmer stage.

VEGETABLE SOUPS

Basic Vegetable Soup   *30 minutes*

2 tbsp (30 ml) margarine   1/2 tsp (2 ml) celery salt
1 large yellow onion, chopped   1/2 tsp (2 ml) dried majoram
1 garlic clove, sliced   2 tsp (10 ml) dried parsley
1 celery stalk, chopped   1/8 tsp (1/2 ml) garlic powder
1 medium carrot, grated   1/2 tsp (2 ml) onion powder
1 small precooked potato, diced   3 tbsp (45 ml) all-purpose flour
8 cups (1920 ml) water   2/3 cups (160 ml) canned ground
2 tbsp (30 ml) vegetable soup   tomatoes
  stock powder   Salt and pepper to taste
1 bay leaf

In a **large saucepan**, melt margarine over a medium-high heat. Add vegetables; quickly sauté while stirring 5 minutes. Pour water, add leaf and seasoning ingredients *(plus ingredients for a recipe variation)*. Bring to a boil over the highest heat setting. Immediately lower heat to a medium-low setting. Add the flour dissolved in a little water; simmer about 10 minutes. Add tomato juice and simmer another 5 minutes. Adjust taste with a little salt and pepper. For crispier soup serve hot immediately. Age twelve hours in refrigerator before serving for a more developed taste. **Makes about 8 average servings of 1 cup (240 ml) each or 2Q/L**

LITE! VERSION *Use only 1/2 tsp (2 ml) margarine in a large non-stick saucepan!*

VEGETABLE SOUP VARIATIONS

Vegetable & Pasta Soup *30 minutes*

1/2 cup (120 ml) uncooked pasta   **1 tsp (5 ml) oregano**
    (any kind)   **1/2 tsp (2 ml) dried fine herbs**

Using *Basic Vegetable Soup* recipe, add pasta when stock mixture has reached a boil. Add oregano and dried herbs with other seasoning ingredients.

Winter Vegetable Soup *30 minutes*

1 small precooked beet, peeled   **1/2 cup (120 ml) precooked parsnip,**
    diced   **diced**
                                                 1/2 tsp (2 ml) dill seeds

Using *Basic Vegetable Soup* recipe, add precooked vegetables *(frozen, unthawed)* when stock mixture has reached a boil. Add dill seeds with other seasoning.

Carrot & Rice Soup *30 minutes*

2 small carrots, thinly sliced   **1 tsp (5 ml) dried thyme**
1/2 cup (120 ml) precooked brown   **Ground sage to taste**
    rice

Using *Basic Vegetable Soup* recipe, sauté carrots too. Add rice when stock mixture has reached a boil. Add thyme with other seasoning and sage at the end to taste.

Vegetables & Bean Soup *30 minutes*

2/3 cup (160 ml) *frozen*   **2 tbsp (30 ml) red wine vinegar**
    precooked Italian or red   **or white vinegar**
    kidney beans, thawed   **1 tsp (5 ml) dried thyme**
                                                  1/4 tsp (1 ml) ground rosemary

Using *Basic Vegetable Soup* recipe, add wine vinegar, thyme and rosemary with other seasoning. Add precooked beans when stock mixture has reached a boil.

BEEF SOUPS

Basic Beef Soup *30 minutes*

2 tbsp (30 ml) vegetable oil   **1 small bare rendering bone**
1 large yellow onion, finely   **2 tbsp (30 ml) beef stock powder**
    chopped or thinly sliced   **1/2 tsp (2 ml) dried mint *(optional)***
1 small carrot, grated   **1 tsp (5 ml) dried parsley**
1 celery stalk, thinly sliced   **1/2 tsp (2 ml) celery salt**
8 cups (1920 ml) water   **1/2 tsp (2 ml) onion powder**
1/3 cup (80 ml) canned ground   **2 tbsp (30 ml) all-purpose flour**
    tomatoes   **Salt and pepper to taste**

In a **large saucepan**, sauté vegetables in oil over a medium-high heat. Stir frequently and sauté a few minutes. Immediately, add water, bare rendering bone, stock powder and seasoning ingredients *(plus ingredients for a recipe variation)*. Bring to a boil on highest setting. Save flour, salt and pepper for later. When boiling, immediately lower heat to medium-low and add flour dissolved in a little water. Cover and simmer about 10 minutes. Add tomato juice and simmer a few more minutes. Add salt and pepper to taste. Serve hot or refrigerate. **Makes about 8 average servings of 1 cup (240 ml) each or 2Q/L**

LITE! VERSION *Use only 1/4 tsp (1 ml) vegetable oil in a large non-stick saucepan. Omit the bone rendering!*

BEEF SOUP VARIATIONS

Beef & Barley Soup   *30 minutes*

2/3 cup (160 ml) barley, soaked
   overnight in cold water
1 large garlic clove, crushed
2 tbsp (30 ml) red wine vinegar
   or white vinegar

1/2 tsp (2 ml) dried basil
1/2 tsp (2 ml) oregano
1/4 tsp (1 ml) rosemary
1/8 tsp (1/2 ml) garlic powder
1 bay leaf

Using *Basic Beef Soup* recipe, add above ingredients immediately after water. *Dried mint in basic recipe may be omitted.*

Hearty Beef Soup   *30-35 minutes*

1/8 cup (30 ml) stewing
   beef, finely chopped
1 large precooked potato,
   peeled and diced
1 small garlic clove, sliced

1/4 pound (100 g) green cabbage,
   shredded
1/16 tsp (1/4 ml) garlic powder
1/4 tsp (1 ml) paprika
1/2 tsp (2 ml) caraway seeds

Using *Basic Beef Soup* recipe, add above ingredients immediately after water. *Dried mint in basic recipe may be omitted.*

Beef & Pasta Soup   *30 minutes*

1/2 cup (120 ml) uncooked pasta,
   any kind *(breaken up if too long)*
1/4 cup (60 ml) *frozen* precooked
   red kidney beans, thawed

1 tsp (5 ml) oregano
1/8 tsp (1/2 ml) garlic powder
1/2 tsp (2 ml) dried fine herbs

Using *Basic Beef Soup* recipe, add above ingredients when stock mixture is boiling.

Brown Potato Soup   *30-35 minutes*

1 tbsp (15 ml) all-purpose flour

3 large precooked potatoes, peeled
   and diced

Using *Basic Beef Soup* recipe, when vegetables *(except potatoes)* are being sautéed add extra flour and stir-fry 5 minutes until brown. Add potatoes during early simmer stage.

CREAM OF VEGETABLE SOUPS

These cream of vegetable soups are low cost and relatively easy and quick to make.

Basic Cream of Vegetable Soup 🐷   *30 minutes*

About 1/2-3/4 pound (225-337 g) of a
  vegetable: carrots, celery,
  or potatoes etc., chopped or sliced
  (pick one or follow a variation)
3 tbsp (45 ml) margarine
1/2 cup (120 ml) chopped yellow onion
4 tbsp (60 ml) all-purpose flour
7 cups (1680 ml) hot tap water

2 tbsp (30 ml) vegetable or
  chicken stock powder
1 bay leaf
2 tsp (10 ml) dried parsley
1 cup (240 ml) *Mock Light Cream*
  (see page 232)
1/2 tsp (2 ml) onion powder
Salt and pepper to taste

In a **large frying pan** or **skillet**, melt margarine over a medium-high heat. Meanwhile, in a **large saucepan**, place water, stock powder, bay leaf and parsley *(plus ingredients for a variation)*. Heat over highest setting.   As   soon   as margarine has melted, sauté the main vegetable and onions a few minutes. Quickly sprinkle skillet with the flour, and stir. When water and stock mixture starts boiling; pour contents of skillet unto saucepan. Stir and lower heat to medium and simmer 10 minutes. In a **blender**, puree half of mixture at once for 10 seconds. ***Do not over-blend.*** Return contents to saucepan and reheat a few minutes over a medium heat. Just before serving stir in the cream and season to taste. **Makes about 8 average servings of 1 cup (240 ml) each or 2Q/L**

LITE! VERSION *Omit the margarine and use reconstituted skim milk and no cream!*

CREAM OF VEGETABLE SOUP VARIATIONS

Cream of Celery Soup   *30 minutes*

3 celery stalks, roughly sliced
1 large precooked potato,
  peeled and coarsely diced

1/2 tsp (2 ml) celery salt
1/8 tsp (1/2 ml) nutmeg

Using *Basic Cream of Vegetable Soup* recipe, use celery as the main vegetable and add potato at the same time. Add celery salt and nutmeg with stock powder.

Cream of Carrot Soup   *30 minutes*

1/2 pound (225 g) fresh or blanched
  carrots, chopped or sliced

1 small garlic clove, sliced
  (optional)

Using *Basic Cream of Vegetable Soup* recipe, use carrots as main vegetable.

Cream of Potato Soup   *30 minutes*

3/4 pound (330 g) *refrigerated* precooked
  potatoes, peeled and very
  coarsely diced

Half a celery stalk with leaves,
  sliced
1/2 tsp (2 ml) dried dill weed

Using *Basic Cream of Vegetable Soup* recipe, use precooked potatoes as main vegetable for this soup and add celery at the same time as onions. Add dried dill weed with the stock powder.

Vichyssoise Soup   30 minutes

4 large *refrigerated* precooked potatoes   **1/4 tsp (1 ml) ground mace**
Add the above to *Basic Cream of Vegetable Soup* recipe.

Cream of Onion Soup   30 minutes

1/2 pound (225 g) yellow onions,   **1 tsp (5 ml) onion powder**
    chopped   ***Replace vegetable or chicken***
Half a celery stalk, chopped   ***stock powder with beef stock***
                                            powder (optional)!

Using *Basic Cream of Vegetable Soup* recipe, use onions as main vegetable and add the celery with the onions. Add onion powder at the same time as the beef stock powder and seasonings.

Cream of Dandelion Soup   30 minutes

4 cups (960 ml) fresh dandelion   **1 garlic clove, sliced**
    greens, coarsely chopped   **Pinch of nutmeg**

Using *Basic Cream of Vegetable Soup* recipe, use dandelion greens as main vegetable. Add the garlic with the onions and season with nutmeg.

Cream of Vegetables Soup   30 minutes

1 celery stalk, sliced   **1/4 tsp (1 ml) celery salt**
1 large precooked potato,   **1/4 tsp (1 ml) dried dill weed**
    peeled and coarsely diced   **1/8 tsp (1/2 ml) nutmeg**
1 medium carrot, thinly sliced   **1 small garlic clove, sliced**

Using *Basic Cream of Vegetable Soup* recipe, add the four vegetables at the same time as onions. Add the 3 spices along with stock powder. Season with salt and pepper to taste.

SUB-VARIATIONS *Replace any or all of above 4 vegetables with fresh vegetable(s) inexpensively in season only, like corn, broccoli, cauliflower, spinach, peas or thinly sliced mushrooms!*

 OTHER SOUP RECIPES

Classic French Onion Soup   30 minutes

2 tbsp (30 ml) margarine   **1 bay leaf**
1 tbsp (30 ml) vegetable oil   **1/8 tsp (1/4 ml) dried thyme**
2 cups (480 ml) yellow onions,   **1 tsp (5 ml) wine vinegar or**
    thinly sliced   **white vinegar**
7 cups (1680 ml) water   **1 tbsp (30 ml) all-purpose flour**
2 tbsp (30 ml) beef stock   **2 tsp (10 ml) onion powder**
    powder   **Salt and pepper to taste**

In a **large frying pan** or **skillet**, heat the margarine and oil over a medium-high setting. Meanwhile, in a **large saucepan**, place water, stock powder, bay leaf, thyme and vinegar; heat over highest setting. When margarine has melted, add onions and sauté for 10 minutes or until light golden brown and slightly caramelized. Stir frequently. Immediately pour contents of skillet to saucepan and reduce heat to medium. Mix the flour with a little water and add to soup at this point. Let simmer 10 minutes. Serve hot with toasted French bread. **Makes about 2Q/L**

Curried Tropical Soup   *20 minutes*

2 tbsp (30 ml) vegetable oil
1 medium yellow onion,
   chopped
1 garlic clove, finely minced
1 tbsp (15 ml) dried shredded
   coconut
1 tbsp (15 ml) curry powder
1 tsp (5 ml) turmeric powder
1/2 tsp (2 ml) ground ginger

7 1/2 cups (1800 ml) water
1 1/2 tbsp (22 ml) chicken soup stock
   powder
1 cup (240 ml) precooked rice
1 tbsp (15 ml) dried parsley
3 tbsp (45 ml) all-purpose flour
Salt and pepper to taste

In a **large frying pan** or **skillet**, heat the vegetable oil over a medium-high setting. Meanwhile, in a **large saucepan**, place water and stock powder; heat over highest setting. When margarine has melted, add onions, garlic, coconut and the three tropical spices. Sauté 5 minutes or until transparent. Stir frequently. Immediately pour contents of skillet, rice and parsley to saucepan and reduce heat to medium. Mix the flour with a little water and add to soup at this point. Let simmer 10 minutes. Serve hot. **Makes about 2Q/L**

Bourbonnaise Cabbage Soup   *30 minutes*

2 tbsp (30 ml) vegetable oil
3/4 pound (330 g) green cabbage,
   shredded
2 precooked potatoes,
   peeled and diced
6 1/2 cups (1560 mL) water

2 tbsp (30 ml) vegetable stock
   powder
1/2 tsp (2 ml) table salt
1 1/2 tsp (7 ml) dried chervil
Black pepper to taste
8 slices rye bread *(optional)*

In a **large saucepan**, place water, stock powder, salt, and chervil. Bring to a boil over highest setting. Meanwhile, in a **large frying pan** or **skillet**, heat the oil over a medium-high setting. Sauté cabbage and potatoes for at least 5 minutes; stir constantly. Add contents of skillet to saucepan. When mixture is boiling, lower heat to medium. Simmer 20 minutes or till vegetables become tender but not soft. Serve hot over a slice of toasted rye and add a dash of pepper. **Makes about 2Q/L**

Traditional Legume Soup   *25 minutes*

2 1/2 cups (600 ml) *frozen* precooked
   green or yellow split peas
6 1/2 cups (1560 ml) hot tap water
2 tbsp (30 ml) chicken stock powder
1 small yellow onion, chopped

6 tbsp (90 ml) all-purpose flour
1/2 cup (120 ml) instant skim milk
   powder
1/4 cup (60 ml) vegetable oil
Salt and pepper to taste

In a **blender**, place all ingredients with only one third of the water; blend on a high speed until smooth for 1 to 2 minutes. Meanwhile, in a **large saucepan**, bring the remaining water to a boil on the highest setting. Add contents of blender to saucepan and when mixture boils lower heat to medium-low. Simmer at least 15 minutes. *Add more water for more but thinner soup.* **Makes about 2Q/L**

Black Bean Soup   *35-40 minutes*

2 tbsp (30 ml) vegetable oil
4 bacon strips, chopped
1 large yellow onion, chopped
1 garlic clove, minced
Half a celery stalk, sliced
7 cups (1680 ml) hot tap water
1/2 tsp (2 ml) dried crushed chilies

2 cup (480 ml) *frozen* precooked
    black beans
1 tbsp (15 ml) beef stock powder
1 tsp (5 ml) prepared mustard
1 tbsp (15 ml) all-purpose flour
1tbsp (15 ml) dried parsley
1/2 tsp (2 ml) celery salt
Dash of dried oregano

In a **large frying pan or skillet**, heat the vegetable oil over a medium-high setting. Meanwhile, in a **large saucepan**, place water, stock powder and seasoning ingredients; heat over highest setting. Thaw bean in a **bowl** of very hot tap water. When margarine has melted, add onions, vegetables, seasonings and beans. Sauté 5-10 minutes or until onions are transparent. Stir frequently. Immediately pour contents of skillet to saucepan and reduce heat to medium. Mix the flour with a little water and add to soup at this point. Let simmer 15-20 minutes. Serve hot. **Makes about 2Q/L**

Old-Fashioned Potato Soup   *35 minutes*

1/4 cup (60 ml) vegetable oil
1 large yellow onion, chopped
1 cup (240 ml) sliced fresh or
    blanched carrots
1 celery stalk, sliced
4 cups (960 ml) *refrigerated*
    precooked potatoes
5 cups (1250 ml) hot tap water

1 tbsp (15 ml) chicken soup stock
    powder
1/2 tsp (2 ml) table salt
2 tbsp (30 ml) instant skim milk
    powder
1 tsp (5 ml) caraway seeds
1 tsp (5 ml) majoram
1/2 tsp (2 ml) dill seeds
1/4 tsp (1 ml) paprika

In a **large frying pan** or **skillet**, heat the vegetable oil over a medium-high setting. Meanwhile, in a **large saucepan**, place water, stock powder and seasoning ingredients; heat over highest setting. When margarine has melted, add onions, vegetables and potatoes. Sauté 5-10 minutes or until onions become transparent. Stir frequently. Immediately pour contents of skillet to saucepan and reduce heat to medium. Mix the flour with a little water and add to soup at this point. Let simmer 15-20 minutes. Serve hot. **Makes about 2Q/L**

Soups! *The great thing about soup is, let's say, you have two empty bowls but enough leftover soup for one bowl only. You just have to add more water, some soup stock powder, salt and pepper. Et voilà...you now have enough to fill two bowls!*

SALADS & DRESSINGS

Salads hold an important place in meal planing. Our salads and dressings are quite varied, quick to make, and low-cost. All are worth trying at least once.

MAYONNAISE SALADS

Popular Pasta Salad   *5-15 minutes*

1 pound (454 g) pasta *(short style)*
1/3 cup (80 ml) *Homemade Mayo-nnaise (see pages 70-1)*
1 tbsp (15 ml*)* sliced green olives, minced
2 tsp (10 ml) pickled hot pepper rings, minced

1 small yellow onion, minced
2 tsp (10 ml) dried parsley
1/4 tsp (1 ml) celery salt
1/4 tsp (1 ml) onion powder
1/16 tsp (1/4 ml) garlic powder
Salt and pepper to taste

Immediately cook the pasta as described in the chapter on pasta dishes *(see page 93)*. In a **small bowl**, mix mayonnaise and seasoning ingredients. When ready, drain pasta. *Alternately, use precooked pasta.* In a **large covered bowl**, add pasta, olives, pepper rings and onion. Pour mayonnaise mixture, toss and cover bowl. Serve immediately or refrigerate a few hours to marinate. **Makes 4 cups (960 ml)**

Popular Potato Salad   *5-6 minutes*

4 large *refrigerated* precooked potatoes, peeled and diced
1/3 cup (80 ml) *Homemade Mayo-nnaise (see pages 70-1)*
1 celery stalk, finely chopped

1 small yellow onion, minced
2 tsp (10 ml) dried parsley
1/4 tsp (1 ml) celery salt
1/4 tsp (1 ml) onion powder
1/16 tsp (1/4 ml) garlic powder

1 tbsp (15 ml) sliced green olives,   Salt and pepper to taste
   minced

In a **large covered bowl**, place diced potatoes, celery, olives and onion. In a **small bowl**, place mayonnaise and seasoning ingredients. Mix together and pour over vegetables. Toss and serve, or cover and refrigerate until needed. **Makes 4 cups (960 ml)**

Exquisite Egg Salad   *7-8 minutes*

5 extra-large or 10 small hard-boiled   1/4 cup (60 ml) sliced green
   (precooked and refrigerated)   or black olives, minced
   eggs, shelled   2 tsp (10 ml) prepared mustard
1/3 cup (80 ml) mayonnaise   2 tsp (10 ml) dried parsley
2 celery stalks, finely chopped   1/4 tsp (1 ml) celery salt
1 medium yellow onion, finely   1/4 tsp (1 ml) onion salt
   chopped   Salt and pepper to taste

 In a **large covered plastic bowl**, quickly mash eggs using a **potato masher**. Add vegetables and toss. In a **small bowl**, place mayonnaise; add mustard and spices. Mix uniformly and pour mayonnaise mixture over eggs. Mix and serve, or cover and refrigerate until needed. **Makes 4 cups (960 ml)**

Tuna & Rice Salad   *5 minutes*

2 cups (480 ml) *refrigerated* precooked   1 celery stalk, chopped
   rice   1 small yellow onion, minced
1/3 cup (80 ml) mayonnaise   2 tsp (10 ml) dried parsley
6 oz (180 ml) canned chunk light   1/4 tsp (1 ml) celery salt
   tuna in water, drained   1/4 tsp (1 ml) onion powder
1/2 cup (120 ml) *frozen* precooked   1/16 tsp (1/4 ml) garlic powder
   whole green peas, thawed   Salt and pepper to taste
   in hot water

In a **large covered bowl**, add rice, tuna, green peas, celery, and onion. In a **small bowl**, place mayonnaise and add spices. Mix well. Pour mayonnaise mixture over ingredients in large bowl and toss. Season to taste. Serve immediately or cover and refrigerate. **Makes 4 cups (960 ml)**

Far East Chicken Salad   *8-10 minutes*

1 cup (240 ml) precooked chicken,   1/2 tsp (2 ml) curry powder
   fine chopped   1/4 tsp (1 ml) ground ginger
2 celery stalks, chopped   1/4 tsp (1 ml) Dijon mustard
2 medium carrots, grated   1 tsp (5 ml) dried parsley
1 small yellow onion, chopped   1/4 tsp (1 ml) celery salt
3 tbsp (45 ml) *Homemade Mayo-*   1/4 tsp (1 ml) onion powder
   nnaise (see page 70-1)   1/16 tsp (1/4 ml) garlic powder
3 tbsp (45 ml) *Homemade Yogurt*   Salt and pepper to taste
   (see pages 232-3)

In a **large covered bowl**, combine chicken and vegetables. In a **small bowl**, blend mayonnaise, yogurt, and remaining dressing ingredients. Pour over vegetables and chicken. Toss and season to taste. Serve immediately or cover and refrigerate. **Makes 4 cups (960 ml)**

Vegetables & Mayonnaise Salad   *5-6 minutes*

3/4 cup (180 ml) green cabbage,
   shredded
2 celery stalks, chopped
1 medium carrot, shredded
   or finely chopped
1 yellow onion, thinly sliced
1 medium precooked potato,
   peeled and sliced

1/2 cup (120 ml) *Homemade*
   Mayonnaise (see pages 70-1)
1 tbsp (15 ml) sliced green olives,
   minced
1 1/2 tsp (7 ml) dried parsley
1/4 tsp (1 ml) celery salt
1/8 tsp (1/2 ml) onion powder
Salt and pepper to taste

In a **large covered bowl**, place all vegetables except olives. In a **small bowl**, mix the mayonnaise with the sliced olives and dressing ingredients together. Pour over vegetables; toss. Season to taste. Serve or refrigerate.
Makes 4 cups (960 ml)

CARROT SALADS

Basic Carrot Salad   *5-8 minutes*

4 cups (960 ml) or 4 large
   carrots, grated
2 tbsp (30 ml) vegetable oil
1 tbsp (15 ml) white vinegar
Pepper to taste

DRY SEASONING:
2 tsp (10 ml) dried parsley
1/4 tsp (1 ml) celery salt or
   table salt
1/4 tsp (1 ml) onion powder
1/16 tsp (1/4 ml) garlic powder

OR 2 tsp (10 ml) PREMIXED DRY SEASONING #5 (see page 27)
In a **large salad bowl**, place grated carrots. In a **small bowl**, whisk together oil, vinegar and dry seasoning ingredients *(plus ingredients for any of the following recipe variations)*. Pour dressing over ingredients in salad bowl. Toss and serve, or let marinate in refrigerator a few hours, with bowl covered with plastic wrap. **Makes 4 cups (960 ml)**

CARROT SALAD VARIATIONS

Oriental Carrot Salad   *7-8 minutes*

1 tbsp (15 ml) lemon juice from
   concentrate
1 tsp (5 ml) granulated sugar
4 tsp (20 ml) pickled hot pepper
   rings, minced

1/8 tsp (1/2 ml) dried crushed
   chillies
1/4 tsp (1 ml) ground ginger
2 tbsp (30 ml) peanuts, chopped
   in blender *(optional)*

Add all of above ingredients to *Basic Carrot Salad* recipe and follow procedure.

Popular Carrot Salad   6-7 minutes

1 tsp (5 ml) granulated sugar
1 tsp (5 ml) Dijon mustard

1/4 tsp (1 ml) ground black
  pepper

Add above ingredients to *Basic Carrot Salad* recipe and follow procedure.

Mediterranean Carrot Salad   7-8 minutes

2/3 cup (160 ml) *frozen* precooked
  green lentils, thawed on
  counter or in hot water

1 celery stack, diced
1 small yellow onion, chopped
1/2 tsp (2 ml) dried thyme
1/4 tsp (1 ml) ground pepper

Add thawed lentils and vegetables to *Basic Carrot Salad* recipe carrots. Add thyme and pepper to and follow procedure.

COLE SLAWS

Basic Cole Slaw   5-7 minutes

1 pound (450 g) green cabbage,
  very coarsely diced
1/4 cup (60 ml) vegetable oil
3 tbsp (45 ml) white vinegar

DRY SEASONING:
2 tsp (10 ml) dried parsley
1/8 tsp (1/2 ml) celery salt or
  table salt
1/4 tsp (1 ml) onion powder
1/16 (1/4 ml) garlic powder

OR 2 tsp (10 ml) PREMIXED DRY SEASONING #5 (see page 27)

BLENDER GRATING In the **covered container** of an **electric blender**, fill two thirds with roughly diced cabbage and barely cover with water. Grate at the lowest speed for a few seconds only until all chunks are gone. Don't over do. Using a **strainer**, drain grated cabbage. *Save the cabbage liquid from the blender grating for soups, cooking or even for your raw vegetable juices.* In a **large salad bowl**, place grated cabbage. In a **small bowl**, whisk together oil, vinegar and dry seasoning ingredients *(plus additional ingredients for any of the following recipe variations).* Pour dressing over cabbage *(and other vegetables)* in salad bowl. Toss and serve, or refrigerate a few hours to marinate. **Makes about 4 cups (960 ml)**

COLE SLAW VARIATIONS

Zesty Cole Slaw   7 minutes

2 medium carrots, grated
1 celery stalk, finely chopped
1 small yellow onion, finely
  chopped

1 tsp (5 ml) dill seeds
1 tsp (5 ml) granulated sugar
1/2 tsp (2 ml) dried basil

Add above vegetables to *Basic Cole Slaw* recipe. Add dill seeds, sugar and basil to dressing and follow instructions in basic text.

Creamy Caraway Cole Slaw   *7 minutes*

1 large carrot, grated
1 small yellow onion, finely
    chopped or sliced
2 tsp (10 ml) caraway seeds

1 tbsp (15 ml) *Homemade*
    Mayonnaise (see pages 70-1)
1 tbsp (15 ml) lemon juice from
    concentrate

Add above vegetables to *Basic Cole Slaw* recipe. Add caraway seeds, mayonnaise
and lemon juice to dressing, and follow instructions in basic text.

TABBOULEHS

Basic Tabbouleh   *5-7 minutes*

1 1/2 cups (360 ml) raw bulgur wheat
3 tbsp (45 ml) vegetable oil
3 tbsp (45 ml) white vinegar
3 tbsp (45 ml) water
Plus vegetables & legumes!
Salt and pepper to taste

DRY SEASONING:
2 tsp (10 ml) dried parsley
1/8 tsp (1/2 ml) celery salt
1/4 tsp (1 ml) onion powder
1/16 tsp (1/4 ml) garlic powder

OR 2 tsp (10 ml) PREMIXED DRY SEASONING #5 (see page 27)
In a **medium-size bowl**, place bulgur wheat and cover with plenty of cold tap water.
Let soak 30 minutes. In a **small bowl**, whisk together oil, vinegar and seasoning
ingredients *(plus ingredients for one of the recipe variations)*. After half an hour the
bulgur will have double in volume; drain. In a **large salad bowl**, add bulgur *(plus
vegetables and legumes)* and pour dressing. Toss and serve or let it marinate one hour
or more. **Makes about 4 cups (960 ml)**

TABBOULEH VARIATIONS

Pea Tabbouleh   *7 minutes*

1 large garlic clove, finely
    minced
1 large yellow onion, finely
    chopped
1 tbsp (15 ml) lemon juice from
    concentrate

1 cup (240 ml) *frozen* precooked
    whole green peas, thawed
1/4 tsp (1 ml) dried mint, crushed
1/2 tsp (2 ml) ground coriander
1/4 tsp (1 ml) ground cumin

Add above vegetables, legumes, lemon juice and spices to *Basic Tabbouleh* recipe.

Tomato Tabbouleh   *7 minutes*

1 fresh tomato, diced
    OR 1/2 cup (120 ml) canned
        diced tomatoes
1 very small yellow onion,
    thinly sliced
1 garlic clove, thinly sliced
1/4 cup (60 ml) chopped cucumber

1 tsp (5 ml) sliced green olives,
    minced
1 tbsp (15 ml) lemon juice from
    concentrate
1/2 tsp (2 ml) dried thyme
1/2 tsp (2 ml) dried mint

Add above ingredients to *Basic Tabbouleh* recipe.

SPROUT SALADS

Basic Sprout Salad   2-4 minutes

2 cups (480 ml) sprouts *(see pages 241-2)* **1/4 cup (60 ml) salad dressing**
Chopped or shredded vegetables!   **Salt and pepper to taste**
In a **salad bowl**, optionally line sides and bottom with green *(when inexpensively in season)* to form a bed. Add sprouts, vegetables and seeds. Pour salad dressing over ingredients; toss and serve. **Makes about 4 cups (960 ml)**

SPROUT SALAD VARIATIONS

Sesame-Sprout Salad   2-4 minutes

Use roughly chopped bean sprouts!   **1 tbsp (15 ml) sesame seeds**
1 large carrot, shredded   *Use French Salad Dressing!*
Use the above in *Basic sprout Salad* recipe.

Sprouted Lentil Salad   2-4 minutes

Use sprouted lentils!   **1 small yellow onion, thinly sliced**
1 celery stalk, thinly sliced   *Use Italian Salad Dressing!*
1/4 tsp (1 ml) ground ginger   *(see page 68)*
Use the above in *Basic sprout Salad* recipe.

Alfalfa Sprout Salad   2-4 minutes

Use half alfalfa seed sprouts and   **1 celery stalk, thinly sliced**
*   half bean sprouts!*   *Use French Salad Dressing!*
1 large carrot, shredded   *(see page 68)*
Use the above in *Basic sprout Salad* recipe.

PASTA SALADS

Basic Pasta Salad   3-12 minutes

Using a **large saucepan**, get about 2 quarts (liters) of hot tap water boiling over the highest heat setting.

1/2 lb (1/4 kg) pasta *about 2 cups*   **1 tsp (5 ml) white vinegar or lemon**
*   (480 ml) of macaroni or shells*   **juice from concentrate**
1 1/2 tbsp (22ml) vegetable oil   **Salt and pepper to taste**

DRY SEASONING:
1 tsp (5 ml) dried parsley   **1/4 tsp (1 ml) onion powder**
1/4 tsp (1 ml) celery salt   **1/8 tsp (1/2 ml) garlic powder**
OR 1 tsp (75ml) PREMIXED DRY SEASONING #5 (see page 27)

In a **small bowl**, whisk together oil, vinegar, and seasoning ingredients *(plus addition ingredient(s) for any of the following pasta salad variations).* Meanwhile, cook pasta in slightly oiled and salted water on a medium-high heat until *al dente. Alternately, use refrigerated precooked pasta (see page 93).* Drain and rinse a minute in running cold tap water. In a **salad bowl,** place all the ingredients, toss and serve. Alternately, marinate in the refrigerator for a few hours before serving. **Makes about 4 cups (960 ml)**

LITE! VERSION *Simply substitute half or two thirds of vegetable oil with water!*

PASTA SALAD VARIATIONS

Warm Penne Salad   3-12 minutes

1 small yellow onion, finely
   chopped or thinly sliced
Half garlic clove, finely minced
1/4 tsp (1 ml) dried mint, crushed

1 tsp (5 ml) pickled hot pepper
   rings, minced
2 tsp (10 ml) pitted green or
   black olives, sliced or minced

Add the above to *Basic Pasta Salad* recipe. Use ***penne rigate or pennine pasta*** *(preferably precooked)* and do not rinse in cold water.

Spicy Macaroni & Bean Salad   3-12 minutes

1/4 tsp (1 ml) red cayenne or black pepper
1 tbsp (15 ml) minced yellow onions
Half a celery stalk, thinly sliced
3 tbsp (45 ml) *Homemade*
   Mayonnaise (see pages 70-1)

2/3 cup (160 ml) *frozen (thawed)*
   precooked red kidney beans
1 tsp (5 ml) prepared mustard
1/2 tsp (2 ml) crushed chilies

Add the above to *Basic Pasta Salad* recipe. *Use **macaroni elbows** as pasta.*

Italian-Sausage & Pasta Salad   3-12 minutes

1/2 cup (120 ml) *Salami Stick*
   or *Pepperoni,* diced *(see page 124)*
1/3 cup (80 ml) canned diced tomatoes
1 garlic clove, minced
A few thin slices of yellow onions

1 tbsp (15 ml) minced black olives
1 tbsp (15 ml) grated dried
   Parmesan cheese
1/4 tsp (1 ml) dried basil
1/2 tsp (2 ml) dried oregano

Add the above to *Basic Pasta Salad* recipe. *Use **rotini** as pasta.*

POTATO SALADS

Basic Potato Salad   4-5 minutes

About 4 cups (960 ml) precooked
   potatoes, diced or sliced
2 tbsp (30 ml) vegetable oil

1 tbsp (15 ml) vinegar or lemon
   juice from concentrate
Salt and pepper to taste

DRY SEASONING:
1 tsp (5 ml) dried parsley
1/4 tsp (1 ml) celery salt

1/4 tsp (1 ml) onion powder
1/8 tsp (1/2 ml) garlic powder

OR 1 tsp (5 ml) PREMIXED DRY SEASONINGS #5 (see page 27)
In a **small bowl**, whisk together oil, vinegar, and seasoning ingredients *(plus additional ingredients for a recipe variation). (Refrigerated precooked potatoes may be warmed after slicing or dicing by placing them in boiling water for about one minute.)* In a **salad bowl,** place all ingredients. Toss and serve, or let marinate refrigerated for a few hours before serving. **Makes about 4 cups (960 ml)**
LITE! VERSION *Simply substitute half or two thirds of vegetable oil with water!*

POTATO SALAD VARIATIONS

Mediterranean Potato Salad   *5 minutes*

1 small yellow onion, thinly sliced
1/4 tsp (1 ml) dried tarragon

1tbsp (15 ml) pitted green or black
   olives, sliced
1/3 cup (80 ml) *frozen* whole green
   peas, thawed

Add the above to *Basic Potato Salad* recipe. *Thaw peas in very hot water!*

Egg & Vegetables Potato Salad   *5 minutes*

2 small or 1 extra-large hard-boiled
   egg(s)
Half a celery stalk, chopped fine

Small yellow onion, finely chopped
2 tbsp (30 ml) *Homemade Mayonnaise (see pages 70-1)*
1 tbsp (15 ml) prepared mustard

Add the above to *Basic Potato Salad* recipe.

Tangy Potato Salad   *5-6 minutes*

Half a celery stalk, thinly sliced
1 small yellow onion, finely chopped
1/4 cup (60 ml) cucumber, chopped
1/3 cup (80 ml) *frozen* red kidney
   beans, thawed *(optional)*

1/4 cup (60 ml) *Homemade Yogurt
   (see pages 232-3)*
1/2 tsp (2 ml) caraway seeds
1 tsp (5 ml) prepared mustard
Dash of mild paprika

Add the above to *Basic Potato Salad* recipe.

RICE SALADS

Basic Rice Salad   *3-4 minutes*

3 cups (720 ml) *refrigerated* precooked
   rice
1 small yellow onion, finely chopped
3 tbsp (45 ml) vegetable oil
More legumes & vegetables!

2 tbsp (30 ml) white vinegar
   and/or lemon juice from
   concentrate
2 tbsp (30 ml) water
Salt and pepper to taste

DRY SEASONING:
1 tsp (5 ml) dried parsley
1/4 tsp (1 ml) celery salt

1/4 tsp (1 ml) onion powder
1/8 tsp (1/2ml) garlic powder

OR 1 tsp (5 ml) PREMIXED DRY SEASONING #5 or 6 (see page 27)

In a **small bowl**, whisk together oil, vinegar, and seasoning ingredients *(plus addition ingredients for any of the following rice salad variations). (Refrigerated precooked rice may be warmed by placing it in boiling water for about 1 minute.)* In a **salad bowl**, place all the ingredients; toss and serve. Alternately, let marinate refrigerated a few hours before serving. **Makes about 4 cups (960 ml)**

LITE! VERSION *Replace half of vegetable oil with water!*

RICE SALAD VARIATIONS

Rice Salad & Green Peas   *3-4 minutes*

1/4 cup (60 ml) chopped cooked ham
  OR 2 slices pre-toasted chopped
    bacon *(see page 26)*

2/3 cup (160 ml) *frozen* precooked
  whole green peas
1 tsp (5 ml) Dijon mustard
1/2 tsp (2 ml) dried fine herbs

Add the above to the *Basic Rice Salad* recipe.

Cajun-Style Rice Salad   *3-4 minutes*

2 small or 1 extra-large hard-boiled
  egg(s)
Half a green bell pepper, chopped
  (peak harvest season only)

1 tsp (5 ml) mild paprika
1/8 tsp (1/2 ml) red cayenne pepper
2 tbsp (30 ml) *Homemade Mayonnaise (see pages 70-1)*

Add the above to the *Basic Rice Salad* recipe.

Chicken & Rice Salad   *3-4 minutes*

1/2 cup (120 ml) chopped precooked
  chicken or turkey
1 celery stalk, finely chopped

1/4 cup (60 ml) *Homemade Yogurt
  (see pages 232-33)*
2 tbsp (30 ml) *Homemade Mayonnaise (see pages 70-1)*

Add the above to the *Basic Rice Salad* recipe.

LEGUME SALADS

Basic Legume Salad   *4-5 minutes*

3 cups (720 ml) precooked thawed
  frozen legumes
3 tbsp (45 ml) vegetable oil

2 tbsp (30 ml) white vinegar
1/2 tbsp (7 ml) lemon juice
1/3 cup (80 ml) water
Salt and pepper to taste

DRY SEASONING:
1 tsp (5 ml) dried parsley
1/4 tsp (1 ml) celery salt

1/4 tsp (1 ml) onion powder
1/8 tsp (1/2 ml) garlic powder

OR 1 tsp (5 ml) PREMIXED DRY SEASONING #5 (see page 27)
In a **salad bowl**, place all ingredients *(plus ingredients for a recipe variation).* Toss and serve at once. Alternately, marinate in refrigerator for a few hours before serving. **Makes about 4 cups (960 ml)**

LEGUME SALAD VARIATIONS

Marinated Soybean Salad   *5 minutes*

1 garlic clove, minced
1 small yellow onion, finely
  chopped

Half a celery stalk, thinly sliced
1/2 tsp (2 ml) dill seeds, crushed

Add the above to *Basic Legume Salad* recipe. *Use soybeans as salad legume.*

Italian Chick Pea Salad   *5 minutes*

1 small yellow onion, chopped or
  sliced
1/2 cup (120 ml) canned diced
  tomatoes

1 tsp (5 ml) dried oregano
1/2 tsp (2 ml) dried Italian herbs

Add the above to *Basic Legume Salad* recipe. *Use chick peas as legume for this salad.*

Easy Lentil Salad   *5 minutes*

1 small yellow onion, chopped
Half a celery stalk, thinly sliced

1 garlic clove, minced

Add the above to *Basic Legume Salad* recipe. *Use precooked liard (or green) lentils as   legume for this salad.*

FRESH VEGETABLE SALADS

These salads should be made only during peak harvest time to be low cost.

Basic Fresh Vegetable Salad   *5-6 minutes*

1 large carrot, shredded or thinly
  sliced
1/2 cup (120 ml) green cabbage, shredded
1 celery stalk, thinly sliced diagonally
1 yellow onion, thinly sliced
Half garlic clove, minced

3 tbsp (45 ml) vegetable oil
2 tbsp (30 ml) vinegar or
  lemon juice from
  concentrate
Salt and pepper to taste

DRY SEASONING:
1 tsp (5 ml) dried parsley
1/4 tsp (1 ml) celery salt

1/4 tsp (1 ml) onion powder
1/8 tsp (1/2 ml) garlic powder

OR 1 tsp (5 ml) PREMIXED DRY SEASONING #5 (see page 27)
In a **small bowl**, whisk together oil, vinegar, and seasoning ingredients *(plus additional ingredients for a recipe variation)*. In a **salad bowl,** place all ingredients. Toss and serve, or let it marinate in refrigerator for a few hours before serving. **Makes about 4 cups (960 ml)**

LITE! VERSION *Substitute half or two thirds of vegetable oil, with water or use a low-fat (lite version) salad dressing (see page 68)!*

FRESH VEGETABLE SALAD VARIATIONS

Fresh Summer Vegetable Salad   *6 minutes*

We recommend that you make this salad during the end of summer when the vegetables are inexpensive because it's their peak season.

Lettuce leaves	1 fresh tomato, diced
Half a green bell pepper, chopped	1 small yellow onion, sliced
1/2 cup (120 ml) cucumber, sliced	

Replace the fresh vegetables from *Basic Fresh Vegetable Salad* recipe with the above ones.

SUB-VARIATIONS *Try with different types of lettuce(s) like Boston, Romaine, and leafy. Replace some vegetables with fresh corn, chopped string beans, broccoli, cauliflower, etc.!*

Fresh Dandelion Greens Salad   *6 minutes*

About 1 pound (454 g) freshly picked dandelion greens	1 celery stalk, thinly sliced
	1 garlic clove, minced
1 large yellow onion, thinly sliced	1/2 tsp (2 ml) ground coriander

Replace the fresh vegetables from *Basic Fresh Vegetable Salad* recipe with the above ones. Add coriander to the seasoning ingredients.

OTHER SALAD RECIPES

Panzanella   *8-10 minutes*

This is an Italian-Style bread salad.

3 cups (720 ml) day-old crusty bread cubes	1 tbsp (15 ml) pitted green or black olives, minced
1 cup (240 ml) fresh diced tomato or canned diced tomatoes	2 tbsp (30 ml) vegetable oil
1/2 cup (120 ml) cucumber with skin, diced	2 tsp (10 ml) white vinegar
	1/2 tsp (2 ml) lemon juice from concentrate
Half a small yellow onion, chopped	1 tsp (5 ml) dried Italian herbs
1 garlic clove, minced	Salt and pepper to taste

In a **small bowl**, whisk together oil, vinegar, lemon juice and seasoning ingredients. In a **salad bowl**, place all remaining ingredients except bread cubes; combine. Just before serving add bread cubes; toss. **Makes 4 cups (960 ml)**

LITE! VERSION *Replace two thirds of vegetable oil with water or tomato juice and use bread made from a lean type of dough!*

Greek Isles Salad

1 1/2 cups (360 ml) fresh tomatoes, diced
    OR canned diced tomatoes
1/2 cup (120 ml) sliced cucumber
    (preferably in peak season)
1 small yellow onion, thinly sliced
1/4 tsp (1 ml) oregano

1 tbsp (15 ml) sliced black olives
1 tbsp (15 ml) vegetable oil
1 tbsp (15 ml) lemon juice from
    concentrate
1 tbsp (15 ml) white vinegar
4 oz (100 g) Feta cheese *(optional)*
Salt and pepper to taste

In a **large salad bowl**, toss together all of the above and serve. **Makes about 2 cups (480 ml) or 8 very small servings**

SALAD DRESSINGS

Basic Salad Dressing   *1-2 minute(s)*

1/2 cup (120 ml) vegetable oil
3 tbsp (45 ml) white vinegar
1 tbsp (15 ml) lemon juice from
    concentrate

1/8 tsp (1/2 ml) onion powder
1/16 tsp (1/4 ml) garlic powder
1/2 tsp (2 ml) dried parsley
Salt and pepper to taste

In a **screw-top jar**, combine all of the above *(plus additional ingredients for a recipe variation).* Shake until all ingredients are suspended in oil and vinegar. **Makes 6 ounces (180 ml) or up to 12 servings**
LITE! VERSION *Replace half or two-thirds of oil with water!*

SALAD DRESSING VARIATIONS

Classic Salad Dressing   *2 minutes*

1/2 tbsp (2 ml) Dijon mustard

Half garlic clove, finely minced
    (optional)

Add the above to *Basic Salad Dressing* recipe.

French 'Vinaigrette' Salad Dressing   *2 minutes*

1 tsp (5 ml) Dijon mustard
1/4 tsp (1 ml) brown sugar

1/4 tsp (1 ml) dried fine herbs
Half garlic clove, minced

Add the above to *Basic Salad Dressing* recipe.

Italian Salad Dressing   *2 minutes*

1 tsp (5 ml) Dijon mustard
1/2 tsp (2 ml) dried oregano
Half small yellow onion,
    finely chopped
    (optional)

1/4 tsp (1 ml) onion powder
1/16 tsp (1/4 ml) crushed dried
    chili
Half small clove garlic, very finely
    minced *(optional)*
Salt and pepper to taste

Add the above to *Basic Salad Dressing* recipe.

Herb Salad Dressing   *2 minutes*

1 tsp (5 ml) dried parsley
1/4 (1 ml) tsp dried chives

1/4 (1 ml) tsp dried tarragon
1/4 (1 ml) tsp dried chervil
Salt and pepper to taste

Add the above to *Basic Salad Dressing* recipe.

Thai Salad Dressing   *2 minutes*

1/2 tsp (2 ml) ground ginger
1 tbsp (15 ml) soy sauce

1 tsp (5 ml) granulated sugar
1 clove of garlic, very finely minced
Salt and pepper to taste

Add the above to *Basic Salad Dressing* recipe.

Zesty Oriental Dressing   *2 minutes*

1/2 tbsp (7 ml) soy sauce
1/2 tsp (2 ml) Worcestershire sauce
1/2 tbsp (7 ml) yellow onion,
    finely chopped *(optional)*

1/8 tsp (1/2 ml) ground ginger
1/2 tbsp (7 ml) granulated sugar
Half clove garlic, finely minced
    (optional)
Salt and pepper to taste

Add the above to *Basic Salad Dressing* recipe.

YOGURT SALAD DRESSINGS

Basic Yogurt Dressing 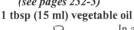   *1-2 minute(s)*

2/3 cup (160 ml) *Homemade Yogurt*
    (see pages 232-3)
1 tbsp (15 ml) vegetable oil

1/2 tbsp (7 ml) lemon juice from
    concentrate
Salt and pepper to taste

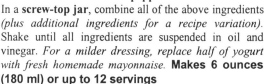
In a **screw-top jar**, combine all of the above ingredients *(plus additional ingredients for a recipe variation)*. Shake until all ingredients are suspended in oil and vinegar. *For a milder dressing, replace half of yogurt with fresh homemade mayonnaise.* **Makes 6 ounces (180 ml) or up to 12 servings**
LITE! VERSION *Replace half or two-thirds of oil with water and use skim milk powder to make the yogurt!*

YOGURT DRESSING VARIATIONS

Oriental Yogurt Dressing   *2 minutes*

1/2 tsp (2 ml) curry powder
1/2 tsp (2 ml) honey *(or sugar)*
1 tbsp (15 ml) minced yellow
    onion *(optional)*

1/4 tsp (1 ml) ground ginger
1/4 tsp (1 ml) onion powder

Add the above ingredients to *Basic Yogurt Dressing* recipe.

Hot Mexican-Style Dressing   2 minutes

1/2 tsp (2 ml) mild paprika
1 tsp (5 ml) pickled hot peppers, minced
1 tbsp (15 ml) yellow onions, finely minced

Add the above ingredients to *Basic Yogurt Dressing* recipe.

Fresh Cucumber Dressing   2 minutes

1/3 cup (80 ml) fresh cucumber, grated *(during peak season only)*
1/4 tsp (1 ml) dried mint leaves, crushed

Add the above ingredients to *Basic Yogurt Dressing* recipe.

Greek Gyro-Style Dressing   2 minutes

2 tbsp (30 ml) chopped cucumber
1/2 tbsp (7 ml) yellow onion, minced
1/4 tsp (1 ml) dry mint, crushed
1/8 tsp (1/2 ml) table salt
Dash of garlic powder

Add the above ingredients to *Basic Yogurt Dressing* recipe.

BUTTERMILK SALAD DRESSINGS

Basic Buttermilk Dressing 🐷   1-2 minute(s)

1/2 cup (120 ml) *Homemade Buttermilk (see page 233)*
2 tbsp (30 ml) vegetable oil
1 tbsp (15 ml) water
1/2 tbsp (7 ml) white vinegar
1/2 tsp (2 ml) dried parsley
Dash of garlic powder
Salt and pepper to taste

In a **screw-top jar**, combine all of the above ingredients *(plus additional ingredients for a recipe variation)*. Shake until all ingredients are suspended in oil and vinegar. **Makes 6 ounces (180 ml) or up to 12 servings**

LITE! VERSION *Replace half or two-thirds of oil with water!*

BUTTERMILK DRESSING VARIATIONS

Dijon & Dillweed Dressing   2 minutes

Half a garlic clove, finely minced *(optional)*
1/4 tsp (1 ml) dried dill weed
1/2 tsp (2 ml) Dijon mustard

Add the above ingredients to *Basic Buttermilk Dressing* recipe.
SUB-VARIATION *Try substituting dill weed and/or mustard with cumin powder!*

HOMEMADE MAYONNAISE

Basic Homemade Mayonnaise   5-6 minutes

Mayonnaise is one of the most used prepared product in the kitchen.

1 extra-large egg *(yolk and white)*
2 tbsp (30 ml) white vinegar
1/2 tsp (2 ml) table salt
1 1/4 cups (300 ml) vegetable oil
Pepper to taste

Place the egg, vinegar, and salt *(plus any additional ingredient for a recipe variation)* in **blender**. Cover and blend at a low speed until ingredients are well combined. With blender still running, very slowly pour oil into mixture; blend until mayonnaise has thickened. If the oil and egg separates during mayonnaise separation, start process all over again using 1 egg and 1 teaspoon (5 ml) of vinegar. Blend these two ingredients well in blender. Add 1 tablespoon (15 ml) of oil drop by drop; very slowly pour in separated mayonnaise. Place in an airtight container or recycled mayonnaise jar. Always keep mayonnaise chilled in refrigerator to 10 days. *Unless homemade mayonnaise contains cooked eggs, since raw eggs may contain salmonella bacteria, use ample care in handling and refrigeration.* **Makes about 12 ounces (360 ml)**

HOMEMADE MAYONNAISE VARIATIONS

Relish Mayonnaise   6 minutes

**3 tbsp (45 ml) dill pickle, very
    finely chopped
1/8 tsp (1/2 ml) dried basil
1/4 tsp (1 ml) dried oregano**

**1/2 tsp (2 ml) turmeric
1/8 tsp (1/2 ml) dried chervil
1 tsp (5 ml) lemon juice from
    concentrate**

Combine the above, in a **bowl**, with *Basic Homemade mayonnaise* recipe.

Old-Fashioned Mayonnaise   6 minutes

**1/2 tsp (2 ml) Dijon mustard
1/8 tsp (1/2 ml) ground black pepper**

**1 tsp (5 ml) granulated sugar
    (optional)**

Add the above ingredients to *Basic Homemade Mayonnaise* recipe.

Lemon-Paprika Mayonnaise   6 minutes

**1/2 tsp (2 ml) dry mustard
1/4 tsp (1 ml) paprika**

**2 tbsp (30 ml) lemon juice from
    concentrate (replaces vinegar)**

Add above ingredients and substitute lemon juice for vinegar in *Basic Homemade Mayonnaise* recipe.

Mustard-Cayenne Mayonnaise   5 minutes

1 tsp (5 ml) dry mustard   **1/8 tsp (1/2 ml) red cayenne**

Add the above ingredients to *Basic Homemade Mayonnaise* recipe.

Thick & Spicy Mayonnaise   6 minutes

**1 tsp (5 ml) honey (or sugar)
1/4 tsp (1 ml) dry mustard
1/16 tsp (1/4 ml) dried chervil
1/16 tsp (1/4 ml) majoram**

**1/16 tsp (1/4 ml) dried thyme
1/16 tsp (1/4 ml) savory
1/8 tsp (1/2 ml) paprika
1/4 tsp (1 ml) onion powder
1/2 tbsp (7 ml) yellow onions,
    finely chopped (optional)**

Add the above ingredients to *Basic Homemade Mayonnaise* recipe.

European-Style Garlic Mayonnaise   6 minutes

2 garlic cloves, crushed or   **2 tbsp (30 ml) lemon juice from**
    finely minced   **concentrate** *(optional)*
1/2 tsp (2 ml) garlic powder
Add the above ingredients to *Basic Homemade Mayonnaise* recipe.

Hamburger Mayonnaise   6-8 minutes

1/4 cup (60 ml) *French Salad Dressing*   **3 tbsp (45 ml) generic-brand relish**
    (see page 68)   **3 tbsp (45 ml) yellow onions, very**
1 tsp (5 ml) granulated sugar   **finely minced**
Make mayonnaise as described in *Basic Homemade Mayonnaise* recipe and
using a **spoon** stir in the above ingredients. *Blend a few seconds only.*
SUB-VARIATION *Add 1/8 tsp (1/2 ml) of cayenne pepper and have this sauce
double as **Mock Tartar Sauce**!*

Simulated Dijon-Mayonnaise   6 minutes

1/2 cup (120 ml) prepared mustard   **1 tsp (5 ml) coarsely ground or**
Dash of *Hot Pepper Sauce (pg. 249)*   **cracked mustard seeds**
Add the above ingredients to *Basic Homemade Mayonnaise* recipe.

OTHER MAYONNAISE RECIPES

New Age Egg-less Mayonnaise   4-5 minutes

1/2 cup (120 ml) cold tap water   **1/2 cup (120 ml) vegetable oil**
1/3 cup (80 ml) skim milk powder   **1/4 tsp (1 ml) table salt**
2 tsp (10 ml) lemon juice from   **1/2 tsp (2 ml) granulated sugar**
    concentrate   **Pepper to taste**
Place all ingredients in a **blender** and run until smooth. Refrigerate before using.
Makes about 12 ounces (360 ml)

Vegetarian Soy Mayonnaise   5-6 minutes

3/8 cup (90 ml) soybean flour   **1/4 tsp (1 ml) onion powder**
3/4 cup (180 ml) water   **1/2 tsp (2 ml) vegetable oil**
1/2 tsp (2 ml) table salt   **3 tbsp (45 ml) lemon juice from**
1/2 tsp (2 ml) mild paprika   **concentrate**
1/16 tsp (1/4 ml) red cayenne
In a **blender**, place all ingredients except oil and lemon juice and run until
smooth. With blender at full speed, very slowly add oil until mixture starts to
thicken. Add remainder of oil faster. Add lemon juice at the end and refrigerate
before use. **Makes about 12 ounces (360 ml)**

EGG DISHES

Eggs are one of the least expensive and most versatile forms of complete proteins available. Some of the egg dishes may be served as a side dish and a couple as hors d'oeuvre (appetizers). Most are meant as the main dish at breakfast.

OMELETS

Basic Omelet   *8-10 minutes*

4 small eggs or 2 large eggs
1/4 cup (60 ml) water
1/2 tbsp (7 ml) vegetable oil

1/2 tbsp (7 ml) margarine
Salt, pepper and parsley to taste

Preheat **large frying pan** or **skillet**, on a low-medium heat. In a **small bowl**, whip the eggs using a **table fork**. Add water and whip again. Place oil and butter in the hot frying pan *(never in a cold pan)* and later pour the egg mixture into pan. When omelet has set and is slightly golden on the underside; top with garnishing on half a side *(for one of the following omelet recipe variations).* **Garnishings are always sautéed simultaneously in a second pan.** Fold the omelet over in half *(with garnish inside).* Slide omelet onto a plate and season. Serve hot. *Do not season or add salt to the egg mixture before or during cooking. Doing so would toughen the eggs. Use only water in the egg mixture. Do not use milk or other liquids because only water blends with the eggs. Using milk would make your omelet watery.* **Makes 1 very large or 2 medium-small serving(s)**

LITE! VERSION *Replace oil and/or margarine for all omelet and garnishing recipes with 1/4 teaspoon vegetable oil in two large or medium non-stick skillets!*

OMELET VARIATIONS

European-Style Omelet   *10 minutes*

1 tbsp (15 ml) margarine or
   vegetable oil

1 medium *refrigerated* precooked
   potato, peeled and coarsely diced

1/2 slice of bacon, finely
   chopped *(or pre-baked)*
1 small yellow onion, chopped
1 small garlic clove, minced

1/2 tsp (2 ml) dried grated
   Parmesan or Romano cheese
Salt and pepper to taste

While the omelet is cooking, heat a second **large frying pan** or **skillet** over a medium-high setting; add fat to hot pan. Sauté the bacon until slightly crisp. Add onion, garlic and potato and cook until hot only. Use this garnish as filling in the *Basic Omelet* recipe. Serve.

Spanish Omelet   *10 minutes*

1 tbsp (15 ml) margarine or
   vegetable oil
Half a *refrigerated* precooked
   potato, peeled and sliced
Half small yellow onion,
   finely sliced

Half a small tomato, sliced
   (inexpensively in season) or
1/4 cup (60 ml)) canned diced
   tomatoes
1/2 tsp (2 ml) white vinegar
Pinch of cayenne pepper

While the omelet is cooking, heat a second **large frying pan** or **skillet** over a medium-high setting; add fat to hot pan. Sauté the onions until become clear. Add potato, tomatoes, vinegar and cayenne; cook until hot only. Use this garnish as filling in the *Basic Omelet* recipe. Serve hot.

Onion & Cheese Omelet   *9 minutes*

1 tbsp (15 ml) margarine
1 small yellow onion, sliced

1 slice of processed cheese for
   burgers *(see shopping list, page 19)*

Sauté onion in margarine and use as filling with cheese in *Basic Omelet* recipe.

Irish Omelet   *10 minutes*

1 tbsp (15 ml) margarine
1/2 slice of pre-baked bacon, chopped
1 small yellow onion, chopped

1 medium *refrigerated* precooked
   potato, diced
Pinch of dried fine herbs

Sauté above ingredients and stuff in *Basic Omelet* recipe.

Chickpea Omelet   *10 minutes*

1 tbsp (15 ml) margarine
1/3 cup (80 ml) precooked chick
   peas, thawed in hot water
   if frozen
Half a small yellow onion,
   chopped

Half garlic clove, minced
2 slices red or green bell
   pepper *(inexpensively in peak
   harvest season, optional)*
1/4 tsp (1 ml) ground turmeric
1/2 tsp (2 ml) dried parsley

Sauté all above ingredients and stuff in *Basic Omelet* recipe.

Pasta Omelet   *10 minutes*

1 tbsp (15 ml) margarine
Half a small yellow onion,
   chopped

1/2 cup (120 ml) *refrigerated*
   precooked pasta
   (fettuccine or elbows)

2 slices of green bell pepper
(when inexpensively in season)

**1 tsp (5 ml) dried grated Parmesan
or Romano cheese
Salt and pepper to taste**

While the omelet is cooking, heat a second **large frying pan** or **skillet** over a medium-high setting; add fat to hot pan. Sauté onion and bell pepper until onion begins to turn brown. Add pasta, dried cheese and seasoning; stir until hot. Stuff in folded *Basic Omelet* recipe.

The Meal Omelet   *10 minutes*

1 tbsp (15 ml) vegetable oil
1 small precooked potato, diced
1 small yellow onion, chopped
1 clove garlic, minced

1/4 tomato, diced *(in peak season)*
OR 2 tbsp (30 ml) canned tomatoes
1/2 tsp (2 ml) dried parsley
Salt and pepper to taste

Sauté all above ingredients, season and stuff in *Basic Omelet* recipe.

French-Style Omelet   *9 minutes*

**1 tbsp (15 ml) margarine or
vegetable oil**
1 small yellow onion, thinly sliced

1 thin slice Mozzarella cheese
1/2 tsp (2 ml) dried mint

Sauté onion and stuff in *Basic Omelet* recipe, along with the cheese and dried mint.

Tomato Sauce Omelet   *9 minutes*

3 tbsp (45 ml) *Instant Tomato
Sauce (see page 98)*

1 thin slice Mozzarella cheese
1/2 tsp (2 ml) Parmesan cheese

When omelet in *Basic Omelet* recipe begins to set, place all above ingredients on one side. When filling is hot and omelet has set, fold in two. Serve hot.

Ham & Cheese Omelet   *10 minutes*

**1 thin slice of low-cost generic-brand
cooked ham, diced**
1 thin slice of processed cheese
(see shopping list, page 19)

**2 thin slices of ripe tomato or
2 tbsp (30 ml) canned diced tomatoes**
Salt and pepper to taste

When omelet in *Basic Omelet* recipe has set, place all filling ingredients on one side. Fold omelet in two and serve immediately.

HARD-BOILED EGGS

Basic Hard-boiled Eggs   *20-25 minutes*

8 small eggs or 4 extra-large eggs
In a **small saucepan**, place eggs and just cover with hot tap water. Heat over a high heat setting; bring to a boil and lower heat. Cook gently for 2 minutes and remove saucepan from the heat. Cover pan and set aside for 15 minutes; then cool eggs immediately in a **plastic bowl** containing running cold tap water. Serve immediately or keep in their shells in the refrigerator.

Alternately, following instructions for one the following hard-boiled eggs variations.
Makes 4 to 8 servings

HARD-BOILED EGGS VARIATIONS

Hard-boiled Eggs & Yogurt Sauce   *25 minutes*

1 tbsp (15 ml) vegetable oil   **1 small yellow onion, chopped**
Garlic clove, minced   **3/4 cup (180 ml)** *Homemade*
          Yogurt (see pages 232-3)

 While eggs are cooking as described in *Basic Hard-boiled Eggs* recipe, in a **second pan or skillet**, sauté the garlic and onion in oil until onion is transparent. Add yogurt, stir, and immediately remove from heat. Pour yogurt sauce over halved eggs and serve hot.

Hard-boiled Eggs & White Sauce   *25 minutes*

Pour 1 cup (240 ml) of hot white sauce or one of the white sauce variations over sliced eggs in *Basic Hard-boiled Eggs* recipe *(see pages 141-3)*.

Deviled Eggs   *25-30 minutes*

3 tbsp (45 ml) *Homemade*   **1 tsp (5 ml) curry powder**
   Mayonnaise (see pages 70-1)   **Salt and pepper to taste**
Slice eggs lengthwise and scoop out yolks. In a **plate**, using a **table fork**, mash yolk with other ingredients. Season and stuff back in the halves.
SUB-VARIATIONS *Substitute curry powder with dried fine herbs or tarragon!*

Stuffed Egg Appetizers   *30 minutes*

3 tbsp (45 ml) *Homemade*   **1/2 tsp (2 ml) dried parsley**
   Mayonnaise (see page 70-1)   **Salt and pepper to taste**
1 tsp (5 ml) prepared mustard
Slice eggs lengthwise and scoop out yolks. In a **plate** using a **large table fork**, mash yolk with other ingredients, season and stuff.

SCRAMBLED EGGS

Basic Scrambled Eggs   *7-8 minutes*

These scrambled egg recipes are suitable as the main portion of a light meal.

1/2 tbsp (7 ml) margarine   **2 tsp (10 ml) skim milk powder**
1/2 tbsp (7 ml) vegetable oil   **2 small eggs, lightly beaten**
3 tbsp (45 ml) water   **Salt and pepper to taste**
Preheat **frying pan** over a medium heat. Meanwhile, in a **small bowl**, mix the eggs, milk (water and milk powder) and salt and pepper together. Place the fat in the pan *(and add ingredient(s) for one of the following variations)*. Fry till golden. Add a little more margarine to the pan at this time if it is dry. Add the egg mixture and cook; stirring until egg mixture sets. Serve hot. **Makes 1 serving**

SCRAMBLED EGGS VARIATIONS

Vegetable Scrambled Eggs   8-9 minutes

1 very small yellow onion, chopped
Half a garlic clove, sliced
1/2 tsp (2 ml) tamari sauce
   (optional)

Quarter tomato, diced *(only in peak harvest season when inexpensive)*
OR 2 tbsp (30 ml) canned diced tomatoes

Sauté the onion and garlic in the fat as described in *Basic Scrambled Eggs* recipe for 5 minutes. Add egg mixture, when eggs have set add tomatoes and optional tamari sauce.

Rice Scrambled Eggs   8 minutes

1/4 cup (60 ml) water
1 tbsp (15 ml) skim milk powder
1/2 tbsp (7 ml) all-purpose flour

3/4 cup (180 ml) *refrigerated* precooked rice
1/2 tsp (2 ml) dried parsley

In a **small bowl**, mix water with skim milk powder and flour. Add to beaten basic raw egg mixture and beat some more. Finally add rice to new mixture and mix well. Cook as described in *Basic Scrambled Eggs* recipe until eggs set. Season.

Ham & Potato Scrambled Eggs   8 minutes

1 thin slice of cooked ham,
   coarsely chopped

1 small *refrigerated* precooked potato, diced

Add ham and potato to egg mixture as described in *Basic Scrambled Eggs* recipe. Cook all ingredients together.

Bacon & Cheese Scrambled Eggs   8 minutes

1 slice pre-toasted bacon, chopped
   (see page 26)

1 processed cheese burger slice
   (see page 19)

Add chopped bacon to *Basic Scrambled Eggs* recipe. Add the cheese last.

Olive & Thyme Scrambled Eggs   8 minutes

1/2 tbsp (7 ml) black or green olives,
   minced

A few thin slices of yellow onions
1/4 tsp (1 ml) dried thyme leaves

Cook as described in *Basic Scrambled Eggs* recipe until eggs set.

OTHER EGG DISHES

Fried Eggs   7-8 minutes

1/2 tbsp (7 ml) margarine
2 small eggs

1/2 tsp (2 ml) water
Salt and pepper to taste

Preheat **frying pan** on a medium-low heat. Place margarine in the pan, moments later when margarine has turned slightly golden; crack eggs and gently drop from shell into pan. Add water and cover. Cook slowly until egg white is firm. Serve sunny side up or turned over.

For a firm yolk eggs, break yolk immediately *(but gently)* after dropping in pan.
Makes one serving

LITE! VERSION *Reduce margarine to 1/4 tsp (1 ml) and use a non-stick skillet!*

Please Note *Cook eggs in as little fat as possible and do not overcook because eggs will be rendered indigestible.*

Shirred Eggs   *10 minutes*

1/2 tbsp (7 ml) vegetable oil or melted margarine	1 tbsp (15 ml) fresh cheese, grated Salt and pepper to taste

2 small eggs

Preheat oven to 400°F(200°C). Put a little liquid fat in the bottom of a **small baking dish**. Carefully crack the eggs into the ovenproof dish. Season and top with the cheese. Place in oven at least 5 minutes until set. Serve very hot. **Makes 1 serving**

Poached Eggs   *9-10 minutes*

2 small eggs

Bring a **small saucepan** of water to a boil; crack eggs and gently drop into boiling water. Immediately remove from heat, cover and let sit 5 to 7 minutes. Yolks must be set yet still runny. Lift out eggs with a **slotted spoon**, let drain. Serve each egg on a piece of toast, if desired. **Makes one serving**

Soft-boiled Eggs    *8-9 minutes*

2 small eggs

In a **small saucepan**, place eggs and barely cover with hot tap water. Bring water to a boil over a high heat. Let water boil no more than 60 seconds; immediately remove from heat. Set aside and let sit 5 minutes. Serve at once. **Makes one serving**

For quiches (egg pies), see page 154
For egg salad, see page 58
For egg spread, see page 117

POTATO DISHES

The potato is the least expensive of all foods. This is so, mainly, because it takes less than a quarter the area of land to grow potatoes than it does to grow grains. Placing its history aside, today, there are hundreds of varieties of potatoes worldwide. You should buy the most popular and least expensive varieties, bought during peak harvest season, usually in autumn. The 'dirt cheap' all-purpose varieties make tasteful potato dishes for pennies a serving. The potatoes used for the boiled and mashed recipes must be precooked (boiled) ahead of time (see page 25). They are then stored in the refrigerator for up to 5 days, a few are taken when needed. They are quickly reheated as described below and served as one of numerous potato side-dish recipes.

BOILED POTATOES

Basic Boiled Potatoes 🐷   *5-7 minutes*

2 large *refrigerated* precooked   1/2 tsp (2 ml) table salt
    potatoes, sliced or diced

In a **large saucepan**, place sliced or diced precooked potatoes and enough hot tap water to barely cover. Bring to a boil over the highest setting and drain immediately. Meanwhile, in a **large frying pan**, sauté *ingredients for any of the following boiled potatoes recipes* over a medium-high heat. Cook and stir until very hot only or until sauce has thickened. No need to simmer. Immediately pour over potatoes and serve hot. **Makes 2 large or 4 small servings**

LITE! VERSION *Reduce fat for all potatoes sauces or dressings by a factor of ten!*

BOILED POTATOES VARIATIONS

French-Style potatoes   *6-7 minutes*

1 tbsp (15 ml) margarine or   1 tsp (5 ml) dried parsley
    vegetable oil   1/4 tsp (1 ml) onion powder

1 tbsp (15 ml) lemon juice from   Dash of ground nutmeg
   concentrate   Salt and pepper to taste

Cook ingredients and serve on *Basic Boiled Potatoes* as described.

Tarragon Potatoes   *6-7 minutes*

1 tbsp (15 ml) vegetable oil   2 tsp (10 ml) all-purpose flour
2/3 cup (160 ml) water   1/2 tsp (2 ml) dried tarragon
3 tbsp (45 ml) instant skim milk powder   Salt and pepper to taste

In a **small bowl**, dissolve milk powder and flour in water. Heat all ingredients until sauce thickens and serve on *Basic Boiled Potatoes* as described.

English-Style Potatoes   *6-7 minutes*

3 tbsp (45 ml) margarine   1/2 tsp (2 ml) white vinegar
1 tsp (5 ml) dried mint   Salt and pepper to taste
2 tsp (10 ml) water

Heat all ingredients together and immediately pour on *Basic Boiled Potatoes* as described.

Old French Style Potatoes   *10-12 minutes*

1 small yellow onion, chopped   1/8 tsp (1/2 ml) ground nutmeg
1 tbsp (15 ml) all-purpose flour   Salt and pepper to taste
1 1/2 tbsp (22 ml) vegetable oil   2 tsp (10 ml) lemon juice from
1 tsp (5 ml) dried parsley   concentrate

Preheat oven broiler and get water for precooked potatoes boiling. In a **large bowl**, mix all ingredients except lemon juice. In a greased **baking dish**, place drained potatoes from *Basic Boiled Potatoes* recipe and mixture; toss. Place under broiler about 5 minutes or until top is browned. Remove from oven and sprinkle with lemon juice. Serve hot.

Potatoes & White Sauce   *8-12 minutes*

Serve about 1/2 cup (120 ml) of white sauce or one of its variations *(see page 141-3)* on *Basic Boiled Potatoes* recipe.

Potatoes & Sauce   *5-15 minutes*

Serve 1/2 cup (120 ml) of non-white sauce *(pages141, 143-4)* on *Basic Boiled Potatoes*.

Potatoes & Vinaigrette   *5-6 minutes*

Serve 2 tbsp (30 ml) of vinaigrette *(salad dressing)* or one of the lite! versions *(see pages 68-9)* over a *Basic Boiled Potatoes* recipe.

Potatoes & Yogurt Dressing   *5-6 minutes*

Serve 2 tbsp (30 ml) of a yogurt salad dressing or one of the lite! versions *(see pages 69,70)* over *Basic Boiled Potatoes*.

Potatoes & Mayonnaise   *5-6 minutes*

Serve 2 tbsp (30 ml) of any mayonnaise over *Basic Boiled Potatoes* recipe.

MASHED POTATOES

Basic Mashed Potatoes    *8-10 minutes*

3 or 4 medium *refrigerated*
   precooked potatoes,
   sliced

1 tbsp (15 ml) margarine
3 tbsp (45 ml) water
1 tbsp (15 ml) skim milk powder
(Salt and pepper to taste)

In a **large saucepan**, place the potatoes and barely cover with water. Quickly bring to a boil over a high setting. Immediately drain. Add remaining above ingredients *(plus additional ingredients for a recipe variation)*. In a **mixing bowl**, roughly mash all with a **potato masher** and whip with an **electric mixer** until creamy. Serve it hot or refrigerate. **Makes 2 average servings**

LITE! VERSION *Replace margarine with 1/2 tsp (2 ml) margarine!*

MASHED POTATOES VARIATIONS

English-Style Potatoes   *8 minutes*

1/16 tsp (1/4 ml) garlic powder
1/8 tsp (1/2 ml) celery seeds

Dash of paprika
Salt and pepper to taste

Add above to the *Basic Mashed Potatoes* recipe ingredients and mash only.

Mashed Potatoes & Carrots   *10 minutes*

1 small precooked *refrigerated*
   or frozen carrot, thaw if frozen
1/2 tsp (2 ml) chicken soup stock
   powder
1 tsp (5 ml) dried parsley

1/2 tbsp (7 ml) lemon juice from
   concentrate
1/16 tsp (1/4 ml) garlic powder
1/4 tsp (1 ml) onion powder
1/16 tsp (1/4 ml) nutmeg

Re-boil precooked sliced carrot along with precooked potatoes. Add all above ingredients with *Basic Mashed Potatoes* ingredients before mashing; mash all ingredients together and serve hot. *Do not whip.*

Piped Potato Contouring   *10 minutes*

Fill a **piping bag** with whipped potato mixture as prepared in *Basic Mashed Potatoes* above. Use it to generous contour when baking a meatloaf (or meatless loaf).

Mashed potatoes & Brown Sauce   *8-9 minutes*

Serve 1/2 cup (120 ml) of the *Brown Sauce* recipe *(see page 143)* over potatoes in the *Basic Mashed Potatoes* recipe.

BAKED POTATOES

Basic Baked Potatoes   *10-15 minutes*

**4 large pre-baked *refrigerated*
low-cost potatoes**

**4 tsp (20 ml) margarine
Salt and pepper to taste**

Preheat oven to 400ºF (200ºC). After a few minutes, place pre-bake potatoes on oven grill and re-bake up to 10 minutes until very hot. Slit each potato. Serve each potato with 1 tsp (5 ml) of margarine and seasoned *(or according to one of the variations). (See page 26 about pre-baking potatoes.)* **Makes 4 baked potatoes or servings**

BAKED POTATOES VARIATIONS

Sour Cream Baked Potatoes   *15 minutes*

2 tbsp (30 ml) *Homemade Sour Cream*   **1 tsp (5 ml) dried parsley**
     (see page 234)

Re-bake potatoes as described in *Baked Potatoes* recipe. Place 1/2 tbsp (7 ml) sour cream and 1/4 tsp (1 ml) parsley in each re-baked potato and serve hot.

Cheese & Bacon Baked Potatoes   *15 minutes*

2 tbsp (30 ml) grated cheddar cheese   **1 tsp (5 ml) simulated bacon bits or
                                                minced pre-toasted bacon *(pg 26)***

Re-bake potatoes as described in *Baked Potatoes* recipe. Place 1/2 tbsp (7 ml) cheese and 1/4 tsp (1 ml) bacon bits in each re-baked potato and serve hot.

Herbed Baked Potatoes   *15 minutes*

4 tsp (20 ml) margarine   **1 tsp (5 ml) dried parsley**
1 tsp (5 ml) lemon juice from   **1 tsp (5 ml) dried fine herbs**
     concentrate

Re-bake potatoes as described in *Baked Potatoes* recipe. Place 1 tsp (5 ml) margarine, 1/4 tsp (1 ml) lemon juice, 1/4 tsp (1 ml) parsley and 1/4 tsp (1 ml) fine herbs in each re-baked potato and serve hot.

Baked Potatoes with Bay Leaf   *15 minutes*

4 small whole bay leaves   **Salt and pepper to taste**
4 tsp (20 ml) margarine

Split each raw potato (before pre-baking) down the middle, and insert a whole leaf. Add 1 tsp (5 ml) margarine, season, and wrap in aluminum foil. Pre-bake in usual way *(see page 26)* and re-bake as outlined in *Basic Baked Potatoes* text. Serve hot.

Stuffed Baked Potatoes   *15-18 minutes*

4 tsp (20 ml) margarine   **2 tbsp (30 ml)** *Homemade Sour*
1 tsp (5 ml) marjoram   *Cream (see page 234)*

Carefully cut a cone-shaped hole on the flatter side of each pre-baked potato. Fill hole with the mashed pulp of removed section mixed with above ingredients. Re-bake until done and broil 2 minutes until stuffing turns brown.

ROASTED POTATOES

Basic Roasted Potatoes   *25-30 minutes*

4 medium raw peeled potatoes,   **1 tbsp (15 ml) vegetable oil**
   thinly wedged, diced or sliced   **Salt and pepper to taste**

Preheat oven to 500°F (260°C). Oil bottom of a **large roasting pan** or **baking sheet** with oil. Wash and peel potatoes, thinly cut pieces on pan or sheet. Bake on top rack 10 minutes, then with a **metal spatula or tongs**, turn potatoes over and bake 10 more minutes. They should be golden on the outside and cooked through. Season. *For following roasted potatoes variations*, place all ingredients and wet potato pieces in a **plastic bag**; shake then bake. **Makes 4 average servings**

LITE! **VERSION** *Replace the oil for the pan or tray with only 1/4 tsp (1 ml) of oil and use a non-stick tray!*

ROASTED POTATOES VARIATIONS

Herbs & Garlic Potatoes   *25-30 minutes*

1 tbsp (15 ml) cornstarch   **1/4 tsp (1 ml) onion powder**
1 tsp (5 ml) table salt   **1 tsp (5 ml) dried parsley**
1/8 tsp (1/2 ml) garlic powder   **2 tsp (10 ml) dried fine herbs**

Place wet cubed potatoes and ingredients in bag; shake and bake.

Hot & Spicy Potatoes   *25-30 minutes*

1 1/2 tsp (7 ml) paprika   **1/2 tsp (2 ml) chili powder**

Place wet wedged potatoes and spices in plastic bag; shake then bake.

Garlic & Rosemary Potatoes   *25-30 minutes*

1 1/2 tbsp (22 ml) vegetable oil   **2 tsp (10 ml) dried rosemary leaves**
2 garlic cloves, finely minced   **1/8 tsp (1/2 ml) garlic powder**

Place dry sliced potatoes and all ingredients in a **large bowl**; toss then bake.

PAN FRIED POTATOES

Basic Pan Fried Potatoes   8-9 minutes

2 large precooked *refrigerated*   **1 tbsp (15 ml) margarine**
potatoes, peeled and sliced   **Salt and pepper to taste**

In a **large frying pan**, melt margarine over a rather high setting. Place potatoes and fry about 3 minutes per side until golden. Turn over using a **metal spatula**. *For the following fried potatoes variations mix additional ingredients with melted margarine before frying potatoes.* Serve immediately. **Makes 2 large or 4 small servings**

LITE! VERSION *Replace margarine with 1/4 tsp (1 ml) of margarine and use a non-stick skillet!*

PAN FRIED POTATOES VARIATIONS

Onion & Tarragon Potatoes   9 minutes

1 small yellow onion, chopped   **1/4 tsp (1 ml) dried tarragon**
Using the *Basic Pan Fried Potatoes* recipe, add onion and tarragon to melted margarine; sauté about 2 minutes. Add sliced potatoes and fry.

Breakfast Potatoes   8 minutes

1/16 tsp (1/4 ml) garlic powder   **1 tsp (5 ml) dried parsley**
Add above ingredients to melted margarine in *Basic Pan Fried Potatoes* recipe and mix. Immediately add sliced potatoes and fry.

Frying Pan French Fries   9 minutes + soaking

Using the *Basic Pan Fried Potatoes* recipe, instead of slicing potatoes, cut lengthwise into sticks about 1/2-inch (1 cm) thick. Soak in a **bowl** of ice water for 15 minutes. Drain thoroughly. Fry each potato stick at least on two sides.

OTHER POTATO RECIPES

Potato Patties   10-12 minutes

3 medium *refrigerated* **precooked**   **Salt and pepper to taste**
    potatoes   **2 tbsp (30 ml) all-purpose flour**
1 tbsp (15 ml) margarine   **1 small egg, beaten**
Half a small yellow onion,   **2 tsp (10 ml) water**
    finely minced   **2 tbsp (30 ml)** *bulk* **wheat germ**
1 tsp (5 ml) dried parsley   **2 tbsp (30 ml) vegetable oil**
1 tbsp (15 ml) grated Cheddar cheese

In a **large bowl**, mash potatoes with a **potato masher**. *Do not whip*. Stir in margarine, onion, parsley, cheese and season. Shape mixture into 8 small patties and dust with flour. Meanwhile, in a **large frying pan or skillet**, heat oil over a medium setting. In a **small bowl**, beat the egg with water. Dip patties, one side at a time, into egg mixture. Using a **plastic bag** containing the wheat germ, coat each patty. Fry each patty about 3 minutes per side until golden. **Makes 4 large servings of 2 patties per person**

Hash Potatoes   *15-20 minutes*

4 large *refrigerated* precooked
   potatoes
1 tbsp (15 ml) vegetable oil
1 yellow onion, thinly sliced
1/8 tsp (1/2 ml) dried sage
1/8 tsp (1/2 ml) dried rosemary

1/4 cup (60 ml) *Homemade Yogurt*
   (see pages 232-3)
1/2 tsp (2 ml) ground mustard
1/4 tsp (1 ml) *Worcestershire-*
   Style Sauce (see pages 243-4)
1/2 tsp (2 ml) dried parsley
1 1/2 tbsp (22 ml) margarine

In a **large frying pan** or **skillet**, heat oil over a medium-high setting. Meanwhile, in a **large bowl**, roughly mash potatoes with a **fork**. Add onion, sage and rosemary to skillet; sauté 5 minutes. Stir as required. Meanwhile, in a **small bowl**, combine remaining ingredients except margarine. Add margarine to skillet (over onion and herbs) and wait for it to melt. Add mash potatoes and stir in the yogurt mixture, flatten out to sides of skillet. Increase heat to high and cook 5 minutes until golden brown. Using **spatula**, turn potato mixture, a little at a time, and cook other side. **Makes 4 large servings**

Potato 'Galettes'   *12-15 minutes*

4 medium raw potatoes,
   peeled, grated or shredded
Half a small yellow onion,
   grated or finely minced
1 small egg, beaten
1 tbsp (15 ml) all-purpose flour

2 tsp (10 ml) *bulk* wheat germ
1 tbsp (15 ml) *bulk* soy flour
1/4 tsp (1 ml) onion powder
1/2 tsp (2 ml) dried parsley
A little water if necessary
Salt and pepper to taste
2 tbsp (30 ml) margarine

In a **large frying pan or skillet**, melt margarine over a medium heat. Meanwhile, in a large bowl, mix all the remaining ingredients. Using a large spoon, scoop about 8 small balls of potato mixture unto frying pan. Flatten into patties using a spatula, fry a few minutes per side until golden. Serve hot. **Makes 8 small servings**

Potato Fritters   *10-12 minutes*

4 large *refrigerated* precooked
   potatoes *(peeled)*
   OR 3 1/2 cups (840 ml) *Basic*
   Mashed Potatoes (see page 81)
4 tbsp (60 ml) all-purpose flour
1 tsp (5 ml) dried parsley
1 tsp (5 ml) dried marjoram

Half a small yellow onion,
   finely chopped
1 small egg, beaten
Salt and pepper to taste
A little water if necessary
1 1/2 tbsp (22 ml) margarine or
   vegetable oil

Mash potatoes using a **potato masher** or use refrigerated mashed potatoes. *Do not use whipped potatoes.* In a **large frying pan** or **skillet**, heat the fat over a medium setting. Meanwhile, In a **large bowl**, add mashed potatoes, half of flour, parsley, marjoram, onion, egg, seasoning and a little water if required. Mix well. Form into eight small patties and roll into remaining flour to give a light coating. Place patties in the skillet and fry about four minutes per side until golden brown. Turn over with a spatula. Serve Immediately. **Makes 8 small servings**

Potato Pancakes    *15-20 minutes*

2 large raw potatoes, peeled and diced	Half a small yellow onion, chopped
1 small egg	1/4 cup (60 ml) all-purpose flour
1 1/2 tbsp (22 ml) water	Salt and pepper to taste

Using a **blender**, in the covered blender container, place all ingredients except half of potatoes and flour. Blend at high speed until smooth. Add flour and remaining potato; blend at high speed until potatoes are just grated. Meanwhile, in a **large cast iron frying pan**, melt margarine over a medium-low setting. Pour out excess fat. Pour about 1/4 cup (60 ml) of potato batter onto pan. Cook until crisp and brown on both sides. Serve with a bit of margarine. **Makes 8 small servings**

Potato Chips 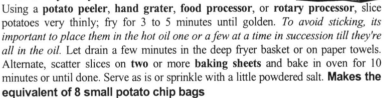   *10-15 minutes*

Preheat oil in **deep-fat fryer** or **heavy, deep saucepan** to 375ºF (190ºC). Or preheat oven to 300ºF (150ºC).

About 4 large low-cost potatoes, peeled and very thinly sliced

Using a **potato peeler**, **hand grater**, **food processor**, or **rotary processor**, slice potatoes very thinly; fry for 3 to 5 minutes until golden. *To avoid sticking, its important to place them in the hot oil one or a few at a time in succession till they're all in the oil.* Let drain a few minutes in the deep fryer basket or on paper towels. Alternate, scatter slices on **two** or more **baking sheets** and bake in oven for 10 minutes or until done. Serve as is or sprinkle with a little powdered salt. **Makes the equivalent of 8 small potato chip bags**

SUB-VARIATIONS *Season them with a little vinaigrette, seasoned salt, powdered salt (see page 247), generic ketchup, red cayenne, chili powder, or garlic powder (or even garlic or onion salt)!*

Homemade Fries    *12 minutes*

French fries almost for free, that is, if potatoes are purchased during peak harvest time in very large sacs.

4 large low-cost potatoes

Simply peel and cut potatoes lengthwise into 3/8-inch (1 cm) wide strips using a **knife** or an inexpensive **'French fries' cutter**. There's no real need to soak them in cold water. *Fry as outlined on pg. 170.* **Makes 4 medium-size servings**

For potato fries or French fries, see page 170

RICE DISHES

Long grain rice (sometimes parboiled) sold in large sacs is by far the least expensive rice available. Instant, converted, wild, or brown rice are all considerably more expensive than long grain rice. Even more expensive are those in boxes, cans, pre-seasoned, or small formats. Apart from long grain rice, the only other rice that justifies its price is brown rice for nutritional reasons.

INSTANT RICE

*These instant rice recipes **do not** use the expensive actual 'Instant Rice' sold in supermarkets but instead use inexpensive long grain rice that you must precook. Real 'Instant Rice" is rice that has been fully cooked and then dehydrated.*

Basic Instant Rice   *4-5 minutes*

2 cups (480 ml) *refrigerated* precooked long grain rice *(see pages 24 or 91)*
1/2 cup (120 ml) hot tap water

1 tbsp (15 ml) vegetable oil or margarine
(Salt and pepper to taste)

DRY SEASONING:
1 tsp (5 ml) chicken or beef soup stock powder
1/4 tsp (1 ml) celery salt

1/4 tsp (1 ml) dried parsley
1/4 tsp (1 ml) onion powder
1/32 tsp (1/8 ml) garlic powder

OR 1/2 tbsp (7 ml) PREMIXED DRY SEASONING #6 (see page 27)

In a **frying pan** or **skillet**, place all ingredients *(plus the ingredients for a variation recipe)*; stir and bring to a boil over the highest heat setting. Immediately lower to a medium-high setting, cover and simmer for a few minutes until most of the liquid has evaporated. Stir when necessary.

Serve hot but plain with a sauce, with basic seasoning *(or as one of the following variations).* **Makes about 2 cups (480 ml) or two average servings**

LITE! VERSION *Simply omit most or all of the vegetable oil and use low-fat soup stock powder!*

INSTANT RICE VARIATIONS

Curried Rice   *4 minutes*
2 tsp (10 ml) curry powder
Add the above *and dry seasoning* to *Basic Instant Rice* recipe.

Mexican Rice   *5 minutes*
1/4 cup (60 ml) canned ground   **1/8 tsp (1/2 ml) red cayenne**
   tomatoes   **pepper**
1/4 tsp (1 ml) mild paprika   **1/4 tsp (1 ml) coriander**
1/3 cup (80 ml) *frozen* precooked   **1 tsp (5 ml) pickled hot pepper**
   whole green peas   **rings, minced**
Add the above *and dry seasoning* to *Basic Instant Rice* recipe.

Buttery-Lemon Rice   *5 minutes*
1 tsp (5 ml) dried fine herbs   **2 tbsp (30 ml) lemon juice from**
1 tbsp (15 ml) margarine *(additional)*   **concentrate** *(replaces same*
                                              amount of water)
Add the above *and dry seasoning* to *Basic Instant Rice* recipe.

Stock Flavored Rice   *4 minutes*
2 tsp (10 ml) chicken or beef soup stock powder
Add the above *and dry seasoning* to *Basic Instant Rice* recipe.

Chinese Rice   *4 minutes*
1 tbsp (15 ml) soy sauce
Add the above *and dry seasoning* to *Basic Instant Rice* recipe.

Herbs & Rice   *4 minutes*
1 tsp (5 ml) dried fine herbs   **1/2 tsp (2 ml) dried thyme**
Add the above *and dry seasoning* to *Basic Instant Rice* recipe.
SUB-VARIATION(S) *Try other herbs like tarragon, Italian herbs, savory, or rosemary alone or in combinations!*

Fine Herbs & Wild Rice   *5 minutes*
1 tsp (5 ml) dried fine herbs   **2 tbsp (30 ml) *frozen* precooked**
                                          wild rice
Add the above *and dry seasoning* to *Basic Instant Rice* recipe.

Italian-Style Rice   *5 minutes*
1 tbsp (15 ml) margarine *(additional)* **2 tsp (10 ml) beef stock powder**
1/2 tsp (2 ml) onion powder   **Dash of saffron**
Half a small yellow onion, sliced   **2 tsp (10 ml) dried Parmesan**
   paper thin *(optional)*   **cheese** *(sprinkled on top)*
Add the above *and dry seasoning* to *Basic Instant Rice* recipe.

Middle-Eastern Multi-Grain Rice   *6-7 minutes*

1 tbsp (15 ml) margarine *(additional)*
1/2 cup (120 ml) medium couscous
1/4 tsp (1 ml) ground cumin

1/4 cup (60 ml) *frozen* precooked
   millet
1/4 tsp (1 ml) mild paprika

Add the above *and dry seasoning* to *Basic Instant Rice* recipe. *Please note that couscous and millet replace the same volume of rice.*

Rice Pilaf   *5-6 minutes*

1 tbsp (15 ml) margarine *(additional)*
Half a small yellow onion, sliced
   paper thin *(optional)*

1/2 tsp (2 ml) turmeric powder

Add the above *and dry seasoning* to *Basic Instant Rice* recipe.

FAST RICE

The fast rice recipes take longer than the instant rice recipes because vegetables and/or legumes must first be sautéed before re-heating the precooked rice.

Basic Fast Rice   *6-12 minutes*

2 cups (480 ml) *refrigerated* precooked
   long grain rice *(see pages 24 or 91)*
3/4 cup (180 ml) hot tap water
Plus vegetables and/or legumes, etc.!

1 tbsp (15 ml) vegetable oil
   margarine
Salt and pepper to taste

DRY SEASONING:
1 tsp (5 ml) chicken or beef soup
   stock powder
1/4 tsp (1 ml) celery salt

1/4 tsp (1 ml) dried parsley
1/4 tsp (1 ml) onion powder
1/32 tsp (1/8 ml) garlic powder

OR 1/2 tbsp (7 ml) PREMIXED DRY SEASONING #6 (see page 27)

In a **frying pan or skillet**, place fat, dry seasoning, and vegetables and/or legumes *(plus additional ingredientss for any of the following recipe variations)*; sauté over a medium-high heat for about 5 minutes until vegetables are done but crisp. Stir frequently. Onions should become transparent. Place rice and water; stir and bring to a boil over the highest heat setting. Immediately lower to a medium-high setting, cover and simmer for a few minutes until most of the liquid has evaporated. Stir if needed. Serve hot. **Make about 2 cups (480 ml) or two average servings**

LITE! VERSION *Simply reduce vegetable oil and use low-fat soup stock powder!*

FAST RICE VARIATIONS

Spanish Rice   *10-12 minutes*

1 cup (240 ml) *Instant Tomato Sauce*
   OR 2/3 cup (160 ml) canned
   ground tomatoes *(see page 98)*
1 very small yellow onion, finely
   minced

1 tbsp (15 ml) green or red bell
   pepper, finely chopped
   (optionally in season only)
1/2 tsp (5 ml) chili powder
1 small garlic clove, minced

Add the above *and dry seasonings* to *Basic Fast Rice* recipe.

French-Style Onion Rice   *10-12 minutes*

1 tbsp (15 ml) margarine *(additional)*   1 tsp (5 ml) white vinegar
1 large yellow onion, thinly sliced   1 tsp (5 ml) beef stock powder

Add the above *and dry seasonings* to *Basic Fast Rice* recipe. *Exceptionally, sauté onion for about 10 minutes instead of 5, until it starts to turn a bit brown and caramelize.*

Fine Herbs Risotto   *8-9 minutes*

1 tbsp (15 ml) margarine *(additional)*   2 small mushrooms, very
1 medium yellow onion,   thinly sliced
    finely chopped   1/4 cup (60 ml) canned diced
1 garlic clove, finely minced   tomatoes
                                              2 tsp (10 ml) grated dried
                                                  Parmesan cheese

Add the above *and dry seasonings* to *Basic Fast Rice* recipe.

Country-Style Mushrooms Rice   *8-9 minutes*

1 small yellow onion, thinly sliced   1 1/2 tsp (7 ml) beef soup stock
2 or 3 medium mushrooms,   powder *(additional)*
    very thinly sliced   1/2 tsp (2 ml) dried tarragon
Half a celery stalk, thinly sliced

Add the above *and dry seasoning* to *Basic Fast Rice* recipe.

Armenian Rice   *10-12 minutes*

1 tbsp (15 ml) margarine *(additional)*   1/4 tsp (1 ml) dried thyme
1/2 cup (120 ml) dried pasta, vermicelli   1/4 tsp (1 ml) dried basil
    or spaghettini, broken short   1/4 tsp (1 ml) black pepper
1 small yellow onion, chopped

Add the above except pasta to *Basic Fast Rice* recipe. The pasta must be cooked in a **separate saucepan** in the usual fashion. Drain when done and add to skillet ingredients; toss and serve. *Dry seasoning is optional here!*

Oriental-Style Vegetable Rice   *7-8 minutes*

1 small yellow onion, chopped   1 tsp (5 ml) soy sauce
1 garlic clove, minced   1 tsp (5 ml) all-purpose flour
Half a celery stalk, sliced   *(sprinkled in)*
                                  1/2 tsp (2 ml) ground ginger

Add the above and *dry seasonings* to *Basic Fast Rice* recipe.

Chinese Fried Rice   *6-7 minutes*

1 tbsp (15 ml) vegetable oil *(extra)*   1 small yellow onion, chopped
1 small garlic clove, minced   1 tbsp (15 ml) soy sauce

Add the above and remove most of the water in *Basic Fast Rice* recipe. Stir-fry to taste. *The dry seasonings are not used in this recipe!*

Red Beans & Rice   *7-8 minutes*

1/2 cup (120 ml) *frozen* precooked
   red kidney beans
1 small yellow onion, chopped
Half a celery stalk, thinly chopped

1 small garlic clove, minced
1 small bay leaf
1 tsp (5 ml) *Worcestershire-Style*
   Sauce (optional, see page 243)

Add the above *and dry seasonings* to *Basic Fast Rice* recipe. Remove bay leaf when done.

Summer Vegetables & Rice   *7-8 minutes*

1/4 cup (60 ml) fresh tomato, diced
1/4 cup (60 ml) green bell pepper,
   chopped

1/4 cup (60 ml) fresh spinach,
   roughly chopped

Add the above *and dry seasonings* to *Basic Fast Rice* recipe.
SUB-VARIATIONS *Try other fresh inexpensive peak season vegetables like broccoli, green beans, cauliflower, fresh corn, etc., etc., etc.!*

CONVERTING FAST RICE RECIPES INTO MAIN DISHES!

Simply by adding to the fast rice recipe about 1/4 cup (60 ml) of precooked chicken, or ground beef or pork, or stewing beef (or pork) cubes sliced very thinly. And for even more proteins (add the meat and legumes in numerous combinations) add about 1/3 cup (80 ml) of a precooked legume like red kidney beans, lima beans, black beans, green lentils, chickpeas, etc., if the recipe doesn't already contain them. Make one very large serving instead of two average ones.

RICE COOKING TECHNIQUE

Traditional Rice   *15-20 minutes*

3 1/3 cups (800 ml) water
1 tsp (5 ml) table salt

1 2/3 cups (400 ml) long grain rice

Absorption Method
In a **large saucepan**, over the highest heat setting, bring the water to a vigorous boil. Add uncooked rice and salt; lower heat to very low; cover and cook 12-15 minutes. Stir every few minutes. Remove from heat and allow to stand a few more minutes. Serve topped with a bit of margarine and season with salt and pepper. Alternately, serve with soy sauce or other sauce. **Makes 4 cups (1 liter) or 4 average servings**

Boiling Method
In a **large saucepan**, over the highest heat setting, bring plenty of hot tap water to a boil. Add uncooked rice and salt; lower heat to medium; do not cover and cook 10-12 minutes. Stir

occasionally. Remove from heat and drain but do not rinse. Serve hot topped with a bit of margarine and seasoned with salt and pepper. Alternately, serve with soy or tamari sauce, or other sauce. ***To prevent rice from sticking,*** *rinse it before cooking in plenty of cold water. After cooking mix with it a small amount of margarine or vegetable oil to prevent rice grains from sticking together as they cool.* **Makes 4 cups (1 liter) or 4 average servings**

Brown Rice *30-35 minutes*

3 1/3 cups (800 ml) hot tap water   1 2/3 cups (400 ml) brown rice
1 tsp (5 ml) table salt

Using the absorption or boiling method; cook rice twice as long as indicated for traditional rice. All other instruction remaining the same.

Pasta Dishes

PASTA

Some of these pasta dishes are light and are more like a side dish. While others may serve as a main course dish. **Makes 3 or 6 servings, 3 as a main course dish or 6 as a side dish**

Pasta Cooking Technique   13-15 minutes

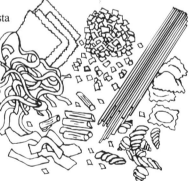

1 pound (450 g) any kind of pasta
In a **large pan** of boiling water, cook pasta with a little vegetable oil and table salt, 8 to 10 minutes. Stir occasionally. When ready it should be cooked but still slightly firm to the bite *(al dente)*. Drain but don't rinse in cold water. Serve immediately with a pasta sauce. *For best results always have sauce ready before the pasta.*

Instant (Precooked) Pasta   4-5 minutes
This pasta is sort of instant but actually is refrigerated (or frozen) precooked pasta.

1 pound (450 g) any kind of pasta
Cook pasta as outlined in the above *Pasta Cooking Technique* and refrigerate in a plastic container, bowl, or bag. Or freeze in portions that you can use. To reheat, place in a **large saucepan** of boiling water; boil until warm or hot. Stir occasionally. Drain and serve immediately covered with pasta sauce.

PASTA & SAUCE

All the pasta sauce recipes were redesigned to reduce cooking time and cost to a minimum. **Makes 3 or 6 servings, 3 as a main course dish or 6 as a side dish. Or from 1/3-3 cups/80-720 ml of sauce plus pasta**

Spaghetti & Meat Sauce   25 minutes

2 tbsp (15 ml) vegetable oil
1/2 cup (120 ml) regular ground
    beef or pork
Small yellow onion, finely chopped
Garlic clove, thinly sliced
1/4 cup (60 ml) carrots, grated
2/3 cup (160 ml) canned diced
    tomatoes
2/3 cup (160 ml) canned ground
    tomatoes

1 1/3 cups (320 ml) hot tap water
1/2 tsp (2 ml) dried parsley
1 tsp (5 ml) dried oregano
1/4 tsp (1 ml) dried fine herbs
3/4 tsp (3-4 ml) chili powder
1/8 tsp (1/2 ml) garlic powder
1 tbsp (15 ml) all-purpose flour
2 bay leaves *(optional)*
Salt and pepper to taste

In a **large frying pan** or **skillet**, heat oil over a medium setting. Add beef (or pork), onions, garlic and carrots; sauté until onions are slightly golden but not brown. Add all spices except bay leaves and stir. Add diced and ground tomatoes, water and bay leaves. Using a **sieve**, sprinkle flour over skillet as you stir. (Meanwhile, get spaghetti cooking as described earlier.) Simmer for about 15 minutes or until sauce has thickened; stir occasionally. Serve hot on *cooked*

or precooked spaghetti or pasta. Add small amounts of grated dried or fresh cheese and/or crushed dried chilies. *Alternately, make sauce in large batches and freeze in smaller size portions!* **Makes 3 large servings**
VARIATIONS *Try this sauce in* **Lasagna,** *or as* **Pizza, Sloppy Joe,** *or* **Hot Michigan Sauce**!

Creamy Bacon Pasta   20 minutes

1 1/2 oz (45 g) pre-toasted bacon, minced
1/3 cup (80 ml) margarine
3 tbsp (45 ml) skim milk powder
1 cup (240 ml) water
2 tbsp (30 ml) white vinegar

2 small eggs, whipped
2 tbsp (30 ml) grated dried
    Pamesan or Romano cheese
Salt or pepper to taste

In a **small saucepan**, heat the milk powder/water mixture then add the bacon and melted margarine. Add the vinegar, this will curd the milk. (Meanwhile, cook pasta as described earlier.) Simmer on low heat for about 10 minutes. Drain *cooked or precooked* pasta. Add whipped eggs, bacon sauce and cheese to it. Season, toss and serve. **Makes 3 large servings**

Vegetarian-Style Pasta   15-18 minutes

1 cup (240 ml) fresh bread
    crumbs
1 garlic clove, thinly sliced

6 tbsp (90 ml) vegetable oil
1 1/2 tbsp (22 ml) sliced marinated
    green/black olives, minced

1 celery stalk, chopped
1 yellow onion, chopped
2/3 cup (160 ml) canned diced
   tomatoes

1/2 cup (120 ml) carrots, grated
1 tbsp (15 ml) lemon juice from
   concentrate
Salt and pepper to taste

In a **large skillet** *(preferably nonstick)*, heat 2 tbsp (30 ml) of oil. Add bread crumbs; stir-fry over medium heat a few minutes until brown. Remove from heat. Meanwhile, get pasta boiling using technique described earlier. In a **large frying pan** or **skillet**, heat 1/2 tbsp (7 ml) of oil. Add garlic, onion, celery, carrots and rosemary. Sauté a few minutes until golden. Add tomatoes and olives; simmer a few minutes. Remove from heat; add lemon juice, salt and pepper. Mix well. Drain *cooked or precooked* pasta. Add remainder of oil to it. Toss until well coated. Serve at once topped with vegetable mixture and browned bread crumbs. **Makes 3 large servings**

Buttery Herbs & Pasta   *5-15 minutes*

1/3 cup (80 ml) margarine
2 tsp (10 ml) dried parsley

1 tsp (5 ml) dried fine herbs
Salt and pepper to taste

Cook or reheat precooked pasta as indicated earlier. Drain when ready. Add margarine and seasoning. Toss and serve hot. **Makes 3 large servings**

Oregano Pasta   *10-15 minutes*

3 slices bread *(day old)*
   crumbed without crust
1/2 cup (120 ml) vegetable oil

2 garlic cloves, finely minced
2 tsp (10 ml) oregano
Salt and pepper to taste

Immediately get pasta cooking as described on page 93. Meanwhile, in a **large frying pan** or **nonstick skillet**, heat 6 tbsp (90 ml) of oil on a medium setting. Sauté the garlic about 30 seconds; add oregano, bread crumbs, a dash of salt and a lot of pepper. Stir-fry up to 5 minutes until evenly browned. Set aside. Drain pasta when al dente. Add remaining oil and bread crumb mix. Toss and serve. **Makes 3 large servings**

Hot Pepper Spaghetti   *20-25 minutes*

1 1/2 tbsp (22 ml) vegetable oil
1 yellow onion, chopped
2 tsp (10 ml) pickled hot pepper
   rings, minced
1 1/2 tsp (7 ml) chicken stock powder
1 garlic clove, thinly sliced

1 1/2 cups (360 ml) water
1 tbsp (15 ml) curry powder
1/8 tsp (1/2 ml) garlic powder
1 tbsp (15 ml) all purpose flour
1 tsp (5 ml) dried parsley
Pepper

Immediately get pasta cooking as described on page 93. Meanwhile, in a **large frying pan** or **skillet**, heat oil over a medium setting. Sauté onion, garlic and pepper rings for about 3 minutes. Set aside. In a **bowl**, mix vegetable stock powder, curry, parsley, flour and water; pour unto skillet. Bring to a boil, lower heat and stir. Simmer at least 5 minutes until sauce starts to thicken. Drain *cooked or precooked* pasta. Top with hot pepper sauce and serve hot. **Makes 3 large servings**

Penne Rigate & Cabbage   20 minutes

1/2 tbsp (7 ml) pickled hot pepper
   rings, chopped
3 tbsp (45 ml) margarine
1 yellow onion, thinly sliced
1 garlic clove, finely minced

Quarter of a green cabbage,
   coarsely shredded or chopped
1 tbsp (15 ml) brown sugar
1 tsp (5 ml) dried parsley
Salt and pepper to taste

In a **large frying pan** or **skillet**, heat margarine over a medium-high, sauté onion and garlic for 5 minutes. Meanwhile, get started by cooking the penne rigate pasta. Quickly shred cabbage. Add cabbage and sugar to onions and garlic; stir in well. Lower heat to medium, cook and stir about 1o minutes until cabbage is golden caramelized and tender. Add a small amount of water if necessary. Drain *cooked or precooked* pasta. Top with cabbage mixture, hot pepper rings, parsley and season. Toss well and serve. **Makes 3 large servings**

Tomato Sauce on Pasta   15-16 minutes

2 tbsp (30 ml) vegetable oil
1 yellow onion, finely chopped
1 garlic clove, finely minced
1 tsp (5 ml) dried fine herbs
1 tsp (5 ml) granulated sugar
1/2 cup (120 ml) canned diced
   tomatoes

1 1/2 cups (360 ml) canned tomato
   juice
1 tbsp (15 ml) tomato paste
2 tsp (10 ml) all-purpose flour
1 tsp (5 ml) dried parsley
1/4 tsp (1 ml) onion powder
Salt and pepper to taste

Get pasta cooking not to lose time. Meanwhile, in a **large frying pan** or **skillet**, heat oil over a medium heat; sauté onion and garlic for 3 minutes. Add remainder of ingredients except flour; increase heat to high. Stir. Bring to a boil; lower heat. Using a **sieve**, sprinkle sauce with flour while stirring. Simmer the sauce about 10 minutes until it thickens. Drain *cooked or precooked* pasta. Top with tomato sauce, season and serve. **Makes 3 large servings**

Mustard Turnips & Pasta   15-18 minutes

3 tbsp (45 ml) vegetable oil
3/4 pound (330 g) turnips
   peeled and diced
2 garlic cloves, minced
1 tsp (5 ml) ground ginger

2 tbsp (30 ml) prepared mustard
1/3 cup (80 ml) water
1 tsp (5 ml) all-purpose flour
Salt and pepper to taste

Immediately get pasta cooking as described on page 93. Meanwhile, In a **large frying pan** or **skillet**, heat oil over a medium-high heat; add turnips, garlic and ground ginger. Sauté for 5 minutes while stirring. Stir the water and flour together, and pour into the pan, lower heat and simmer up to 5 minutes until sauce thickens. Set aside. Drain pasta. Coat sauce with mustard and mix. Top the *cooked or precooked* pasta with sauce and serve hot immediately. **Makes 3 large servings**

European-Style Garlic Liguine   15 minutes

6 garlic cloves, sliced
1/2 tsp (2 ml) garlic powder

1 cup (240 ml) water
2 tbsp (30 ml) dried grated

1/3 cup (80 ml) vegetable oil Parmesan or Romano cheese
3 tbsp (45 ml) skim milk powder Salt and pepper to taste

Immediately start boiling water for pasta. Meanwhile, in a **frying pan** or **skillet**, sauté the garlic over high heat in 4 tbsp (60 ml) of vegetable oil until brown in color. Set aside. In a **blender**, pour water, add skim milk powder and remaining oil. Blend to make a cream on high for 15 second. Return pan to a low-medium heat; add blender cream, garlic powder and cheese. Simmer 2 minutes. Set aside. Drain pasta. Toss sauce on *cooked or precooked* pasta and serve hot. **Makes 3 large servings**

Pasta & Vegetables   *15-18 minutes*

1 tbsp (15 ml) vegetable oil
1 small yellow onion, chopped
1 cup (240 ml) canned diced
    tomatoes
1/2 tsp (2 ml) dried basil
1/2 tsp (2 ml) oregano
2 garlic cloves, finely minced

2 zucchini, coarsely grated
    (only in peak season when
    inexpensive)
1 small egg, beaten
2 tbsp (30 ml) dried grated
    Parmesam cheese
Salt and pepper to taste

Immediately get pasta cooking as described on page 93. Meanwhile, in a **large frying pan** or **skillet**, heat oil over a medium-high heat. Sauté garlic until golden. Add onions and sauté until transparent. Add tomatoes, basil, and oregano. Simmer a few minutes, and add the zucchini. Cook on a high heat and stir, until most of the liquid has evaporated. Add the egg and cheese. Drain *cooked or precooked* pasta. Toss over pasta and serve. Do not refrigerate or keep. **Makes 3 large servings**

Macaroni & Cheese Dinner   *5-15 minutes*

2/3 cup (160 ml) *Cheese (Stretcher)*   1/3 cup (80 ml) water or *Reconst-*
    Sauce (see page 142)   *ituted Skim Milk (see page 231)*

Cook or reheat precooked pasta as described earlier. Drain when ready. Add above ingredients, heat and stir on medium-high about a minute. Serve hot.
Makes 3 large servings
VARIATIONS *Try with cheese sauce stretchers made from processed burger cheese slices (see page 19) or old Cheddar!*

OTHER PASTA SAUCE RECIPES

Tomato & Meat Sauce   *15 minutes*
*This sauce is fast to make even though taste like it was simmered for hours. It's great on pasta and convenient on **Hot Michigan** and **Sloppy Joe**.*

2 tbsp (30 ml) vegetable oil
1/2 cup (120 ml) regular grade ground
    beef, pork, or sausage *(pages 122-4)*
1 large yellow onion, finely chopped

1/3 tbsp (80 ml) canned ground
    tomatoes
3/4 cup (180 ml) hot tap water
3 tbsp (45 ml) *'Quick'* rolled oats

A quarter of a green pepper, finely
   chopped *(optionally in peak season)*
1 1/3 cup (320 ml) canned diced tomatoes

1 tsp (5 ml) chili powder
1/8 tsp (1/2 ml) garlic powder
1 tsp (5 ml) *Worcestershire-Style Sauce (see page 243)*
Salt and pepper to taste

In a **large skillet**, sauté meat and vegetables in oil over a medium-high heat till meat is brown. Don't drain fat and stir in canned tomatoes, water, oats, and remainder of ingredients. Bring to a boil; reduce heat. Simmer at least 5 minutes or till mixture is of the proper consistency. Sprinkle in some flour if necessary. Meanwhile, in a second **large saucepan**, reheat precooked pasta *(see Instant Pasta, page 93)*. Serve at once. *Multiply and freeze this sauce recipe.* **Makes about 2 1/2 cups (600 ml) or 20 very small servings**

LITE! VERSION *Use a nonstick skillet, omit oil and drain fat from pan when meat is fully cooked!*

Instant Tomato Sauce   *4-5 minutes*

2 cups (500 ml) canned tomato juice
   AND 1 cup (250 ml) hot tap water
OR 1 cup (240 ml) canned ground
   tomatoes
   AND 2 cups (480 ml) water
1/2 tsp (2 ml) onion powder

1 tbsp (15 ml) chicken or beef soup
   stock powder
1/3 cup (80 ml) *bulk* cornstarch
   (or all-purpose flour)
1 1/2-3 tbsp (22-45 ml) vegetable oil
Salt and pepper to taste

Place all ingredients in a **large saucepan** or **skillet**, quickly whisk together; then heat over the highest setting. Whisk occasionally until thickened. Meanwhile, in a second **large saucepan**, reheat precooked pasta *(see Instant Pasta, page 93)*. Serve at once. **Makes 3 large servings**

VARIATION(S) *Brown 2/3 cup (160 ml) regular ground beef or pork in skillet before making sauce, and/or back with same amount of a frozen precooked legume!*

LITE! VERSION *Use a nonstick skillet, omit or reduce oil and drain fat from pan when meat turns brown if, you're using meat as a variation!*

TIPS & HINTS: *For any recipe, 1 tbsp (15 ml) of ground canned tomatoes may be replaced with 1 tsp (5 ml) of canned tomato paste and 2 tsp (10 ml) of canned tomato juice...or 1/2 tbsp (7 ml) canned tomato paste and 1/2 tbsp (7 ml) water!*

BREAD MAKING

We are proud of this chapter, the basic bread technique allows you to bake quality, light well-risen yeast bread very inexpensively. Specifically, you can make **three large bread loaves for about one dollar** (Canadian). The method uses the cheapest flour on the market and very little yeast, and is not labor intensive.

Freshly baked bread within the hour…

Using the methods outlined in this chapter, you can bake fresh bread, anytime, often in less than an hour. This is true only, if the proper preparations in advance have been made. It's accomplished with any of three techniques. The first is the 'always ready' refrigerated dough, which can be shaped, final raised, and baked into bread or small rolls any time you need it. ('Pita' bread takes less than 15 minutes.) The second way is to re-bake semi-baked refrigerated or frozen bread. If stored in refrigerator instead of freezer, a loaf can be re-baked in less than 20 minutes. Finally, there's quick bread, which take well under an hour to prepare and bake, sometimes less than 30 minutes. These three bread-baking options virtually eliminate the problem of day-old or stale bread. This chapter is sure to turn your kitchen into a small but very efficient bread bakery.

About 'Always Ready' Refrigerated Dough!

*We recommend that you always have unshaped pre-risen refrigerated dough in your refrigerator. This way you can enjoy daily, without a long wait, freshly baked items like bread loaves, pita, bagels, rolls, buns, flat bread, and even pizza. For example pita made with **unshaped** refrigerated dough takes about 10 minutes, compared to the usual two hours. Most refrigerated doughs will last only 4-7 days, and this is where frozen unshaped dough comes in. When you're almost out of refrigerated dough, simply thaw a piece of frozen dough (placed in a zipper-lock bag with most of the air expelled) in the refrigerator and the next day it's ready to use. When dough is needed, shape and final rise it as you normally would before baking. Dough must always be risen once and deflated before freezing or refrigeration. Microwave oven dough rising (proofing) makes 'Always Ready' refrigerated dough even more convenient and fast, see page 110. **Having 'Always Ready' refrigerated dough (or frozen) is so convenient that it's almost unbelievable!***

Traditional/Sponge Method

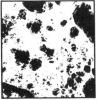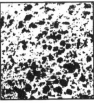

We included two mixing methods because each one yields a very different and interesting crumb texture. Generally speaking, leaving aside dough types, where a light and airy textured crumb is desired, use the **sponge method** *for mixing the dough (see STEP 3. Sponge Starter and Traditional Method(s), page 103). If a denser and more uniformly textured*

SPONGE METHOD	TRADITIONAL METHOD
AIRY AND	*DENSE AND*
IRREGULAR TEXTURE	*UNIFORM TEXTURE*

crumb is needed, use the **traditional method** *to mix the dough (see illustrations). The longer a sponge rises or ferments, the more irregular the inner crumb texture will be. Sourdough starters are sponge starters left to sour a few days.*

Making a sourdough sponge starter!

Why use a sourdough sponge starter? To obtain bread with an open airy texture and a superior flavor. Most books on bread making which include sourdough recipes will recommend making a sourdough starter that you must use or feed continually. We tested the technique and found it unreliable since many things can go wrong. Its easy to forget that you even have a sourdough starter in your refrigerator and let it waste by not using or feeding it for weeks or months. Other things can and do go wrong when perpetuating those starters. Thus, we recommend that you make a sourdough starter, let it age at room temperature for a few days, use it (or some of it) immediately or freeze it in loaf-size portions. It's that simple with little that can go wrong. The method uses very little fresh yeast and is essentially the same as the sponge starter method in our basic yeast bread instructions except that its left at room temperature a few days.

Sourdough Sponge Starter   *2-5 days*

Use this sourdough starter with any bread recipe. Use it, freshly made or thawed, interchangeably with the sponge method in the basic yeast bread recipe (see pages, 102-3). This recipe is good for four large loaves, multiply as needed.

MAKING STARTER

1 tsp (5 ml) fresh compressed yeast	7 cups (1680 ml) generic all-purpose
OR *(1/2 tsp/2 ml active dry yeast)*	flour *(bleached or unbleached)*
5 cups (1200 ml) lukewarm water	2 tsp (10 ml) granulated sugar

SOUR-
DOUGH
STARTER

In a **very large plastic bowl** or **gallon jar** *(or any non-metal container)*, add the yeast and lukewarm water *(110° to 115° F/43° to 46° C)* and stir to dissolve the yeast. After proofing the yeast 5 minutes add remaining ingredients and stir with a **plastic mixing spoon** until smooth. *Always use a non-metallic spoon and the plastic bowl and glass jar should have a plastic lid.* Alternately, cover the jar or bowl with its lid loose-fitting or plastic wrap or a few layers of cheesecloth secured with a sting or rubber band. *Remember that it must breathe.* Let stand at room temperature for 2-5 days till mixture develops a fermented scent; stir it down once or twice daily. After a few days, if you judge the aroma is just right, stir it down one last time and divide it into four equal portions. Use it immediately or store portions in separate plastic containers or plastic bags frozen till needed. **Makes sourdough sponge starter for 4 large loaves**

USING FROZEN SOURDOUGH STARTER
Thaw the frozen sourdough starter in refrigerator, at room temperature, or in oven incubator at 75-85°F/24-29°C *(see page 104)*. *When using a sourdough starter that has been frozen, always add an addition 1/8 tsp/1/2 ml of dry active yeast (double for fresh yeast) per loaf.* Use it as directed in *Basic Yeast Bread* recipe. *About 2 cups (480 ml) of stirred-down sourdough starter or of ordinary sponge starter (see page 103) is good for one loaf.*

POPULAR BREAD SHAPES

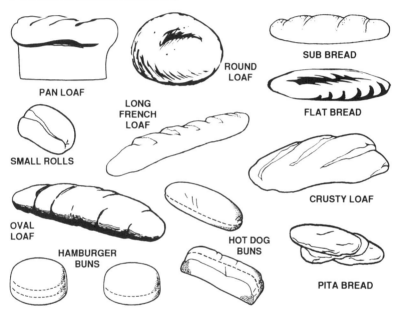

PAN LOAF

ROUND LOAF

SUB BREAD

LONG FRENCH LOAF

FLAT BREAD

SMALL ROLLS

OVAL LOAF

CRUSTY LOAF

HOT DOG BUNS

HAMBURGER BUNS

PITA BREAD

POPULAR BREAD GLAZES AND TOPPINGS
Glazes and/or toppings add a finishing touch to bread. They have a direct effect on the taste, texture and appearance of the bread though they are by no means necessary. Glazes are applied with a brush before and/or after baking. Toppings are usually sprinkled on by hand or with a fine mesh sieve or even pressed on gently in some cases. The least expensive ones are list below, use them sparingly.

GLAZES	TOPPINGS
Whole egg and water glaze	Blender cracked wheat topping
Egg white and water glaze	Poppy seed topping
Egg yolk and water glaze	Sesame seed topping
Vegetable oil glaze	All-purpose flour topping
Reconstituted milk glaze	Cornmeal topping (or for bottom)
Salted water glaze	Sautéed minced yellow onion topping
	Ground spice or coarse salt topping

YEAST BREADS

The following bread-making method will give you the best well-risen bread for the money. It uses one of the least expensive flour on the market, which usually is generic-brand bleached all-purpose flour purchased in 22 lb/10 kg bags. It uses very little fresh or dry active yeast, which amounts to barely a couple of pennies a loaf. **Yes, you can make three large loaves of bread for one Canadian dollar!** *In addition, we'll tell you how little kneading you can get away with and still get professional results. Accordingly, you must use the 'Sponge Starter Method' as used only in this book. The 'Traditional Method' is also included for reference's sake; it won't yield the same results and low cost. When possible, commercial small bakery techniques are employed or adapted to a smaller scale. Depending on whether you're single, a couple or a family of 4 or more, you might want to use the basic yeast bread method several times a month.*

Basic Yeast Bread   *4-6 hours*

The basic yeast bread recipe and its variations uses some commercial food technology know-how along with old forgotten methods to get the best results. Resulting in the most rise and volume, from very little yeast given in two doses and the least expensive flour on the market (sometimes unbleached is least expensive). Double this recipe and freeze the pre-risen dough. **Makes 4 loaves**

SPONGE STARTER INGREDIENTS ONLY:

1/2 tsp (2 ml) any active dry yeast
    OR 1 tsp/5 ml fresh yeast
    (the yeast is used in two doses)
5 cups (1200 ml) lukewarm water

7 cups (1680 ml) generic all-purpose
    flour *(bleached or unbleached)*
2 tsp (10 ml) granulated sugar

REMAINING DOUGH INGREDIENTS:

7 cups (1680 ml) generic all-purpose
    flour *(bleached or unbleached)*
2 tsp (10 ml) granulated sugar
2 tsp (10 ml) table salt

1/4 tsp (1 ml) ascorbic acid crystals
    (optional, see list on page 22)
2 tsp (10 ml) liquid (soya) lecithin
    (optional, see list on page 22)

Buying and storing yeast...*Fresh yeast is sold in one very large plastic mixing bowl... Fresh yeast is sold in compressed blocks weighing about 2 lb/1 kg at small local bakeries. You can make over 400 bread loaves from it (1¢ a loaf). Refrigerate a small portion for up to a month. Divide the rest into 1 tsp (5 ml) portions, loose-pack freeze and store them bagged in freezer. Buy the dry yeast (any kind) in packets or a small jar, stored refrigerated. Once a packet has been opened, its content should be placed in a tiny airtight glass jar. One packet (2 tsp/10 ml) makes 16 loaves (3¢ each).*

> **How to incorporate lecithin into dough?**
> *Take no more than a quarter cup (60 ml) of flour, add the lecithin and mix both with small wooden stirrer or a utensil. Combine.*

STEP 1. *Testing and Dissolving the Yeast*

In **one very large plastic mixing bowl (with an non-airtight lid)**, pour all of the warm water *(100-110°F/38-43°C)*. Add half the dry or fresh yeast and sugar to the water. Stir to dissolve. For dry yeast, let it stand **only** 5 minutes. If it foams on top of the water its good! In contrast, fresh yeast cannot be tested but is almost always good. *Leaving the yeast more than 15 minutes in water will **kill** it!*

STEP 2. *Using a Sponge Starter to Cultivate the Yeast*
FOR SPONGE STARTER METHOD ONLY (omit this step for traditional method) *The sponge method refers to a starter made of two doses of yeast, all of the water in recipe and half of the flour in recipe, mixed together in a bowl. It is left to ferment and increase in size over time till it looks like a sponge. This bread making method that we developed will give well-risen bread from very little yeast.* After dissolving half of the yeast as described in step 1, add exactly half (7 cups/1680 ml) of flour and half of the sugar (2 tsp/10 ml). Using a **plastic mixing spoon**, quickly turn it into a paste. Cover the bowls with their **lids** or with **plastic wrap**. Let it ferment *(and slowly cultivate the yeast)* overnight for 24 hours at room temperature (65-75°F/18-24°C). Midway or after say 12 hours, add the remaining yeast *(dissolved in very little water)* for a second dose. Over 24 hours will make sourdough starter.

WAIT 24 hrs.

STEP 3. *Mixing the Dough*
SPONGE STARTER METHOD Using the same bowl or bowls, add flour *(preferably warm)* and remaining ingredients *(including those for a recipe variation)*. With a **plastic mixing spoon**, stir to combine ingredients. Inevitably, there's going to be some loose dough pieces and flour. Turn out bowl contents unto a non-floured surface. Mix and incorporate loose flour and pieces with dough by tearing dough often. Gather dough bits and pieces and **hand-mix** a minute or so *(see hand-mixing ill.)*. Separate dough into four equal portions, now its ready for kneading. *(Alternately, separate dough in four before hand-mixing, or use one bowl per loaf method.)*
TRADITIONAL METHOD (omit step 2 for traditional method) *We've included the traditional method but it yields inferior results and requires a lot more yeast. You have to use four to eight times more yeast, so if you do use it, make the adjustments.* In a **very large mixing bowl**, combine warm flour

HAND-MIXING

and remaining ingredients *(including those for a recipe variation)*. With a **plastic mixing spoon**, stir to combine ingredients. Inevitably, there's going to be some loose dough pieces and flour. Turn out bowl contents unto a non-floured surface. Gather dough bits and pieces and **hand-mix** a minute or so *(see hand-mixing ill.)*. Separate dough into four *(or 8)* equal portions, now its ready for kneading.

STEP 4. *Kneading the Dough*
Kneading is essential for well-risen bread. Experience has shown us that hand kneading the required dough for each bread energetically about 4 minutes till smooth and uniform will result in a well-risen quality product. More kneading doesn't improve quality much, but less will drastically reduce bread quality. Alternately, knead half of the entire bread dough at once for about 8 minutes with a **heavy-duty mixer**.

HAND KNEADING

How to hand knead? *Fold one half of flattened dough over the other; very lightly dust with flour. Using the heel of your hand, push into the dough in a shearing motion. Using the other hand, fold it again in half and rotate about a quarter turn. Repeat kneading the dough 3 to 4 minutes per loaf till smooth and elastic in texture. Incidentally, kneading half bread dough portions is far easier than full bread portions. Warm dough kneads easiest!*

STEP 5. Initial Rise

75-85°F/24-29°C

OVEN RISE

The initial rise period is necessary for quality well-risen bread. Lightly oil the pieces of dough with a bit of vegetable oil using oiled hands. *This prevents a crust from forming.* Place the pieces of dough in **four** *(wet)* **mixing bowls**, cover with **lids** or **plastic wrap**, and let rise in a warm oven *(see illustration)* at a temperature of 75-95°F/24-35°C for about 2½ hours till almost tripled in size. *(Warmer would slowly bake and dry the dough, cooler would take too long to rise.)* The 'Traditional Method' will require less time for the initial rise, usually no more than 1½ hours. Do not allow it to over-rise beyond that point. If it's under-risen, allow more time. If it's over-risen, use it just the same. Once the dough has risen completely, deflate by pressing on it. Remove dough from bowls, and *optionally* knead each piece again as you had done before for about a minute before shaping and the final rise. *When using 'Refrigerated Dough', omit initial rise, it already had its initial rise.*

How to oven-rise your dough? *To pre-warm an oven, turn it on at any low setting and maintain about 30 seconds; turn it off. Now switch on oven light (60-100 watts) and place a large saucepan lid or metal pie pan over the stovetop element where the oven vent is located. Place bowl of dough in it. An oven used in this manner, heated by the oven light, should maintain a temperature of about 85°F (29°C). If the temperature is too low use a higher wattage bulb. If the oven light socket is inaccessible, place a small lamp in the oven and careful lead the electric wire to a plug outside the oven. If it gets too hot remove pan covering oven vent and keep oven door slightly opened using a small utensil.*

OPTIONS AT THIS STAGE!
Please consider the following choices at this point.

Option 1. Proceed to shape, final rise, and immediately bake everything. Alternately, bake some of it, and freeze and/or refrigerated the rest.

Option 2. Deflate, shape and immediately freeze and/or refrigerate everything without a final rise. To freeze shaped dough, use the *'Loose-pack'* method by placing all the pieces on one or more baking sheets and let them freeze immediately without cover. After a few hours place all pieces in large zipper or twist-tie plastic bags. If the pieces of dough are frozen they won't stick together. When needed, remove the frozen dough from the bag and place them in baking pans or sheets, covered, to thaw and rise. This thaw and final rise is either done at room temperature or in warm oven; bake when the final rise is completed. If you want to refrigerate the dough, shape it and place it in baking pans or on baking sheets while covered. When needed, final rise the dough on counter or in warm oven and bake as directed. *(See text 'The best way to keep refrigerated dough'.)*

Option 3. Deflate *(but do not shape),* and immediately freeze and/or refrigerate all the dough that you have prepared. *(See text in 'Option 2' for how to freeze the dough.)* The 'always ready' refrigerated dough falls into this category *(see text on 'The best way to keep refrigerated dough')*. When you need to make bread or rolls, remove the required amount of dough from the zipper or plastic bag, shape it and place it in baking pans or on baking sheets, covered with plastic wrap or a very large plastic bag. Final rise the dough as long as needed and bake.

The best way to keep refrigerated dough...*is to place the mass of unshaped dough in a zipper or plain plastic bag with twist-tie. Use more than one*

bag if necessary. Shut the zipper about 90% all the way and force out most of the air by using your hands. Then zip it all the way. This keeps the dough from drying and allows any expansion due to gases. When removing a portion of the dough repeat air removal step before zipping close again. Refrigerate up to 6 days and renew.

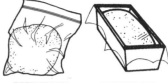

REFRIGERATE
'ALWAYS READY'
UNSHAPED DOUGH
UP TO 4-5 DAYS

REFRIGERATE
(COOLRISE)
PRE-SHAPED DOUGH
UP TO 24 HOURS

STEP 6. Shaping

A. On a lightly floured surface, gather both hands around the dough, rotating it slowly and applying pressure to give it a round and semi-spherical shape. Then flatten the dough with the palm of your hands, or using a lightly floured **rolling pin**, to expel any gas bubbles. Keep the dough in a round but flat shape. **B.** Take the edge of the dough and fold it at the center. **C.** Fold the other half of the dough into the center, as to overlap the previously fold half. Gently press along the seam to seal it and make surface contact between the folds. **D.** With the palms of both hands, roll the dough back and forth to achieve the desired size and length of dough. *(See illustrations.) In summary, the dough is never placed in a pan or on a baking sheet as is. It must be flattened and then folded twice or rolled up as needed. For most bread shapes, the dough is either folded in two, in three, rolled up, or for round loaves the skin of the dough is pulled towards the bottom. Dough is never folded in four. The seam is then pinched with enough pressure to prevent the dough from unfolding during the final rise or baking. Sometimes the shaped is rolled back and forth as when making long-thin bread. Finally, it is transferred to a loaf pan or baking sheet with its fold usually placed underneath it. **If dough resists shaping or rolling out, slap it (flat) against kitchen counter a few times.***

A   B   C   D

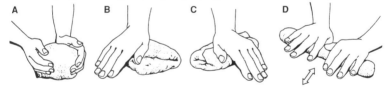

STEP 7. Final Rise, Glazing, and Toppings

PLASTIC CONTAINER
OR BOWL *(WET)*

SHAPED
DOUGH

BAKING SHEET/PAN

After shaping the dough is either placed in **baking pans** or **baking sheets**, usually the seam of the dough is kept on the underside. Use dark dull metal, preferably non-stick pans and avoid shiny metal ones. Use a large plastic container to cover the shaped dough in pans *(see ill.)*. Wet and let drip inside of container for added humidity. *(Or cover it with plastic wrap sprayed with cooking spray.)* Final rising of dough at 75-95°F/24-35°C takes up to 3 hours *(sometimes longer)* till at least tripled in volume. After final rise you can gently glaze and add toppings to the dough. All glazes are placed on the upper exposed surface of dough and most are done before baking, applied with a **soft pastry brush**. Toppings are sprinkled on top of dough using your fingers and its always done before baking, after the final rise and glazing. The bread recipe variations specify which to use, or go by taste *(see glazes and toppings, page 101)*.

STEP 8. *Baking*

Before baking, after the final rise, glaze, and toppings comes the optional slashing. It serves a functional and decorative purpose. It prevents the loaf from cracking or breaking at the sides. It is best to cut the slashes with an extremely shape blade and use a quick and firm stoke to avoid sticking and tearing. Most slashes should be about 1/2-inch (1 cm) deep. About 5 minutes before the end of the final rise preheat oven unless you have some glazing and/or topping to add. *Under-risen dough should not be baked but instead given more time!* Placed loaf pans or sheets on one or two oven rack(s) depending on type of bread you're baking and the oven temperature *(see page 37)*. Individual bread recipe variations will specify the oven temperature and number of racks. Always set a **timer** when baking bread. When making crusty bread the presence of steam in the oven is required. This is accomplished by placing a metal or glassware pan containing, water and ice, on the lowest level oven rack. When testing for doneness, the best indicator is the color of the crust. It should be golden brown, not dark brown nor too pale. Small or thin bread can be baked at higher temperatures, while larger and thick breads must bake more slowly at moderate temperatures. *See recipes for baking temperatures.*

STEP 9. *Cooling & Storage*

Freshly baked bread loaves should be removed from pans or baking sheets and thoroughly cooled on **wire racks**. This not only saves time but also prevents the bottom portion from becoming damp and soggy. Turn bread upside down to dry bottom. Warm bread should be sliced using a sharp, *serrated* **bread knife** to avoid tearing or crushing the loaf. Store bread in plastic bags, or plastic containers with lid in refrigerator, freezer, or breadbox.

LITE! VERSION *Simply exclude any fats from recipes such as shortening, pure lard, margarine, or vegetable oil. The resulting fatless bread is more than acceptable!*

For an even more voluminous bread...

For higher risen bread loaves use high-gluten bread flour which is about twice as expensive as generic bleached all-purpose flour. The resulting bread will be noticably higher with a superior flavor. In addition, using even more yeast with the sponge starter method will give balloon-like loaves of bread. A third rise and more kneading helps towards this end. The Dinner Rolls *recipe gives the most rise.*

YEAST BREAD VARIATIONS

Whole Wheat Bread   *4-6 hours*

Substitute half of all-purpose flour with 7 cups (1680 ml) generic-brand whole-wheat flour!

3/8 cup (90 ml) dark brown sugar
1/3 cup (80 ml) instant skim milk powder

1/4 cup (60 ml) margarine *(optional)*

Add or use the above ingredients in the *Basic Yeast Bread* recipe. *Initial Rise...*1½ hours. Divide into four equal portions and shape to make four pan loaves, *Final Rise...*2-2½ hours, *Bake...*40-45 minutes at 375°F (190°C) using one or 2 rack(s) placed in a preheated oven. Cool thoroughly on wire racks and store in plastic bags. **Makes 4 medium pan loaves**

SUB-VARIATIONS *For **Multi-Grain Bread**, try substituting small amounts of rolled oats, flax, cornmeal, and other low-cost grains for the all-purpose flour!*

Dinner Rolls *(Crescent-Shaped)* *4-6 hours*

1/3 cup (80 ml) instant skim milk powder
1/4 cup (60 ml) granulated sugar
    (instead of 2 tsp/10 ml in remaining
    ingredients portion of basic recipe)

4 small or 2 large eggs, beaten
3/4 cup (180 ml) margarine,
    melted

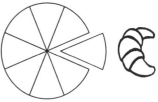

Add the above ingredients to the *Basic Yeast Bread* recipe. *Don't forget to use the optional ascorbic acid crystals and lecithin. Initial rise…*2 hours. Divide into 8 equal round balls and roll each into an 8-inch (20 cm) circle. Using a **pizza/pastry cutter** cut each circle into 8 equal wedges. Beginning with the wide end, firmly roll up each wedge toward the point. Place them point down on four baking sheets with ends curved inwards. *Final rise…*2-3 hours, **Bake**…10-15 minutes at 375ºF (190ºC) using one or 2 rack(s) placed in a preheated oven. Cool till warm on wire racks and serve. Likewise, store in plastic bags and reheat if desired. Rolls may be shaped after the initial rise and then frozen or refrigerated for later use *(see Option 2, page 104).* **Makes 64 rolls**
SUB-VARIATION(S) *Shape them as Parker House rolls, round or oval dinner rolls, bow knot rolls, cloverleaf rolls, snail rolls, twist rolls, or butterfly rolls!*

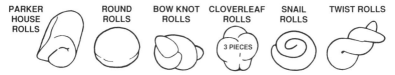

PARKER HOUSE ROLLS   ROUND ROLLS   BOW KNOT ROLLS   CLOVERLEAF ROLLS   SNAIL ROLLS   TWIST ROLLS   3 PIECES

Hamburger and Hot Dog Buns, or Sub Bread *4-6 hours*

Use the previous *Dinner Rolls* recipe and follow shaping instructions *(see ill's page 101).* Always place them on 4 flour dusted or greased **baking sheets** and placed so that when they expand they'll be touching slightly. **HAMBURGER BUNS:** Divide dough into 48 and quickly shape each into ball and flatten with the floured bottom of a **large jar**. *Final bun size: 3½"(9 cm) round x 2"(5 cm) high.* **STEAMED HOT DOG BUNS:** Divide dough into 48 pieces and flatten each into an oval about 5"(13 cm) long. Fold twice, pinch seam and roll with palm to proper shape. Place seams on underside. *Final bun size: 5½"(14 cm) long x 1¾"(4.5 cm) wide.* **TOASTED HOT DOG BUNS:** Divide dough into 8 piece. Shape and flatten each piece into a rectangle 4½"(11.5 cm) x 7"(18 cm) x ½"(1.25 cm) high. Place two per baking sheet. When baked, cut the center slots while each six are still in one piece. Sever in 5 places to make 6 buns from each rectangle, see illustration.

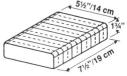

Final bun size: 5½"(14 cm) long x 1¼"(3.25 cm) wide x 1¾"(4½ cm) high. **SUBMARINE BREAD:** Divide dough into 16 pieces and flatten each into an oval about 9"(23 cm) long. Fold twice, pinch seam and roll with palm to proper shape. Place seam on underside. *Final sub bread size: 10"(25 cm) long x 2¼"(5.75 cm) wide x 2"(5 cm) high.* These buns will cost you only a few cents each to make! **Makes 48 buns or 16 subs**

Sandwich Bread Loaf   *4-6 hours*

Use the *Dinner Rolls* recipe, but omit eggs. Divide
dough in 4 and shape as pan loaves *(no slashes)*; bake
about 30 minutes instead of 15. **Makes 4 loaves**

European-Style Rye Bread   *4-6 hours*

5 cups (1200 ml) rye flour *(replaces
same amount of all-purpose flour)*
**1/4 cup (60 ml) melted low-cost
margarine or vegetable oil**
**1/4 cup (60 ml) instant skim milk
powder** *(optional)*

1/2 tbsp (7 ml) caraway seeds
(optional)
3/8 cup (90 ml) dark brown sugar
1/4 cup (60 ml) cornmeal *(sprinkled
on baking sheets before baking)*

 Add the above ingredients to the *Basic Yeast Bread*
recipe. *Initial rise*…2-2½ hours. Divide into four equal
portions and shape to make four oval or round rye
loaves, *Final rise*…2 hours, *Bake*…35-40 minutes at
375°F (190°C) using one or 2 rack(s), covered in cornmeal, placed in a preheated
oven. Cool on racks and store in plastic bags. **Makes 4 large oval rye loaves**
SUB-VARIATION *To make **Pumpernickel Bread** replace the brown sugar with
same amount of molasses, add 1 1/2 tbsp (22 ml) of instant coffee granules and 3
tbsp (45 ml) of cocoa powder dissolved in hot water. Use the sourdough method
for **Sourdough Rye Bread**. Make **Onion Rye Bread** or **Garlic Rye Bread** by
topping the dough, before baking, with some sautéed chopped onions or garlic!*

French-Style Crusty Bread   *4-6 hours*

1/8 cup (30 ml) molasses *(optional)*
Exclude the lecithin and ascorbic acid crystals, and add the above *optional*
ingredient in the *Basic Yeast Bread* recipe. *Initial rise*…2 to 3 hours. Divide
into equal portions, and shape to make 3 or 4 large crusty loaves or 8 long and
thin French 'Baguette' loaves. Place on **baking sheets**, *final rise*…2-3 hours, cut
a few slash diagonally, *bake*…15-30 minutes at 400°F (200°C) using one rack
only placed in the middle of preheated oven. Place a pan containing water and ice
on bottom rack. Cool at least several minutes on wire racks and consume, or store
in plastic bags. **Make 3 or 4 large crusty loaves or 8 French 'Baguettes'**

Middle-Eastern Pita Bread   *4-6 hours*

2 tbsp (30 ml) vegetable oil *(optional)*
To make real pita bread, the *Basic Yeast Bread* recipe should include the above
optional ingredient and don't use ascorbic acid and lecithin. *Initial Rise*…2
hours. Divide into 36 equal portions, using **rolling pin**, roll out into 7-inch (18
cm) rounds. *Final Rise*…10 minutes *(optional)*, *Bake*…about 3 minutes per side
(till puffed and light brown spots appear) at 475°F (245°C) on preheated baking
sheets. Use one rack only placed mid-level in preheated oven. Place on cooling
racks several minutes, store in plastic bags. **Makes 48 pieces of pita bread**
SUB-VARIATION *Make **Whole-wheat Pita Bread** by substituting half of the
all-purpose flour with whole-wheat flour!*

New York-Style Bagels   *4-6 hours*

*This recipe is similar to the basic bread recipe. What creates the
chewy texture & glazed surface is the broiling, boiling, and baking.*

1/2 cup (120 ml) sugar   **2 tbsp (30 ml) *bulk* sesame seeds**
    (instead of second 2 tsp/10 ml)

Add more sugar in the
Basic Yeast Bread
recipe but save 25 %
of sugar for boiling
water. *No Initial Rise!*
Divide into 48 equal
portions and shape as
dough rings *(see ill's.).* Place on baking sheets. *Final Rise*...15-20 minutes, and
Broil...2 minutes per side. Meanwhile, in a large saucepan bring plenty of water
(with sugar) to a boil on highest setting. Reduce heat to medium and simmer
bagels several at once. When bagel begin to float, boil 2 minutes per side. Place
on baking sheets again and sprinkle 1/8 tsp (1/2 ml) of sesame seeds on each
bagel.. *Bake*...20-30 minutes at 375°F (190°C) using 2 racks placed in a
preheated oven. Cool till warm on wire racks and serve. Or store the bagels in
plastic bags and reheat. Bagels may be shaped without an initial rise and then
stored frozen. *Try bagels made from Refrigerated Dough!* **Makes 48 bagels**
SUB-VARIATIONS *Make **Rye Bagels** by substituting 1/3 of the flour with rye
flour. Make **Whole-wheat Bagels** by substituting half of the flour with whole-
wheat flour. Try making **Onion Bagels** by adding small amounts of onion powder
and/or dried minced onions into flour, and top with sautéed minced onions.
Alternately, try toping with poppy seeds or cornmeal!*

San Francisco Sourdough Bread   *4-6 hours*

8 cups (1920 ml) *Sourdough Sponge*   ***Double the amount of table salt!***
    Starter *(replaces the sponge starter)*   **2 cups (480 ml) whole-wheat flour**
1 tsp (5 ml) fresh compressed yeast   *(replaces same amount of flour)*
    OR *(1/2 tsp/2 ml active dry yeast)*

Add or use the above to substitute certain ingredients in
the *Basic Yeast Bread* recipe. *Initial Rise*...2-2½ hours.
Divide and shape to make 3 very large loaves and place on
baking sheets. *Final Rise*...2-4 hours. *A San Francisco
sourdough loaf is traditionally shaped as an oval/round loaf with crisscrossing
slashes on top (see ill.). Bake*...45 minutes at 375°F (190°C) using one rack only
placed in the middle of preheated oven. Let cool on wire racks and serve; or store
in plastic bags. **Makes 3 very large or 4 large sourdough loaves**
SUB-VARIATIONS *Try the sourdough technique with any yeast bread recipe!*

Flat Bread(s)   *4-6 hours*

*Barbari, Nan, Pide, pain Tunisien, and Ekmek are all popular flat breads from
the Middle East. Due to limited space, we'll concentrate mostly on typical flat
breads. The basic bread recipe is more than suitable for making any flat bread.*

3/8 cup (90 ml) vegetable oil *(optional)*   ***Glazes & toppings are optional!***

Add the above to the *Basic Yeast Bread* recipe. Some recipes call for honey or milk *(reconstituted)* instead of sugar or water. ***Initial Rise...***2 hours. Divide and shape to make 3, 6, or 12 flat breads *(see illustrations)* and place on **baking sheets**. ***Final Rise...***1½-2½ hours. Some flat bread, traditionally, have four crisscrossing lines usually done with the blunt edge of a knife, others have 9 dimples made with a fingertip. Some are plain in shape *(and have no glaze or topping).* ***Bake...***20-40 minutes at 400°F (200°C) using one or two rack(s) placed in a preheated oven. Let cool on wire racks and serve; or store in plastic bags. **Makes 3 or 4 large, 6 to 8 medium, or 12 to 16 small flat breads SUB-VARIATIONS** *Try the whole-wheat & sourdough recipes with flat bread!*

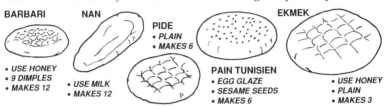

BARBARI
- USE HONEY
- 9 DIMPLES
- MAKES 12

NAN
- USE MILK
- MAKES 12

PIDE
- PLAIN
- MAKES 6

PAIN TUNISIEN
- EGG GLAZE
- SESAME SEEDS
- MAKES 6

EKMEK
- USE HONEY
- PLAIN
- MAKES 3

Semi-baked Bread   *10-20 minutes*
Any time you want freshly baked bread, without waiting, this is the solution.

Use any of the previous recipes and bake the bread about three-quarters of recommended time. Cool loaves, dinner rolls, or even bagels and store in plastic bags refrigerated or frozen. When hot bread is needed, reheat bread in a preheated oven at the same recipe temperature for 5 to 15 minutes. If using frozen semi-baked bread that isn't thawed, reheat at a lower temperature for a longer time. Alternately, wrap bread in aluminum foil for a softer crust. *This works best with baguette, flat bread, small rolls or buns!*

How to quickly proof dough with a microwave oven?

Many microwave ovens can very quickly proof (raise) dough at their lowest setting. This is done by placing the covered dough and a bowl of very hot water in microwave oven for about 15 minutes. Some microwave ovens are too hot even at their lowest setting and kill the yeast which is unfortunate.

How to use bread machines with our recipes?

Simply place all ingredients for one loaf only as they are after following 'Step 3' on page 103, into bread machine and follow manufacturer's instructions.

QUICK BREADS

The following quick breads are very different than the usual quick bread recipes found in many cookbooks, we like to think that we've improved them. Unlike typical quick bread, ours contain yeast along with baking powder.

Basic Quick Bread   50-60 minutes

*These '**CookMISER**' quick breads have an unusual texture and great taste. They're reminiscent of English muffins.*

2 cups (480 ml) generic-brand bleached all-purpose flour
1 cup (240 ml) warm tap water
2 tsp (10 ml) *bulk* instant skim milk powder
1 tsp (5 ml) baking powder

2 tsp (10 ml) granulated sugar
1/32 tsp (1/8 ml) ascorbic acid crystals
1/8 tsp (1/2 ml) dry active yeast OR 1/4 tsp (1 ml) fresh yeast
1/2 tsp (2 ml) table salt

In a **large mixing bowl**, place all ingredients and mix with the **electric mixer** or **whisk**. Remove from bowl and roughly shape into about half a dozen buns, rolls, muffins, cup cakes, or English muffins. Lightly flour the top of this dough and your hands for shaping and keep in mind that you cannot shape this sticky dough as you would ordinary yeast bread dough. Place the shaped dough on a lightly floured *(non-stick)* **baking sheet** and cover with a wet but well dripped **plastic container** or **bowl**. Let it raise in a warm oven at a temperature of 90-100°F(32-38°C) for 30-40 minutes. Bake at 400°F (200°C) in a preheated oven (center rack) for about 12 minutes. Serve warm and not hot.
Makes 6 quick buns or rolls

SOYA FLOUR OPTION! *For any bread recipe you may add 10% of soybean flour for more nutrition without overly affecting the taste and properties of bread.*

NON-YEAST BREAD RECIPES

Flour Tortillas   20 minutes

They cost 1/3rd the supermarket price. They're easy to make and better tasting than corn tortillas. Make your efforts worthwhile by making a large batch.

2 cup (480 ml) all-purpose flour (*generic-brand & bleached*)
1 tbsp (15 ml) instant skim milk powder

2/3 cup (160 ml) water
1 tbsp (15 ml) vegetable oil
1/2 tsp (2 ml) table salt

In a **mixing bowl**, combine flour and salt. In a **small bowl**, dissolve milk powder in water and add oil. Pour into the flour and stir well with a **mixing spoon**. Knead or hand-mix a minute or two till uniform. Divide into 8 balls; roll out on a lightly floured surface using a light floured **rolling pin**, until 8-inches (20 cm) in diameter. *Alternately, roll out with a plastic bag or piece of waxed paper between rolling pin and dough.* Use a **tortilla press** if you have one. Meanwhile, heat a **cast iron frying pan** or **griddle**, over a medium-high setting *(do not*

TORTILLA PRESS

grease it). Gently pick up the rolled out dough using the fingers of both hands and place in hot pan without making folds. Cook about 1 minute per side until brown spots appear. Place them immediately in a plastic bag, refrigerate or freeze. **Makes eight 8-inch (20 cm) or a dozen 6-inch (15 cm) tortillas**
VARIATION *Replace half of flour with generic-brand whole-wheat flour!*

Corn Tortillas   *20-30 minutes*

They are not the real thing but you'll get use to their inferior quality and taste with time. They're a low-cost, easy to make substitute with 50% all-purpose flour.

1 cup (240 ml) all-purpose flour *(generic-brand & bleached)*	7/8 cup (210 ml) water
1 cup (240 ml) *bulk* corn flour	2 tbsp (30 ml) vegetable oil
	1/2 tsp (2 ml) table salt

Use the same directions as in previous *Flour Tortillas* recipe but with above ingredients. Divide into 12 balls and roll out to 6-inch (15 cm) rounds. Using at least **two frying pans**, or a **large griddle**, cook them on **_high_** instead of medium-high for about 2 minutes per side. **Makes a dozen**

Taco Shells   *17-20 minutes*

Another good substitute, that's fast and fun to make.

Use the same ingredients and directions as in previous *Corn Tortillas* recipe except that they are fried. In a **medium skillet** or **frying pan**, heat about 1/4 inch (.6 cm) of vegetable oil, to 375°F/190°C. Quickly slip one tortilla dough in the hot oil, and using a **spatula**, immediately fold it in half. Hold down one half of tortilla with the spatula and fry for about 30 seconds. Turn over and fry the other half. Drain them standing up on paper towels *(see ill.)* or **wire racks**. Cool them thoroughly before storing in plastic bags. **Makes a dozen**
VARIATION *Cut Corn Tortillas into 8 wedges for fried **Corn Chips**!*

Irish Soda Bread   *50-55 minutes*

This is a no-knead version. Since this bread is better eaten on the same day that its baked we recommend you make one only.

1 3/4 cups (420 ml) all-purpose flour *(generic-brand)*	1 1/4 tsp (6 ml) baking soda
1 3/4 cups (420 ml) whole-wheat flour *(generic-brand)*	1 tsp (5 ml) table salt
1/8 cup (30 ml) low-cost margarine	1 3/4 cups (420 ml) *Homemade Buttermilk* or *Recipe-Grade Sour Milk (see page 233)*

 In a **mixing bowl**, mix all the dry ingredients. Add buttermilk or sour milk, and margarine to make sticky dough. Mix with a **mixing spoon** and knead for a minute. Preheat oven to 375°F190°C. Meanwhile, roughly shape the dough with floured hands as a round loaf. Patting on it to make a round loaf will help. *Whatever shape you give it, don't expect it to look as good as a shaped yeast bread loaf.* Place it on an **8-inch/20 cm ceramic baking bowl** or **cast iron pan**, and cut two deep slashes to form an 'X'. Dust with flour. Bake in center of oven for about 45 minutes or till brown in color and bottom sounds hallow when tapped. Cool thoroughly on wire racks before serving or store in plastic bag for up to one day. **Makes one loaf**
VARIATION *For **Rye Soda Bread**, substitute a portion of the whole-wheat or all-purpose flour with the same amount rye flour!*

SPREADS, DIPS, & SANDWICH FILLINGS

SPREADS

The spread and paté recipes may double as dips or sandwich fillings. The recipe yields are relatively small and should be doubled or quadrupled when (or if) they pass your taste-bug test.

MEAT SPREADS

Basic Meat Paté   *15-20 minutes*

1/2 cup (120 ml) regular ground beef
1 slice of generic-brand salami,
    pepperoni, or bacon
1 tbsp (15 ml) vegetable oil
1/4 cup (60 ml) flour
1/2 cup (120 ml) water
2 tsp (10 ml) skim milk powder

1 tbsp (15 ml) corn flour
1/2 tsp (2 ml) granulated sugar
1/8 tsp (1/2 ml) garlic powder
1/8 tsp (1/2 ml) onion powder
1/2 tsp (2 ml) gelatin
1/4 tsp (1 ml) table salt
Pepper to taste

Heat a **large frying pan** or **skillet** over a medium-low setting. When pan gets hot, add the oil. Cook ground beef about 10 minutes until all pink is gone. In a **blender**, place all ingredients. *(Gelatin must be softened in the water 5 minutes before use.)* Blend at the lowest speed into a puree. Do not over blend. Place in a **serving dish** and cover with **plastic wrap**. Alternately, if you have a plastic bag sealer, stuff meat spread in a plastic bag tube and tie both ends *(see illustration)*. Refrigerate immediately and serve later when chilled. **Makes 1 cup (240 ml)**

LITE! VERSION Replace economical regular ground beef with lean ground beef and replace oil or margarine with 1/4 tsp (1 ml) of vegetable oil in a non-stick skillet!

MEAT SPREAD VARIATIONS

Chicken Spread   *17-20 minutes*

Using *Basic Meat Paté* recipe, replace ground beef with same quantity of chopped chicken. Omit salami, pepperoni, or bacon.

Pork Spread   *15-17 minutes*

Using *Basic Meat Paté* recipe, replace ground beef with same quantity of ground pork. All remaining ingredients are the same.

Pork Liver Spread   *17-20 minutes*

1/2 cup (120 ml) pork Liver,   1 garlic clove, sliced
    diced   1/2 tsp (2 ml) dried parsley
1 yellow onion, chopped   1/2 tsp (2 ml) fine herbs

Using *Basic Meat Paté* recipe, replace ground beef with same quantity of pork liver. Sauté all of the above ingredients together.

LEGUME SPREADS

Middle East Spread (Hummus)   *5 minutes*

1 cup (240 ml) *frozen* precooked   1 1/2 tbsp (22 ml) lemon juice from
    chick-peas, thawed in water   concentrate
1 garlic clove, sliced   1/8 tsp (1/2 ml) garlic powder
2 tbsp (30 ml) sesame butter   1/2 tsp (2 ml) soy sauce
    (also called Tahini)   1/4 tsp (1 ml) table salt

In a **blender**, fill the container with all of the above ingredients and cover. Blend at a low speed until smooth. Stop and use **rubber spatula** if necessary. Try adding 1 tsp (5 ml) of water to get ingredients circulating. Chill in a serving dish. Serve with toast, pita bread or crackers.

Makes about 1 cup (240 ml)

White Bean Spread   *5 minutes*

1 cup (240 ml) *frozen* precooked   1/4 tsp (1 ml) ground cumin
    beans, thawed   1/2 tsp (2 ml) lemon juice from
1 very small yellow onion, chopped   concentrate
1 small garlic clove, chopped   1/4 tsp (1 ml) white vinegar
2 tsp (10 ml) water   2 tsp (10 ml) vegetable oil
1/2 tsp (2 ml) dried basil   Salt and pepper to taste

Into a **blender**, place ingredients except salt and pepper; blend at a low speed to form a smooth paste. Taste and season; blend several more seconds. Repeat if required. Serve with bread or vegetables and rice. Refrigerate. **Makes about 1 cup (240 ml)**

Creamed Lima Beans   *5-7 minutes*

1 cup (240 ml) *frozen* precooked
  lima beans, thawed
1 very small yellow onion,
  chopped
1 tbsp (15 ml) skim milk powder
1 tbsp (15 ml) white cheddar
  cheese, grated

2 tbsp (30 ml) water
1/2 tsp (2 ml) chicken stock
  powder
1 tsp (5 ml) dried parsley
1/2 tsp (2 ml) dried tarragon
2 tsp (10 ml) vegetable oil
1 tsp (5 ml) white vinegar
Salt and pepper to taste

In a **small bowl**, mix water and milk powder. Add vinegar; stir and set aside a few minutes. In a **blender**, place beans and water mixture. Add grated cheese and remaining ingredients, except salt and pepper. Blend at a low speed to form a smooth paste. Do not over- blend. Season if necessary; transfer to a **serving dish** and cover with **plastic wrap**. Serve immediately or chill. Serve with bread, and raw or cooked vegetables.

Makes about 1 cup (240 ml)

Red Kidney Bean Spread   *5 minutes*

1 cup (240 ml) *frozen* precooked
  red kidney beans, thawed
3 tbsp (45 ml) fresh tomatoes,
  chopped (or canned diced
  tomatoes)
1 tbsp (15 ml) yellow onion,
  chopped

1 tbsp (15 ml) lemon juice from
  concentrate
1 tbsp (15 ml) *Homemade
  Mayonnaise (see pages 70-1)*
1/2 tsp (2 ml) chili powder
Salt and pepper to taste

In a **blender**, puree all ingredients at a low speed until smooth. Better if chilled in a **serving bowl** covered with **plastic wrap**. *This recipe is as much a dip as a spread.*
Makes about 1 cup (240 ml)

Lentil Spread   *5 minutes*

1 cup (240 ml) *frozen* precooked
  lentils *(any kind)*, thawed
1 garlic clove, chopped
2 tbsp (30 ml) *Homemade Yogurt
  (see pages 232-3)*

1 tbsp (15 ml) lemon juice from
  concentrate
1 tsp (5 ml) oregano
1/2 tsp (2 ml) dried dill weed
Salt and pepper to taste

In a **blender**, puree all ingredients at a low speed until smooth. Place in a **serving dish**. Serve immediately or chill. **Makes about 1 cup (240 ml)**

Chick-pea Spread   *5 minutes*

1 cup (240 ml) *frozen* precooked
  chick-peas, thawed
1 garlic clove, sliced
1 tbsp (15 ml) vegetable oil

2 tbsp (30 ml) lemon juice from
  concentrate
1/2 tsp (2 ml) dried parsley
1/8 tsp (1/2 ml) table salt

In a **blender**, puree all ingredients at a low speed until smooth. Place in a **serving dish**. Serve immediately or chill. **Makes about 1 cup (240 ml)**

MORE SAUCES AND DIPS! *Legume spread recipes can also serve as a cold or hot sauce when diluted with a little water. These same recipes may double as dips if diluted. They are recommended on tortilla stuffing, salad, rice, raw vegetable appetizers, and cooked vegetables.*

DIPS

The few low cost dips we selected are of the cold variety and meant to be served mostly with inexpensive crudités as dippers. This French culinary term means raw and refers to vegetables. Sticks made from carrots and celery are the least expensive year-round, even more so in late summer. Slices from cucumbers and radishes during peak harvest season are inexpensive too. Homemade potato chips, fries, pretzels, crackers, bread, and corn chips (or broken-up tacos shells and corn tortillas) also make good low cost dippers, see pages 86, 106-112, 170. Other inexpensive though seductive snacks may include, popcorn, salted peanuts and homemade soynuts, or pickled (marinated) vegetables, see pages 245 and 247. **Both recipes make 1 cup (240 ml)**

Chunky Salsa-Style Dip   *3-7 minutes*

7/8 cup (210 ml) generic-brand canned diced tomatoes

1 tbsp (15 ml) canned ground tomatoes *(see tips... pg.98)*

1/8 cup (30 ml) chopped fresh yellow onions *(or boiled a few minutes)*

1/2 tsp (2 ml) all-purpose flour

1 tbsp (15 ml) white vinegar

1 tsp (5 ml) low-cost vegetable oil

1/4 tsp (1 ml) pickled pepper rings, chopped

1/8 tsp (1/2 ml) crushed chilies

1/16 tsp (1/4 ml) garlic powder

Salt to taste

Combine all the ingredients in a **bowl**; mix well. Refrigerate.

HOT! **VERSION** *Add 1/4 tsp (1 ml) red cayenne pepper or Hot Pepper Sauce (see page 249). This hot version develops more strength after a few hours!*

Sour Mayonnaise Dip   *3-4 minutes*

1/2 cup (120 ml) *Basic Homemade Mayonnaise (see pages 70-1)*

1/2 cup (120 ml) *Homemade Yogurt (see pages 232-3)*

1 tsp (5 ml) curry powder

1 tsp (5 ml) vinegar or lemon juice from concentrate

1/8 tsp (1/2 ml) garlic powder

1/4 tsp (1 ml) onion powder

1/4 tsp (1 ml) soy sauce *(optional)*

Combine all the ingredients in a **bowl** and mix well. Refrigerate until needed.

VARIATIONS *Substitute with other styles of mayonnaise, and try replacing yogurt with of homemade sour cream or sour milk, see pages 70-2, 234. Alternately, substitute dried thyme, fine herbs, or Italian herbs for curry powder!*

For even more dips *(cold and hot)*, try the mayonnaise, yogurt and buttermilk dressing, cheese (stretcher) sauce, white and other sauce, recipes, pg. 69-72, 141-4

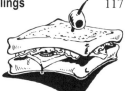

SANDWICH FILLINGS

All the previous spreads were also sandwich fillings, and most of the following sandwich filling recipes are simply different and more varied spreads.

Egg Salad Spread   *7-8 minutes*

Use *Exquisite Egg Salad* recipe as a sandwich spread *(see page 58)*.

Chicken Salad Spread   *8-10 minutes*

Use *Far East Chicken Salad* recipe as a sandwich spread *(see page 58)*.

Scrambled Eggs Filling   *8 minutes*

Use the *Basic Scrambled eggs, Vegetable Scrambled Eggs,* or *Bacon & Cheese Scrambled Eggs* recipes as a sandwich filling *(see pages 76-7)*.

Burger Filling   *15 minutes*

Use one of the *Meat or Meatless Burger* recipes as a sandwich filling *(see pages 125-131)*.

Meatloaf Filling   *2 minutes*

Use one of the *Meat or Meatless loaf* recipes as sandwich filling *(see pages 132-7)*.

Vegetable Spread   *5 minutes*

3/4 cup (180 ml) cabbage, shredded   1 tbsp (15 ml) *Homemade*
1/4 cup (60 ml) carrot, grated   *Mayonnaise (see pages 70-1)*
1 tbsp (15 ml) onion, chopped   Salt and pepper to taste
In a **bowl**, place all ingredients and mix. This spread will fill four sandwiches.
Makes about 1 cup (240 ml)
VARIATIONS *Substitute one of the fresh vegetables with finely chopped celery or sprouted alfalfa seeds, if in peak season, finely chopped green or red bell pepper!*

Tuna & Vegetable Spread   *6 minutes*

3 oz (90 g) *(about 1/2 can)*   1 tsp (5 ml) sliced green olives,
    tuna in water, drained   minced
Add tuna and olives to previous *Vegetable Spread* recipe. **Makes 1 cup (240 ml)**

Hamburger & Vegetable Stuffing   *10 minutes*

1/2 cup (120 ml) regular ground beef
In a **large frying pan or skillet**, cook beef over a medium-low heat about 5 minutes until all pink is gone. Break ground beef into small pieces. Mix with previous *Vegetable Spread* recipe. **Makes about 1 cup (240 ml)**
VARIATION *Replace ground beef with ground pork!*

Chicken & Vegetable Stuffing   *6 minutes*

1/4 cup (60 ml) *refrigerated* **pre-**   **1/4 tsp (1 ml) dried parsley**
   cooked chicken, chopped

Add above to previous *Vegetable Spread* recipe. **Makes about 1 cup (240 ml)**

Sardine Spread   *3-4 minutes*

6 oz (180 g) canned sardines   **1 tsp (5 ml) sliced green olives**
1 small yellow onion, finely   **2 tbsp (30 ml)** *Homemade*
   chopped   *Mayonnaise (see pages 70-1)*
Half a celery stalk, finely chopped   **Salt and pepper to taste**

In a **plate**, mash sardines using a **fork**. Add remaining ingredients and
mix well. Serve as sandwich filling or refrigerate. **Makes about 1
cup (240 ml)**

VARIATION *Make at half the cost and comparable
taste,* **Maqueral Spread** *with canned pacific jack
maqueral instead of sardines!*

SAUSAGE MAKING, BURGERS, LOAVES, & MUCH MORE

SAUSAGE MAKING

Generic brand wieners and bologna are very inexpensive and need not be made at home, unless you want old-fashioned quality. Many other store-bought sausages like fresh or dried sausages can be very pricey and are prohibitive. We will concentrate on those expensive types that can be made quickly and naturally at home. Unlike their supermarket counterpart, our sausages do not contain curing agent (unless you want them to), emulsifying or flavoring agents, anti-oxidants, artificial coloring, anti-molding and preserving chemicals, or binders and extenders. Also included are sausages that contain only a third meat (or that are vegetarian) but are great tasting and cost next to nothing to make. We don't smoke our sausages yet they have a light smoked taste because a slice or two of finely chopped bacon is added. Non of our sausages are hang-dried in a cool place, since that would take 6 to 8 weeks. Instead, we dry them in the oven for a few hours. Non of them take longer than six hours to make unless you cure them. All recipes call for supermarket ground meat so you don't really have to grind your own. Its not specified whether the meat is ground course, medium or fine, or grind twice, since we recommend that you use whatever the large supermarkets have to offer.

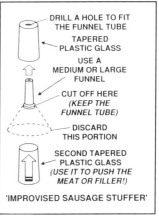

DRILL A HOLE TO FIT THE FUNNEL TUBE

TAPERED PLASTIC GLASS

USE A MEDIUM OR LARGE FUNNEL

CUT OFF HERE (KEEP THE FUNNEL TUBE)

DISCARD THIS PORTION

SECOND TAPERED PLASTIC GLASS (USE IT TO PUSH THE MEAT OR FILLER!)

'IMPROVISED SAUSAGE STUFFER'

Sausages and equipment!

Most books on sausage making will classify all sausages into two main categories, fresh and cured. We categorized them as four types of sausages, fresh, dried, pre-cooked, and cured. We included recipes for the first three types, and left the cured ones as an option only. This way all our recipes are natural if you don't cure them and can be made quickly, within six hours plus the chilling period. Cured sausages use saltpeter or Prague powder and contain nitrates and nitrites. The methods outlined are simple and the least expensive, yet based on true sausage-making techniques. You might need some of the following items:

1. **Plastic funnels**
2. *OPTIONAL* meat grinder & sausage stuffing attachment
3. *OPTIONAL* sausage stuffer

Stuffing sausages

We recommend that you use mostly small pork casings (1¼ inch/30-32 mm). They are a convenient size, least expensive, and easy to obtain. For large or medium sausages, use beef casings. Regardless of the type of casing or stuffer you use, the basic principles are the same. Cut a few lengths of casing of about 3-4 feet (1 meter). Soak them in cool water at least 15 minutes while you prepare the meat *(or meatless)* stuffing. Then rinse them inside and out. The inside of the casing can be flushed, by running cold faucet water through it. *The rinsing and soaking can be omitted without grave consequences.* Fill the sausage funnel, sausage stuffer, large plain funnel *(or new 'wide mouth' radiator funnel)*, or our improvised sausage stuffer with the meat *(or non-meat)* stuffing, stop when you can see the meat at the opening. Load the tube by gathering the entire length of casing over the tube accordion-style and tie the end of the casing into a knot, being careful not to trap any air. Force the meat by various means into the casing until the entire length is filled. Pull back casing occasionally to pack sausage filling *(stuffing)* properly and squeeze with entire hand to assure good contact between filling and casing *(see ill's)*. Try to avoid air pockets or over-packing. Make a knot at the other end. Now make numerous links by twisting as required. Remove trapped air, if any, by making small holes with a needle and forcing it out. Links can be severed with a knife. *Your local butcher shop should be able to supply you with typical lengths of about 30 ft (10 meters) of small natural pork (or synthetic) casing. At any rate, the casing shouldn't cost more than a dime a foot (1/3 meter). Any leftover length of casing should be stored in a solution of water and a lot of salt dissolved in it. Refrigerated, it should last months if it well covered with the solution.*

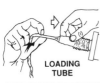
LOADING TUBE

PULL BACK CASING...
TO PACK SAUSAGE...

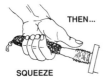
THEN...
SQUEEZE

SAUSAGES

Basic Sausage   15 minutes to 6 hours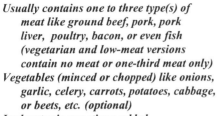

Usually contains one to three type(s) of meat like ground beef, pork, pork liver, poultry, bacon, or even fish (vegetarian and low-meat versions contain no meat or one-third meat only)
Vegetables (minced or chopped) like onions, garlic, celery, carrots, potatoes, cabbage, or beets, etc. (optional)
Iced water is sometimes added

May contain fillers like cornmeal, flour, seeds, legumes, tofu, bread crumbs, grains, etc.
Spices and herbs
Always contains salt
May also contain ascorbic acid, saltpeter, sugar, etc.
Casing(s) to suit!

FRESH UNCOOKED SAUSAGE: In a **large mixing bowl**, combine all stuffing ingredients including water in some cases. *If grinding you own meat, do so according to your taste, whether its course, medium or fine.* Work ingredients well together using your hands, keep this up at least a minute. Stuff into small casings. *(fresh uncooked sausages are never large)* as described earlier. The fresh sausage is now ready to be cooked or stored. It may be grilled, boiled, sautéed, baked or broiled. Refrigerate up to 2 days, or freeze for longer storage. Fully thaw in refrigerator before cooking. **TIME REQUIRED:** *15-20 minutes*
Makes 2 lb (1 kilo) of sausage(s)

ELIMINATING THE TRICHINOSIS & SALMONELLA RISK IN RAW PORK & CHICKEN MEAT!
Fresh pork can be host to the parasitic roundworm known as trichina, which is responsible for a disease known as trichinosis. The parasite can be killed by freezing raw pork meat at 5°F/-21°C (or colder) for thirty days. Or cooking it to an internal temperature of 140°F/60°C or higher. Any sausages preserved by curing, smoking, or drying should have its pork treated this way. Fresh sausages do not required this but should be very well cooked (to 140°F/60°C +). Never taste raw pork or sausage! □ Never taste raw sausage made from raw poultry. The meat may contain salmonellae.

FAST DRIED SAUSAGE: Preheat oven to 175°F/80°C. In a **large mixing bowl**, combine all stuffing ingredients. *If grinding you own meat do so according to your taste, whether its course, medium or fine.* Work ingredients well together using your hands, keep this up at least a minute. Stuff into small casings for sausage sticks or medium ones for medium sausages *(about 2-inch/5 cm diameter)* as described earlier. Make sure the sausages are not punctured and do not make pin holes. They must retain their fat or will be too dry. Place them on **wire racks** placed on **lipped baking sheets**, and let dry in oven. Dry the small sausage stick at least 3 hours and fatter ones up to 6 hours. **TIME REQUIRED:** *3-6 hours*
Makes 4 or 5 sausage sticks

For a saltpeter meat cure!
This meat curing option preserves and gives your sausages a professional look, color, and taste. Mix 1/4 tsp (1 ml) of saltpeter powder for every 2.2 lb/1 kg of ground meat. Place covered bowl in refrigerator for twenty-four hours and use it in the recipe. Precooked (or cooked by smoke) and dried sausages may or may not contain saltpeter but fresh sausages rarely do. Saltpeter is always used with ascorbic acid, in proportions of 1/8 tsp (1/2 ml) per 2.2 lb/1 kg of ground meat.

PRE-COOKED SAUSAGE: In a **large mixing bowl**, combine all stuffing ingredients including water in some cases. Work ingredients well together using your hands, keep this up a minute or so. For recipes calling for ice water add about 2 tbsp (30 ml) of it at on several occasions as you continue working the mixture. In a **non-stick saucepan**, over a low heat setting, slowly cook the sausage stuffing about 10 -15 minutes *(until all pink is gone if it contains meat)* but don't overcook. . Some pre-cooked sausages are partially or completely emulsified, use a blender or food processor to accomplish this. Individual recipe variations will specify what percentage of sausage is emulsified or pureed. In a **blender** (or **food processor**), place the desired percentage of hand mixed ingredients. Blend or process at the lowest speed into a puree. Do not overpuree. Add a little water if difficult to process. Stuff filling into large *or sometimes small* casings to mold and shape them, or shape into small sausages or patties using your hands. *Some sausages are partially boiled in their watertight casing from 15 to 45 minutes.* Refrigerate up to 5 days, or freeze for longer storage. **TIME REQUIRED:** *30-40 minutes* **Makes about 2 pounds/1 kilogram of sausage(s)**

LITE! VERSION *Use leaner ground meats but it isn't recommended!*

All sausages prepared as outlined in the CookMISER should be eaten or cooked within 2 days (5 days if pre-cooked) or frozen up to 3 months...this applies to fresh, pre-cooked, & dried sausages!

UNIVERSAL SAUSAGE STRETCHER

This sausage stretcher or meatless filler works well with most meat sausages, and can be used to replace each pound (half kilogram) of ground meat. These combined ingredients below will supply protein, texture, firmness, and bonding qualities.

3/4 cup (180 ml) Homemade Firm
  Tofu or High-Yield Pulp Tofu
  (mashed or unpressed, pg. 239-40)
1/2 cup (120 ml) Fine Breadcrumbs
  (see page 246)

3/4 cup (180 ml) *'Quick'* **rolled oats**
1/8 cup (30 ml) **corn flour**
1/8 cup (30 ml) **all-purpose flour**
A little boiling water to suit!

In a **mixing bowl**, combine the above ingredients and just enough hot water to process. *Keep the water to a minimum to prevent sogginess.* Stir well *(or use your hands to work the ingredients)* and use the resulting mixture to replace each pound of sausage. The meat in most sausage recipes can be replaced in a ratio anywhere between 10-75% according to taste. Aside from this universal sausage stretcher, you may use any of the following fillers in combinations of two ingredients or more, with or without the above ones. For any given sausage recipe the spice and herb seasonings usually stay about the same but may require adjusting in certain cases. **Makes almost 2 cups/480 ml**

More sausage stretching ingredients...

1.   **Mashed cooked or precooked beans, peas, or lentils**
2.   **Roughly mashed potatoes**
3.   **Whole-wheat and non-wheat flours**
4.   **Polenta (pg. 193) or cornmeal with a bit more hot water**
5.   **Low-cost bulk seeds**

SAUSAGE VARIATIONS

Country-Style Fesh Sausage   10-15 minutes

About 2 pounds/1 kilogram ground
    pork
No vegetables or fillers!
1/2 tsp (2 ml) ground white pepper
1 tsp (5 ml) dried sage

1/4 tsp (1 ml) dried thyme
1/8 tsp (1/2 ml) dried savory
1/4 tsp (1 ml) crushed chilies
1 tsp (5 ml) coarse salt
1/2 tsp (2 ml) granulated sugar
1 1/4 "(32 mm) natural hog casings

Use above to make *fresh sausages* in *Basic Sausage* recipe and follow the <u>fresh uncooked sausage</u> directions.

Italian-Style Fresh Sausage   10-15 minutes
This is a sweet sausage recipe and can be made hot if cayenne pepper is added.

About 2 pounds/1 kilogram ground
    pork or pork butt
2 garlic cloves, minced
1/2 tsp (2 ml) ground white pepper
No fillers!

1 tsp (5 ml) fennel seed, crushed
1/4 tsp (1 ml) ground sage
1/4 tsp (1 ml) ground coriander
1 tsp (5 ml) coarse salt
1/2 tsp (2 ml) red cayenne (optional)
1 1/4 "(32 mm) natural hog casings

Use above to make *fresh sausages* in *Basic Sausage* recipe and follow the <u>uncooked</u> directions.

SUB-VARIATION(S) *Substitute some of the above seasoning with small quantities of nutmeg, anise seeds, ground cloves, cumin, oregano, thyme, etc.*

Ham Sausage   60 minutes
The next time your supermarket offers a great deal on fresh ham, try this recipe.

About 2 pounds/1 kilogram ground
    fresh ham
No fillers!
1/2 tsp (2 ml) ground black pepper

1/2 tsp (2 ml) nutmeg
1/2 tsp (2 ml) ground cinnamon
1/4 tsp (1 ml) ground cloves
1 tsp (5 ml) table salt
1 1/4 "(32 mm) natural hog casings

Use above to make *fully cooked sausages* in *Basic Sausage* recipe and follow the <u>pre-cooked</u> directions. *Parboil them 45 minutes.*

Pepperoni Stick or Sausage   1-12 hours
A great tasting and quick to make imitation of dried pepperoni.

1 1/3 pound/600 grams ordinary ground
    pork
2/3 pound/300 grams regular ground
    beef
1 garlic clove, minced
1/4 cup (60 ml) red wine *(optional)*
No fillers!
1/8 tsp (1/2 ml) garlic powder

1/2 tsp (2ml) crushed anise seed
1/2 tbsp (7 ml) mild paprika
1/2 tsp (2 ml) cayenne pepper
1/2 tsp (2 ml) crushed chilies
1 tbsp (15 ml) table salt
1 tsp (5 ml) granulated sugar
1 1/4" (32 mm) OR 2" (50 mm)
    synthetic or hog casings

Use above to make *quickly dried sausages* in *Basic Sausage* recipe and follow the <u>uncooked</u> and <u>fast sausage drying</u> directions. Make links 12"/30 cm long with small casings for sticks. *Refrigerate up to one week only.*
SUB-VARIATION *Convert it to an **All-Beef Pepperoni** by using beef only as meat, replace cayenne with black pepper, add 1/2 tsp (2 ml) each of fennel and mustard seed, and double amount of garlic!*

Salami Sausage or Stick   *50 minutes*
This fully cooked salami has a lightly smoked taste due to the smoked bacon.

1 1/3 pound/600 grams regular ground beef	1 tsp (5 ml) crushed red chilies
2/3 pound/300 grams ordinary ground pork	1/2 tsp (2 ml) black pepper
2 slices smoked bacon, finely chopped	1/2 tsp (2 ml) ground coriander
1 garlic clove, minced	1/4 tsp (1 ml) cardamom
1/3 cup (80 ml) ice water	1/4 tsp (1 ml) ground mace
1/8 tsp (1/2 ml) garlic powder	1 tbsp (15 ml) table salt
No fillers!	*1 1/4" (32 mm) OR 3" (75 mm) hog, synthetic, or homemade casing(s)*

Use above to make *quickly dried sausages* in *Basic Sausage* recipe and follow the <u>uncooked</u> and <u>fast sausage drying</u> directions. Make sticks *(links)* about 12"/30 cm long and use small casings. *Refrigerate up to one week only.*
SUB-VARIATION *Convert it to an **All-Beef Salami** by using beef only as meat (omit bacon), replace crushed red chilies with whole white peppercorns, omit cardamom and mace!*

'LOW-MEAT AND VEGETARIAN SAUSAGES'

Swedish Potato Sausage   *60 minutes*
*Called **Potatis Korv** and contains 50% meat only. A complete meal in a sausage!*

About 1/2 pound/227 grams regular ground beef	1/2 tsp (2 ml) ground black pepper
About 1/2 pound/227 grams ground pork	1/8 tsp (1/2 ml) allspice
About 3 cups (720 ml) coarsely mashed *low-cost* potatoes	1/8 tsp (1/2 ml) ground mace
1 medium yellow onion, chopped	1/8 tsp (1/2 ml) nutmeg
1 small garlic clove, finely minced	1/2 tbsp (7 ml) chicken stock powder
No fillers!	3/4 tsp (3 ml) table salt
	Large casing(s)

Use above to make *fully cooked sausages* in *Basic Sausage* recipe and follow the <u>pre-cooked</u> directions. *Parboil them at least 45 minutes in water with or without chicken stock powder.*

Soy-Pulp Sausage   *45-50 minutes*

3 cups (720 ml) soy pulp *(from
   making soymilk, see page 231)*
1 cup (240 ml) all-purpose flour
1/3 cup (80 ml) *bulk* wheat germ
3 tbsp (45 ml) *bulk* wheat bran
1/3 cup (80 ml) vegetable oil
1/2 tbsp (7 ml) tamari, soy, or
   Worcestershire sauce
1/2 tbsp (7 ml) prepared mustard
About 1/2 cup (120 ml) ice water

1 tsp (5 ml) crushed fennel seed
1/2 tsp (2 ml) ground black pepper
1 tsp (5 ml) dried oregano
1/2 tsp (2 ml) onion powder
1/4 tsp (1 ml) garlic powder
1/4 tsp (1 ml) red cayenne pepper
1 tsp (5 ml) coarse or table salt
1/2 tbsp (7 ml) granulated sugar
*1 1/4" (32 mm) synthetic casing(s)
   or homemade muslin bag or casing*

Use above to make *fully cooked sausages* in *Basic Sausage* recipe and follow the pre-cooked directions. Or follow the uncooked and fast sausage drying directions. If making links make them 12"/30 cm long. *Stuffing can be emulsified in blender or food processor (from 50 to 100%). Parboil at least 30 minutes. Keeps about a week when refrigerated.*

SUB-VARIATIONS *Substitute soy pulp with course mashed precooked soybeans and/or add one finely chopped yellow onion and/or garlic clove.*

MORE SAUSAGE-MAKING VARIATIONS!
Most of the recipes for the following, meat or meatless, burgers and some of the meatloaves are good if not great for sausage making. Please try them!

BURGERS & MEATLOAVES

All meat burgers and meatloaves are boosters or stretchers, and contain 1/3 to 1/2 meat only. This ratio can be increased or decreased to suit your taste and needs. These burgers and meatloaves retain their fluids and fat, nothing is lost. Every calorie, or gram of fat, you paid for is used!

MEAT BURGERS

Basic Meat (Stretcher) Burgers   *12-20 minutes*

1 tbsp (15 ml) vegetable oil or
   margarine
1/2-2 /3 cup (120-160 ml) regular
   ground beef *(or pork)*
1/2 extra large egg or 1 small egg,
   lightly beaten *(optional)*
May contain some flour as binder!
May also contain sautéed onion/garlic!
1/4 tsp (1 ml) baking powder *(optional)*

1/2 tsp (2 ml) beef soup stock
   powder
*Filler(s) like vegetables, tofu, grains,
   or legumes (pick one or two, or
   those in a recipe variation)!*
Some boiling water to give mixture
   consistency of fresh ground beef
Seasonings!
Salt and pepper to taste

1/4 cup (60 ml) homemade breadcrumbs (see page 246), wheat germ, or flour for coating (optional)

In a **mixing bowl**, place all ingredients *(including any additional ingredients for one of the following variations)* except fat and coating material *(if using frozen legumes or ingredients, thaw them in a bowl containing very hot tap water).* Mix well *(use your hands if desired).* Alternately, some cooks prefer to let sit the mixture in refrigerator for about half an hour before use. *We recommend that you double or quadruple the recipe yield and store them uncooked with small wax paper separators in freezer, see illustration.*

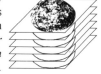

Meanwhile, heat a **large skillet** or **frying pan** over a medium heat; add oil or margarine. Shape four patties out of the mixture. In a **small bowl**, containing a little coating material, quickly dip patties in coating. Do the same for both sides of both patties. Place all 4 patties in skillet and cook until each side is brown. Turn once only. *Do not press on them with spatula because pressing forces the liquid out of them and results in dry patties or burgers. Alternately, fry patties in a deep fryer.* Serve hot between halved homemade *(or bargain-packed store-bought ones)* hamburger buns, bagels, or pita pockets *(see pages 107, 108, 109, 110, 111)* with your favorite condiments or our salads orcole slaws. **Makes about 2 cups (500 ml) or 4 medium-large patties**

LITE! VERSION *Reduce the fat to 1 tsp (5 ml) and use a non-stick skillet. Use lean ground beef instead of the economical regular ground beef!*

TIPS & HINTS: *Always heat pan before adding vegetable oil or margarine to avoid or reduce food from sticking to pan.*

MEAT BURGER VARIATIONS

Simulated Beef Burgers   *15-17 minutes*

This ground beef stretcher recipe is the best of the lot and is recommended as a hamburger substitute as used in the chapter on fast food. It looks and has the texture of cooked ground beef. It actually taste better than 100% ground beef!

1 small yellow onion, coarsely grated or finely minced	1/4 tsp (1 ml) *Caramelized Sugar Coloring (see page 243)*
1/4-1/2 cup (60-120 ml) *Homemade Firm Tofu (mashed), High-Yield Pulp Tofu,* or soybean pulp *(see pages 231, 239, 240)*	1/4 tsp (1 ml) soy sauce **OR** 1/8 tsp (1/2 ml) soy sauce and 1/4 tsp (1 ml) tamari sauce
1/3-2/3 cup (80-160 ml) regular rolled oats *(don't use quick or instant)*	1/2 tsp (2 ml) all-purpose flour *Do not use eggs or baking powder! Use very little boiling water!*

Use the above in *Basic Meat (Stretcher) Burgers* recipe. Start by sautéing onions in the vegetable oil and caramelized sugar coloring a few minutes on medium-high. Add the sautéed onions without the oil to the remaining ingredients. Work and knead it well using hands. Shape as rather thin patties and cook in oil on medium-low instead of medium heat while covered. These usually don't require a breadcrumb or flour coating. *Use tofu that hasn't been pressed or is mashed.*

Vegetable Meat Burgers   *18-20 minutes*

1 cup (240 ml) carrots, grated
1 garlic clove, minced
1/4 cup (60 ml) *'Quick'* rolled oats
1 small yellow onion, finely chopped

Quarter celery stalk, fine chopped
1 tbsp (15 ml) *bulk* wheat germ
1 tsp (5 ml) dried parsley
1/8 tsp (1/2 ml) garlic powder

Add the above to *Basic Meat (Stretcher) Burgers* recipe.

Bombay-Style Burgers   *16-18 minutes*

1/2 cup (120 ml) *frozen* precooked
    whole green peas
1/4 cup (60 ml) *'Quick'* rolled oats
2 tbsp (30 ml) corn flour

1 small yellow onion, chopped
1 tbsp (15 ml) curry powder
1 tsp (5 ml) turmeric

Add the above to *Basic Meat (Stretcher) Burgers* recipe. Serve with a bit of yogurt as sauce or with yogurt dressing.

Garbanzos & Meat Burgers   *16-18 minutes*

2/3 cup (160 ml) *frozen* precooked
    (garbanzo beans) chick peas
1/4 cup (60 ml) fresh bread crumbs
2 tbsp (30 ml) any flour
1 garlic clove, minced

1/2 tsp (2 ml) dried parsley
1/4 tsp (1 ml) onion powder
1 tsp (5 ml) cumin powder
1/4 tsp (1 ml) ground coriander
1/8 tsp (1/2 ml) garlic powder

Add the above to *Basic Meat (Stretcher) Burgers* recipe.

Multi-Grains & Meat Burgers   *15-17 minutes*

1/4 cup (60 ml) *'Quick'* rolled oats
1/4 cup (60 ml) precooked brown rice
2 tbsp (30 ml) corn flour
2 tbsp (30 ml) *bulk* wheat germ

1 tbsp (15 ml) *bulk* wheat bran
1 tsp (5 ml) soy sauce
1 tsp (5 ml) peanut butter
1/2 tsp (2 ml) onion powder

Add the above to *Basic Meat (Stretcher) Burgers* recipe.

Tomato-Oregano Meat Burgers   *18-20 minutes*

2 tbsp (30 ml) yellow onion, fine chopped
1/4 cup (60 ml) blanched carrots, chopped
1 tbsp (20 ml) canned ground tomatoes
1 tbsp (15 ml) sunflower seeds

1/3 cup (80 ml) rolled oats
3 tbsp (45 ml) *frozen* lima
    beans, mashed
1 /2 tsp (2 ml) oregano

Add the above to *Basic Meat (Stretcher) Burgers* recipe.

Tofu & Meat Burgers   *16 minutes*

1 cup (240 ml) tofu, shredded

2 tbsp (30 ml) *'Quick'* rolled oats
1 tsp (5 ml) tamari or soy sauce

Add the above to *Basic Meat (Stretcher) Burgers* recipe.

Carrots & Beef Burgers   16-18 minutes

1/2 cup (120 ml) carrots, grated
1/2 tbsp (7 ml) instant milk powder
1/4 cup (60 ml) *bulk* wheat germ
1/4 tsp (1 ml) ground sage

1/4 cup (60 ml) *Homemade Firm Tofu,* mashed
1/4 cup (60 ml) yellow onions, minced

Add the above to *Basic Meat (Stretcher) Burgers* recipe.

Tofu & Beef Burgers   15-17 minutes

2/3 cup (160 ml) *Homemade Firm Tofu,* mashed

2 tsp (10 ml) soy sauce *(mixed with the water)*
2 tbsp (30 ml) flour

Add the above to *Basic Meat (Stretcher) Burgers* recipe.

Gyros-Style Meat Burgers   16-18 minutes

3/4 cup (180 ml) whole wheat or
   all-purpose flour
1 tbsp (15 ml) table salt or
   sea salt
1/3 cup (80 ml) *Homemade Firm Tofu* or *'Quick'* rolled oats

1/8 tsp (1/2 ml) garlic powder
1/4 tsp (1 ml) onion powder
1/4 tsp (1 ml) ground cumin
1/4 tsp (1 ml) ground rosemary
1/8 tsp (1/2 ml) ground sage

Add the above to *Basic Meat (Stretcher) Burgers* recipe.

MEATLESS BURGERS

These vegetarian burgers cost about a tenth of the store-bought ones and are of better quality. Meatless burgers will cook faster than those containing meat.

Basic Meatless Burgers   13-17 minutes

2 tbsp (30 ml) vegetable oil or
   margarine
1 extra large egg or 2 small eggs,
   lightly beaten *(optional)*
*Fillers for one of the recipe
   variations like breadcrumbs,
   tofu, rolled oats, rice, wheat germ,
   wheat bran, flour(s), cornmeal,
   precooked legumes, fresh or
   blanched vegetables, etc.
   (pick a few or those in a variation)!*

1/2 tsp (2 ml) vegetable soup stock
   powder
1/8 tsp (1/2 ml) baking powder
*Enough boiling water to get
   consistency of minced beef!*
*Spices to taste or those from a recipe
   variation!*
Salt and pepper to taste

1/4 cup (60 ml) bread crumbs (see page 246), wheat germ, or flour for coating

In a **medium-size mixing bowl**, place all ingredients *(including any additional ingredients for a recipe variation)* except fat and coating material *(if using frozen legumes or ingredients, thaw them in a bowl containing very hot tap water)*. Mix well *(use your hands if desired)*. *Alternately, some cooks prefer to let the mixture sit in refrigerator for about half an hour before use.* Meanwhile, in a **large skillet** or **frying pan**, heat fat over a medium heat. Shape four patties out of the mixture.

In **2 small bowls**, one containing a litter water and the other containing a little coating material; quickly dip patties, first in the water and then in coating. Do the same for both sides of both patties. Place all 4 patties in skillet and cook until each side is brown. Turn once only. *Do not press on them with spatula because pressing forces the liquid out of them and results in dry patties or burgers. Alternately, fry them in deep fryer instead of pan.* Serve hot between halved homemade *(or store-bought)* hamburger buns, bagels, or pita pockets *(see pages 107, 108, 109, 110, 111)* with your favorite condiments. *Some meatless burgers do not require any boiling water.* **Makes about 2 cups (480 ml) or 4 medium-large patties**

LITE! VERSION *Reduce the fat to 1 tsp (5 ml) and use a non-stick skillet and heat over a medium-low setting!*

MEATLESS BURGER VARIATIONS

Falafel Burgers ·   *15-17 minutes*

1 cup (240 ml) *frozen* precooked
   chickpeas
1 cup (240 ml) *frozen* precooked
   yellow peas
1 large garlic clove, chopped
Half a small yellow onion, chopped

1 tbsp (15 ml) dried parsley
1/2 tsp (2 ml) ground cumin
1 tsp (5 ml) ground coriander
1/4 tsp (1 ml) onion powder
1/4 tsp (1 ml) garlic powder
1/8 tsp (1/2 ml) ground pepper

Grind thawed legumes, garlic and onion in blender or food processor. Add the above and following directions in *Basic Meatless burgers* recipes.

Spiced Millet Burgers   *15-17 minutes*

1 1/3 cups (320 ml) precooked millet
1/3 cup (80 ml) carrots, grated
3 tbsp (45 ml) whole-wheat flour
2 tbsp (30 ml) sunflower seeds

1/4 tsp (1 ml) ground cumin
1/4 tsp (1 ml) ground coriander
1 tsp (5 ml) dried parsley
1/2 tsp (2 ml) dried oregano

Add the above to *Basic Meatless Burgers* recipe.
SUB-VARIATIONS *Try with rice or bulgur wheat instead of millet!*

Veggie Tofu Burgers   *15-17 minutes*

1 1/4 cups (300 ml) *Homemade Firm
   Tofu,* mashed *(see pages 239-40)*
1 tbsp (15 ml) sunflower seeds
1/2 cup (120 ml) *'Quick'* rolled oats
2 tbsp (30 ml) yellow onions,
   chopped

1 tbsp (15 ml) tamari sauce
  OR 1 tsp (5 ml) soy sauce
1 tsp (5 ml) dried parsley
1/4 tsp (1 ml) celery salt
1/8 tsp (1/2 ml) sage
1/4 tsp (1 ml) marjoram

Add the above to *Basic Meatless Burgers* recipe.

Sprouted Grain Burgers   15-17 minutes

1 cup (240 ml) sprouted wheat berries,
   chopped *(see page 242)*
1/2 cup (120 ml) *frozen* precooked barley
3/8 cup (90 ml) *'Quick'* rolled oats
1/4 cup (60 ml) fresh breadcrumbs

1 tbsp (15 ml) peanut butter
1/2 tbsp (7 ml) tamari sauce
   OR 1/2 tsp (2 ml) soy sauce
1 tsp (5 ml) onion powder
1/2 tsp (2 ml) dried parsley

Add the above to *Basic Meatless Burgers* recipe.

Nuts & Oats Burgers   15-17 minutes

1 1/4 cup (300 ml) *'Quick'* rolled oats
1/2 cup (120 ml) fresh bread crumbs
1/4 cup (60 ml) chopped peanuts
2 tbsp (30 ml) whole-wheat flour

1/2 tsp (2 ml) dried parsley
1 small yellow onion, finely
   chopped

Add the above to *Basic Meatless Burgers* recipe.

Frugal Lentil Burgers   14-16 minutes

1 cup (240 ml) *frozen* precooked lentils
5/8 cup (150 ml) *'Quick'* rolled oats
1/4 cup (60 ml) fresh bread crumbs

1/2 tsp (2 ml) onion powder
1/4 tsp (1 ml) garlic powder
1/2 tsp (2 ml) fine herbs

Add the above to *Basic Meatless Burgers* recipe.

Onion-Tofu Burgers   15-17 minutes

1 1/2 cups (360 ml) *Homemade Firm
   Tofu,* mashed *(see pages 239-40)*
1/4 cup (60 ml) whole-wheat flour
1 tsp (5 ml) peanut butter

1 small yellow onion, chopped
1/2 tsp (2 ml) onion powder
1/2 tsp (2 ml) celery salt
2 tsp (10 ml) prepared mustard
1 tsp (5 ml) dried parsley

Add the above to *Basic Meatless Burgers* recipe.

Spicy Rolled Oats burgers   15-17 minutes

1 1/2 cups (360 ml) *'Quick'* rolled oats
2 tbsp (30 ml) sunflower seeds
1 small yellow onion, chopped
1 garlic clove, minced

1/4 tsp (1 ml) garlic powder
1/4 tsp (1 ml) oregano
1/8 tsp (1/2 ml) basil
1 tsp (5 ml) dried parsley
1/2 tbsp (7 ml) tamari sauce

Add the above to *Basic Meatless Burgers* recipe.

Fresh Garden Burgers   15-17 minutes

1 cup (240 ml) *Homemade Firm
   Tofu,* mashed *(see pages 239-40)*
1/2 cup (120 ml) *'Quick'* rolled oats

1 small carrot, grated
1 small yellow onion, chopped
1 garlic clove, minced
1 tsp (5 ml) soy sauce

Add the above to *Basic Meatless Burgers* recipe.

Vegetarian Millet Burgers   15-17 minutes

3/4 cup (180 ml) *'Quick'* rolled oats
1 cup (240 ml) precooked millet
1/4 cup (60 ml) whole-wheat flour
1 small carrot, grated
1 garlic clove, minced

2 tbsp (30 ml) sunflower seeds
1/2 tsp (2 ml) ground cumin
1 yellow onion, finely chopped
1 tbsp (15 ml) soy sauce

Add the above to *Basic Meatless Burgers* recipe.

Bulgar & Tofu Burgers   22-25 minutes

1 cup (240 ml) *Homemade Firm Tofu,*
   mashed *(see pages 239-40)*
1/3 cup (80 ml) bulgur wheat,
   presoaked in water 10 minutes
1 small yellow onion, finely chopped

1 small carrot, grated
1 tbsp (15 ml) canned ground
   tomatoes
1 tbsp (15 ml) tamari sauce
1/2 tsp (2 ml) dried oregano

Add the above to *Basic Meatless Burgers* recipe.

White Bean Burgers   15-17 minutes

1 1/2 cups (360 ml) precooked white
   (navy) beans, mashed
1/2 cup (120 ml) fresh bread crumbs

1 small yellow onion, chopped
2 tbsp (30 ml) grated aged Cheddar
   cheese

Add the above to *Basic Meatless Burgers* recipe. *Its good using most legumes.*

Red Chili Bean Burgers   15-17 minutes

1 1/2 cups (360 ml) *frozen* red or pink
   precooked kidney beans, mashed
   or blender pureed
1/4 cup (60 ml) *bulk* wheat germ

Small yellow onion, chopped
2 tbsp (30 ml) canned ground
   tomatoes
1/2 tsp (2 ml) chili powder

Add the above to *Basic Meatless Burgers* recipe.

Oriental Soy Burgers   15-17 minutes

1 1/2 cups (360 ml) *frozen* precooked
   soybeans, mashed or blender chopped
1/3 cup (80 ml) precooked brown rice
1 tbsp (15 ml) sunflower seeds
1 tsp (5 ml) sesame seeds
2 tbsp (30 ml) whole-wheat flour

1 green onion, completely
   chopped except roots
   (or very small yellow onion)
1 tsp (5 ml) soy sauce
1/4 tsp (1 ml) ground ginger
1/2 tsp (2 ml) dried parsley

Add the above to *Basic Meatless Burgers* recipe.

Oregano & Tofu Burgers   15-17 minutes

1 cup (240 ml) *Homemade Firm Tofu,*
   mashed or un-pressed *(see page 239)*
1/2 cups (120 ml) *frozen* precooked
   soybeans, mashed or blender chopped
1/4 cup (60 ml) fresh bread crumbs
1 very small yellow onion, chopped

1 tsp (5 ml) dried parsley
1/4 tsp (1 ml) table salt
1/4 tsp (1 ml) oregano
Use beef stock powder
   instead of vegetable
   soup stock powder!

Add the above to *Basic Meatless Burgers* recipe.

Fresh Garden Tofu burgers   *15-17 minutes*

1 1/2 cup (360 ml) *Homemade Firm*
   Tofu, mashed *(see pages 239-40)*
1 small yellow onion, minced
1 small carrot grated

Quarter celery stalk, minced
1 tbsp (15 ml) chopped peanuts
   or sunflower seeds
1 tsp (5 ml) dried parsley

Add the above to *Basic Meatless Burgers* recipe.

Greek Gyros-Style Burgers   *13-15 minutes*

1/2 cup (120 ml) whole-wheat or
   all-purpose flour
1 tbsp (15 ml) table salt or sea salt
1 1/4 cup (300 ml) *Homemade Firm*
   Tofu, mashed *(see pages 239-40)*

1/8 tsp (1/2 ml) garlic powder
1/4 tsp (1 ml) onion powder
1/4 tsp (1 ml) ground cumin
1 tsp (1 ml) ground rosemary
1/8 tsp (1/2 ml) ground sage

Add the above to *Basic Meatless Burgers* recipe.

OTHER BURGER SHAPES

Meatballs (or meatless): *Most meat, veggie and fish burgers may be shaped as meatballs and either deep-fried or fried in frying pan. Adding a tiny piece of garlic inside them is a must do for added flavor. For super moist meatballs, a small ice cube inside them does the trick, unfortunately it doesn't work with flat patties. Make meatballs about 1 1/4-inch (3 cm) in size and coat as you would burgers.*

Meat or meatless shish-kabobs: *Most meat, veggie and fish burgers may be shaped as shish-kabobs with or without a stick and either oven broiled or fried in frying pan.*

MEATLOAVES

Basic Meat (Stretcher) Loaf   *30-35 minutes*

3 tbsp (45 ml) vegetable oil
1 1/2 pounds (3/4 kg) *(3 cups/720 ml)*
   regular ground beef or pork
2 large raw carrot, shredded
1 large yellow onions, chopped
Fillers for one of the recipe variations
   like rice, breadcrumbs, rolled oats,
   legumes, wheat germ, wheat bran,
   tofu, cornmeal, flour(s), grains,
   or more vegetables, etc.!

2 small eggs, beaten
2 tsp (10 ml) soup stock powder
   (chicken or beef)
1/3 cup (80 ml) boiling water
Seasoning!
Salt and pepper to taste

Place a rack mid-level in oven. Preheat oven to
400°F (200°C). Heat a **large skillet** or **frying pan** over
a medium-high setting. Within a minute or two, add fat.
Then add ground meat and vegetables only; sauté about 10
minutes until meat looses its red or pink color. Vegetables must

be cooked through yet still quite firm and break up ground meat into small pieces. Remove from heat at once. In a **large mixing bowl** quickly combine using your hands all the remaining ingredients *(including those for any of the following variations)*; mix thoroughly. Place in **two** *(greased)* or **non-stick loaf pans** or **oven dishes.** Make the loaves no more than about one inch (2.5 cm) thick *(if thicker they will take much longer to bake)* and place in oven; set timer to 20 minutes. Bake till brown on top and cooked throughout. May be served hot or chilled *(with or without a sauce or condiment)* with salad, a side dish or in sandwiches. **Makes 2 meatloaves, 8 average or 16 small servings**

LITE! VERSION *Reduce the amount of oil to 1 tsp (5 ml) and use 1/4 cup (60 ml) water in a non-stick skillet. Use leaner beef instead of regular ground beef!*

MEATLOAF VARIATIONS

Tomato-Garbanzos Meatloaf   *30-35 minutes*

1 1/2 cups (360ml) *refrigerated*
  precooked rice
1 cup (240 ml) precooked *(frozen)*
  chick peas
2 strips of bacon, finely chopped

1/2 tsp (2 ml) ground nutmeg
3 tbsp (45 ml) lemon juice from
  concentrate
1 cup (240 ml) *Inst. Tomato Sauce*
  or tomato juice *(see page 98)*

Add the above to *Basic Meat (Stretcher) Loaf* recipe. Omit water and replace with the tomato sauce or juice. Serve hot or chilled as sandwich filling.

Siberian-Style Meatloaf   *30-35 minutes*

4 hard-boiled eggs, chopped
2 cups (480 ml) precooked rice

1 tsp (5 ml) dried parsley

Remove carrots and raw eggs, and add the above ingredients to *Basic Meat (Stretcher) Loaf* recipe. Sprinkle top with the parsley. Serve hot or chilled.

Traditional Meatloaf   *30-35 minutes*

1/2 cup (120 ml) all-purpose flour
2 tbsp (30 ml) skim milk powder
3 cups (720 ml) soft bread crumbs

1/2 tsp (2 ml) paprika
1/4 tsp (1 ml) nutmeg
Dash of allspice

Add above to *Basic Meat (Stretcher) Loaf* recipe.

Old-Fashioned Glazed Meatloaf   *30-35 minutes*

1 1/2 cups (360 ml) canned tomato juice
5 cups (1200 ml) soft bread crumbs
1/4 cup (60 ml) ham, finely chopped
1/4 cup (60 ml) water

1/3 (80 ml) dark brown sugar
1/4 cup (60 ml) white vinegar
1/2 tsp (2 ml) dry mustard
1 tbsp (15ml) Worcestershire sauce
Dash of cayenne

Add the above ingredients except sugar, vinegar, dry mustard, cayenne, water and Worcestershire sauce to *Basic Meat (Stretcher) Loaf* recipe. In a **small bowl**, mix sugar, vinegar, dry mustard, cayenne, water and Worcestershire sauce and pour in both oven dishes beside the meatloaves. This liquid is to be spooned over loaves, before and during baking and serves to glaze.

Lima Beans & Rice Meatloaf   *30-35 minutes*

2 cups (500 ml) *refrigerated*
  precooked rice
2 cups (500 ml) *frozen* precooked
  lima beans, whole

1 tsp (5 ml) turmeric powder
1 tsp (5 ml) paprika
2 tbsp (30 ml) dried parsley
Dash of cayenne

Omit carrots and raw eggs, add above ingredients in *Basic Meat (Stretcher) Loaf* recipe. Serve it hot or warm only.

Vegetable Meatloaf   *30-35 minutes*

2 medium raw potatoes,
  roughly grated
1 celery stalk, thinly sliced or chopped

2 tbsp (30 ml) instant skim milk
  powder
2 tsp (10 ml) dried parsley

Add the above ingredients to *Basic Meat (Stretcher) Loaf* recipe.

VEGETARIAN LOAVES

Basic Vegetarian Loaf 🐷   *30-35 minutes*

4 tbsp (60 ml) vegetable oil
2 tsp (10 ml) vegetable stock powder
*Fillers for one of following recipe
  variations like precooked rice,
  precooked legumes, homemade
  tofu, fresh or blanched vegetables,
  bulk wheat germ or bran, flour(s),
  cornmeal, other grains and seeds,
  bread crumbs, etc.!*

2 extra-large eggs, lightly
  beaten *(optional)*
*Enough boiling water to make
  ingredients stick together
  and give it the consistency
  of raw ground beef
  (usually from 1/4 cup/60 ml
  to 1 cup/240 ml)!*
Seasoning (spices and herbs)!
Salt and pepper to taste

Place an oven rack on a medium-high level. Preheat oven to 450ºF (230ºC). Heat a **large skillet** or **frying pan** over a medium-high setting. Within a minute or two, add fat. Then add frozen legume(s) and vegetables, sauté about 5 minutes until vegetables are cooked through yet still quite firm. Add all the remaining ingredients *(including those for any of the following variations)*; continue to sauté and stir until hot only. Remove from heat at once. Place in **two** *(greased)* or **non-stick loaf pans** or **oven dish**. Make the loaves about two inches thick *(if thicker they will take much longer to bake)* and place in oven; set timer. Bake at least 20 minutes or until brown on top and cooked throughout. May be served hot or chilled *(with or without a sauce or condiment)* with salad, a side dish or in sandwiches. **Makes 2 medium-size (semi-flat) loaves (6 cups/1440 ml), 8 average or 16 small servings**
LITE! VERSION *Reduce amount of oil to 1 tsp (5 ml) and use 1/4 cup (60 ml) water in a non-stick skillet for preheating ingredients before baking in oven!*

VEGETARIAN LOAF VARIATIONS

Curried Vegetarian Loaf   30-35 minutes

2 cups (480 ml) *frozen* precooked
    black-eyed peas, mashed
1 cup (240 ml) yellow onions, coarse
    chopped
1/2 cup (120 ml) *'Quick'* rolled oats
1 cup (240 ml) cornmeal

1 celery stalk, diced
1/2 cup (120 ml) soft bread crumbs
1 tsp (5 ml) dried parsley
2 tsp (10 ml) curry powder
A little more water may be
    needed for this one!

Add above ingredients to *Basic Vegetarian Loaf* recipe. When loaf is done, cool and chill a few hours. Serve sliced cold or fry slices in vegetable oil or deep fryer.

Legume-Vegetable Loaf   30-35 minutes

2 cups (480 ml) *frozen* precooked
    lima beans, mashed or chopped
1 cup (240 ml) bread crumbs
1 1/2 cups (360 ml) raw carrots,
    shredded
1 garlic clove, minced

1 large yellow onion, chopped
1 celery stalk, diced
1 tsp (5 ml) celery salt
1/4 tsp (1 ml) garlic powder
1/4 cup (60 ml) *Mock Heavy*
    Cream (see page 232)

Add the above to *Basic Vegetarian Loaf* recipe. Serve with your favorite sauce.

Tomato Veggie Loaf   30-35 minutes

2 cups (480 ml) *frozen* precooked
    green lentils, mashed or chopped
1 cup (240 ml) soft bread crumbs
2/3 cup (160 ml) canned tomato juice
    (instead of water)
1/3 cup (80 ml) canned diced
    tomatoes, slightly mashed

1 large yellow onion, chopped
1 celery stalk, diced
2 tsp (10 ml) dried grated
    Parmesan cheese
1 tsp (5 ml) celery salt
2 tsp (10 ml) dried oregano

Add above ingredients to *Basic Vegetarian Loaf* recipe.

Savory Red Bean Loaf   30-35 minutes

2 cups (480 ml) *frozen* precooked
    red kidney beans, mashed
1 cup (240 ml) bread crumbs
1/2 cup (120 ml) canned diced
    tomatoes
1/2 cup (120 ml) canned ground
    tomatoes

1 yellow onion, chopped
1 celery stalk, diced
1/4 cup (60 ml) *bulk* wheat germ
1 tsp (5 ml) savory

Add the above ingredients in *Basic Vegetarian Loaf* recipe. Serve hot with a sprinkle of lemon juice from concentrate.

Carrot & Legume Loaf   *30-35 minutes*

2 cups (480 ml) *frozen* precooked
    pinto, garbanzo, lima, or black
    beans, mashed or chopped
1 cup (240 ml) fresh bread crumbs
2 large carrots, shredded

1 large yellow onion, chopped
1 celery stalk, diced
2 tbsp (30 ml) sunflower seeds
1/4 tsp (1 ml) rosemary
1 tsp (5 ml) savory

Add above ingredients to *Basic Vegetarian Loaf* recipe. Serve hot or cold.

Savory Carrot & Rice Loaf   *30-35 minutes*

2 cups (480 ml) grated carrots
1 1/2 cups (360 ml) *refrigerated* pre-
    cooked long grain or brown rice
3/4 cup (180 ml) fresh bread crumbs

1 large yellow onion, chopped
1/2 tsp (2 ml) fine herbs
2 tbsp (30 ml) instant skim milk
    powder

Add above ingredients to *Basic Vegetarian Loaf* recipe.

Tomato Lentil Loaf   *30-35 minutes*

2 1/2 cups (600 ml) *frozen* precooked
    lentils, mashed
1/2 cup (120 ml) canned ground
    tomatoes
1 cup (240 ml) *'Quick'* rolled oats

2 tbsp (30 ml) sunflower seeds
2 tbsp (30 ml) whole-wheat flour
1 cup (240 ml) minced yellow onion
1/2 tbsp (7 ml) minced olives
1/2 tbsp (7 ml) tamari sauce

Add above ingredients to *Basic Vegetarian Loaf* recipe.

Potatoes & Veggies Loaf   *30-35 minutes*

2 cups (480 ml) *refrigerated* precooked
    potatoes, peeled and chopped
1 cup (240 ml) fresh bread crumbs
1 large yellow onion, chopped
1 medium carrot, grated

1/2 cup (120 ml) soybean flour
2 tbsp (30 ml) sunflower seeds
1 tsp ((5 ml) dried parsley
1/2 tsp (2 ml) sage
1/2 tsp (2 ml) celery salt

Add above ingredients to *Basic Vegetarian Loaf* recipe.

Carrot & Grain Roast   *30-35 minutes*

2 cups (480 ml) precooked carrots
1 larger yellow onion, chopped
1 garlic clove, minced
Half of a celery stalk, diced
1 cup (240 ml) *'Quick'* rolled oats
1 cup (240 ml) bread crumbs

2 tbsp (30 ml) sunflower seeds
1 tsp (5 ml) caraway seeds
1 tsp (5 ml) peanut butter
    (dissolved in the water)
2 tsp (10 ml) lemon juice from
    concentrate

Add above ingredients to *Basic Vegetarian Loaf* recipe.

Spiced Tomato Carrot Loaf   *30-35 minutes*

3 cups (720 ml) grated carrots
1 large yellow onion, chopped
2 cups (480 ml) small bread cubes

2 tbsp (30 ml) sunflower seeds
1/2 cup (120 ml) canned diced
    tomatoes
1/4 cup (60 ml) ground tomatoes

Add above ingredients to *Basic Vegetarian Loaf* recipe.

Cheese Vegetarian Loaf   30-35 minutes

1 1/4 cups (300 ml) *'Quick'* rolled oats
2 tbsp (30 ml) sunflower seeds
2 tbsp (30 ml) blender chopped peanuts

2 tbsp (30 ml) instant skim milk
   powder
1/4 cup (60 ml) any strongly
   flavored cheese

Add the above to *Basic Vegetarian Loaf* recipe. Serve topped with the cheese.

Soybean Loaf   30-35 minutes

2 1/2 cups (600 ml) *frozen* precooked
   soybeans, mashed or chopped
1 cup (240 ml) soft bread crumbs
1 large yellow onion, chopped

1 cup (240 ml) *'Quick'* rolled oats
2 tbsp (30 ml) sunflower seeds
1 small grated carrot
1/2 tsp (2 ml) dried basil

Add above ingredients to *Basic Vegetarian Loaf* recipe.

SKILLET FILLETS

Skillet fish fillets, that is! The least expensive frozen fish fillets are Turbot and Alaskan Cod. As for frozen whole fish, although, we don't cover fish preparation (scaling, etc.), the least expensive usually are Herring, Macquerel, and Merlan. There are many exceptions, so keep an open eye for fish (and seafood) bargains. Anything under two dollars a pound/four dollars a kilo (Canadian) can be considered as inexpensive though not necessarily a bargain.

Basic Skillet Fillets   12-15 minutes
Serve the fish fillet recipes with a rice, potato, salad, or pasta dish.

1 tbsp (15 ml) vegetable oil or
   margarine
1/4 cup (60 ml) flour
   (battered version only)

1/3-1/2 pound (150-227 g) frozen fish
   fillets *(Turbot, Alaskan Cod, etc.)*
1/8 tsp (1/2 ml) table salt *(for batter)*

WITHOUT BATTER: Heat a **frying pan** or **skillet** over a medium-high setting till hot. Add the fat, and the fish fillets *(and variation ingredients)* when the oil or margarine is hot. Sauté at least 4-5 minutes on the first side and 3-4 minutes on the second side. *Add a little water to reduce dryness and shrinkage.*

BATTERED: Heat a **frying pan** or **skillet** over a medium-high setting till hot. Add the fat only when the skillet is hot. Meanwhile, in a shallow **bowl**, combine optional flour and salt. Dredge wet fillets in flour mixture to coat. *At this point, add the ingredients for a variation to serve as seasoning or make a small amount of sauce in the same skillet!* Place fillets in skillet and fry for 5-6 minutes, or until golden brown. Turn over once and fry the other side 4-5 minutes until cooked throughout. **Makes 2 average servings**

LITE! VERSION *Reduce fat to 1 tsp (5 ml) and use a non-stick skillet and heat over a medium-low setting!*

SKILLET FILLETS VARIATIONS

Sautéed Fish Fillet & Mushrooms   *12-13 minutes*

Use Turbot or Alaskan Cod!
2 medium mushrooms, sliced
    paper thin
1/4 tsp (1 ml) chicken stock powder

1/4 cup (60 ml) hot tap water
1 tsp (5 ml) lemon juice from
    concentrate
Black pepper to taste

Add the above to *Basic Skillet Fillets* recipe. Follow the without batter directions.

Fish Steak with Tomato & Basil   *12-13 minutes*

Use low-cost fish steaks instead of
    fillets (any low-cost salmon)!
1 very small yellow onion,
    course chopped
1 garlic clove, minced

1/2 tsp (2 ml) dried basil leaves
1/3 cup (80 ml) canned diced
    tomatoes
1-2 tbsp (15-30 ml) water
Salt and pepper to taste

Add the above to *Basic Skillet Fillets* recipe. Follow the without batter directions.

Garlic Fried Fillets   *14-15 minutes*

Use Turbot or Alaskan Cod!
1/4 tsp (1 ml) garlic powder
2 garlic cloves, minced

1/4 cup (60 ml) *Fine Bread Crumbs*
    (replaces the flour, see page 246)

Add the above to *Basic Skillet Fillets* recipe. Follow the battered directions.

Sweet & Sour Fried Fillets   *13-14 minutes*

Use Turbot or Alaskan Cod!
1 tbsp (15 ml) granulated sugar
1 tbsp (15 ml) white vinegar
1 tbsp (15 ml) chopped yellow onions
2 tbsp (30 ml) water

1/2 tbsp (7 ml) cornstarch
1/2 tbsp (7 ml) generic catsup
1/2 tsp (2 ml) soy sauce
1/4 tsp (1 ml) ground ginger
Dash of tabasco sauce

Add the above to *Basic Skillet Fillets* recipe. Follow the without batter directions.

Italian-Style Fried Fillets   *14-15 minutes*

Use Turbot or Alaskan Cod!
1/2 tsp (2 ml) dried parsley
1/8 tsp (1/2 ml) dried oregano leaves

1 tbsp (15 ml) red wine vinegar
    (optional)

Add the above to *Basic Skillet Fillets* recipe. Follow the battered directions.

Oriental Whitefish Fillets   *12-13 minutes*

Use any low-cost whitefish fillet!
1/8 tsp (1/2 ml) ground ginger

2 tsp (10 ml) soy sauce
1/2 tsp (2 ml) dark brown sugar

Add the above to *Basic Skillet Fillets* recipe. Follow the without batter directions.

Dijon-Mustard Fish Fillets   *14-15 minutes*

Use Turbot or Alaskan Cod, etc.!   3 tbsp (45 ml) *Recipe-Grade*
1 tbsp (15 ml) minced yellow onions   *Sour Milk (see page 233)*
1/2 tbsp (7 ml) Dijon mustard

Add the above to *Basic Skillet Fillets* recipe. Follow the <u>without batter</u> directions.

Lemon Fish Fillets   *12 minutes*

Use Turbot or Alaskan Cod, etc.   1/2 tsp (2 ml) dried fine herbs
2 tsp (10 ml) lemon juice from   1/4 tsp (1 ml) chicken stock powder
   concentrate   Dash of salt

Add above to *Basic Skillet Fillets* recipe. Follow the <u>without batter</u> directions.

Mustard Cod Fillets   *12-15 minutes*

Use low-cost cod fillets!   1 tbsp (15 ml) white vinegar
1/2 tbsp (7 ml) prepared mustard   1 tbsp (15 ml) water
1/2 tsp (2 ml) dried parsley   1-2 tsp (5-10 ml) all-purpose flour
          Salt and pepper to taste

Add the above to *Basic Skillet Fillets* recipe. Follow the <u>without batter</u> directions. Dust the wet fillet with flour before cooking them.

SAUTÉED PORK LIVER

Basic Sautéed Pork Liver   *10-12 minutes*

Pork liver is the least expensive of the supermarket sold liver meat. Its very nutritious but unfortunately has a strong odor and flavor that must be covered. Despite that, its well worth cooking with and is the only variety meat fit to be in this book.

1 tbsp (15 ml) margarine or   1/2 pound (227 g) pork liver *(fresh*
   vegetable oil   *or frozen thawed in refrigerator)*

Heat a **frying pan** or **skillet** over a medium-high setting till hot. Add the fat, and the liver *(and variation ingredients)* when the margarine has melted. Sauté at least 5-6 minutes on the first side and 3-4 minutes on the second side. Chop it up when cooked. **Makes 2 average servings**

SAUTÉED PORK LIVER VARIATIONS

Liver & Onions   *10-12 minutes*

1 medium yellow onion, sliced and   1 tsp (5 ml) tap water
   separated into rings   1/2 tsp (2 ml) prepared mustard
1 tsp (5 ml) lemon juice from   1/4 tsp (1 ml) *Worcestershire-Style*
   concentrate   *Sauce (see page 243)*

Add the above to *Basic Sautéed Pork Liver* recipe.

Liver with Tomatoes 12 minutes

1 very small yellow onion, finely
    chopped
1 garlic clove, minced

1/2 cup (120 ml) canned diced
    tomatoes
1/2 tsp (2 ml) dried thyme

Add the above to *Basic Sautéed Pork Liver* recipe.

Marinated Sautéed Liver 12 minutes + marinating

2 tbsp (30 ml) water
2 tbsp (30 ml) white vinegar
1 tbsp (15 ml) red wine vinegar

1 tbsp (15 ml) all-purpose flour
Salt and pepper to taste

Add the above to *Basic Sautéed Pork Liver* recipe. Marinate liver in water and vinegar at least one hour before drenching in flour and sautéing.

RELATED RECIPES

Fried Battered Fillets 15-20 minutes

1/2 pound (227 g) small low-cost
    fish fillets, 3-inch (8 cm) lengths

1 cup (240 ml) *Batter Mix (pg. 244)*
1/2-5/8 cup (120-150 ml) water

 In a deep **bowl** or **jar**, combine batter mix with cold tap water *(plus optional egg and fat)*. Stir until smooth. *If too thick add more water and if too thin add more batter mix.* Heat the oil in deep fryer or frying pan to about 375°F (190°C). Meanwhile, prepare fillets to be battered and fried. *Fillets must not be wet; pat them dry if they are.* Dip and rotate items in batter until evenly coated. Remove from batter and drain off excess. Immerse gradually one at a time into hot oil. Fry half a dozen at a time for 5-6 minutes or till golden and fish is thoroughly cooked. **Makes 2 large servings**

Coated Fried Chicken 15-30 minutes

Serve one or two pieces of chicken from this recipe with homemade or low-cost frozen fries, homemade coleslaw, fried chicken gravy sauce, hot rolls made from refrigerated dough, pop, and you still fall within the **CookMISER** *cost/time range.*

6 precooked or uncooked chicken
    pieces, refrigerated or frozen/
    thawed in refrigerator *(2 small
    drumsticks, 2 wings, and 2 thigh
    sections)*
Oil to fry!

1/4 cup (60 ml) *Reconstituted
    Skim Milk* **or water** *(page 231)*
1/2 cup (120 ml) all-purpose flour
3/4 tsp (3 ml) table salt
1/4 tsp (2 ml) paprika
1/4 tsp (1 ml) ground black pepper

If using uncooked chicken, boil pieces for 12-15 minutes in a **large saucepan**. *Save liquid for soup.* Quickly pat-dry the freshly cooked or precooked chicken. Meanwhile, heat the oil in deep fryer or frying pan to about 375°F (190°C). Using a **spray bottle** *(see ill. on page 245)* and a **soup bowl**, place milk or water in bottle, combine flour and seasonings in the bowl. Spray a chicken piece with milk or water and then dip it in the flour. Repeat. Fry chicken pieces for 4 to 8 minutes *(depending if its pre-cooked or not)* till cooked throughout, and crisp outside. **MAKES 3 SERVINGS**

SAUCES

INSTANT SAUCES

Instant Chicken BBQ Sauce   4-5 minutes

1 cup (240 ml) hot tap water
1/4 cup (60 ml) canned tomato juice
    OR 1 1/2 tbsp (22 ml) canned
      ground tomatoes
1 tbsp (15 ml) vegetable oil
1 1/2 tbsp (22 ml) *bulk* cornstarch

1/2 tbsp (7 ml) chicken stock powder
1/4 tsp (1 ml) onion powder
1/4 tsp (1 ml) mild paprika
1/16 tsp (1/4 ml) black pepper
1/8 tsp (1/2 ml) Worcestershire sauce
Dash of red cayenne pepper

Place all ingredients in a **large saucepan** or **skillet**, quickly whisk together and heat over the highest setting till thickened. **Makes about 1-1 1/2 cups (240-360 ml)**

Instant Hot Chicken Gravy   4-5 minutes

Same as *Instant Chicken BBQ Sauce* recipe, except omit paprika, Worcestershire sauce, and cayenne. **Makes about 1-1 1/2 cups (240-360 ml)**

Instant Fried Chicken Gravy   4-5 minutes

1 cup (240 ml) hot tap water
1 1/2 tbsp (22 ml) vegetable oil
1 1/2 tbsp (22 ml) all-purpose flour

2 tsp (10 ml) beef soup stock powder
1/4 tsp (1 ml) onion powder
Salt and pepper to taste

Place all ingredients in a **large saucepan** or **skillet**, quickly whisk together and heat over the highest setting till thickened. **Makes about 1-1 1/2 cups (240-360 ml)**

WHITE SAUCES

Basic White Sauce   7-9 minutes

1 1/2 tbsp (22 ml) margarine
1 1/2 tbsp (22 ml) all-purpose flour
1 cup (240 ml) cold tap water

3 tbsp (45 ml) instant skim milk
    powder *(optional)*
Salt and pepper to taste

Melt margarine over a medium heat in a **saucepan**. Remove from heat. Add flour and mix. Add water (or skim milk) at once and return to heat. Stir continuously until thickened. *(Add ingredients for any of the following variations.)* Cook while stirring for another 3 minutes. Season to taste. Serve on fish, eggs, rice, pasta, potatoes, side dishes, and meatloaves. *See text about thickeners, on page 149, in* **TIPS & HINTS**.

Makes 1 to 1 1/2 cups (250-360 ml)

LITE! VERSION *Double amount of skim milk powder and omit margarine; scald 3/4 of milk, mix flour with remainder of milk, stir into scalded milk and stir continuously until low-fat sauce thickens!*

WHITE SAUCE VARIATIONS

Cheese (Stretcher) Sauce   8-10 minutes

1/3 cup (80 ml) grated old Cheddar,   2 tbsp (30 ml) skim milk powder
    mild Cheddar, or Mozzarella cheese   1 1/2 tbsp (22 ml) margarine or
1/4 tsp (1 ml) dry mustard   vegetable oil
1/4 tsp (1 ml) table salt   Dash of Worcestershire sauce

Add above ingredients to *Basic White Sauce* recipe. This recipe is more effective with strong cheese. Do not use pepper. Serve this sauce on pasta, vegetables, meatloaf, eggs, omelets, toasts, pizza, or in sandwiches and hamburgers.

LITE! VERSION *Reduce margarine or vegetable oil, and use low-fat cheese!*

Curry Sauce   7-8 minutes

1 tbsp (15 ml) curry powder
Add above ingredient to *Basic White Sauce* recipe. Serve on rice.

Herb Sauce   7-8 minutes

1 tsp (5 ml) dried fine herbs   2 tsp (10 ml) dried parsley
Add above to *Basic White Sauce* recipe. Serve on cooked vegetables or potatoes.

Onion White Sauce   8-9 minutes

1 yellow onion, finely chopped   1 1/2 tbsp (22 ml) water
1/2 tbsp (7 ml) margarine   1/2 tsp (2 ml) chicken stock powder

In a **large frying pan** or **skillet**, heat oil over a medium-high heat. Add onions and sauté a few minutes. Add water and stock powder; stir. Combine with white sauce from *Basic White Sauce* recipe. Serve on hot vegetables, rice or meatloaf.

Garlic White Sauce   8-9 minutes

Same as *Onion White Sauce* recipe except onion is replaced with 2 finely chopped garlic cloves and 1/4 tsp (1 ml) garlic powder is added.

Hungarian-Style Sauce   8-9 minutes

1 small yellow onion, finely chopped   1/2 tsp (2 ml) paprika
1/2 tbsp (7 ml) tomato paste   1/4 tsp (1 ml) nutmeg
Add above to *Basic White Sauce* recipe. Serve on hot vegetables or meatloaf.

Sour Pickle Sauce   *7-8 minutes*

2 1/2 tbsp (37 ml) pickled dills, minced   1 tsp (5 ml) lemon juice from
                                          concentrate

Add above to *Basic White Sauce* recipe. Serve on vegetables, grains, or meatloaf.

French-Style Sauce   *9-10 minutes*

1 tbsp (15 ml) margarine   1/8 tsp (1/2 ml) dried thyme
1 tbsp (15 ml) grated carrots   1/4 cup (60 ml) water
1 tbsp (15 ml) yellow onions,   1/4 tsp (1 ml) chicken stock powder
    very finely chopped   1 bay leaf

In a second **saucepan** or **skillet**, heat margarine over a medium-high setting. Sauté carrots and onions for 2 minutes; add water and remaining ingredients. Stir. When water has evaporated, add about 1 1/4 cups (300 ml) of white sauce. Simmer a few minutes while stirring occasionally. Remove bay leaf. Serve over meatloaf or fish.

Brown Sauce   *9-11 minutes*

Use same ingredients as *Basic White Sauce* recipe but the procedure is different. Heat margarine until brown. Add flour. Stir and cook both until brown or dark brown in color. Add water or skim milk and cook while continuously stirring till thickened. Serve over french-fries, rice and grain dishes, certain meatloaves or burgers.

OTHER SAUCES

Mild Yogurt Sauce   *15 minutes*

1 1/2 tbsp (22 ml) all-purpose flour   1 tbsp (15 ml) red wine vinegar
2/3 cup (160 ml) water   1/2 tsp (2 ml) chicken stock powder
1/3 cup (80 ml) *Homemade Yogurt*
   (see pages 232-3)

In a **saucepan**, combine the flour and water. Add remaining ingredients. Stir. Simmer for 10 minutes over a medium heat. Stir constantly as the sauce thickens. Serve over vegetables or meatloaf. **Makes about 1-1 1/2 cups (240-360 ml)**

HOT! **VERSION** *Try with 1/8 tsp (1/2 ml) of cayenne pepper and crushed chilies!*

Chickpea Sauce   *5 minutes*

2/3 cup (160 ml) precooked chickpeas   1 garlic clove, finely chopped
2 tbsp (30 ml) lemon juice from   1/3 cup (80 ml) hot tap water
   concentrate   Salt and pepper to taste

Blend all ingredients in an **electric blender** until smooth. Season. It can be served cold over salads or warm on cooked vegetables, patties or meatloaves. **Makes about 1-1 1/2 cups (240-360 ml)**

Spiced Pepper Sauce   *10-12 minutes*

1 tbsp (15 ml) vegetable oil   1/4 cup (60 ml) water
   or margarine   1 tsp (5 ml) all-purpose flour

1 yellow onion, chopped
1 garlic clove, sliced
2 tbsp (30 ml) hot pepper rings, minced
    OR half a green bell pepper, thinly
    sliced *(in peak season only)*

1 tsp (5 ml) dried parsley
1/4 tsp (1 ml) dried basil
Salt and pepper to taste

In a **large frying pan** or **skillet**, heat the fat over a medium-high heat. Sauté onion, garlic and hot pepper rings *(or paper-thin sliced green bell pepper)* for 5 minutes; stir frequently. Meanwhile, in a **small bowl**, mix water, flour and seasoning. Pour on sautéed vegetables and cook 1 to 2 minutes until sauce thickens. Puree in a **blender** and serve hot or at room temperature. This sauce goes well over vegetables, pasta, rice or fish. Spread on toasts. **Makes about 1/2 cup (120 ml)**

Legume-Caraway Sauce   *12 minutes*

3/4 cup (180 ml) precooked split
    peas *(frozen and thawed, or
    refrigerated)*
5/8 cup (150 ml) water

3 tbsp (45 ml) skim milk powder
1/4 tsp (1 ml) table salt
1 tsp (5 ml) caraway seeds
1 tbsp (15 ml) all-purpose flour

In a **blender**, puree peas. In a **small bowl** or **measuring cup**, mix water and milk powder. In a **small saucepan**, combine milk and split pea puree. Stir. Cook over a low-medium heat; add salt and caraway seeds *(crushed, ground or whole)*. After 5 minutes sprinkle in the flour, stir and simmer a few minutes until sauce thickens. Serve hot with rice and/or cooked vegetables. **Makes about 1-1 1/2 cups (240-360 ml)**

Spicy Pinto Sauce   *10 minutes*

1/2 cup (120 ml) water
1/2 tsp (2 ml) chicken stock powder
3/4 cup (180 ml) *frozen* precooked
    pinto beans
1 small yellow onion, chopped

Half a celery stalk, coarsely chopped
1/4 tsp (1 ml) ground turmeric
1/2 tsp (2 ml) dried tarragon
1/2 tsp (2 ml) table salt
1/2 tsp (2 ml) granulated sugar
Pepper to taste

In a **blender**, puree the beans in the water. Add onion, celery and remainder of ingredients; blend till smooth. In a **small saucepan**, pour the mixture; cook over a medium heat. Stir. Cook at least 5 minutes until hot and raw onion taste has gone. Serve on cooked vegetables and rice. **Makes about 1-1 1/2 cups (240-360 ml)**

Onion Sauce   *15-18 minutes*

2 tbsp (30 ml) margarine
1 tbsp (30 ml) vegetable oil
2 large yellow onions, thinly sliced

2 tsp (10 ml) beef soup stock powder
1/2 tsp (2 ml) onion powder
1 tsp (5 ml) dark brown sugar
1/2 tsp (2 ml) *Caramelized Sugar
    Coloring (see page 243)*

Heat a **large frying pan** or **skillet**, over a medium-high setting. When hot add fat, margarine has melted, add onions and sauté for 10 minutes or till light golden and slightly caramelized. Stir frequently. *Use it mostly to top pizza.* **Makes about 1-1 1/2 cups (240-360 ml)**

DESSERT & DISH PIES

Pies as baked in the **CookMISER** *require less time as compared to conventional pie making techniques. Part of the reason lies in the filling, it is preheated and thinner than usual. Higher than average cooking temperature accounts for the rest. The pie shell may be referred to as pie pastry or dough before baking and piecrust after baking.*

PIE PASTRIES

All pie pastry recipes are suitable for two or four 8 or 9-inch (20-23 cm) pies.

Basic Pie Pastry   10-12 minutes

4 cups (960 ml) generic-brand
   bleached all-purpose flour
1/2-1 tsp (2-5 ml) table salt

1 cup (240 ml) generic-brand or
   low-cost margarine
3/4 cup (180 ml) cold tap water

In a **large bowl**, combine flour and salt *(plus variation ingredients)*. Cut in the cold margarine with a **table fork** or **pastry blender** for about a minute until it looks like gravel of various sizes. *Its texture will not be uniform and will contain small and larger bits and pieces.* Sprinkle the water all over it and not just one spot. Mix very lightly for a few seconds only.

Turn the contents of bowl unto the counter and gather with both hands to make a ball. Separate in four balls without working the dough. *The less you work it and the less uniform it is, the flakier the crust.* Cut two square pieces of wax paper and place one on a slightly wet counter area. *You can use a hand that's dripping wet for this; it prevents the wax paper from slipping as the dough is rolled out.* Place a hand-flattened round piece of dough on it and cover with the second piece of wax paper. Using a **rolling pin**, roll out into a thin circle of almost 12-inches (30 cm). Remove the top piece of wax paper; pick up the bottom paper with the pie pastry on it, invert it and place against the **pie pan** or **plate**. Pressing it lightly against the pie pan will make it stick to the pan as you can pull off the wax paper. Repeat the procedure three more times using the same pieces of wax paper. Layer **2** or **4 pie pans or plates,** or refrigerate *(or freeze)* rolled-up with separator waxed papers in a plastic bag for later use. Crimp edges if making a double-crust pie *(see illustrations on pages 146-7).* **Makes 4 pie pastries**

TIPS & HINTS: *For well-baked piecrusts use dull metal pie pans or glass pie plate. Shiny metal (or thin aluminum) pans will not properly bake them (especially the bottom) and should be used for crumb crust pies only.* □
*When preparing the pie pastry, it must **not** be blended into a uniform paste but instead have bits of shortening with flour of varying size, for a flaky crust.*

PIE PASTRY VARIATIONS

Herbed Pie Pastry   *10-12 minutes*

1 1/2 tsp (7 ml) vegetable stock powder   1 tsp (5 ml) dried fine herbs
Add the above to *Basic Pie Pastry* recipe.
SUB-VARIATIONS *Try instead with dried Italian herbs, or parsley!*

Lemon-Taste Pie Pastry   *10-12 minutes*

2 tbsp (30 ml) lemon juice from concentrate
Substitute same amount of water with the above in *Basic Pie Pastry* recipe.

Sweetened Pie Pastry

2 tbsp (30 ml) granulated sugar
Add the above to *Basic Pie Pastry* recipe.

Wheat Germ Pie Pastry   *10-12 minutes*

1/4 tsp (1 ml) ground nutmeg   1 cup (240 ml) *bulk* wheat germ
                                      2 tsp (10 ml) skim milk powder
Replace same amount of flour with wheat germ, and add other above ingredients in *Basic Pie Pastry* recipe.

Whole Wheat Pie Pastry   *10-12 minutes*

1/4 cup (60 ml) *bulk* wheat germ   1/4 cup (60 ml) wheat bran
Replace same amount of flour with wheat germ/bran or replace all the all-purpose flour with same amount of whole-wheat flour in *Basic Pie Pastry* recipe.

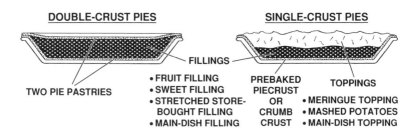

DOUBLE-CRUST PIES   **SINGLE-CRUST PIES**

FILLINGS

TWO PIE PASTRIES
• FRUIT FILLING
• SWEET FILLING
• STRETCHED STORE-
  BOUGHT FILLING
• MAIN-DISH FILLING

PREBAKED
PIECRUST
OR
CRUMB
CRUST

TOPPINGS
• MERINGUE TOPPING
• MASHED POTATOES
• MAIN-DISH TOPPING

OTHER PIECRUST RECIPES

Crumb Crust   *5-18 minutes*

**2 cups (480 ml) fine cookie crumbs   1/2 cup (120 ml) melted margarine
1/2 cup (120 ml) granulated sugar**

Using **blender**, turn homemade graham-like or other cookies into fine crumbs.
Line **two metal 9-inch pans** with it and refrigerate. Or bake at 450ºF (230ºC) for
about 5-7 minutes until lightly golden. *It may be used baked or unbaked!*

Oiled Refrigerated Dough Pie Pastry   *1 hour plus*

Enough 'Refrigerated Dough' to suit   Enough veg. oil to cover pastry

Roll out to as thin as possible to fit a pie pan. Soak in oil at least a half hour/side.

DOUBLE-CRUST PIE STYLES

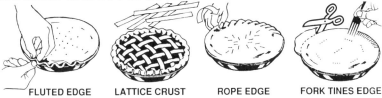

FLUTED EDGE   LATTICE CRUST   ROPE EDGE   FORK TINES EDGE

FRUIT PIE FILLINGS

Basic Plain Fruit Filling   *15-18 minutes*

About 3 cups (720 ml) fresh fruit, course   **1 cup (240 ml) white sugar**
chopped, diced, or thinly sliced   **1/4 cup (60 ml) all-purpose flour**
(peeled, cored, or washed if required)
3 cups (720 ml) hot tap water

In a **large skillet** or **saucepan**, pour water and all ingredients except fruit; whisk
well. Add fruits *(plus variation ingredients)*, cook mixture over a medium-high
heat about 10 minutes or until fruit is tender. *More water may be necessary for
longer cooking periods!* Stir or whisk as required. The thickened pie filling is
now ready for immediate use or freezer/refrigerator storage. Use as is or add
ingredients like spices and flavoring for a pie recipe. *Fruit filling recipes can be
flavored in numerous ways!* **Makes 4 cups (960 ml) or enough for 2 pies**

FRUIT PIE FILLING VARIATIONS

Apple Filling   *17-18 minutes*

*Use low-cost apples suitable for cooking,
preferably, during peak apple season!*
Use the above in *Basic Plain Fruit Filling* recipe.

Rhubarb Filling   *15-16 minutes*

Use rhubarb, preferably during peak season!
Use the above in *Basic Plain Fruit Filling* recipe. ***Discard the poisonous leaves!***

Pumpkin Filling   16-18 minutes

Use pumpkin, only during peak harvest season!
Use the above in *Basic Plain Fruit Filling* recipe.

Raisin Filling   5-20 minutes

Use 2 cup (480 ml) presoaked raisins (equals 1 1/4 cups/300 ml dried raisins)
    Or boil them at least 15 minutes!
Use the above in *Basic Plain Fruit Filling* recipe. Replace half of sugar with
brown sugar. The soaking *(or boiling)* water replaces the hot tap water.

OTHER DESSERT PIE FILLINGS & TOPPINGS

Pie Filling Stretcher    7-9 minutes

*This recipe will double your store-bought pie filling, or good for two double-
crust 8-9"(20-23 cm) pies. It's also recommended as low-cost dessert topping or
cake filling. If you're out of generic pie-filling, try jam instead (see page 248)!*

19 fl oz (540 ml) generic-brand pie filling *(apple, cherry, strawberry, or blueberry)*	**1/4 cup (60 ml) cornstarch or all-purpose flour**
2 1/4 cups (560 ml) water	**1/2 cup (120 ml) granulated sugar**
2 tsp (10 ml) lemon juice from concentrate	**3 tbsp (45 ml) sweetened flavored drink crystals**
1 tbsp (15 ml) margarine	

In a **heavy saucepan or skillet**, pour the water, lemon juice and
dissolve the cornstarch *(or flour)* with a **whisk**. *Cornstarch
works much better than flour with this recipe!* Heat over a
medium heat setting and dissolve sugar while stirring; add
margarine. Within a few minutes the mixture will thicken
and become bubbly, cook another 2 minutes. Remove
from heat and pour-in the store-bought pie filling; stir about 30
second. Pie filling stretcher is now ready for use in pie making or be refrigerated
well covered. These pie-filling stretchers are a bit thinner than unstretched pie-
fillings when hot, so pies made from them should be eaten at room temperature or
colder. *If stretching a cherry or strawberry pie filling, stretch the color too with
cherry or strawberry flavored drink crystals. For a blueberry pie filling stretch
the color with grape flavored crystals. It's not necessary for apple pie filling.* **Try
tripling recipe yield by doubling all the above ingredients except the store-
bought filling.** **Makes about 4 cups (960 ml) or enough filling for 2 pies**
LITE! VERSION *Omit margarine for a low fat but more foggy pie filling!*

Lemon Filling   10 minutes

1 1/3 cups (320 ml) granulated sugar	**2 2/3 cups (640 ml) hot tap water**
1/4 cup (60 ml) all-purpose flour	**1 extra-large or 2 small egg yolk(s)**
3 tbsp (45 ml) *bulk* cornstarch	**3 tbsp (45 ml) margarine**
Pinch of salt	**6 tbsp (90 ml) lemon juice from concentrate**

In a **large saucepan**, combine sugar, flour, cornstarch, and salt. Stir in the water and cook over a medium-high heat till thickened and bubbly; whisk. Remove from heat. Beat the yolks *(save whites for meringue)* gradually stir into saucepan mixture. Bring to a gentle boil again and cook two more minutes. Remove from heat and stir in margarine, and then lemon juice. Pour into two pre-baked piecrusts and cover with meringue or double recipe and use for three double-crust pies. *Alternately, try the Lemon Pudding recipe as pie filling (see page 207).*
Makes about 4 cups (960 ml)

Sugar Pie Filling   *7-8 minutes*

3 1/2 cup (840 ml) hot tap water   1/2 cup (120 ml) all-purpose flour
1/4 cup (60 ml) molasses or table syrup   Pinch of salt
1 cup (240 ml) granulated sugar   1 tsp (5 ml) artificial vanilla extract
1/2 cup (120 ml) dark brown sugar   3 tbsp (45 ml) margarine

In a **blender**, blend all ingredients except margarine for 30 seconds on a high speed. Pour in a **large saucepan** and heat over a medium-high setting till thickened and bubbly. Stir in margarine and cook another 2 minutes. Use as filling for double-crust pies. **Makes about 4 cups (960 ml)**

> **TIPS & HINTS:** *Thickening agents such as all-purpose flour and cornstarch must be used in a specific manner to obtain professional results. To thicken a liquid with flour, you must make a **roux**. For this the flour is mixed with melted margarine (shortening or butter) over a low heat, stirred and cooked for two minutes. At this point the liquid (preferably hot) is added to the melted fat/flour mixture and further cooked until thickened and bubbly. To thicken a liquid with cornstarch, it must be dissolve in that liquid while it is cold. If the liquid or mixture is hot, the resulting sauce or pudding will be lumpy. After the cornstarch has dissolved, the liquid can be cooked until thickened and bubbly.*

Meringue Topping   *7-9 minutes*

4 extra-large or 8 small egg whites,   1/2 cup (120 ml) granulated sugar
    at room temperature   1/4 tsp (1 ml) table salt

In a **metal mixing bowl**, add the egg whites, and sugar and place the bowl in a **second bowl** of very hot tap water. Stir constantly until the egg whites feel warm, then add the salt; remove from hot water. Using an **electric mixer** beat at a medium speed until meringue is stiff with glossy peaks. Immediately, using a wet **spatula**, spread meringue over two baked pie shells half filled with still warm filling making sure to touch the crust rim to prevent shrinkage. Bake under broiler a minute or two just long enough to lightly brown the meringue peaks.
Makes about 4 cups (960 ml)

For flavored crystals filling, see page 216

DESSERT PIES

Total time to make pie recipes assumes pie pastry and filling are ready.

Basic Dessert Pie   20-30 minutes

FILLING:

For a double-crust pie *use about 2 cups (480 ml) of a fruit or sweet pie filling!*
OR

For a single-crust pie *use about 1 cup (240 ml) of a fruit or sweet pie filling recipe and top with a meringue (see illustrations pages 146)!*

PIE PASTRY:

Use 2 or 4 suitable pie pastry or crumb crust for a single-crust or double-crust pie!

GLAZING:

To suit your taste (see text below)!

Preheat oven to 450°F (230°C) about 5 minutes before you think pies will be ready for baking. **For a double-crust pie**, prepare filling as directed in one of the filling recipes or reheat it. Meanwhile, line **two dull metal pie pans** or **glass pie plates** with pie pastries; try to adjust it to the pan by stretching or pulling it back as much as possible. *This stretching and pulling back will minimize wastage.* Place hot filling in pastry lined pie pan; cover with second pie pastry. Using a **fork**, crimp to seal the pie edge. To obtain a pie glazing, brush unbaked top pie pastry with either milk, water, melted margarine or a little of beaten egg/water mixture. Optionally sprinkle the wet glaze with some sugar. Bake up to three pies at a time on one rack only placed lower than middle of oven. Set **timer**, and bake at 450°F (230°C) for about 15 minutes until crust is light golden-brown. If top crust gets too brown, cover it with a square sheet of aluminum foil for remainder of baking time. Cool to room temperature in pan on a **cooling rack** before covering with aluminum foil for storage in freezer or refrigerator. Serve our pies at room temperature or chilled only.

For a single-crust pie, prepare filling *(half the amount)* as directed in one of the filling recipes or reheat it. Meanwhile, line **two dull metal pie pans** or **glass pie plates** with pie pastries. Adjust each pastry to the pan by stretching or pulling it back as much as possible. Pre-bake up to three piecrusts at a time on one rack only in the middle of oven or slightly higher. Set **timer**, and pre-bake them at 450°F (230°C) for 5-10 minutes until crust is light golden-brown. Let cool several minutes. Place hot filling in pastry lined pie pan; top with meringue but be sure it touches the entire edge of pie pastry to avoid shrinkage. Set timer again, and broil for a few minutes until the meringue peaks are browned. Let cool. Can be refrigerated for storage up to two days but serve at room temperature. **Makes two 8-9 inch (20-23 cm) single or double-crust pies**

DESSERT PIE VARIATIONS

American Apple Pie   25-30 minutes

1 tsp (5 ml) ground cinnamon
1/2 tsp (2 ml) ground nutmeg

1/8 tsp (1/2 ml) allspice *(optional)*
2 tbsp (30 ml) margarine

Add the above to *Apple Filling* recipe, then use in *Basic Dessert Pie* recipe.
SUB-VARIATION *For **Strawberry Flavored American Apple Pie**, add 2 tbsp (30 ml) of sweetened strawberry crystals to this recipe variation!*

Spiced Pumpkin Pie   *25-30 minutes*

2 tbsp (30 ml) margarine
2/3 cup (120 ml) skim milk powder
Dark brown sugar *(instead of
    granulated sugar)*

1/2 tsp (2 ml) nutmeg
1tsp (5 ml) ground cinnamon
1 tbsp (15 ml) lemon juice from
    concentrate

Add the above to *Pumpkin Filling* recipe, and follow *Basic Dessert Pie* recipe.

Sweet Rhubarb Pie      *25-30 minutes*

2 tbsp (30 ml) molasses or table syrup
2 tbsp (30 ml) margarine

2 tbsp (30 ml) strawberry flavored
    sweetened drink crystals

Add the above to *Rhubarb Filling* recipe, and follow *Basic Dessert Pie* recipe.

Raisin Pie   *20-25 minutes*

2 tbsp (30 ml) lemon juice from
    concentrate

1/4 cup (60 ml) dark brown sugar
    OR 2 tbsp (30 ml) molasses

Add the above to *Raisin Filling* recipe, and follow *Basic Dessert Pie* recipe.

POTATO PIES

Basic Potato Pie   *20-30 minutes*

*FILLING: Use 4 cup (1 liter) of the basic boiled potato recipe or any of its first 5
variations. Alternately, use 4 cups (1 liter) of a mashed potato recipe (see pg 81)*
PIE PASTRY: Use basic pie pastry, either the herbed or whole-wheat variation!
Preheat oven to 450ºF (230ºC) about 5 minutes before the pies will be ready to be
placed in oven. In a **large saucepan**, place about four large halved precooked
(refrigerated) potatoes; bring about 2 quarts (2 liters) of hot tap water to a boil
using the highest heat setting. Immediately, turn off heat and set aside while you
work on pie pastry if it's not yet ready. *For some potato pie variations, a **frying
pan or skillet** may be required to sauté meat and/or vegetables.* In a **pie pan** or
pie plate, place the lower pie pastry. Adjust it to the pan by stretching or pulling
it back as much as possible. Drain potatoes and prepare *(sliced, diced or mashed)*
them as outlined in the chapter on potatoes. Place prepared potatoes *(and
additional ingredients for a potato pie variation)* in pastry lined pie pans; cover
with second pie pastries. Seal the edge. Set **timer**, and bake at 450ºF (230ºC) for
15-20 minutes until crust is light golden-brown. Let cool several minutes before
serving or wrap for freezer or refrigerator. *If using leftover mashed or boiled
potatoes reheat quickly in a **frying pan** or **skillet**, add a little water if necessary.*
Makes two 8-9 inch (20-23 cm) single or double-crust pies

POTATO PIE VARIATIONS

Potato & Salmon Pie   *20-25 minutes*

**About 8 ounces (200 g) canned Keta
    salmon, drained**
Mix above with 3 cups (720 ml) of mashed potatoes in *Basic Potato Pie* recipe.

Potato & Meat Pie   *25-30 minutes*

1 tsp (5 ml) vegetable oil
1 cup (240 ml) regular ground
   beef or pork

1 large yellow onion, chopped
Half celery stalk, thinly sliced
Small garlic clove, minced
Salt and pepper to taste

Add the above to *Basic Potato Pie* recipe. Layer each pie with half of the sautéed meat and vegetables *(drain excess liquid),* and top each pie with 1 1/2 cups (360 ml) of a mashed or sliced boiled potato recipe.
SUB-VARIATIONS *Try ground pork, or diced chicken!*

Potato & Onion Pie   *25-30 minutes*

2 or 3 large yellow onions, thinly
   sliced

1/4 tsp (1 ml) ground rosemary
1/2 tsp (2 ml) caraway seeds

Add the above to *Basic Potato Pie* recipe. Layer each pie with half of the sautéed onions at bottom, cover with 1 cup (240 ml) sliced boiled potatoes *(plain or seasoned)* and top with 1 cup (240 ml) basic mashed potatoes.

Potato & Legume Pie   *25-30 minutes*

2/3 cup (160 ml) precooked
   (frozen/thawed) chick peas
1/2 cup (120 ml) *Homemade* or
   Recipe-Grade Sour Milk
   (see pages 233-4)

2 tbsp (30 ml) margarine
1/2 tsp (2 ml) dried basil
1/2 tsp (2 ml) dried thyme
2 tbsp (30 ml) grated fresh Feta or
   other strongly flavored cheese

Add the above to *Basic Potato Pie* recipe. Layer pies with half of the mixture from the above ingredients, top each pie with 1 1/2 cups (360 ml) of basic mashed potatoes.

Spicy Carrot-Potato Pie   *20-30 minutes*

1 cup (240 ml) mashed carrots
Add the above to *Basic Potato Pie* recipe. Layer pies with half of mashed carrots, top each pie with 1 1/2 cups (360 ml) of basic mashed potatoes.

VEGETABLE PIES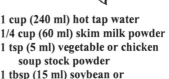

Basic Vegetable Pie   *25-30 minutes*

PIE FILLING:
2 tbsp (30 ml) vegetable oil
2 medium yellow onions,
   thinly sliced or finely chopped
1 garlic clove, minced
2 or 3 other vegetables *(about
   1 cup /240 ml each)*

1 cup (240 ml) hot tap water
1/4 cup (60 ml) skim milk powder
1 tsp (5 ml) vegetable or chicken
   soup stock powder
1 tbsp (15 ml) soybean or
   all-purpose flour
1 tbsp (15 ml) dried parsley

PIE PASTRY: **Use basic pie pastry, either the herbed or whole-wheat variation!**

Preheat oven to 450°F (230°C) about 5 minutes before you think pies will be ready for oven. In a **skillet** or **iron frying pan**, heat oil over a medium-high heat; sauté vegetables covered for at about 5 minutes. Stir occasionally and don't allow vegetables to brown. Meanwhile, in a **large bowl**, mix all remaining ingredients and pour into frying pan; cook mixture another 2 minutes. In **2 pie pans**, place lower pie pastry or dough; try to adjust it to the pan by stretching or pulling it back as much as possible. *This stretching and pulling back will avoid wastage.* Place vegetable mixture *(and additional ingredients for a potato pie variation)* in pastry lined pie pans; cover with second pie pastries and seal pie rims. Set **timer**, and bake at 450°F (230°C) on the middle or slightly lower shelf for 15-20 minutes until crust is light golden-brown. Let cool on wire rack several minutes before serving, or wrap for freezer or refrigerator. Remove from pan(s) before slicing.

Makes two 8-9 inch (20-23 cm) single or double-crust pies

LITE! VERSION *Sauté vegetables in large non-stick skillet with only 1 tsp (5 ml) of vegetable oil (add a little water if necessary) and use a low-fat pie pastry!*

VEGETABLE PIE VARIATIONS

Winter Vegetable Pie   *25-30 minutes*

1 cup (240 ml) fresh or *frozen*
   blanched carrots, diced
1 cup (240 ml) *refrigerated* precooked
   potatoes, diced
2 tbsp (30 ml) canned ground
   tomatoes

1/2 cup (120 ml) *frozen* precooked
   whole green peas
1 tsp (5 ml) dried fine herbs
1 tbsp (15 ml) white vinegar
1 tsp (5 ml) dried fine herbs

Add the above to *Basic Vegetable Pie* recipe. Ground tomatoes and vinegar replaces same amount of water.

SUB-VARIATIONS *Try other early winter vegetables when inexpensively in season like beets, parsnip, turnips and green cabbage!*

Summer Vegetable Pie   *25-30 minutes*

1 cup (240 ml) broccoli, chunks
1 cup (240 ml) zucchini or eggplant,
   sliced or diced *(in season only)*

Half red or green bell pepper,
   sliced or chopped
1/2 tsp (2 ml) dried basil

Add the above to *Basic Vegetable Pie* recipe.

SUB-VARIATIONS *Try other fresh late summer vegetables when inexpensively in peak season like, snow peas, cauliflower, corn, green beans, spinach, etc.!*

Beef-Vegetable Pie   *25-30 minutes*

2/3 cup (160 ml) stewing beef
   cubes, minced or finely diced
1 cup (240 ml) fresh or blanched
   frozen carrots, diced
1 cup (240 ml) *refrigerated*
   precooked potatoes, diced

1 tsp (5 ml) beef soup stock powder
   (instead of vegetable soup stock)
1/2 cup (120 ml) *frozen* precooked
   whole green peas

Add the above to *Basic Vegetable Pie* recipe.

SUB-VARIATION *Try low cost pork cubes instead of beef!*

Chicken-Vegetable Pie   25-30 minutes

2/3 cup (160 ml) low-cost turkey or
   chicken, finely chopped
1 cup (240 ml) fresh or *frozen*
   blanched carrots, diced
1 cup (240 ml) *refrigerated* precooked
   potatoes, diced

1 tsp (5 ml) beef soup stock powder
   (instead of vegetable soup stock)
1/2 cup (120 ml) *frozen* precooked
   whole green peas

Add the above to *Basic Vegetable Pie* recipe.

OTHER MAIN-DISH PIES

Egg (Quiche) Pie   25-30 minutes

1 pre-baked pie pastry *(see page 145)*
3 extra-large or 6 small eggs,
   at room temperature
1 1/2 cups (360 ml) fresh milk (3.25%)

1/4 tsp (1 ml) nutmeg
1/8 tsp (1/2 ml) table salt
Dash of ground black pepper
1 tbsp (15 ml) all-purpose flour

EGG MIXTURE

Preheat oven to 450°F (230°C) or 375°F (190°C) if piecrust is already baked. If unbaked, line a **pie pan** with pie pastry *(do not prick)* and bake at 450°F (230°C) on the middle rack for about 5 minutes. Meanwhile, in a **mixing bowl**, stir together eggs, milk, seasonings, and flour. Alternately, use an **electric hand mixer** but don't over mix. Pour the egg mixture into the pie shell. *Now, you can add ingredients for a recipe variation (see variations below) either below the egg mixture, mixed with it, or on top of it.* Bake at 375°F (190°C) for about 20 minutes till set. A knife or skewer inserted close to the center should come out clean. *Do not over bake.* If necessary, cover edge of crust with foil to prevent over-browning. Serve a quiche portion with potatoes & small salad. *Recipe doesn't work well with reconstituted skim milk.* **Makes one 8-9" (20-23 cm) quiche pie or 4 large servings**
VARIATIONS *Add to recipe one or two of the following taste stuffing's: 1 or 2 thin slices of cheese or chopped bacon, sautéed chopped or sliced yellow onions, or other vegetables in season, precooked legumes, grated fresh cheese, varied seasonings, etc. Use no more stuffing's than is required for added taste!*

Pot Pies   25-35 minutes

Turn ordinary chicken, turkey or beef (vegetable) pies into pot pies (also called deep-dish pies) by doubling or tripling previous Basic Vegetable Pie recipe or one of its variations. Using a 1 1/2 to 2 Q/L baking dish covered with one pie pastry only pressed to the dish. Follow the same basic instructions and bake a bit longer if necessary. Include vents in pastry for the steam to escape.

Legume Pies   30-35 minutes

Using one of the legume spread recipes on pages 114-5, line the bottom half of a pie. Or combine legume spread half with tofu. Top with one of the mashed or boiled potato recipes from pages 79-81. See single-crust pie ill., on page 146.

MAIN-COURSE DISHES

MEAL-IN-ONE-PAN

Meal-in-one-pan (also called stovetop meals, skillet meals or dinners, or one-pan meals) means the whole meal, usually of one person, is quickly prepared in one pan only. This means, no mixing bowls, or separate procedures apart from the

precooked ingredients. They should include ingredients from the major food groups like carbohydrates, proteins, fats, and vegetables. These one pan meals are so fast to make, they're almost instant.

Basic Meal-In-One-Pan

5-7 minutes

1 tbsp (15 ml) margarine or veg. oil
*About 1/3 cup (80 ml) regular ground
    beef, pork, chopped cooked poultry,
    chopped stewing beef or pork cubes,
    bacon, sausage, fish fillets, or even
    mashed, sliced, cubed, or mashed
    homemade tofu (pick one only)!*
*About 2/3 cup (160 ml) fresh or blanched
    inexpensive vegetables like yellow
    onions, celery, carrots, cabbage, clove
    of garlic, or vegetables at peak
    harvest season(pick one to three
    or those in a recipe vartation)!*
About 1/2 cup (120 ml) hot tap water
    (omit water if stir-frying)

*1/3 cup (80 ml) precooked/frozen
    legumes like soybeans, red
    kidney beans, chickpeas, or
    lima beans, etc. (pick one)!*
*2 cups (480 ml) refrigerated pre-
    cooked rice, potato, or pasta
    OR a combination of three
    OR 1 cup (240 ml) rice,
        potatoes, or pasta
        AND 1 cup (240 ml)
            couscous or millet*
Seasonings!
1/2 tsp (2 ml) all-purpose flour
Salt and pepper to taste

Heat a **large frying pan** or **saucepan** over a medium-high setting, when hot add margarine or oil. Sauté the meat *(or tofu)*, vegetables *(including those from a variation too)* for a few minutes till meat has lost its pink color, and vegetables are lightly cooked and crisp. Stir. Add water and remainder of ingredients *(plus the variation ingredients that were not meat or vegetables)*; simmer a few minutes on a medium heat setting till most of the liquid has been absorbed. Serve hot with bread. **Makes one very large serving or about 2-2 1/2 cups (480-600 ml)**

LITE! VERSION *Use a non-stick skillet on a medium-low heat, omit or reduce fat. Use lean beef, and avoid bacon, ham, or pork!*

MEAL-IN-ONE-PAN VARIATIONS

Beef Stroganoff   *6-7 minutes*

Use regular ground or finely chopped
   or diced stewing beef!
1 small yellow onion, finely chopped
2 medium mushrooms, very
   thinly sliced
Legumes are optional here!
Use precooked rice or pasta!

2 tbsp (30 ml) skim milk powder
1/2 tbsp (7 ml) white vinegar
2 tbsp (30 ml) canned ground
   tomatoes
1/2 tsp (2 ml) beef stock powder
1/8 tsp (1/2 ml) nutmeg

Add or use the above ingredients in *Basic Meal-In-One-Pan* recipe. *Stir together cold (instead of hot) water, milk powder and vinegar; set aside a few minutes to sour the milk.*

Chicken Dijon Rice   *6-7 minutes*

Use precooked refrigerated chopped
   chicken (or turkey)!
1 small yellow onion, finely chopped
Legumes optional here!
Use precooked long grain rice!
2 tbsp (30 ml) skim milk powder

1 tbsp (15 ml) lemon juice from
   concentrate
1/4 tsp (1 ml) onion powder
1 tsp (5 ml) all-purpose flour
2 tsp (10 ml) Dijon mustard
1/2 tsp (2 ml) dried parsley

Add or use the above ingredients in *Basic Meal-In-One-Pan* recipe.

Hearty Sausage & Potatoes   *6-7 minutes*

Use 1 or 2 breakfast pork sausage(s) or
   1 homemade sausage, chopped
   or sliced (see pages 121-5)!
1 small yellow onion, finely chopped
Use frozen precooked whole green peas!
1/4 tsp (1 ml) Worcestershire sauce

1/2 cup (120 ml) canned diced
   tomatoes
Use precooked refrigerated
   cubed potatoes!
1 tbsp (15 ml) all-purpose flour
1/4 tsp (1 ml) onion powder

Add or use the above ingredients in *Basic Meal-In-One-Pan* recipe.

Spiced & Creamy Chicken Rice   *7-10 minutes*

Double the margarine or oil!
Use chopped precooked chicken or turkey!
1 small yellow onion, finely chopped
1 small clove of garlic, minced
Half a celery stalk, thinly sliced
3 tbsp (45 ml) skim milk powder
1/2 tbsp (7 ml) white vinegar

Use frozen precooked lima beans!
Use precooked refrigerated rice!
1/2 tsp (2 ml) chicken soup stock
   powder
1/2 tsp (2 ml) curry powder
1/4 tsp (1 ml) ground ginger
1/16 tsp (1/4 ml) garlic powder

Add or use the above ingredients in *Basic Meal-In-One-Pan* recipe. *Stir together water, milk powder and vinegar; set aside a few minutes to sour the milk.*

Hamburger-Rice & Green Peas   *6-7 minutes*

Use economical regular ground beef!   *Use refrigerated precooked rice!*
1 small yellow onion, finely chopped   1 tsp (5 ml) dried parsley
Use frozen precooked whole green peas! 1 tsp (5 ml) chicken stock powder
Add or use the above ingredients in *Basic Meal-In-One-Pan* recipe.

Vegetarian Bean Stroganoff   *6-7 minutes*

No meat here!   1/2 cup (120 ml) *Homemade*
1 small yellow onion, finely chopped   *Yogurt (see pages 232-3)*
2 or 3 small mushrooms, very   1/2 tsp (2 ml) *Worcestershire-*
    thinly sliced   *Style Sauce (see page 243)*
Use double the amount frozen precooked 1 tsp (5 ml) prepared mustard
    soybeans!   1 tsp (5 ml) white vinegar
Use precooked rice or bulgur wheat!   2 tbsp (30 ml) canned ground
1/2 tbsp (7 ml) all-purpose flour   tomatoes
1/2 tsp (2 ml) vegetable *(or chicken)*   1/8 tsp (1/2 ml) nutmeg
    stock powder
Add or use the above ingredients in *Basic Meal-In-One-Pan* recipe.

Lemon Mackerel & Potatoes   *6-7 minutes*

Triple amount of margarine!   *Use refrigerated precooked potatoes!*
Use 4 oz (100 g) of mackerel!   1 tsp (5 ml) prepared mustard
1 garlic clove, minced   1 tbsp (15 ml) lemon juice from
Use frozen precooked lima beans!   concentrate
                                         1 tsp (5 ml) dried parsley
Add or use the above ingredients in *Basic Meal-In-One-Pan* recipe.

Rice Provençale & Fillets   *6-7 minutes*

Use 2 small Alaskan cod or turbot fillets! 1/4 cup (60 ml) canned diced
1 small yellow onion, finely chopped   tomatoes
Half a garlic clove, minced   1 tbsp (15 ml) canned ground
Use frozen precooked red kidney beans!   tomatoes
Use refrigerated precooked rice!   1/2 tbsp (7 ml) green or black
1/2 tsp (2 ml) dried parsley   sliced olives, finely chopped
1/2 tsp (2 ml) dried thyme *(optional)*
Add or use the above ingredients in *Basic Meal-In-One-Pan* recipe.

Spiced Potatoes & Turkey   *6-7 minutes*

Use precooked chopped turkey...double 1/2 tbsp (7 ml) lemon juice from
    the amount!   concentrate
1 very small yellow onion, chopped   1 tbsp (15 ml) skim milk powder
Legumes optional here!   1/2 tsp (2 ml) chili powder

Use refrigerated precooked potatoes!   1/4 tsp (1 ml) ground cumin
Add or use the above ingredients in *Basic Meal-In-One-Pan* recipe.

Pasta-Fish & Black beans   *6-15 minutes*

Use any medium fish fillet!   *Use frozen precooked black beans!*
1 fresh tomato, sliced *(inexpensively*   *Use penne rigate or macaroni pasta!*
in peak harvest season only)   1/2 tsp (2 ml) dried parsley
OR 1/4 cup (60 ml) canned diced   1/4 tsp (1 ml) onion powder
tomatoes   1 tsbp (15 ml) grated old Cheddar
1 small garlic clove, minced   cheese
Add or use the above ingredients in *Basic Meal-In-One-Pan* recipe.

Beef & Pasta Stir-Fry   *6-7 minutes*

Use vegetable oil instead of margarine   *Omit the water in this one!*
but double amount!   *Use frozen precooked whole*
Use thinly sliced stewing beef!   *green peas!*
1 small yellow onion, thinly sliced   *Use spaghetti or linguine pasta!*
Half celery stalk, thinly sliced   1 tbsp (15 ml) soy sauce
1 small carrot, shredded   1 tsp (5 ml) brown sugar
1 small garlic clove, minced   1/4 tsp (1 ml) ground ginger
Add or use the above ingredients in *Basic Meal-In-One-Pan* recipe.

Meat-Potatoes & Gravy   *5-6 minutes*

Use economical regular ground beef   *Use refrigerated precooked potatoes,*
or pork!   *sliced or diced!*
1 small yellow onion, finely chopped   1 tbsp (15 ml) all-purpose flour
1/2 tbsp (7 ml) beef stock powder   1/4 tsp (1 ml) dried parsley
Use frozen precooked whole green peas!   1/4 tsp (1 ml) Worcestershire sauce
Add or use the above ingredients in *Basic Meal-In-One-Pan* recipe.

Speedy Chili & Rice   *6-7 minutes*

Use regular ground beef or pork!   1 tsp (5 ml) chili powder
1 small yellow onion, chopped   1/4 tsp (1 ml) ground cumin
1 garlic clove, minced   1/2 tsp (2 ml) oregano
Use frozen precooked red kidney   1/3 cup (80 ml) canned diced tomatoes
beans...double amount!   2 tbsp (30 ml) ground tomatoes
Use refrigerated precooked rice!   1/2 tsp (2 ml) beef stock powder
Add or use the above ingredients in *Basic Meal-In-One-Pan* recipe.

Pork & Potatoes   *7-8 minutes*

Use marinated stewing pork, sliced thin!   *Use refrigerated precooked potatoes!*
1 small yellow onion, sliced thin   1/2 tsp (2 ml) beef stock powder
Half a small carrot grated   1/2 tsp (2 ml) caraway seeds
1/2 cup (120 ml) shredded cabbage   1/2 tsp (2 ml) all-purpose flour
Legumes optional here!   1/2 tsp (2 ml) dried parsley
Add or use the above ingredients in *Basic Meal-In-One-Pan* recipe.

Pork Liver & Rice   6-7 minutes

Double amount of margarine!
*Use one medium-sized slice of pork
   liver, chop it up when cooked!*
1 medium yellow onion, chopped

A few dandelion leaves, chopped
Legumes optional here!
Use refrigerated precooked rice!
1 tsp (5 ml) beef stock powder
1/2 tbsp (15 ml) red wine vinegar

Add or use the above ingredients in *Basic Meal-In-One-Pan* recipe.

Carbonara Pasta   6-7 minutes

Double amount of margarine!
Use chopped cooked pork or ham!
1 sliced green onion
3 tbsp (45 ml) skim milk powder
1/2 tsp (2 ml) chicken soup stock
   powder

*Use frozen precooked whole green
   peas!*
*Use (precooked if possible) pastas
   like spaghettini or vermicelli!*
1 tsp (5 ml) dried Italian herbs
1/4 tsp (1 ml) onion powder

Add or use above in *Basic Meal-In-One-Pan* recipe. Serve with hot rolls.

Tex-Mex Chicken & Rice   6-7 minutes

Use precooked chopped chicken!
1 small yellow onion, chopped
Half a celery stalk, sliced
1 small garlic clove, minced
Quarter green bell pepper, chopped
   (optionally in season only)
*Use frozen precooked red kidney
   beans or whole green peas!*

Use refrigerated precooked rice!
1/2 tsp (2 ml) chicken stock powder
1/3 cup (80 ml) canned diced
   tomatoes, not drained
1 small bay leaf
1/2 tsp (2 ml) ground cumin
1/2 tsp (2 ml) chili powder
Dash of cayenne

Add or use above ingredients in *Basic Meal-In-One-Pan* recipe. *Remove bay
leaf before serving.*

Vegetarian Tofu Stroganoff   6-7 minutes

Use tofu instead of meat...doubly!
1 very small yellow onion, chopped
2 medium mushrooms, very thinly sliced
Legumes optional here!
Use precooked rice or pasta!
1 tbsp (15 ml) canned ground tomatoes

2 tbsp (30 ml) skim milk powder
1/2 tbsp (7 ml) white vinegar
1 tsp (5 ml) all-purpose flour
2 tbsp (30 ml) lemon juice from
   concentrate
1/2 tsp (2 ml) dried parsley

Add or use the above ingredients in *Basic Meal-In-One-Pan* recipe. *Stir
together cold (instead of hot) water, milk powder and vinegar; set aside a few
minutes to make sour milk.*

Quick Chili   7-10 minutes

Use regular ground beef!
*Use 1 cup (240 ml) of frozen precooked
   red kidney beans (instead of
   1/3 cup/80 ml)!*
1 yellow onion chopped

1/4 tsp (1 ml) garlic powder
1/2 cup (120 ml) canned diced
   tomatoes
2 tbsp (30 ml) canned ground
   tomatoes *(see tip on page 98)*

1/8 cup (30 ml) finely chopped green bell pepper *(optional)*
1 tsp (5 ml) chili powder
1 tsp (5ml) all-purpose flour

1/8 tsp (1/2 ml) Worcestershire sauce
No rice, potatoes, or pasta!

Use the above in *Basic Meal-In-One-Pan* recipe. Serve with lots of bread.

Shepherd's Pie   10-12 minutes

This is our cheap (and fast) but good tasting version of a shepherd's pie (which incidentally is not a pie at all). Time assumes mashed potatoes are refrigerated and ready.

Use regular ground beef!
1 small yellow onion, chopped
Half a small garlic clove, minced
1/2 cup (120 ml) *frozen* precooked lentils *(optional)*

1/4 tsp (1 ml) rosemary
1/2 tsp (2 ml) beef stock powder
1 tsp (5 ml) all-purpose flour
1-1 1/2 cup(s) 240-360 ml) *Basic Mashed Potatoes (see page 81)*

Add or use above ingredients in *Basic Meal-In-One-Pan* recipe. When beef gravy has thickened, top with mashed potatoes. In a preheated oven, place all metal frying pan directly under broiler for a few minutes to brown the mashed potatoes.

MORE COMBOS & VARIATIONS!

Using the information contained in the Basic Meal-In-One-Pan *recipe and its variations as examples, you can come up with hundreds, if not thousands, of different recipe combinations and variations.*

FAST STEWS

These stews or ragouts are simple and quick to make as stovetop meals. They are very inexpensive, great tasting and all have thick gravy. Much of the time is save with these fast stews by using many precooked ingredients store frozen or refrigerated. Additional cooking time is gain by using less liquid than usual. The lack of flavor due to undercooking is reinforced with a greater range and more seasonings. Chili powder helps give the dish an aged or simmered for hours taste.

Basic Fast Stew   15-20 minutes

2 tbsp (30 ml) vegetable oil or margarine
Use fresh or blanched vegetables!
About 2/3 cups (160 ml) meat, poultry, or meat or meatless meatballs, etc.!
Precooked vegetables or legumes!
May also contain additional ingredients like breadcrumbs, eggs, canned tomato products, sauce, sugar, vinegar, dumplings, etc.!

3/4 cup (180 ml) cold tap water
2 tbsp (30 ml) all-purpose flour
2 tsp (10 ml) beef soup stock powder
1/2 tsp (2 ml) chili powder
1 tsp (5 ml) dried parsley
Salt and pepper to taste

Over a medium-high setting, heat **frying pan or skillet** and when pan is hot add the fat. As soon as margarine is melted, add fresh or blanched vegetables and meat *(as indicated in stew recipe variations).* Sauté and stir for at least 5 minutes. Meanwhile, in a **small bowl**, combine water, flour, stock powder, seasonings and spices *plus possible additional ingredients like eggs, hot sauce, etc.* Pour mixture unto the pan; add precooked vegetables and legumes *plus any remaining ingredients for recipe variations.* Lower heat to medium and simmer partially covered for at least 10 minutes or until vegetables like carrots are tender but firm. At this point, the gravy should have thickened. Stir occasionally and add a little water only if necessary. Serve stew with bread and soup or salad if desired. Alternately, refrigerate and serve later as a more flavorful leftover. *If using stewing beef in your stew cut each cube into smaller cubes.*

Makes about 4 cups (960 ml) or 4 average servings
LITE! VERSION *Use only 1/4 tsp (1 ml) fat in a large non-stick skillet and leaner meat. Use lower temperatures with non-stick pans and to allow more time!*

FAST STEW VARIATIONS

Veggie Meatballs Stew   *20 minutes*

1 cup (240 ml) fresh or blanched sliced carrots *(very thinly sliced if fresh)*
About a dozen small vegetarian meatballs *(see pages 128-32)*
2 cup (480 ml) *refrigerated* precooked potatoes, coarsely cubed

2/3 cup (160 ml) *frozen* pre-cooked whole green peas
1/3 cup (80 ml) high yield pulp or mashed tofu
1/8 tsp (1/2 ml) garlic powder
1/4 tsp (1 ml) celery salt

Use and add the above as outlined in the *Basic Fast Stew* recipe.

Winter Vegetables & Beef Ragout   *20 minutes*

1/2 cup (120 ml) fresh or blanched sliced carrots *(very thinly sliced if fresh)*
About 1/4 cup (60 ml) each, turnips and parsnip *(bought cheap end of fall)*
2/3 cup (160 ml) ground beef or tiny marinated stewing beef cubes
1/4 cup (60 ml) *frozen* precooked diced beet roots

2 cup (480 ml) *refrigerated* pre-cooked potatoes
2 tbsp (30 ml) white vinegar
1/2 tsp (2 ml) Worcestershire-Style Sauce *(see page 243)*
1/4 cup (60 ml) canned ground tomatoes
1/2 tsp (2 ml) onion powder

Use and add the above as outlined in the *Basic Fast Stew* recipe.

Bavarian-Style Stew   *20 minutes*

1 cup (240 ml) fresh or blanched carrots *(sliced thin if fresh)*
1/2 cup (120 ml) fresh cabbage, sliced
1 large yellow onion, thinly sliced
2/3 cup ((160 ml) tiny stewing beef cubes
1 cup (240 ml) *refrigerated* precooked potatoes, diced or sliced

1/3 cup (60 ml) *frozen* whole green peas
2 tbsp (30 ml) white vinegar
1 large bay leaf
1/2 tsp (2 ml) caraway seeds
1 tbsp (15 ml) brown sugar

Use and add the above as outlined in the *Basic Fast Stew* recipe. *Leave in the bay leaf if refrigerating dish.*

MORE STEW VARIATIONS AND SUB-VARIATIONS!

Hundreds of combinations can be created, by using the above basic recipe guidelines with a whole range of other ingredients and seasonings. A small sample list would include precooked red kidney beans, lima, lentils and countless legumes...also pastas, rice, pork breakfast sausages, ground pork, chopped chicken, etc., etc., etc. Stew recipes from other cookbooks can be converted to suit guidelines of this book and allow you to very inexpensively cook stews in less than twenty minutes!

QUICK CASSEROLES

Basic Quick Casserole   *25-30 minutes*

2 tbsp (30 ml) vegetable oil
1 1/3 cups (320 ml) regular grade ground beef or pork, cooked ham cubes, or fish fillet, etc. Or 2/3 cup (160 ml) canned fish or seafood like, tuna, crabmeat, keta salmon, or precooked chicken (use one only)!
About 7 cups (1750 ml) fillers like rice, bread crumbs, raw or blanched vegetables, frozen legumes, potatoes, pasta, etc. (according to recipe variations or make your own recipes by picking your own)!

All contain about 1 1/2 cup (360 ml) of liquid like hot tap water, milk, sour cream or milk, tomato juice, cream soup, whey liquid, etc.!
2 tsp (10 ml) stock powder *(chicken and beef)*
1 or 2 tbsp (15-30 ml) flour
May contain misc.. ingredients for a recipe variation like lemon juice, soy, Worcestershire or tabasco sauce, hot pepper rings, etc.!
Seasonings for one of the recipe variations!
Salt and pepper to taste

If using *frozen* precooked legumes, thaw them in a **medium-sized bowl**, containing very hot tap water. In a **large heavy saucepan**, heat the oil over a medium-high setting. If casserole contains pasta, get water boiling in a second **large saucepan**. Meanwhile, chop, slice, dice or mince vegetables or potatoes if any. Preheat oven to 450°F (230°F). If casserole contains meat, fish, onions, garlic, celery, cabbage or carrots, sauté them along with seasonings about 5 minutes until almost cooked. Stir occasionally. Add all remaining ingredients except liquid and flour; cook or sauté a few more minutes while stirring. In a **small bowl**, mix liquid(s) ingredients and flour. Transfer ingredients from saucepan to **casserole dish(s)**; pour in liquid-flour mixture. Place in oven; bake 15 to 20 minutes uncovered or until golden-brown on top and very hot throughout. There should be very little liquid left in dish. Cover midway only if top is cooking faster than it should. Serve with bread or salad after a soup and you have a complete meal. **Makes 2 medium or 1 large casserole(s), or about 2 quarts/liters, 8 average or 4 very large servings**

LITE! VERSION *Utilize only 1 tsp (5 ml) of oil in a non-stick heavy deep skillet or saucepan. Use low-fat but expensive lean ground beef!*

QUICK CASSEROLE VARIATIONS

Wild Rice & Beef Casserole   25-30 minutes

1 1/3 cups (320 ml) regular groud beef
1/4 cup (60 ml) *frozen* precooked wild rice
3 1/2 cups (840 ml) *refrigerated* precooked long grain rice
1/2 cup (120 ml) *frozen* whole green peas

1 yellow onion, chopped
2 celery stalks, thinly sliced
1 1/2 cups (360 ml) *Cream of Celery Soup* or *Mock Light Cream (see pages 53, 232)*
1 tsp (5 ml) *Worcestershire-Style Sauce (see page 243)*
2 tbsp (30 ml) white vinegar

Add the above to the ingredients in *Basic Quick Casserole* recipe.

Hot Mexican Pork Casserole   25-30 minutes

1 1/3 cups (320 ml) ground pork
2 bacon strips, chopped
2 cups (480 ml) yellow onions, chopped
1/2 cup (120 ml) green bell pepper, chopped *(in peak season only)*
4 cups (960 ml) *refrigerated* pre-cooked long grain rice
1 cup (240 ml) *frozen* precooked red kidney beans

1 cup (240 ml) hot tap water
1/2 cup (120 ml) canned ground tomatoes
2 tsp (10 ml) dried parsley
1 tbsp (15 ml) pickled hot pepper rings
1/2 tsp (2 ml) paprika

Add the above to the ingredients in *Basic Quick Casserole* recipe.

Tuna Casserole   25-30 minutes

1 large yellow onion, chopped
1 celery stalk, thinly sliced
1 cup (240 ml) *frozen* whole green peas
4 cup (960 ml) *refrigerated* pre-cooked long grain rice
1 can (6-7 oz/170 g) tuna, not drained

2 tbsp (30 ml) margarine
1 tbsp (15 ml) pickled hot pepper rings, minced
1/2 cup (120 ml) *Homemade Mayonnaise (see pages 70-1)*
1 cup (240 ml) *Cream of Celery Soup* or *Mock Light Cream (see pages 53, 232)*

Add the above to the ingredients in *Basic Quick Casserole* recipe.

Spicy Olive & Beef Casserole   25-30 minutes

1 1/3 cups (320 ml) regular ground beef
1 small yellow onion, chopped

1/2 cup (120 ml) *Queso Blanco* soft cheese *(see page 237)*
1 cup (240 ml) hot tap water

1 garlic clove, minced
2 tbsp (30 ml) pitted green or
  black olives, minced
5 cups (1200 ml) cooked penne rigate
  (equals 2 1/4 cups/560 ml uncooked)

1/4 cup (60 ml) instant skim milk
  powder
1 tsp (5 ml) *Worcestershire-Style
  Sauce (see page 243)*
1/2 tsp (2 ml) paprika
Dash of Tabasco sauce

Add the above ingredients to *Basic Quick Casserole* recipe.

Winter Vegetables & Beef   25-30 minutes

1 1/3 cups (320 ml) regular ground
  beef
1 cup (240 ml) *frozen* precooked
  sliced or chopped beets
2 cups (480 ml) *frozen* blanched
  sliced or diced carrots

4 cups (960 ml) *refrigerated*
  precooked potatoes, sliced
1 tbsp (15 ml) margarine
1/4 tsp (1 ml) garlic powder
1/2 tsp (2 ml) onion powder
1/2 tsp (2 ml) celery salt

Add the above ingredients to *Basic Quick Casserole* recipe.

Tomato Pasta & Beef Dish   25-30 minutes

1 1/3 cups (320 ml) regular ground
  beef
5 cup (1200 ml) cooked ready-cut or
  elbow macaroni *(about
  2 1/4 cups/540 ml uncooked)*
1 large yellow onion, thinly sliced

1/2 cup (120 ml) canned diced
  or whole tomatoes
1 cup (240 ml) *Pizza Tomato
  Sauce* or other tomato sauce
  (see pages 182-3, 93-8)
1/4 tsp (1 ml) garlic powder

Add the above ingredients to *Basic Quick Casserole* recipe.

Madrid Rice & Beef   25-30 minutes

2 slices of bacon, chopped
1 1/3 cups (320 ml) regular ground
  beef
6 cups (1440 ml) *refrigerated*
  precooked long grain rice
1 medium yellow onion,
  chopped

1tsp (5 ml) dried thyme
1/4 tsp (1 ml) dried basil
1/2 tsp (2 ml) paprika
1 1/2 cups (360 ml) canned
  tomato juice
1/2 cup (120 ml) *frozen* whole
  green peas

Add the above ingredients to *Basic Quick Casserole* recipe.

Cabbage & Beef Casserole   25-30 minutes

1 1/3 cups (320 ml) regular ground
  beef
One 2 lb (1 kg) green cabbage,
  thinly sliced
1 small yellow onion, thinly
  sliced

1 cup (240 ml) *Fine Breadcrumbs
  (see page 246)*
1/2 cup (120 ml) hot water
1/4 cup (60 ml) instant skim milk
  powder

Add the above ingredients to *Basic Quick Casserole* recipe.

Potato & Beef Casserole   25 minutes

1 1/3 cups (320 ml) regular ground
  beef
5 cups (1200 ml) *refrigerated* precooked
  potatoes, peeled and sliced
1 large yellow onion, sliced

4 medium mushrooms, thinly
  sliced
1/2 cup (120 ml) hot water
1 cup (240 ml) canned
  ground tomatoes
1 tsp (5 ml) dried fine herbs

Add the above ingredients to *Basic Quick Casserole* recipe.

Moroccan Chicken Casserole   25-30 minutes

2/3 cup (160 ml) cooked chicken,
  finely chopped
1 cup (240 ml) *frozen* precooked
  chick-peas
1/2 cup (120 ml) *frozen* precooked
  lima beans
1 large carrots, thinly sliced
1 cup (240 ml) yellow onions, chopped
1 garlic clove, minced

5 cups (1200 ml) cooked
  couscous *(see page 189)*
1 cup (240 ml) canned diced
  tomatoes
1 cup (240 ml) hot tap water
1 tbsp (15 ml) dried parsley
1/4 tsp (1 ml) ground cloves
1/2 tsp (2 ml) coriander
1/4 tsp (1 ml) garlic powder

Add the above ingredients to *Basic Quick Casserole* recipe.

Sardines & Pasta Casserole   25-30 minutes

6 cups (1440 ml) cooked elbow
  macaroni or bucatini
About 7 oz/ 200 g sardines in oil
  or pacific jack mackerel
1/2 cup (120 ml) vegetable oil

1 cup (240 ml) yellow onion,
  finely chopped
2 tbsp (30 ml) *Fine Breadcrumbs*
  (see page 246)
Dash of saffron

Add the above ingredients to *Basic Quick Casserole* recipe. *Use only 1/2 cup
(120 ml) of water for this recipe.*

Vegetables & Meat Casserole   25-30 minutes

1 1/3 cups (320 ml) regular
  ground beef or finely diced
  cooked ham
2 garlic cloves, finely chopped
1 large yellow onion, chopped
2 cups (480 ml) *refrigerated* precooked potatoes, diced
2 celery stalks, sliced

2 cups (480 ml) sliced blanched
  carrots
1/2 tsp (2 ml) dry mustard
1/2 tsp (2 ml) ground pepper
2 tbsp (30 ml) instant skim milk
  powder

Add the above ingredients to *Basic Quick Casserole* recipe.

Penne-Hamburger Casserole   25-30 minutes

3 cups (720 ml) uncooked penne pasta
  (about 6 cups/1440 ml cooked)
1 1/3 cups (320 ml) regular
  ground beef or pork

2 tsp (10 ml) instant skim milk
  powder
2 tsp (10 ml) dried grated
  Parmesan cheese

1 garlic clove, finely chopped
1 large yellow onion, chopped
1 celery stalk, thinly sliced

1/2 tsp (2 ml) dried Italian
  herbs
2 small bay leaves

Add the above ingredients to *Basic Quick Casserole* recipe. *Discard bay leaves before serving.*

Spiced Potato-Meat Casserole   25 minutes

1 1/3 cups (320 ml) regular ground
  beef or very finely cubed
  marinated stewing beef
1 garlic clove, thinly sliced
6 large *refrigerated* precooked
  potatoes, peeled and sliced

1 cup (240 ml) canned diced
  tomatoes
2 small bay leaves
2 tsp (10 ml) dried thyme
1/4 tsp (1 ml) garlic powder

Add the above ingredients to *Basic Quick Casserole* recipe. *Use only 1/2 cup (120 ml) of water for this one and discard bay leaves before serving.*

Vegetables-Lentil Casserole   25-30 minutes

4 cups (960 ml) *frozen* precooked
  lentils
1 cup (240 ml) yellow onions, chopped
1 cup (240 ml) sliced fresh or blanched
  carrots

2 medium mushrooms, very thinly
  sliced
2 large *refrigerated* precooked
  potatoes, sliced
1 tbsp (15 ml) dried parsley

Add the above ingredients to *Basic Quick Casserole* recipe.

Vegetarian Lentil Casserole   25 minutes

1 medium yellow onion, chopped
1 garlic clove, minced
6 cup (1440 ml) precooked liard lentils
1/4 cup (60 ml) homemade cheese,
  crumbled

3/4 cup (180 ml) canned diced or
  whole tomatoes
1 tsp (5 ml) chili powder
1/4 tsp (1 ml) garlic powder

Add the above ingredients to *Basic Quick Casserole* recipe. *Use only 1/2 cup (120 ml) of water for this one.*

Concerning recipes calling for marinated stewing beef cubes...
See marinade for meat on page 247!

CONVERT CASSEROLES INTO STOVETOP DISHES!

Many casseroles can be converted into one-pan meal dishes by incorporating their ingredients into the Basic Meal-In-One-Pan *instructions. Divide amounts by four and proceed.*

There are many more main dishes in this book!

For many, more main course dishes see the chapters on pizza, restaurant foods, pasta, pies and pot pies, rice and side dishes with meat, poultry and fish variations.

FAST FOOD

HAMBURGERS

Low-cost versions of numerous hamburger styles that do taste (or almost) as if they're 100% beef.

Basic Hamburger 🐷   18-20 minutes

2 store-bought *bargain-packed* hamburger buns or home-baked buns *(see pages 107, 110)*
1/2 tbsp (7 ml) vegetable oil

2 or 4 *Simulated Beef Burger* patties *(see page 126)*
2 tsp (10 ml) margarine
Salt and pepper to taste

Toppings, dressing, and seasonings to taste!

Heat a **frying pan** or **skillet**, oil over a medium setting; add oil when hot. Meanwhile, in a **bowl**, mix the burger ingredients. Divide the mixture into 2 equal portions, and press down on wax paper to a diameter of about 4 inches (10 cm). Cook each side of patties about 5 minutes, with a **spatula** turn them once only and *do not* press on them. Toward the end of cooking, butter up the cut sides of buns, toast lightly in skillet. Alternately, place buns in skillet directly over patties, cover and steam them a few minutes. Alternately, toast buns in a **toaster oven** or **wide slotted toaster**. To serve, place toppings on top or below patties or half over and below *(see the following variations for more details). Ideally, the patties should be thawed from freezer and buns pre-baked and refrigerated if not using the bargain-pack store-bought ones. If using hamburger mayonnaise, it too should ready ahead of time.* **Makes 2 hamburgers of any style**

LITE! VERSION *Use lean beef, low-fat or fat-free dressings or mayonnaise, omit cheese and margarine!*

POPULAR HAMBURGER TOPPINGS

- ❑ *Hot pickled pepper rings*
- ❑ *Thinly sliced, diced or chopped yellow onions*
- ❑ *Thinly sliced dill pickles or olives*
- ❑ *Sprouted alfalfa, radish, or mustard seeds*

❑ *Shredded lettuce (in peak season only)*
❑ *Thinly sliced tomatoes (in peak season only)*
❑ *Processed cheese burger slice*
❑ *One pre-baked bacon slice (see page 26)*

POPULAR HAMBURGER DRESSINGS
❑ *Generic catsup*
❑ *Homemade Mayonnaise (see pages 70-2)*
❑ *Mustard (see page 246)*
❑ *Dijon mustard*
❑ *Salad or Slaw (see pages 59-61, 66)*
❑ *Any Vinaigrette (see pages 68-70)*
❑ *Hamburger Mayonnaise (see page 72)*

HAMBURGER VARIATIONS

Classic Hamburger   *18-20 minutes*

2 generic-brand *bargain* hamburger
     buns or home-baked buns *(pg. 107)!*
2 *Simulated Beef Burger(s) (pg. 126)!*
2 large but thin yellow onion slices
Use the above in *Basic Hamburger* recipe.

1/4 cup (60 ml) shredded
     iceberg lettuce *(in season)*
6 thin dill pickle slices
Mustard and ketchup to taste

SUB-VARIATIONS *For a **Cheese Hamburger,** add a
slice of processed cheddar cheese (from a 180 burger slice
pack), or cheese and a pre-toasted slice of bacon halved in
two for a **Bacon & Cheese Hamburger**!*

Fast Food Style Hamburger   *18-20 minutes*

Same as the above *Classic Hamburger* recipe with the
exception that, sesame buns are used, and the onion slices
must be separated into rings. Add a large but thin tomato
slice to each hamburger, and replace mustard with
homemade mayonnaise and generic ketchup.

Double Decker Style Hamburger   *18-20 minutes*

2 sesame seed buns as burger
     buns, each sliced twice to make
     three pieces *(see page 107)!*
4 thin *Simulated Beef Burger*
     (instead of two, see page 126)
2 slices of processed cheddar cheese
     (180 burger slice pack)

2 tsp (10 ml) finely diced yellow
     onion
1/2 cup (120 ml) chopped Iceberg
     lettuce *(in peak season only)*
A few very thin dill pickle slices
1/4 cup (60 ml) *Hamburger
     Mayonnaise (see page 72)*

Use the above in *Basic Hamburger* recipe. Exceptionally,
toast the sliced face of all buns using dry **frying pan** or
griddle. Prepare and assemble buns and other ingredients
while patties are cooking. Wrap assembled hamburger in wax
paper and microwave 15 seconds before serving.

ADDITIONAL HAMBURGER COMBINATIONS!

Thousands of hamburger combinations can be made using the numerous burger patty recipes in chapter on burgers. Toppings for buns like sesame or poppy seeds, cornmeal, and glazes with egg-wash, and oil, should be explored. Buns may also contain whole-wheat, multi-grains, sourdough, soda, corn or crusty bread. Alternately, make hamburger buns using Pita, Naan, bagels, kaiser buns, or English muffins (see bread-making chapter). Many sauces, dressings, mayonnaise, or spread-able cheeses may be used. Hamburger toppings like cooked sliced beets or raw radish, sprouts, or dressed fresh salads offer new taste potentials too.

HOT DOGS

The hot dog recipes are enough for two if accompanied with side orders of fries and pop.

Basic Hot Dogs   10-12 minutes

4 generic-brand beef or chicken wieners

**4 generic-brand wiener buns
    OR homemade** *Hot Dog Buns* **(see page 107)**
2 tsp (10 ml) margarine *(optional)*

Toppings, dressing, and seasonings to taste!

STEAMED HOT DOGS: In a **large saucepan**, place hot dog wieners and barely cover with hot tap water. Bring to a boil over the highest heat setting; lower to medium. Add a **steamer basket** or improvise and use a **sieve or colander**, add buns and cover. Steam a few minutes until done. *Alternately, microwave the wieners and buns to steam them, or wrap buns in aluminum or enclose between two pie pans in a hot oven until steamed.*

TOASTED HOT DOG: In a **large saucepan**, place hot dog wieners and barely cover with hot tap water. Bring to a boil over the highest heat setting; boil a few minutes until wieners are done. Meanwhile, using a **large frying pan (or griddle)** heated to a medium setting, melt margarine. Brown buns on both sides. Alternately, cook wieners on griddle too. **Makes 4 hot dogs**

LITE! VERSION *Buy low-fat wieners and omit margarine!*

HOT DOG VARIATIONS

Steamed Hot Dog   10 minutes

Use the steamed hot dog instructions in the *Basic Hot Dog* recipe. Dress with mustard, chopped onions, coleslaw, etc.

Toasted Hot Dog   12 minutes

Use the toasted hot dog instructions in the *Basic Hot Dog* recipe. Dress with mustard, chopped onions, coleslaw, etc.

Chili Dogs   10-15 minutes

Use the steamed hot dog instructions in the *Basic Hot Dog* recipe. Dress each dog with 1/8 cup (30 ml) of *Tomato & Meat Sauce* recipe *(see page 97).*

Corn Dogs (Pogo)   10-12 minutes

1 pound (454 g) generic-brand beef or chicken wieners *(one dozen)*

2 cups (480 ml) *Batter Mix (pg. 244)*
1 1/8-1 1/4 cups (270-300 ml) water
12 *bulk* wooden coffee stirrers

In a **deep bowl** or **jar**, combine batter *optional egg and fat)*. Stir until water; if too thin add more dry fryer or frying pan to about prepare wieners *(sticks must* and fried. *Wieners must* and rotate items in batter and drain off mix with cold tap water *(plus* smooth. *If too thick add more batter mix.* Heat the oil in deep 375°F (190°C). Meanwhile, *go in most of the way)* to be battered *not be wet, pat dry them if they are.* Dip batter until evenly coated. Remove from excess. Immerse them gradually one at a time into hot oil. Fry half a dozen at a time for about 3 minutes or till golden. *The inside wiener will be extremely hot!* Store refrigerated or frozen any leftover corn dogs. **Makes 12 corn dogs**

LITE! **VERSION** *Do not use the optional margarine (for batter), and try baking instead of frying them!*

POTATO FRIES

Basic Potato Fries   9-10 minutes

Preheat **deep-fat fryer** *(a least 5 minutes).*
2 cups (480 ml) or *6 oz/170 g* generic-brand
**   *frozen* potato fries *(regular, julienne,***
**   *or rippled)***

Place frozen fries in fryer basket and deep-fry 4 to 5 minutes or until golden brown. Drain with basket over fryer about a minute and serve at once. *Use as one of following variations.* Alternately, fry in pan or roast fries in oven. **Makes about 2 cups (480 ml), 2 average or 1 very large serving(s)**

POTATO FRIES VARIATIONS

French Fries   9-10 minutes

Same as the previous *Basic Potato Fries* recipe.

French Fries

Gravy & Fries   10-12 minutes

1/4 cup (60 ml) of instant sauce *(see page 141)*
Add the above to *Basic Potato Fries* recipe.

French-Canadian 'Poutine'   *11 minutes*

1/3 cup (80 ml) of instant sauce   1/3 cup (80 ml) pieces of firm unripen
(see page 141)   curd cheese or Mozzarella

Add above to *Basic Potato Fries* recipe. Using a **small bowl**, you must first mix
the curds with hot fries and top with hot sauce. *Fries and sauce must be very hot!*

For fried onion rings, see page 192.

SOFT DRINKS

*For convenience and savings, you can't beat pop in the 2
liters (quarts) plastic bottle format of generic brand. Often
times, the large supermarkets have well-known brand-
name pop that don't cost that much more. Even generic
brand cases of pop in cans will cost at least twice as much.
Alternately, brew or make your own and save even more.
Homemade soft drinks are fresher tasting and of better
quality. If you rebottle them in small bottles, you will avoid
the flatness from half-emptied large bottles.* **A typical
average serving would be 10 fl oz/270 ml**

For colas
*Serve from 2 liters/quarts bottles, rebottled, or make your own (see
pages 224-7).*

For uncolas
Serve from 2 liters/quarts bottles, rebottled, or make your own (see pages 224-7).

For ginger ales
Serve from 2 liters/quarts bottles, rebottled, or make your own (see pages 224-7).

For root beers
Serve from 2 liters/quarts bottles, rebottled, or make your own (see pages 224-7).

For other flavors
*Serve from 2 liters/quarts bottles, rebottled, or make your own (see
pages 224-7).*

COLD SUB SANDWICHES

Basic Cold Sub Sandwich 5 minutes

One 10" *Sub Bread (pg. 107)*   1 slice of cheese *(from 80 processed
   (pre-baked, semi-baked, or made)*   cheese sub slice pack, see pg. 21)*
   fresh from refrigerated dough)   *Filling & toppings sparingly to taste!*

Cut a "V" shape section off the submarine roll, in a way that is customary *(see ill.)*. Place the sub cheese slice in roll. *Add required cold ingredients or toppings for one of the variations.* Fold cold cuts once or twice for added thickness. ***Thaw small frozen portions of sliced cold cuts under running water.*** Top with condiments, season and dress to taste. Place "V" shaped section on garnished sub sandwich and serve. *Costs half a buck each to make!* **Makes 1 cold sub**

POPULAR COLD SUB SANDWICH TOPPINGS

- ❑ *Hot pickled pepper rings (minced)*
- ❑ *Thinly sliced onions*
- ❑ *Thinly sliced dill pickles*
- ❑ *Sliced green or black olives*
- ❑ *Shredded lettuce (in peak season only)*
- ❑ *Thinly sliced green peppers (in peak season only)*
- ❑ *Thinly sliced tomatoes (in peak season only)*

POPULAR COLD SUB DRESSINGS & SEASONINGS

- ❑ *Vegetable oil*
- ❑ *Homemade mayonnaise*
- ❑ *Mustard*
- ❑ *Dijon mustard*
- ❑ *Any salad dressing (see pages 68-70)*
- ❑ *Dried oregano or/and parsley*
- ❑ *Salt and pepper*

COLD SUB SANDWICH VARIATIONS

Sub Sandwich Supreme   *3 minutes*

3 thin slices of generic-brand   **1 thin slice of generic-brand**
     salami or pepperoni   **cooked ham**
2 thin slices of mock chicken
Add the above to the ingredients in *Basic Cold Sub Sandwich* recipe.

Tuna Delight Sub Sandwich   *3-5 minutes*

1 cup (240 ml) *Tuna & Rice Salad (see page 58)*
Add the above to the ingredients in *Basic Cold Sub Sandwich* recipe.

Exquisite Egg Sub   *3-8 minutes*

1 cup (240 ml) *Exquisite Egg Salad (see page 58)*
Add the above to the ingredients in *Basic Cold Sub Sandwich* recipe.

Far East Chicken Sub   *3-10 minutes*

1 cup (240 ml) *Far East Chicken Salad (see page 58)*
Add the above to the ingredients in *Basic Cold Sub Sandwich* recipe.

Turkey & Ham Sub   *3-5 minutes*

3 thin slices cooked ham   **3 thin slices precooked turkey**
Dijon mustard!   *French vinaigrette!*
Condiments to taste!
Add the above to the ingredients in *Basic Cold*
Sub Sandwich recipe.

HOT SUB SANDWICHES

Basic Hot Sub Sandwich   *8-10 minutes*

Stewing beef cubes that are very thinly sliced is our solution to low-cost sandwich steak. The large pack sub slices cut in two amounts to less than a dime for cheese. Homemade sub bread buns and dressings, and low-cost generic brand or homemade cold cuts amounts pretty much to the remainder of savings. Our steak and non-steak hot subs all cost well under a dollar.

One 10" *Sub Bread (see page 107)*   **One slice of cheese** *(processed cheese*
1 tbsp (15 ml) margarine   *sub slices, see page 21)*
Plus a variation filling and toppings!   **Some salad dressing** *(see pg. 68-70)*

Preheat toaster oven to 475ºF (245ºC). Slice submarine bread lengthwise, though not right through, in a way that is customary. Line the sub bread with a sub cheese slice placed lengthwise. *Alternately, use some thinly sliced non-processed cheese like Mozzarella or Cheddar.* Place

submarine roll in preheated toaster oven (or oven) for 5 minutes or until slightly toasted. Meanwhile, using a **cast iron pan** or **griddle**, melt margarine when surface gets hot over a medium-high heat. *Sauté ingredients for any of the following recipe variations like stewing beef slices (marinated or non-marinated), cold cut slices, green pepper and onion slices.* When ready, place the cheese in toasted roll add sautéed ingredients. To this, add **shredded lettuce** *(in peak season only)*, raw **thinly sliced onions**, a few **thin tomato slices** *(in peak season only),* plus seasoning and dressing to taste. Serve hot at once. *Stewing beef or pork cubes are used as an inexpensive and convenient replacement for sandwich steak commonly used in hot steak submarine sandwiches. Slice the cubes using a very sharp knife into thin sliced. For more flavor and tenderness, marinate them about one hour. Do this in advance, drain and store them uncooked refrigerated or 'Loose-Pack' frozen till needed, see pages 247, 31.* **Makes 1 sub**

LITE! **VERSION** *Use a non-stick skillet with little or no margarine and a little water. Use low-fat cheese and cold cuts when practical!*

HOT SUB SANDWICH VARIATIONS

Steak & Pepperoni Sub Sandwich   *8-10 minutes*

1/4 cup (60 ml) stewing beef or pork,   **3 thin slices of generic or home-**
   very thinly sliced *(marinated)*   **made pepperoni** *(or salami)*
Sauté the above ingredients and use as directed in *Basic Hot Sub Sandwich* recipe.

Steak & Green Pepper Sub
8-10 minutes

1/4 cup (60 ml) stewing beef or pork,
very thinly sliced

A quarter of a green bell pepper,
thinly sliced *(in season only)*
Several thin yellow onion slices

Sauté the above ingredients and use as directed in *Basic Hot Sub Sandwich* recipe.

Hot Bologna Submarine
7-8 minutes

5 or 6 slices of low-cost bologna

Sauté the above ingredient and use as directed in *Basic Hot Sub Sandwich* recipe.

Vegetarian Cheese Sub Sandwich
5-6 minutes

Another slice or two of cheese
A quarter of a green bell pepper,
thinly sliced,
Several thin yellow onion slices

1/2 cup (120 ml) shredded iceberg
lettuce
4 thin slices of tomatoes
Alfalafa sprouts *(optional)*

Sauté green pepper and onion only, follow the *Basic Hot Sub Sandwich* recipe.

Hot Sub Sandwich
7-8 minutes

2 thin slices of generic-brand pepperoni
or salami
Several thin yellow onion slices

2 thin slices of generic-brand
cooked ham
3 slices of bologna

Sauté the above ingredients and use as directed in *Basic Hot Sub Sandwich* recipe.

BURRITOS & TACOS

Burritos and tacos have never been cheaper to make. A couple of dimes each! Double or quadruple the recipe yield and turn it into a small production line for freezer purposes. Store them frozen wrapped in aluminum foil for an oven reheat, or in plastic wrap or sandwich bags for a microwave reheat. The time given assumes tortillas (or taco shells) and sauce are ready.

Basic Burritos & Tacos
12-15 minutes

Four 8-inch (20 cm) *Tortillas*
OR six 6-inch (15 cm) *Tortillas*
or *Taco Shells (pages 111-12)*
3/4 cup (180 ml) of a *Burrito-Taco*
Filling (see pages 176-7)

1-2 cup(s) (240-480 ml) *Spanish*
Rice (Instant) (see page 89)
1/4 tbsp (60 ml) *Cheese (Stretcher)*
Sauce or Yogurt Dressing
(see pages 69, 70, 142, 249)

Steam tortillas or tacos in a **steamer** *(or improvise one with a sieve, saucepan and lid)*. Alternately, steam them in a **plastic bag** in the **microwave** for about 30 seconds on high. Assemble your costume-made burrito or taco by first adding using a **spoon** a burrito-taco filling, followed by a rice filling, and topped by a cheese (stretcher) sauce or

sauce *(not necessarily containing yogurt).* For burritos, fold one side over filling. Then fold a small portion of the bottom upwards, and then finish rolling it up *(see illustration).* Make sure to tuck flap under the rolled up tortilla. For tacos, just scoop in the fillings. Serve hot with more rice and a salad, if desired. **Makes 4 or 6 burritos (or tacos)**

LITE! **VERSION** *Exclude oil when making tortillas or tacos, use the lite versions for the burrito-taco, rice, or sauce fillings!*

BURRITOS & TACOS VARIATIONS

Breakfast Burritos   *12-15 minutes*

Use a double portion of a Scrambled Eggs *or a single portion of an* Omelet *recipe (pages 76-7, 73-5)!*
No rice in these!

1/4 cup (60 ml) *Cheese (Stretcher)* Sauce *(Cheddar)* **or a** *Yogurt* Dressing **or a Mayonnaise** recipe *(pages 142, 249, 69, 70-2)*
1 pork breakfast sausage, chopped

Use above in *Basic Burritos & tacos* recipe. Cook chopped sausage with eggs.

Mexican Beef Burritos   *12-15 minutes*

Use Beef Filling *recipe (see page 176)!*
1 cup (240 ml) Spanish Rice *(see page 89)*

1/2 cup (120 ml) shredded lettuce *(optionally in peak season only)*
1/4 cup (60 ml) *Cheese (Stretcher)* Sauce *(see pages 142 or 249)*

Use the above in *Basic Burritos & tacos* recipe.

Classic Chicken Burritos   *12-15 minutes*

Use Chicken Filling *(page 176)!*
1 cup (240 ml) Spanish Rice *(see page 89)*

1/2 cup (120 ml) *frozen* precooked pinto beans
1/4 cup (60 ml) Cheese (Stretcher) Sauce *(see pages 142 or 249)*

Use the above in *Basic Burritos & tacos* recipe. Boil the bean at least 5 minutes and season with salt and pepper.

Vegetarian Rice & Beans Burritos   *12-15 minutes*

Use Vegetarian Bean Filling *(pg. 176)!*
2 cups (480 ml) Spanish Rice *(see page 89)*

1/4 cup (60 ml) Cheese (Stretcher) Sauce *(see page 142)*

Use the above in *Basic Burritos & tacos* recipe.

Beef Soft Tacos   *12-15 minutes*

Use Beef Filling *(see page 176)!*

1/2 cup (120 ml) shredded lettuce

1 cup (240 ml) *Spanish Rice*   *(optionally in peak season only)*
  (see page 89)   1/4 cup (60 ml) *Cheese (Stretcher)*
                                              Sauce (see page 142)

Use the above in *Basic Burritos & tacos* recipe.

SUB-VARIATION *Try some of the above burritos fillings in crisp or steam-softened tacos!*

BURRITO & TACO FILLINGS

Basic Burrito & Taco Filling   *10-12 minutes*

1-2 tbsp (15-30 ml) vegetable oil
1/4 cup (60 ml) regular ground beef
  (or pork), or precooked poultry
4-8 tbsp (60-120 ml) of fillers like rolled-oats, tofu, or precooked legumes!
  (see variations for fillers)
1/4 cup (60 ml) minced yellow onion

1/2 cup (120 ml) hot tap water
1/2 tbsp (7 ml) all-purpose flour
1/8 tsp (1/2 ml) table salt
1/8 tsp (1/2 ml) onion powder
1/16 tsp (1/4 ml) garlic powder
Dash of cayenne pepper

Heat a **frying pan** or **skillet** over a high setting. After a couple of minutes lower heat to medium-high and add oil, meat *(if any)*, and minced onion *(plus ingredients and seasoning for a recipe variation)*. Cook until ground meat has lost its pink color and onions are transparent, about 3-4 minutes. Dissolve flour in water; add water/flour mixture and any remaining ingredient for a recipe variation. Lower heat to medium and simmer another few minutes or until thickened. **Makes almost 1 cup (240 ml) or 4-6 burrito or taco fillings**

LITE! VERSION *Omit or reduce amount of vegetable oil and use a non-stick skillet with lower heat settings, and if affordable, leaner beef or pork!*

BURRITO & TACO FILLING VARIATIONS

Beef Filling   *10-12 minutes*

Use regular ground beef!
1/8 tsp (1/2 ml) paprika
1/2 tsp (2 ml) chili powder
3-4 tbsp (45-60 ml) ground tomatoes

2-3 tbsp (30-45 ml) *'Quick'* or
  'Regular' rolled oats *(not instant)*
3-4 tbsp (45-60 ml) *Brown Tofu*,
  mashed or un-pressed *(pg. 240)*

Use and add the above in *Basic Burrito & Taco Filling* recipe.

SUB-VARIATIONS *Substitute rolled oats with 1/4 cup (60 ml) of mashed tofu, or tofu before pressing (or high-yield pulp tofu), or precooked kidney or pinto beans. Try replacing beef with ground pork or chopped homemade sausage!*

Chicken Filling   *10-12 minutes*

Use precooked chopped chicken or turkey!
1/4 tsp (1 ml) soy sauce

1/2 tsp (2 ml) dark brown sugar
1/4 tsp (1 ml) chili powder
1 extra-large egg white, unbeaten
  but scrambled *(optional)*

Use and add the above in *Basic Burrito & Taco Filling* recipe.

SUB-VARIATIONS *Substitute optional egg white with 1/4 cup (60 ml) of mashed tofu or high-yield pulp tofu (page 240), or precooked plain beans!*

Vegetarian Bean Filling   *10-12 minutes*

Use 1/2 cup (120 ml) frozen precooked   1 tbsp (15 ml) *'Quick'* **rolled oats**
    pinto beans (no meat in this one)!   1/4 cup (60 ml) **canned ground**
1/8 tsp (1/2 ml) **paprika**   **tomatoes OR**
1 tsp (5 ml) **chili powder**   2 tbsp (30 ml) **tomato paste**

Use and add the above in *Basic Burrito & Taco Filling* recipe.
SUB-VARIATIONS *Substitute with kidney beans, chickpeas, or lentils!*

MORE TORTILLA (& TACO) WRAPPER COMBOS!

*Try a multitude of stuffing combinations using
various rice, egg, sauce (or dressing),
sausage,meatloaf, meatballs, side-dish,
or salad recipes!*

OTHER FAST FOOD FAVORITES

Club Sandwich   *5-6 minutes*

3 slices of generic-brand *(bargain)*   2 thin slices ripe, firm tomato
    or homemade white bread, toasted   *(inexpensively in season)*
1 1/2 tbsp (22 ml) *Homemade Mayo-*   1/4 cup (60 ml) **shredded lettuce**
    nnaise (see pages 70-1)   *(inexpensively in season)*
3 tsp (15 ml) margarine *(optional)*   2 pre-toasted *refrigerated*
3 tbsp (45 ml) chopped *refrigerated*   bacon slices, chopped
    precooked chicken   Salt and pepper to taste

Spread mayonnaise and optional margarine on one side of each slice of
toast. Cover with chicken, and cover with a slice of toast. Add
remaining ingredients *(reheat bacon if desired)*, season and
cover with last slice of toast. Diagonally cut in quarters
and serve with coleslaw, fries and pop *(see pages 60,
170-1, 224-6)*. **Makes one**

Grilled Cheese Sandwich   *7-8 minutes*

4 slices of generic enriched white   2 slices of processed cheddar cheese
    sandwich bread or *Sandwich*   *(from a 180 burger slice pack)*
    Bread Loaf (see page 107)   1 tsp (5 ml) **margarine**

Heat a **frying pan or skillet**, over the highest setting for 2
minutes. Lower heat to medium and add 1 tsp (5 ml) of
margarine at a time; when melted add the sandwich. Press it
down with a **spatula** during grilling. Do the same for each side of the
sandwich so that cheese melts and each side golden brown. **Makes two**

VARIATIONS *Make a* **Grilled Cheese & Bacon Sandwich** *by adding a pre-
toasted slice of bacon cut in two. Or add one item like thin slice of ham, onion, or
tomato!*

LITE! **VERSION** *Use a non-stick skillet and omit or reduce amount of margarine.
Use low fat processed cheese!*

Hot Chicken Sandwich   5-6 minutes

4 slices of generic sandwich bread
    or homemade bread, toasted
1/3-1/2 cup (80-120 ml) *refrigerated*
    precooked chicken or turkey

2/3 cup (160 ml) *frozen* precooked
    whole green peas
1 cup (240 ml) Instant Hot
    Chicken Gravy *(see page 141)*

Place one toast in each of two plates. Cover with chicken, and cover with a slice of toast. Pour the hot sauce and top with the green peas *(thawed in hot water that was boiled)*. Serve with a side order of French Fries, Cole Slaw, and Pop *(see pages 60, 170-1, 224-6)*. **Makes two sandwiches**

Sloppy Joe's   6-16 minutes

2 generic-brand *bargain-pack* hamburger
    buns or home-baked buns, each
    bun split and toasted *(page 107)*

1 cup (240 ml) Tomato & Meat
    Sauce *(see page 97-8)*

Reheat sauce if refrigerated and serve in hamburger buns. *Sauce is either made from scratch or reheated from refrigerator.* **Makes two**

Pizzas
See chapter on pizza, page 179!

Pastas
See chapter on pasta, page 93!

Chinese Food
See chapters on rice and side dishes, etc.!

Middle-Eastern Food
See couscous, Middle-Eastern rice dishes, falafel burgers, etc.!

Fried Chicken Meal
See Coated Fried Chicken, page 140!

Pizza

Working within certain monetary and equipment constraints, the following techniques come as close as possible to making pizza the professional way. They rival those baked in large brick-lined ovens. You can even make a first-rate medium-size all-dressed pizza for about one dollar, see Frugal All-Dressed Pizza *recipe on page 186.*

PIZZA DOUGH

The all-purpose flour we used for the pizza dough recipes was bleached. Although unbleached flour gives a better flavor and quality, the bleached flour is far cheaper.

Basic Pizza Dough   1 1/2 hours

This is a New York style pizza dough which is lean and requires no oil. It is the least expensive to make and requires less yeast.

1 tsp (5 ml) granulated sugar
1 1/4 cup (270 ml) warm tap water
1 tsp (5 ml) *refrigerated or frozen/thawed fresh yeast (see pages 22, 102)*
1/2 tsp (2 ml) lecithin *(see pages, 22, 102)*

3 1/2 cup (840 ml) bleached all-purpose flour
1 tsp (5 ml) table salt
1/16 tsp (1/4 ml) ascorbic acid crystals *(see page 22)*

In a **large mixing bowl**, dissolve sugar and fresh yeast in all of the warm tap water 110-115°F (43-47°C). Using a **plastic mixing spoon**, combine all of the flour and salt *(plus any additional ingredient(s) if making one of the variations)* with the liquid. Now turn the dough out onto a lightly floured surface. Knead the dough by working and pulling it and repeatedly folding it over. Knead it energetically for 4 to 5 minutes until it feels smooth and springy. No more, no less. Lightly oil the pieces of dough with a bit of vegetable oil using oiled hands. *This prevents a crust from forming during the initial rise.* Place the dough in a conductive **metal bowl**, covered with with **plastic wrap**, and let oven-rise in oven at 90-100°F (32-38°C), see page 104. Let it rise one hour and

HAND KNEADING

15 minutes until doubled in volume. After the initial rise, punch down and deflate it. Either shape it to make pizza *(see page 184)*, or refrigerate or freeze by placing it in storage plastic bags. If you are making pizza(s) immediately with the dough, keep in mind that you must give it a final rise for 45 minutes after shaping the dough but without the toppings. *If you don't intend to bake a pizza within the 2*

hours following the first rising, punch it down store refrigerated in a covered bowl (or zipper bag) till needed. Shape it to make a variety of pizza(s). Depending if you're making one extra large or two medium pizzas make one ball of dough or divide it in two. Place the dough on a lightly floured surface and dust the top of the dough

too. Dust the rolling pin and roll it out in a circle about 1/4 inch *(.64 cm)* thick. Using your knuckles *(see ill.)*, stretch the inside portion of the pizza dough, rotate as you're stretching and stop when it's stretched enough. Pick it up by the rim using both hands and make it rotate *(see ill.)*. Its own weight will stretch it even more. Continue until it's at least the needed diameter, which should take about 30 seconds. Keep in mind that the outer rim of the dough should be much thicker than the inside area *(see ill.)*. In **one 17-inch (43 cm) or**

two 12-inch (30 cm) nonstick pizza pan(s), place the dough and adjust it to the diameter of pan(s). The adjusting is usually done by pulling back the over-stretched dough to suit the pan or gives it the size you want it to be if that size happens to be smaller than the pan. For square or rectangular pizzas, use the same method but work towards a square or rectangular shape. For deep-dish pan pizzas *(see ill.)*, place the stretched dough in oiled deep pan(s) and using fingers make a ridge about 1 inch (2.5 cm) high all around the rim resting against the pan's rim wall. *If all fails, simply shape it entirely using a rolling pin!* Regardless

of the shape you give your pizza(s), once its shaped and in the pan it must be allowed to rise a final (second) time for 45 minutes before adding the toppings, see page 184 for further instructions. *You can't beat refrigerated dough as pizza dough, see page 181!* **Makes 1 extra-large (16 to 17 inches) or 2 medium- size (12-inch) pizza dough or 3 medium-size (12-inch) super-thin pizza dough or 4 mini (8-inch) pizza dough**

PIZZA DOUGH VARIATIONS

Whole-Wheat Pizza Dough   1 1/2 hours

1 3/4 cups ((420 ml) whole wheat flour
Or use the following…
3 tbsp (45 ml) *bulk* wheat germ
3 tbsp (45 ml) *bulk* wheat bran
Replace the same amount of all-purpose flour with either the whole-wheat flour, or wheat germ and bran *(blender ground)* in *Basic Pizza Dough* recipe.

Authentic Pizza Dough   *1 1/2 hours*

1 tbsp (15 ml) granulated sugar
(instead of 1 tsp/5 ml)

1/4 cup (60 ml) olive or vegetable oil
(if using olive oil, use extra-virgin)

Use more sugar and replace 2 tbsp (30 ml) of water with oil. Substitute the bleached all-purpose flour with either semolina, bread, or unbleached all-purpose flour or try a combination in the *Basic Pizza Dough* recipe.

Cornmeal Pizza Dough   *1 1/2 hours*

1 tbsp (15 ml) granulated sugar
(instead of 1 tsp/5 ml)

1/4 cup (60 ml) vegetable oil
1 cup (240 ml) yellow cornmeal
(replaces same amount of flour)

Use more sugar and add the oil. Substitute same amount of the bleached all-purpose flour with yellow cornmeal in the *Basic Pizza Dough* recipe.

OTHER PIZZA DOUGH

Refrigerated (Bread) Pizza Dough   *2 minutes*
When it comes to pizza-making, you can't beat this for convenience and quality.

Use the refrigerated bread dough *(see pages 99, 105)*, the same amount that is required for an average loaf of bread or about 3 1/2 cups (840 ml) deflated. Follow shaping, final rise and baking instructions outlined in *Basic Pizza Dough* recipe. **The recipe on page 102 makes the most convenient and inexpensive pizza dough!** **Makes dough for 2 medium or 4 small pizzas** **VARIATION** *Try with **Sourdough** refrigerated dough (pages 100-1)!*

Quick (Non-Yeast) Pizza Dough   *5-6 minutes*
This recipe comes close to the readymade 'Pizza Crust' type dough sold refrigerated in a tubular packaging.

1 3/4 cups (420 ml) cold tap water
1/2 cup (120 ml) *bulk* instant skim
  milk powder
1/8 cup (30 ml) white vinegar
4 cups (960 ml) *bleached* all-purpose
  flour

1/2 tsp (2 ml) *bulk* baking soda
1 tsp (5 ml) generic baking powder
1 tsp (5 ml) table salt
1/16 tsp (1/4 ml) ascorbic acid
  crystals
1/4 cup (60 ml) low-cost margarine

In a **small mixing bowl**, combine water, milk powder, and vinegar; let sit up to 5 minutes till slightly thickened. In a **large mixing bowl**, combine all remaining dry ingredients and top with the unmelted margarine. Add the recipe-grade sour milk mixture to it and mix with a **spoon** or **electric mixer**. Quickly remove from bowl and shape into two or four round-flat lumps of dough about an inch (2.5 cm) thick on a lightly floured surface. Lightly flour the top of this dough and roll out to the diameter of the pizza pan. Place in pans while adjusting the size. Because this quick dough contains much more water than yeast pizza dough recipe, you cannot manipulate it in the air or stretch it. It's more suitable for small pizzas. Add toppings and bake at 425°F (215°C) instead of 500°F(260°C) in oven (center rack) 15 minutes. **Makes 4 small 8-9" (20-22 cm) pizza dough**

TOMATO PIZZA SAUCES

Basic Tomato Pizza Sauce 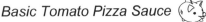   *30-50 minutes*

2 tbsp (30 ml) vegetable oil
1 garlic clove, minced
3/4 cup (180 ml) canned diced tomatoes
1 cup (240 ml) canned tomato juice
1/2 cup (l20 ml) can ground tomatoes
1 1/2 cups (360 ml) hot tap water

2 tbsp (30 ml) all-purpose flour
1/8 tsp (1/2 ml) garlic powder
1 tsp (5 ml) dried oregano
1/4 tsp (1 ml) dried basil
1/2 tsp (2 ml) chili powder
Salt and pepper to taste

If you're short on time, try the Non-cooked Pizza Sauce, page 183! In a **large frying pan** or **skillet**, sauté garlic and spices in the oil over a medium-high heat for a few minutes. Add flour and mix well with oil; then add the tomato products. Bring to a simmer, lower heat and let it simmer partially covered for about 15-20 minutes. A **splashguard** or **simmer plate** may be useful here. All pizza sauces may be stored in the refrigerator for several days or frozen up to 3 months. Better to reheat or bring to room temperature before using. **Makes enough sauce for 8 medium (12-inch) round flat pizzas or about 2 2/3 cups (640 ml)**

TOMATO PIZZA SAUCE VARIATIONS

Authentic Pizza Sauce   *50 minutes*
This sauce is more expensive than the basic recipe (almost twice the cost) but is better.

3 1/2 cups (840 ml) canned diced tomatoes
     (instead of 1 cup (240 ml)
Use the above but omit flour, water, tomato juice and chili powder in *Basic Pizza Sauce* recipe. Simmer up to 40 minutes on a low setting instead of 15-20 on medium.

Mexican-Style Pizza Sauce   *25-30 minutes*

2 medium yellow onions, finely chopped
1 garlic clove, minced *(additional)*
1 cup (240 ml) regular ground beef
1/4 tsp (1 ml) garlic powder *(additional)*

1/4 cup (240 ml) all-purpose flour *(additional)*
1 1/2 tbsp (22 ml) chili powder *(additional)*
1 tsp (5 ml) ground cumin
1 tsp (5 ml) paprika

Add the above to *Basic Pizza Sauce* recipe.

Chicago-Style Pizza Sauce   *25-30 minutes*

1 garlic clove, minced *(additional)*
1/4 tsp (1 ml) garlic powder *(additional)*

1 tsp (5 ml) dried oregano *(additional)*

Add the above to *Basic Pizza Sauce* recipe.

OTHER TOMATO PIZZA SAUCES

Non-cooked Tomato Sauce   1 minute

It actually is, we think, the best pizza sauce in the entire chapter. And convenient!

1/3 cup (80 ml) canned ground tomatoes	1/16 tsp (1/4 ml) chili powder
1/3 cup (80 ml) canned diced tomatoes, lightly mashed	1/16 tsp (1/4 ml) *Worcestershire-Style Sauce (see page 243)*
1/4 tsp (1 ml) dried oregano	Dash of garlic powder

In a **small bowl**, combine above ingredients. Use as pizza sauce under toppings.
Makes enough sauce for 1 extra-large pizza or 2/3 cup (160 ml)
VARIATIONS *Substitute the canned ground and diced tomatoes with 5/8 cup (150 ml) of canned diced tomatoes, 1 tbsp (15 ml) tomato paste, oregano, and garlic powder. Omit the other ingredients. For a **Plain Tomato Sauce**, use canned ground and diced tomatoes only (with salt and pepper), forget the rest!*

NON-TOMATO PIZZA SAUCES

For spiced pepper sauce, see pages 143-4
For onion sauce, see page 144

PIZZA SHAPES OR TYPES

- ❑ *Conventional round pizza*
- ❑ *Super-thin round pizza*
- ❑ *Deep-dish round pan pizza*
- ❑ *Turnover semi-round pizza (calzone)*
- ❑ *Rectangular or square pizza*
- ❑ *Deep-dish rectangular or square pan pizza*
- ❑ *Mini, triangular, or odd-shaped pizza*

'MINI PIZZA'

POPULAR PIZZA TOPPINGS

- ❑ *Thinly sliced generic-brand or homemade pepperoni, salami, etc.*
- ❑ *Fresh grated generic-brand Mozzarella or Cheddar cheese*
- ❑ *Very thinly sliced green or yellow sweet bell pepper*
- ❑ *Very thinly sliced mushrooms*
- ❑ *Mozzarella Cheese Stretcher (see page 249)*
- ❑ *Sliced green or black olives*
- ❑ *Finely sliced or chopped yellow onion*
- ❑ *Sliced or chopped fresh vegetables*
- ❑ *New age style toppings like fresh white (crumbled) cheeses, sprouts, chopped chicken, etc.*

PIZZA

The time given is based on the assumption that the dough is not ready but the sauce is ready to be used. If sauce isn't ready, use the Non-cooked Tomato Sauce *recipe on page 183, you'll be surprised how good it is.*

Basic Pizza   1/3-2 1/2 hours

Choose a pizza dough recipe or use the one suggested in a pizza recipe variation!
Choose a pizza sauce recipe 2/3 cups/180 ml or the one suggested in a pizza recipe variation!

Choose a shredded cheese or cheese stretcher 1 cup/240 ml
Choose your own toppings or those from a variation!
Use 1 tbsp (15 ml) vegetable oil to drizzle pizza!

ASSEMBLING PIZZA: Once the dough is properly placed in a **pizza pan** (or on **pizza screen**) allow about 45 minutes for the final rise. Failing to do so may result in a poorly risen crust. *Refrigerated dough may come in handy here!* Using a **measuring cup**, place 1/3 cup (80 ml) of tomato sauce on each medium pizza, or 2/3 cups (320 ml) for a round extra-large pizza, in center of dough. Spoon outwards the sauce to about one-inch (2.5 cm) from the outer rim. If making an all-dressed pizza, add the slices of pepperoni second. Third, comes the grated cheese and/or cheese stretcher. Then top with the thinly sliced vegetables like bell pepper, mushrooms, onions, etc. Finally, evenly drizzle the pizza with the oil. *Some pizzas have a combination of ingredients that do not include sauce, cheese, or vegetables.*

BAKING PIZZA: Preheat oven to 500°F (260°C) about 5 minutes before placing the assembled pizza in it. Place the pizza pan on either, on the middle oven rack position. *Never place the pizza(s) lower or higher than the middle of oven.* Only use one oven rack when baking pizzas, either using two medium round pans, or one extra large pizza pan. Baking sheets suit rectangular pizzas well. To bake pizzas properly and professional, use **non-stick dull metal pans**. Conventional pizzas should be baked about 8 to 10 minutes. Super-thin crust pizzas will take a couple of minutes less. Deep-dish pan pizzas or 'calzone' may take up to 15 minutes or more. Always set timer to 1 or 2 minutes less than required time and watch the color of crust as to avoid over-baking. When ready, optionally brush some vegetable oil on pizza rim when baked but still in pan(s). Let cool in pan(s) about 5 minutes covered with another pizza pan or plastic sheet if a softer crust is desired. Remove from pan(s) to a cutting board or serving platter. Cut each pizza into 6 or 8 slices using a **pastry-pizza cutter**. **Makes 1 extra-large (16 to 17 inches/42 cm) or 2 medium-size (12-inch/30 cm) pizza(s)or 3 medium-size super-thin pizzas or 4 to 8 mini pizzas**

LITE! VERSION *Use the basic pizza dough as is, with no oil or shortening. Cook pizza sauce in a non-stick skillet or saucepan with very little or no oil. Use only low-fat cheese, low-fat pepperoni, or low-fat sausages as pizza toppings!*

RE-HEATING LEFTOVER PIZZA: *Place leftover pizza in dull metal pan, for frozen pizza bake at 275°(135°C) 12-15 minutes, or 7-8 minutes if refrigerated.*

PIZZA VARIATIONS

New York Pizza   *30-35 minutes*

*Use Basic Pizza Dough (shaped
    as 1 or 2 round pizza(s))!*
2/3 cup (180 ml) *Authentic Pizza
    Sauce (see page 182)*

TOPPINGS:
1/4 lb (110 g) large or small
    pepperoni, very thinly sliced
1 cup (240 ml) generic Mozzarella
    cheese, loosely grated
2 medium mushrooms, very
    thinly sliced
Quarter green bell pepper, very
    thinly sliced

Use the above as outlined in *Basic Pizza* recipe.

Chicago-Style Pizza   *35-40 minutes*

*Use Cornmeal Pizza Dough (to
    accommodate 1 or 2 deep-dish
    round pan pizzas, page 181)!*
2/3 cup (180 ml) *Chicago-Style or
    Basic Pizza Sauce (page 182)*
2 tbsp (30 ml) vegetable oil
    (to brush and drizzle)

TOPPINGS:
One Italian sausage, removed
    from casing and finely
    broken apart *(do not slice it)*
3/4 cup (180 ml) generic Mozzarella
    cheese, loosely grated
2 tbsp (30 ml) dried grated
    Parmesan cheese
Dash of dried parsley

Use the above as outlined in *Basic Pizza* recipe except that Mozzarella cheese is
place directly on dough, then cover with tomato sauce and toppings. Drizzle
evenly with half of the oil. Use **two 9-inch round cake
pans** or **one 15-inch round deep-dish pan.** Brush
remaining half of the oil on pizza crust when
baked but still in pan(s). Remove from pan(s) to
a cutting board or tray, slice and serve
immediately.

Mexican-Style Pizza   *30-35 minutes*
This pizza is chili on a crust covered with Cheddar cheese and chopped onions.

*Use Cornmeal Pizza Dough (shaped
    as a 2 deep-dish pan pizzas)!*
1 cup (240 ml) *Mexican-Style
    Pizza Sauce (see page 182)* or
    Chunky Salsa-Style Dip (pg. 116)
1 cup (240 ml) shredded yellow
    Cheddar cheese or *Cheese
    (Stretcher) Sauce (Cheddar
    flavored, see page 142)*

2 tbsp (30 ml) vegetable oil
    (to brush and drizzle)
1/2 cup (120 ml) yellow onion,
    minced

Use the above as sole ingredients, assemble and bake
pizza as outlined in *Basic pizza* recipe.

Traditional Tomato Pizza    *35-45 minutes*

Use Basic, Authentic, Instant, or
   Sourdough Pizza Dough (shaped
   as 1 large or 2 medium rectangular
   pizzas)!
2-3 cups (480-720 ml) *Authentic*
   Pizza Sauce (see page 182)
1/4 cups (60 ml) *vegetable oil*
   (to brush and drizzle)

Use the above as sole ingredients, assemble and bake pizza as outlined in *Basic pizza* recipe. *Its better to bake this one at 375ºF(190ºC) for about 20 minutes.*

SUB-VARIATION *For a* **Fast Tomato Pizza** *don't precook the tomato sauce, instead follow directions for the* Non-cooked Tomato Sauce *recipe or its variation on page 183!*

Tomato & Cheese Pizza 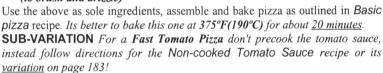   *30-35 minutes*

Use Basic, Authentic, Quick, or
   Sourdough Pizza Dough (shaped
   as 1 large or 2 medium round
   pizzas, see pages 179-81, 100)!

1 2/3 cups (320 ml) *Basic Pizza*
   Sauce (see page 182)
2 tbsp (30 ml) *vegetable oil*
   (to brush and drizzle)
1 cup (240 ml) *Mozzarella cheese,*
   loosely grated

Use the above as sole ingredients, assemble and bake pizza as outlined in *Basic pizza* recipe.

'Calzone' Pizza   *35-40 minutes*

Use Basic, Authentic, Quick, or
   Sourdough Pizza Dough (shaped
   as 4 small or 2 medium folded
   pizzas, see pages 179-81, 100)!

Use any sauce or toppings as
   calzone pizza filling!
2 tbsp (30 ml) *vegetable oil*
   (to brush and drizzle)

Use the above as sole ingredients, fill, fold and seal; bake pizza as outlined in *Basic pizza* recipe. Do not slice or cut in two. *Bake calzones for 15 minutes!*

Frugal All-Dressed Pizza   *30-35 minutes*

This is the recipe that will make a quality medium all-dressed pizza for a buck.

Use Basic Pizza Dough or Refri-
   gerated (Bread) Pizza Dough
   (shaped as 2 medium pizzas)!
2/3 cup (180 ml) *Basic Pizza*
   Sauce or Non-cooked
   Tomato Sauce
   (see pages 181-3)

TOPPINGS:
About 1/4 lb (100 g) *low-cost* **pepperoni,**
   very thinly sliced *(or homemade)*
1/4 cup (60 ml) generic Mozzarella
   cheese, grated
1 cup (240 ml) *Mozzarella*
   Cheese Stretcher (see page 249)
1 medium mushroom, sliced paper thin

**6 paper thin slices of green bell pepper
OR several very thin slices of yellow
onion, with rings separated**

Use the above as sole ingredients, assemble and bake pizza as outlined in *Basic pizza* recipe. *Serve a large pizza slice with a side order of fries or chips, & pop!*

Vegetarian Pizza   *35-40 minutes*

*Use Basic Pizza Dough (shaped
as 1 large or 2 medium round
pizzas)!*
2/3 cup (180 ml) *Basic Pizza
Sauce* or *Non-cooked
Tomato sauce (pages181-3)*

TOPPINGS:
1/2 cup (120 ml) *Homemade Firm
Tofu,* shredded
1/2 cup (120 ml) generic **Mozzarella
cheese, loosely grated**
1/2 cup (120 ml) *Mozzarella Cheese
Stretcher (optional, see page 249)*
**2 medium mushrooms, very thinly
sliced**
**1 tbsp (15 ml) green or black pitted
sliced olives, minced**
Small yellow onion, very thinly sliced
2/3 cup (160 ml) *frozen* **whole green
peas** *(thawed in hot water)*

Use the above as sole ingredients, assemble and bake pizza as outlined in *Basic pizza* recipe. Don't brush or drizzle oil on this pizza.
SUB-VARIATIONS *Try other fresh vegetables when inexpensively in their peak season like sliced green or red bell pepper, broccoli, asparagus, squash, etc.!*

Fresh Tomato Pizza   *30-35 minutes*

*Use Basic Pizza Dough (Shaped
as 1 large or 2 medium round
pizza, see page 179)!*
2 tbsp (30 ml) **vegetable oil**
(to brush and drizzle)

TOPPINGS:
**4 medium fresh ripe tomatoes,
thinly sliced** *(peak season only)*
1/4 tsp (1 ml) **garlic powder**
2 garlic cloves, thinly sliced
1 tsp (5 ml) dried oregano
Salt and pepper to taste

Use the above ingredients only and prepare as outlined in *Basic pizza* recipe.

Fast All-Dressed Pizza   *20 minutes*
With this recipe you can make a decent all-dressed pizza in about 20 minutes.

*Use Quick (Non-yeast) Pizza Dough
or Refrigerated (Bread) Pizza
Dough (shaped as 1 large,
2 medium, or 4 small pizzas,
see pages 99, 102, 105, 179)*
2/3 cup (180 ml) *Non-cooked
Tomato Sauce (see page 183)*

TOPPINGS:
**1/4 lb (110 g) large generic-brand
pepperoni, very thinly sliced**
**1 cup (240 ml) generic Mozzarella
cheese, loosely shredded**
2 medium mushrooms, sliced thinly
**Quarter green bell pepper, very
thinly sliced**

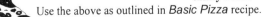 Use the above as outlined in *Basic Pizza* recipe.

NON-TOMATO PIZZA

French Onion Pizza   30-35 minutes

Use Basic, Cornmeal, Quick, or
    Sourdough Pizza Dough (shaped
    as 1 large or 2 medium rectangular
    pizza(s) see pages 179-81, 100)!

1 1/3 cups (320 ml) Onion
    Sauce (see page 144)
1/4 cups (60 ml) vegetable oil
    (to brush and drizzle)

Use the above as sole ingredients, assemble and bake pizza as outlined in Basic pizza recipe.

Thailand-Style Pizza   30-35 minutes

Use Basic, Cornmeal, Instant, or
    Sourdough Pizza Dough (shaped
    as 1 large or 2 medium round
    pizza(s) see pages 179-81, 100)!
2 tbsp (30 ml) vegetable oil
    (to brushing and drizzle)

TOPPINGS:
1/2 cup (120 ml) Mozzarella
    cheese, loosely grated
1/2 cup (120 ml) Queso Blanco
    cheese (see page 237)
1/2 cup (120 ml) precooked
    chopped chicken
1/4 cup (60 ml) peanuts, coarse
    chopped in blender
1 medium carrot, finely
    julienne or shredded
1/2 cup (120 ml) bean sprouts
1 green onion, thinly sliced

Use the above as sole ingredients, assemble and bake pizza as outlined in Basic pizza recipe.

Fresh Vegetable Pizza   30-35 minutes

Use Basic, Cornmeal, Quick, or
    Sourdough Pizza Dough (shaped
    as 1 large or 2 medium round
    pizza(s), see pages 179-81, 100)!
2 tbsp (30 ml) vegetable oil
    (to brush and drizzle)

TOPPINGS:
1/2 cup (120 ml) Mozzarella
    cheese, loosely shredded
1/2 cup (120 ml) Queso Blanco
    cheese (see page 237)
About 2 cups (480 ml) fresh
    vegetables like broccoli,
    green onions, squash, etc.

Use the above as sole ingredients, assemble and bake pizza as outlined in Basic pizza recipe. Vegetables that are not low cost staples should be purchased when inexpensively in season only!

There are hundreds, if not thousands of pizza combinations you can make using the information in this chapter...so have fun!

SIDE DISHES

Side dishes as opposed to main dishes are generally lighter and complementary, and quite often do not contain meat, poultry or fish. All the recipes in this chapter are stovetop, fast to make and very inexpensive. Many of the dishes are grain dishes; likewise, most rice and potato dishes are side dishes.

COUSCOUS

Basic Plain Couscous   *8-9 minutes*

1 cup (240 ml) medium couscous
1 cup (240 ml) hot tap water
1/2 tsp (2 ml) table salt

1 tbsp (15 ml) vegetable oil
2 tbsp (60 ml) margarine
Salt and pepper to taste

Set large element on stove to highest setting. In a **large saucepan**, add hot tap water, salt and oil. Bring to a boil; remove from heat. Immediately stir in uncooked couscous in pan. Set aside; allow it to swell for 2 minutes. Add margarine and heat again over a low setting for about 2 minutes more while stirring with a **fork** to prevent grains from sticking.
Couscous will have at least double in volume at this point. Serve as is, with sauce or a bit of salad dressing, or as one of the following variations. **Makes about 3 cups (720 ml) or 6 small servings**

LITE! VERSION *Reduce amount of oil and margarine or 1/2 tsp (2 ml) vegetable oil and 1 tsp (5 ml) margarine!*

COUSCOUS VARIATIONS

Middle-Eastern Couscous & Legumes   *10 minutes*

1/3 cup (80 ml) *frozen or refrigerated*
  precooked lima beans
1/3 cup (80 ml) *frozen or refrigerated*
  precooked whole green peas

1/4 tsp (1 ml) paprika or
  spanish paprika
1 tsp (5 ml) dried parsley
1/2 tbsp (7 ml) lemon juice from

1/4 tsp (1 ml) ground cumin   concentrate

Using a **medium-size bowl** containing very hot tap water, place the frozen or refrigerated legumes; thaw or warm up about a minute. Quickly drain. Add legumes and remainder of ingredients to *Basic Plain Couscous* recipe. Stir over a medium-low heat about 2 minutes. Serve at once.

SUB-VARIATION(S) *Try with 2/3 cup (160 ml) of one legume only or other combinations of legumes like lentils, chick peas, red kidney beans, etc.!*

Buttery Couscous Pilaf   *8-9 minutes*

1/2 tbsp (7 ml) vegetable oil   1/4 tsp (1 ml) onion powder
1 small yellow onion, chopped   1 tsp (5 ml) dried parsley
1 tsp (5 ml) chicken or beef soup
    stock powder

Onion can be sautéed in vegetable with the same pan before cooking the plain couscous, or in a **second sauce pan** or **skillet** sauté onion about 3 minutes on a medium heat until transparent. Add the cooked onion *(if using a second saucepan)* and remaining above ingredients to *Basic Plain Couscous* recipe. Stir and serve at once.

SUB-VARIATIONS *Add one minced garlic clove & a dash of garlic powder!*

Vegetables & Couscous   *8-9 minutes*

1/2 tbsp (7 ml) vegetable oil   1 small yellow onion, chopped
1 small carrot, diced *(fresh or frozen   or sliced
    blanched)*   1 tsp (5 ml) vegetable stock powder
Half a celery stalk, diced   1/2 tsp (2 ml) dried parsley
1/4 cup (60 ml) shredded green cabbage

If using frozen blanched vegetables, thaw in a **bowl** containing very hot tap water. The four above vegetables can be sautéed in the vegetable oil in the same pan before cooking plain couscous, or in a **second saucepan** or skillet. Sauté vegetables about 5 minutes until cooked but crisp. Add the cooked vegetables and remaining above ingredients to *Basic Plain Couscous* recipe. Stir and serve hot.

SUB-VARIATIONS *During peak harvest season when vegetables are much cheaper replace above staple vegetables with other varieties like chopped green bell pepper, broccoli, fresh green peas, etc.!*

BARLEY DISHES

Basic Plain Barley   *18-20 minutes*

2 cups (480 ml) *frozen or refrigerated   2 cups (480 ml) hot tap water
    presoaked pot or pearl barley*   1 tbsp (15 ml) margarine
2 tsp (10 ml) chicken or beef soup   Salt and pepper to taste
    stock powder

In a **large saucepan**, place stock powder and water; bring to a boil over a high heat. Add barley; reduce heat to medium and simmer uncovered about 15 minutes or until all the liquid is absorbed. Stir occasionally. Add margarine and season to taste. Serve hot with a sauce or as one of the following variations. **Makes about 3 cups (720 ml) or 6 small servings**

LITE! VERSION *Reduce amount of margarine to 1/2 tsp (2 ml)!*

BARLEY DISHES VARIATIONS

Barley & Mushroom Pilaf   *18-20 minutes*

1/2 tbsp (7 ml) vegetable oil
1 medium yellow onion, finely
    chopped
2 or 3 medium mushrooms, very
    thinly sliced

1 tsp (5 ml) dried parsley
1/2 tsp (2 ml) ground turmeric

Onion and mushroom may be sautéed in vegetable oil in the same pan as the one used to cooked the barley or in a **second pan** or **skillet**. Sauté vegetables 3 to 4 minutes on a medium heat. Add the vegetables and remainder of above ingredients to *Basic Plain Barley* recipe. Stir and serve hot.

SUB-VARIATIONS *Try other vegetables like fresh or blanched celery, broccoli, etc.!*

CHOP SUEY DISHES

Basic Chop Suey   *9-10 minutes*

1 tbsp (15 ml) vegetable oil
2 tbsp (30 ml) hot tap water
1 medium yellow onion,
    chopped
Half celery stalk, sliced

1 garlic clove, minced
1/8 tsp (1/2 ml) garlic powder
3 cups (720 ml) homegrown
    mung bean sprouts
(see pages 241-2)

In a **wok, frying pan** or **saucepan**, heat the oil over a medium-high setting; add water, vegetables and garlic powder. Stir-fry a few minutes. Add sprouts and stir-fry another 3 or 4 minutes until they're warm and tender. Serve at once with soy, or tamari sauce. **Makes about 3 cups (720 ml) or 6 small servings**

LITE! VERSION *Use only 1/2 tsp (2 ml) of oil to allow for at least some taste!*

VARIATIONS *Try other legume sprouts and try with a (non-white sauce) sauce!*

CHOP SUEY VARIATIONS

Cantonese 'Chop Suey'   *9-10 minutes*

1/4 tsp (1 ml) ground ginger
2 green onions, completely chopped
    up including green part *(preferably
    in peak season)*

1/4 tsp (1 ml) table salt

Add the above ingredients to *Basic Chop Suey* recipe.

Saucy Vegetable Chop Suey   9-10 minutes

1 tbsp (15 ml) sesame seeds
1/4 tsp (1 ml) ground ginger
2 medium mushrooms, very
   thinly sliced
1 small bunch of broccoli, cutted
   in bite-size pieces *(preferably in*
   peak season)

1/3 cup (80 ml) hot tap water
1/4 tsp (1 ml) chicken soup stock
   powder
1 tbsp (15 ml) corn flour or
   all-purpose flour
1 tsp (5 ml) soy sauce

In a **second skillet**, toast sesame seeds on a medium heat *(without oil)* for 5 minutes, stir frequently. Meanwhile, add remainder of the above ingredients to *Basic Chop Suey* recipe and stir-fry as outlined. Sprinkle with toasted seeds and serve.

OTHER SIDE DISHES

Fried Onion Rings   15 minutes

2 large yellow onions, thickly sliced
1 cup (240 ml) hot tap water
1/3 cup (80 ml) skim milk powder
1/2 tsp (2 ml) table salt

1 cup (240 ml) all-purpose flour
Salt and pepper to taste
2/3 cup (160 ml) vegetable oil for
   frying pan (or use deep-fryer)

OR 1 1/3 cups (320 ml) of Batter Mix recipe, see page 244

Cut onions into 1/4-inch (5 mm) thick slices; separate into rings. In a **medium-size bowl**, whisk together hot water, milk powder and salt; add onion rings and soak 7 to 10 minutes. Stir occasionally. In a **medium-size plastic bag**, combine flour, salt and pepper to taste. Add raw onion rings in batches and shake to coat. Meanwhile, put the heat on a **large saucepan** or **deep fryer**. Fry or deep-fry rings in batches and without crowding, for about 3 minutes or until golden brown. Place in a **plastic bowl** with **lid** until all are done. Season and serve hot. Reheat leftovers in oven. **Make 4 medium or 8 small servings**

LITE! VERSION *Use 1/2 tsp (2 ml) of oil in a non-stick skillet over moderate heat!*

VARIATIONS *Try with red or white onions when inexpensively in season!*

Black Beans Venezuela-Style   20-22 minutes

3 cups (720 ml) *frozen* precooked
   black beans
1 tbsp (15 ml) vegetable oil
1 small yellow onion, finely chopped
1 tsp (5 ml) pickled hot pepper rings,
   minced

1 garlic clove, minced
1/2 tsp (2 ml) ground cumin
1/2 tbsp (7 ml) granulated sugar
Salt and pepper to taste

In a **frying pan** or **skillet**, over a medium setting, heat the pan and add oil when hot. Meanwhile, using a **medium-size bowl**, containing very hot tap water, place

frozen or refrigerator thawed black beans; thaw or warm-up about 2 minutes. As soon as oil is hot, place the vegetables and spices in pan; sauté a few minutes. Drain the beans and place in pan, add the water, cover partially; simmer over a medium heat about 15 minutes or until most of the water has evaporated. Season, and stir occasionally. Serve hot with various dishes. Better if served as a leftover after several hours of refrigeration. **Makes almost 3 cups (720 ml)**
VARIATIONS *Try adding half a sweet red bell pepper (chopped) when inexpensively in peak season!*

Curried Carrots   *10 minutes*

3 cups (720ml) fresh *or frozen*
   blanched carrots, sliced
1/2 tbsp (7 ml) honey *(or sugar)*
1 tsp (5 ml) lemon juice from
   concentrate
1/2 tsp (2 ml) Dijon mustard

1 tsp (5 ml) curry powder
1 tbsp (15 ml) vegetable oil
1 tsp (5 ml) margarine
1/2 tbsp (7 ml) dark brown sugar
Salt and pepper to taste

Using a **large bowl**, containing very hot tap water, place frozen /blanched carrots; thaw a few minutes. Meanwhile, in a **small bowl**, combine honey, lemon juice, mustard and curry powder. In a **large frying pan** or **skillet**, over a medium setting, heat oil and margarine until margarine is melted. Drain carrots and add to pan. Sauté while occasionally stirring about 2 minutes. Add brown sugar and the honey mixture, stirring constantly. Sauté another two or three minutes, or until carrots are well glazed. Season to taste and serve hot. **Makes 3 cups (720 ml)**
VARIATIONS *Try with frozen/blanched beets, or fresh vegetables inexpensively in season like broccoli or cauliflower!*

Plain Polenta   *9-10 minutes*

1 1/4 cup (300 ml) cornmeal *(# 250)*
3 cups (720 ml) hot tap water

1/2 tsp (2 ml) table salt

In a **frying pan** or **heavy skillet**, bring water to a boil over the highest heat setting. Lower heat to medium and gradually add the cornmeal, stirring at the same time. Stir until polenta is smooth and thick, about 5 minutes. Mold in a rectangular dish; let cool and slice or cut into squares. Alternately, serve immediately as a mushy side dish. **Makes almost 3 cups (720 ml)**

West Coast-Style Chick Peas   *15 minutes*

2 1/2 cups (600 ml) *frozen* precooked
   chick peas
1 tbsp (15 ml) vegetable oil
1 tbsp (15 ml) green or black
   pitted olives, chopped
Half a celery stalk, chopped

1/2 cup (120 ml) canned diced
   tomatoes
1 small yellow onion, finely
   chopped
1 tbsp (15 ml) white vinegar
1 tsp (5 ml) Worcestershire sauce
Salt and pepper to taste

In a **large bowl**, containing hot tap water, place the frozen chickpeas, thaw and warm-up for 2 to 3 minutes. In a **frying pan** or **skillet**, heat oil over a medium-high setting. Place all ingredients, including drained chickpeas, in pan and combine. Sauté while stirring occasionally for about 10 minutes until liquid has thickened. Serve while hot. **Makes almost 3 cups (720 ml)**

Black Beans & Vegetables · 15 minutes

2 cups (480 ml) *frozen* precooked
   black beans
2 tbsp (30 ml) margarine
1 small yellow onion, chopped
2 garlic cloves, minced
1/2 cup (120 ml) fresh *or frozen*
   blanched sliced celery

1/4 cup (60 ml) fresh *or frozen*
   blanched diced or sliced carrots
2 tbsp (30 ml) hot tap water
2 tsp (10 ml) dried parsley
1 bay leaf
1 tsp (5 ml) dried thyme
1/4 tsp (1 ml) garlic powder
1 tbsp (15 ml) white vinegar
Salt and pepper to taste

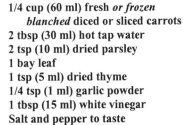

Using a **large bowl**, containing a lot of very hot tap water, place frozen legumes and *(if frozen)* vegetables; thaw a few minutes. Meanwhile, in a **large frying pan** or **skillet**, over a medium-low setting, melt margarine; add drained legumes and vegetables and all the remaining above ingredients. Sauté and stir the mixture for about 6 to 7 minutes. Remove bay leaf and serve hot. **Makes 3 cups (720 ml)**
VARIATION *Try with red kidney beans!*

Stuffed Vine Leaves · 40-45 minutes

A one-pound (454 g) jar contains about 100 leaves, which comes out to less than a nickel each. A couple of cents more each for the stuffing makes them very affordable.

24 grapevine leaves in brine
1 1/2 cups (360 ml) *refrigerated* precooked rice
1 yellow onion, finely chopped
1 garlic clove, minced
1/4 tsp (1 ml) garlic powder

1 tbsp (15 ml) dried parsley
3 tbsp (45 ml) vegetable oil
2 tbsp (30 ml) lemon juice from
   concentrate
1/8 tsp (1/2 ml) allspice
2 tbsp (30 ml) white vinegar

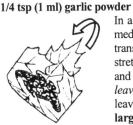

In a **large skillet or frying pan**, combine and heat over a medium setting. Simmer about 10 minutes until onion is transparent *(add a little water if necessary)*. On each stretched-out leaf place at least 1 tbsp (15 ml) of stuffing and fold as illustrated. *If properly folded the stuffed vine leaves should not unfold themselves.* Pack the stuffed vine leaves tightly together in cheesecloth tied or wrapped. In a **large saucepan**, place the stuffed vine leaves bundle at bottom of pan; barely cover with water; place a **heavy plate** on them. If necessary, add vegetable oil and a little more lemon juice from concentrate. Cook on medium-low until done. **Makes 24 stuffed vine leaves**

For more side dishes, see the chapters on potatoes, rice, pastas, and certain salads and pies!

MUFFINS, CAKES, COOKIES, CEREAL BARS, & DOUGHNUTS

MUFFINS

Basic Muffins   *25-35 minutes*

Preheat oven to 425°F (215°C) before starting.

DRY INGREDIENTS:

2 1/2 cups (600 ml) all-purpose flour
   (generic-brand bleached)
1-1 1/4 cups (240-300 ml) sugar

2 tsp (10 ml) baking powder
2 tbsp (30 ml) instant skim milk
   powder
1/2 tsp (2 ml) table salt

Or 3 7/8 cups (660 ml) of premixed dry ingredients #1 (see page 26)

NON-DRY INGREDIENTS:

1 1/8 cups (270 ml) cold tap water   **2 tbsp (30 ml) margarine**

In a **large mixing bowl**, place dry ingredients *(flours today are pre-sifted before packaging and do not have to be sifted)* and quickly mix. Add water and margarine. Using an **electric hand mixer** beat on high speed up to one minute until a uniform batter result. *(For the muffin recipe variations below, include the additional ingredients too.) Large or bulky ingredients are better added after beating and then hand mixed with spoon.* Add batter to greased or paper cup lined **muffin pans** to about 2/3rd full. Bake them on the middle rack of preheated oven (425°F/215°C). Set a **timer** for 12-20 minutes *(depending on muffin size)*, verify if well baked using a **test stick**. If it comes out clean without wet batter, it's baked. *Please keep a close eye on cakes at the end of baking period because of the higher than average oven temperature.*

Makes 12 large or 24 small muffins, or 24 large cupcakes

LITE! VERSION *Its already low-fat but reduce it more by omitting margarine!*
<u>*HI-FIBER*</u> OPTION! *Substitute half of the flour with generic whole-wheat flour!*

> **TIPS & HINTS** *Baking soda, unlike baking powder, cannot be used by itself and needs an acid ingredients like sour milk, buttermilk, yogurt, vinegar, lemon or citrus juice, tartaric acid or molasses to react with it to produce gases to make the batter rise. Try to use baking powder & baking soda within a year of purchase. To test baking powder, place some in hot water, if it bubbles vigorously its good!*

MUFFIN VARIATIONS

Spiced Apple-Carrot Muffins   25-35 minutes

2 tbsp (30 ml) *bulk* wheat germ
2 tbsp (30 ml) *bulk* wheat bran
1/4 tsp (1 ml) nutmeg
1 tsp (5 ml) cinnamon
1/4 tsp (1 ml) allspice

2 tbsp (30 ml) dark liquid honey
1/4 tsp (1 ml) artificial vanilla
   extract
1/2 cup (120 ml) carrots, grated
1 apple, grated with skin

Add above ingredients to those in *Basic Muffins* recipe.

Raisin-Bran Muffins   25-35 minutes

1/3 cup (80 ml) *bulk* wheat bran
2/3 cup (60 ml) *Homemade Butter-
   Milk* or *Recipe-Grade Sour
   Milk (see page 233)*
2 tbsp (30 ml) *bulk* wheat germ

1 tsp (5 ml) cinnamon
1/2 tsp (2 ml) nutmeg
1/4 tsp (1 ml) allspice
1/4 cup (60 ml) dried raisins, *frozen*
   presoaked

Add above ingredients to *Basic Muffins* recipe. *Frozen presoaked raisins should be thawed in very hot tap water a minute. Use half of water only in basic recipe.*

Yogurt & Protein Muffins   25-35 minutes

3/4 cup (180 ml) *Homemade Yogurt
   (see pages 232-3, replaces same
   amount of water)*
1/4 cup (60 ml) molasses
2 tbsp (30 ml) *bulk* wheat germ
2 tbsp (30 ml) *bulk* wheat bran

2 tbsp (30 ml) soy flour
1 tbsp (15 ml) dried raisins, finely
   minced
2 tbsp (30 ml) peanuts, blender
   chopped

Add above ingredients to *Basic Muffins* recipe.

Oatmeal Muffins   25-35 minutes

3/4 cup (180 ml) *'Quick'* rolled oats
   (replaces same amount of flour)
1/2 tsp (2 ml) artificial vanilla extract
2 tbsp (30 ml) molasses

2 tbsp (30 ml) *bulk* wheat germ
2 tbsp (30 ml) *bulk* wheat bran
1/2 tbsp (7 ml) cinnamon
1/2 cup (120 ml) dark brown sugar

Add above to *Basic Muffins* recipe. *Use only 1/2 cup (120 ml) of white sugar.*

Chocolate Chip Muffins   25-35 minutes

1/3 cup (80 ml) generic chocolate-flavored
   or semi-sweet chocolate chips
Add above ingredients to *Basic Muffins* recipe.

Corn-Bread Muffins   *25-35 minutes*

1 cup (240 ml) cornmeal *(replaces the same amount of flour)*

1 1/3 cups (320 ml) *Homemade Buttermilk* **or** *Recipe-Grade Sour Milk (see page 233)*

Add above ingredients to *Basic Muffins* recipe.

CAKES

The following cakes were inspired by actual wartime cake recipes. Such cakes were egg-less, milk-less, and almost without fat due to wartime shortages. Therefore, our cakes are egg-less, and very low in milk and fat. War-cakes were made with baking soda which is 4 times cheaper than baking powder (see Tips & Hints on page 196). These cakes are delicious even without icing. The reduced batter thickness and higher temperatures in the following cake recipes, cut baking time in half. These add up to maximum savings, both money and time. The instructions use the 'one-mixing bowl only' method, and electric mixer. Make a small production of it, double or quadruple the required recipe quantities .

Basic Plain Cake   *20-22 minutes*

Preheat oven to 450ºF (230ºC) before starting.

DRY INGREDIENTS:

2 1/2 cups (600 ml) all-purpose flour *(generic-brand bleached flour)*
1 1/4 cups (300 ml) granulated sugar

2 tsp (10 ml) generic baking powder
2 tbsp (30 ml) generic instant skim milk powder
1/2 tsp (2 ml) table salt

Or 3 7/8 cups (660 ml) of premixed dry ingredients #1

NON-DRY INGREDIENTS:

1 1/4 cups (300 ml) cold tap water
1/2 tsp (2 ml) artificial vanilla extract

2 tbsp (30 ml) low-cost margarine *(melted or chilled)*

In a **large mixing bowl**, combine dry ingredients *(flours today are pre-sifted before packaging and do not have to be sifted)*. Add water, vanilla and margarine *(no need to melt it)* in that order. Using an **electric hand mixer** beat on high speed about one minute until a uniform batter result. *(For the cake recipe variations below, include the additional ingredients too.)* Large or bulky ingredients are better added after beating and then hand mixed with spoon. In **two** greased and lightly floured **square** *(or round)* **dull-metal baking pans**, add batter. *Non-stick pans are useless here!* Place them in the middle *(use one rack only)* of preheated oven; bake at 450ºF (230ºC) for about 15 minutes till top is golden brown. *This temperature is for thin cakes, for thicker cakes use lower temperatures and longer baking.* Set a **timer** and verify if well baked using a **test stick** *(like a skewer)*. If it comes out clean without wet batter it's baked. Cool cakes on cooling racks, serve, or refrigerate and/or freeze in storage plastic bags. **Makes two cakes (8"x8"x1" or 20x20x2.5 cm) or 32 small servings**

LITE! VERSION *Its already low-fat but reduce it more by excluding margarine!*

HI-FIBER OPTION! *Substitute half of the flour with generic whole-wheat flour!*

CAKE VARIATIONS

Chocolate-Flavored Cake   20-22 minutes

*It was included for use in the small **Chocolate-Coated Cake with Filling** recipe (see page 220).*

1/3 cup (80 ml) *bulk* cocoa powder   *Double the amount of vanilla!*
Add the above to *Basic Plain Cake* recipe.

Buttermilk-Raisin Cake   20-22 minutes

1/2 cup (120 ml) *frozen* presoaked   1 1/3 cups (320 ml) *Recipe-Grade*
   dried raisin *(or 1/4 cup (60 ml)*   *Sour Milk* or *Homemade Butter-*
   dried raisins)   *milk (replaces water, see page 233)*
1 tsp (5 ml) ground cinnamon

Add or replace the above ingredients in *Basic Plain Cake* recipe.

Date & Orange Cake   20-22 minutes

1/4 cup (60 ml) dried dates, chopped   1 tbsp (15 ml) lemon juice from
2 tsp (10 ml) orange peel, grated   concentrate
Add the above ingredients in *Basic Plain Cake* recipe.

Divine Carrot Cake   20-22 minutes

3/4 cup (180 ml) carrots, grated   2 tbsp (30 ml) lemon juice
1/2 tsp (2 ml) ground cinnamon   from concentrate
Add the above ingredients in *Basic Plain Cake* recipe.

Spiced Cake   20 minutes

This recipe is very similar to an actual low-cost, ingredient-shortage war cake.

1 tbsp (15 ml) <u>each</u> *bulk* wheat germ   3 tbsp (45 ml) molasses
   and *bulk* wheat bran   3 tbsp (45 ml) dried raisins, coarse
1/4 tsp (1 ml) ground cloves   chopped
1/8 tsp (1/2 ml) allspice   1 tbsp (15 ml) peanuts, blender
1/2 tsp (2 ml) ground cinnamon   chopped
Add the above to *Basic Plain Cake* recipe. *Top with the chopped peanuts and use baking soda instead of baking powder to maintain the tradition.*

Apple & Cinnamon Cake   20-22 minutes

One apple, peeled and diced   2 tsp (10 ml) ground cinnamon
Dash of allspice
Add the above ingredients in *Basic Plain Cake* recipe.

For cheesecakes, see pages 218-9
For super-fast cakes, see page 250

ICINGS

The following two types of icings or frostings are the least expensive we were able to come up with. One is low fat, bulky and airy, it goes the distance. While the other is very basic and simple, it uses low-cost margarine.

Basic Plain Icing 🐷   *3-8 minutes*

TYPE 1

1/2 cup (120 ml) low-cost margarine	2 cups (480 ml) granulated sugar
1 1/2-2 tbsp (22-30 ml) cold tap water	*(or very expensive icing sugar)*
2 tsp (10 ml) instant skim milk powder	

In a **blender**, grind *(one cup at a time only)* the granulated sugar till powdered. In a **mixing bowl**, beat margarine with a **hand-held electric mixer** on medium speed for 30 seconds. Slowly add half of the powdered sugar while beating. In a **glass**, dissolve the milk powder in water. Add half of reconstituted milk while beating. Now add remaining sugar *(plus additional ingredients for a recipe variation)* and enough milk to make it spread-able. This type is especially good for piping. Wait until cake has cooled to room temperature before frosting *(frost certain spots only of cake for economy and added taste). For further economy frost the top of cake or in-between two cakes only, or lightly ice individual cake portions using the 'Easy Icing Technique', see page 200.* **Makes at least 1 cup (240 ml) or enough for a few cakes**

TYPE 2

1 cup (240 ml) granulated sugar	1/4 tsp (1 ml) cream of tartar
1/3 cup (80 ml) cold tap water	2 small or 1 extra-large egg white

In a **small saucepan**, place sugar, water, and cream of tartar *(or baking powder)*; combine. Cook while stirring with a **whisk** till bubbly and sugar has dissolved. Set aside. In a **small mixing bowl**, place the egg white(s) *(plus the ingredients for a recipe variation).* Pour the hot sugar mixture very slowly into the egg white(s), beating on high speed with an **electric hand mixer** at least 5 minutes till stiff peaks form. *Always store refrigerated.* **Makes at least 1 cup (240 ml)**

CAKE ICING VARIATIONS

Vanilla Icing   *3-8 minutes*

2/3 tsp (3 ml) artificial vanilla extract
Add the above to *Basic Plain Cake Icing* recipe, type 1 or 2.

Lemony Icing   *3-8 minutes*

1-2 tbsp (15-30 ml) lemon juice	1/8 tsp (1/2 ml) artificial vanilla extract
from concentrate	

Add the above to *Basic Plain Cake Icing* recipe, type 1 or 2.

Chocolate Frosting   *3-8 minutes*

2 tbsp (30 ml) *bulk* cocoa powder   1/8 tsp (1/2 ml) artificial vanilla extract
Add the above to *Basic Plain Cake Icing* recipe, type 1 or 2.

Easy Caramel Icing   3-8 minutes

1/3 cup (80 ml) dark brown sugar
   (replaces 1/3ʳᵈ of granulated sugar)
Add the above to *Basic Plain Cake Icing* recipe, type 2 only.

Instant Coffee Icing   3-8 minutes

1 tbsp (15 ml) instant coffee
Add the above to *Basic Plain Cake Icing* recipe, type 1 or 2. Grind the instant coffee granules and the granulated sugar at the same time in blender.

EASY ICING TECHNIQUE

Try this simple icing solution on Danish pastries, doughnuts, cereal bars, cake portions, etc. Don't try applying the icing with a pastry tube, it's a hassle and troublesome to clean. Leftover icing in a pastry tube is almost impossible to remove and wasteful. This technique is simply a small plastic bag (storage or freezer bag) with a tiny scissors made hole in one corner, 1 or 2 tbsp (15-30 ml) of icing is squeezed out with hand pressure (see illustration). Refrigerated leftover icing for next snack or breakfast. The small plastic bag is discarded when empty with no wastage.

COOKIES

We opted for more commercial-style cookies that are bulkier, leaner, and drier than the usual home-style cookies found in most cookbooks. Making one batch of this cookie recipe will fill you oven and use both racks. Doubling or quadrupling the recipe will make your efforts more worth while. They come to less than one-quarter of the cost of the least expensive generic-brand cookies (including electricity) you can buy.

Basic Plain Cookies   20-25 minutes

Preheat oven to 350ºF (180ºC) before starting.

DRY INGREDIENTS:

2 1/2 cups (600 ml) all-purpose flour	**2 tsp (10 ml) baking powder**
(generic-brand bleached flour)	**1/2 tsp (2 ml) table salt**
1 1/4 cups (300 ml) granulated sugar	

Or 3 3/4 cups (630 ml) of premixed dry ingredients #1 (see page 26)

NON-DRY INGREDIENTS:

1/4 cup (60 ml) margarine	**1/2 tsp (2 ml) artificial vanilla**
5/8 cups (150 ml) cold tap water	**extract**

In a **large mixing bowl**, combine dry ingredients. Quickly cut the margarine *(do not melt it)* into the flour mixture using a **fork** or hands. Add water, vanilla in that order. *(For the cookie and biscuit variations below, include the additional* *ingredients also.) Large or bulky ingredients are better added after the water has been mixed in and then mixed with spoon.* Separate the dough into 10 pieces and from each piece, working with wet hands, quickly make 20 tiny balls *(or 10 small ones)* about 5/8-inch (1½ cm) in diameter. *You must make the tiny balls real fast, perfection is not important!* Using **four medium non-stick baking sheets**, place tiny dough ball about 1¼ inches (4.5 cm) apart; very quickly flatten them using the *greased (or wet)* bottom of a **glass** to a thickness of 1/8-inch (3 mm). *It should not take more than about a second each to flatten.* Place the four baking sheets near the middle of preheated oven on two racks, bake at 350ºF (180ºC) for about 10 minutes till golden brown. *Use an even lower oven temperature for a more uniform bake.* Set a **timer.** They will at least double in size during baking. Let cool while still in baking sheets but place them on cooling racks for 5-10 minutes. For harder, dryer cookies, cool them on cooling rack only for about one hour before storing them in plastic bags. Store in a dry place, refrigerator, or freezer. For softer cookies cool till warm only before bagging them. Cookies left on cooling racks for several hours will become quite hard. *No egg(s) means that they're safe to store at room temperature.*

Makes about 100 small cookies or 200 bite-size cookies

LITE! VERSION *Omit or reduce margarine, or any fat altogether!*

MOISTER COOKIE OPTION! Double water and spoon them out on baking sheets!

COOKIE VARIATIONS

Oatmeal-Raisin Cookies   *20-25 minutes*

3/4 cup (180 ml) *'Quick'* rolled oats
  (replaces same amount of flour)

1/3 cup (80 ml) *frozen* presoaked
  raisins
1/2 tbsp (7 ml) dark liquid honey

Add or replace above ingredients in *Basic Plain Cookies* recipe.

Homemade Graham Crackers   *20-25 minutes*
This recipe comes close to the real McCoy and at 1/5ᵗʰ the cost.

1 1/4 cups (300 ml) *bulk* graham flour
  OR 1 cup (240 ml) whole wheat
  flour & 1/4 cup (60 ml) *bulk* bran
  (replaces half of all-purpose flour)
1/4 cup (60 ml) instant skim milk
  powder

1/2 tbsp (7 ml) white vinegar (5%)
1/2 tsp (1 ml) baking soda
3 tbsp (45 ml) strongly flavored
  dark liquid honey
  AND 3 tbsp (45 ml) molasses
  (both replace all the sugar)

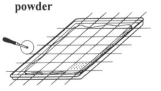

Add and substitute above ingredients in *Basic Plain Cookies* recipe. *If using bran, grind it in blender till fine.* Dissolve milk powder in water, stir in vinegar and set aside 5 minutes. Meanwhile, in a **small bowl**, beat margarine, honey, and molasses together. Omit vanilla. In a **large mixing bowl**, combine flour, baking powder, soda, and salt. Combine all ingredients in large bowl mixing well; separate in four. Preheat oven to 400ºF (200ºC). Meanwhile, using **4 non-stick baking**

sheets and a **rolling pin**, roll out each piece of dough directly in a baking sheet to a thickness of 1/16-inch (1.5 mm). *Remove the handles of rolling pin if they get in the way and dust it with flour as often as necessary!* Using a **pastry cutter** *(pizza wheel),* quickly but gently cut into 2-inch (5 cm) squares & prick all over with fork. **Makes about 80 graham crackers**
SUB-VARIATIONS *Substitute all of flour with whole-wheat or graham flour. For **Chocolate Coated Graham Crackers**, see pages 210-11!*

Chocolate Chip & Oatmeal Cookies   20-25 minutes

3/4 cup (180 ml) *'Quick'* rolled oats *(replaces same amount of flour)*	1/4 cup (60 ml) generic-brand chocolate flavored chips

Add the above ingredients to *Basic Plain Cookies* recipes.
SUB-VARIATION *For **Plain Chocolate Chip Cookies** omit the rolled oats!*

Natural Sunflower Seed Cookies   20-25 minutes

3/4 cup (180 ml) *'Quick'* rolled oats *(replaces same amount of flour)*	2 tbsp (30 ml) sunflower seed kernels
1/4 cup (60 ml) wheat germ	2 tbsp (30 ml) dark brown sugar

Add the above ingredients to *Basic Plain Cookies* recipes.

Spiced Ginger Cookies   20-25 minutes

1 tsp (5 ml) ground ginger	1/4 tsp (1 ml) cinnamon
2 tbsp (30 ml) molasses	1/4 tsp (1 ml) nutmeg
	1/8 tsp (1/2 ml) allspice

Add the above ingredients to *Basic Plain Cookies* recipe.

Sesame-Oatmeal Cookies   20-25 minutes

2 tbsp (30 ml) sesame seeds	2 tbsp (30 ml) yellow cornmeal

Add the above ingredients to *Basic Plain Cookies* recipe.

Nutty-Banana Cookies   20-25 minutes

1/2 cup (120 ml) *'Quick'* rolled oats *(replaces same amount of flour)*	1/4 tsp (1 ml) nutmeg
	1/4 tsp (1 ml) cinnamon
Half a banana, mashed	1 tbsp (15 ml) *bulk* peanuts, blender chopped

Add or substitute the above ingredients in *Basic Plain Cookies* recipe.

Spiced Carrot Cookie   20-25 minutes

1/2 cup (120 ml) carrots, grated	1 tbsp (15 ml) instant skim milk powder
1/2 cup (120 ml) *'Quick'* rolled oats *(replaces same amount of flour)*	1/4 tsp (1 ml) cinnamon
2 tbsp (30 ml) molasses	Dash of nutmeg

Add or replace the above ingredients in *Basic Plain Cookies* recipe.

Date & Applesauce Cookies   *20-25 minutes*

1/3 cup (80 ml) applesauce *(page 217)*
   (replaces same amount of water)
2 tbsp (30 ml) dates, chopped

1/2 cup (120 ml) *'Quick'* rolled oats
   (replaces same amount of flour)

Add or replace the above ingredients in *Basic Plain Cookies* recipe.

Old-Fashioned Molasses Cookies   *20-25 minutes*

1/2 cup (120 ml) *bulk* wheat germ
   (replaces same amount of flour)
1/2 cup (120 ml) *'Quick'* rolled oats
   (replaces same amount of flour)
1/4 cup (60 ml) molasses

1 tbsp (15 ml) dried raisins,
   finely chopped
1/4 tsp (1 ml) ground ginger
1/8 tsp (1/2 ml) ground cloves
Dash of allspice

Add or replace the above ingredients in *Basic Plain Cookies* recipe.

Peanut & Coconut Cookies   *20-25 minutes*

2 tbsp (30 ml) peanut butter
1 tbsp (15 ml) shredded coconut

1/2 cup (120 ml) *'Quick'* rolled oats
   (replaces same amount of flour)

Add or replace the above ingredients in *Basic Plain Cookies* recipe.

CEREAL & FRUIT BARS

Basic Cereal & Fruit Bars   *35-40 minutes*

*These cereal bars come out to about one-third the cost of the
least expensive generic-brand/bargain-pack cereal bars that
you can buy. Feel free to double or quadruple recipe! Time
given assumes filling is ready.*

1 1/2 cups (360 ml) all-purpose flour
   (generic-brand bleached)
1 1/2 cups (360 ml) *'Quick'* rolled oats
1/2 cup (120 ml) granulated sugar

1/3 cup (80 ml) dark brown sugar
1/2-1 tsp (2-5 ml) baking powder
3/4 cup (180 ml) margarine
3-4 tbsp (45-60 ml) cold tap water
About 1 cup (240 ml) of fruit filling!

FOR FILLINGS *See Pie Filling Stretcher page 148, Fruit Pie Filling page 147,
Flavored Crystals Filling page 216, or Old-Fashioned Applesauce page 217!*

In a **mixing bowl**, combine flour, oats,
sugars, and baking powder. Cut in the
margarine till mixture resembles course
cornmeal. Add water and shape into a ball
using hands. On a floured surface, flatten the
ball into roughly a flat thick square with your
palms. Roll out until it's at least 14" x 21" (36 x 54 cm) square. Using a **pastry
cutter** *(pizza wheel)*, cut dough into 24 squares of 3½" x 3½" (9 x 9 cm).
*Alternately, divide dough into 24 pieces and shape each by hand into a flat
square.* Quickly place about 2 tsp (10 ml) of filling on each square piece and fold
each side *(see illustration)*; press lightly to seal seam. Preheat oven to 400°F
(200°C). Meanwhile, on **2 medium non-stick baking skeet**, place the assembled
bars. Bake for 15 to 20 minutes or till golden brown. Cool in the baking sheet on a

cooling rack till warm only and immediately place in plastic bag(s). **Makes about 24 bars**

LITE! VERSION *Substitute margarine with 2/3 the amount of homemade buttermilk or recipe-grade sour milk and use baking soda instead of baking powder!*

CEREAL & FRUIT BARS VARIATIONS

Blueberry Cereal Bars   *35-40 minutes*

Use (blueberry) Pie Filling Stretcher *recipe!*
   (see page 148)
Use the above as filling in the *Basic Cereal & Fruit Bars* recipe.

SUB-VARIATIONS *Try the cherry, apple, strawberry, raspberry, or raisin store-bought pie fillings (stretched of course)!*

Homemade Filling Cereal Bars   *35-40 minutes*

Use one of the Basic Fruit Pie Filling
   recipe variations (see page 148)!
Use the above as filling in the *Basic Cereal & Fruit Bars* recipe.

Chocolate-Coated Cereal Bars   *55-60 minutes*

About 2 cups (480 ml) *Chocolaty*
   Coating Dip (see pages 210-11)
Using any of the *Basic Cereal & Fruit Bars* recipe variations, coat each bar with chocolate as described in *Chocolaty Coating Dip* recipe *(see pages 210-11).* Let cereal bars cool on wire racks to room temperature before coating.

RELATED RECIPES

Quick Doughnuts   *20-30 minutes*

1 3/4 cups (420 ml) all-purpose flour	1/4 tsp (1 ml) ground cinnamon
(generic-brand & bleached)	1/8 tsp (1/2 ml) nutmeg
1/3 cup (80 ml) granulated sugar	5/8 cup (150 ml) cold tap water
2 tbsp (30 ml) instant skim milk powder	1/4 tsp (1 ml) vanilla extract
1/2 tbsp (7 ml) baking powder	1 small egg, slightly beaten
1/4 tsp (1 ml) table salt	1 tbsp (15 ml) melted margarine

Or 3 3/4 cups (630 ml) of premixed dry ingredients #2 (see page 26)
Plug-in deep fryer, set at 375°F (190°C). Meanwhile, in a **mixing bowl**, stir together the dry ingredients. Add water and remainder of ingredients and, using a **mixing spoon**, quickly stir till uniform *(don't use an electric mixer and use hands if necessary).* On a floured surface, roll out dough to a 3/8-inch (1 cm) thickness. Using a **doughnut**

cutter or a **drinking glass** and **small cap**, cut out the doughnuts. *Don't make center holes for jelly-filled doughnuts.* Fry doughnuts 3 to 6 at a time for about 2 minutes per side or till golden, turning once with a **slotted spoon**. *Save frying oil in a covered plastic container refrigerated for the next time, and don't use oil that was used for frying meat.* Let them drain and cool on cooling racks. Using a **plastic bag** containing *Powdered sugar (page 247)*, place a few semi-cooled doughnuts and shake to coat, or simply dust them. Alternately, glaze or ice tops only. **Makes about one dozen doughnuts**

VARIATION(S) *For **Jelly-filled Doughnuts** fill dough (using a pastry bag) before frying with up to 1 tbsp (15 ml) of* Flavored Crystal Filling, Jam Stretcher, Pie Filling Stretcher, Custard Filling, Crème Filling, *or applesauce (see pages 148, 216, 217, 248)! For **Chocolate Doughnuts** omit cinnamon & nutmeg, add 1/2 cup (120 ml) generic-brand chocolate drink mix or half that amount of unsweetened cocoa to recipe! **Refrigerated dough** is also great for doughnuts, just knead in 2 tbsp (30 ml) of granulated sugar per 1 cup (240 ml) of dough to sweeten; cut, rise and fry!*

Pancakes    *15 minutes*

1 cup (240 ml) all-purpose flour *(generic enriched bleached)*	1 cup (240 ml) cold tap water
3 tbsp (45 ml) skim milk powder	1 1/2 tbsp (22 ml) vegetable oil or melted margarine
1 tbsp (15 ml) granulated sugar	1 small egg or half an extra large egg, slightly beaten
1/2 tbsp (7 ml) baking powder	
1/4 tsp (1 ml) table salt	*Small amount additional margarine or oil for frying pan or griddle*

Or 3 3/4 cups (630 ml) of premixed dry ingredients #3 (see page 27)

Heat **frying pan** or **griddle** over a medium setting. Meanwhile, in a **mixing bowl**, stir together the dry ingredients. Add water and remainder of ingredients. Using an **electric hand mixer**, beat until smooth on a medium speed. Add oil or margarine to the hot iron surface. Pour unto surface about 1/4 cup (60 ml) of batter for each pancake. Cook until golden brown *(when bubbles pop)* and flip for second side. **Makes about 6 pancakes**

VARIATIONS *For **Buckwheat Pancakes**, replace half of the flour with buckwheat flour! For **Buttermilk Pancakes**, replace water and milk powder with* Homemade Buttermilk *or* Recipe-Grade Sour Milk *(see page 233), and reduce baking powder by half and add 1/2 tsp (2 ml) of baking soda, add a little more water if necessary! For **Sourdough Pancakes**, simply add 1/2 cup (120 ml) of thawed frozen sourdough (for taste only) to the above plain pancake batter and mix, see pages 100-1!*

Waffles    10-12 minutes

Use the same ingredients and mixing directions as in previous *Pancakes* recipe, except that they're baked in a **waffle iron or baker** according to the manufacturer's directions. **Makes 4 to 6 waffles**

Crepes   20-30 minutes

Crepes are very thin French pancakes and may be served plain and sweetened, stuffed and rolled as wrappers with sweet or more main course fillings.

Use the same ingredients and mixing directions as in previous *Pancakes* recipe, with the exception of the sugar and baking powder that are omitted, and use 50% more water for a thinner batter. Rub hot pan with very little margarine using a paper towel. Use 2 tbsp (30 ml) of batter per crepe, lift and tilt frying pan to spread batter. Flip crepe after 1 to 2 minutes when golden brown, invert pan to remove crepe when done. **Makes about a dozen crepes**

Fruit Danish   1½ hours

1/2 cup (120 ml) *Reconstituted Skim Milk*, scalded *(see page 231)*
1/4 cup (60 ml) melted margarine or vegetable oil
2 tbsp (30 ml) granulated sugar
1/2 cup (120 ml) cold tap water
1/2 tbsp (7 ml) active dry yeast

1/2 tbsp (7 ml) baking powder
1 small egg, slightly beaten
3 cups (720 ml) all-purpose flour *(generic-brand & bleached)*
3/4 cup (180 ml) *Pie Filling Stretcher (serves as topping, see page 148)*

Or about 3 cups (720 ml) of refrigerated dough and knead in some sugar
In a **large mixing bowl**, mix the hot milk, margarine or oil, sugar, and cold water. Stir in the yeast into lukewarm mixture, then beat in egg; cover and let stand in oven incubator *(see pages 232-3)* for 10 minutes. Add flour and baking soda and knead about 5 minutes until dough is soft and uniform. Quickly shape into 12 flat and round buns. Place buns on **2 non-stick baking sheets**, cover with plastic wrap, and let rise for at least 45 minutes in warm oven *(see page 104)* till light. Preheat oven to 400° (200°C) at least 5 minutes before placing assembled buns in it. Press deep indentations into center of each bun and place about 1 tbsp (15 ml) of fruit filling in them. Bake for 20 minutes in center of oven and cool on wire racks. **Makes a dozen**

LITE! VERSION *Omit or greatly reduce the margarine or oil content!*
VARIATIONS *Glaze top of buns with beaten egg whites, sprinkle on cinnamon on apple Danish or use* Flavored Crystals Filling *instead of* Pie Filling Stretcher, *or top with custard, dessert cheese, or applesauce recipes all from this book! Ice lightly on top, (see pages 200, 216-17, 237)!*

DESSERTS, SNACK BARS, & FROZEN TREATS

PUDDINGS

These very low cost and fast to make puddings are a sort of variation of 'Blanc Mange'. And since the 'Proof of the pudding is in the eating', try our puddings.

Basic Pudding

5-7 minutes + chilling

2 tbsp (30 ml) generic vegetable oil
2 cups (480 ml) cold tap water
1/4 cup (60 ml*) bulk* **cornstarch**

1/4 cup (60 ml) instant skim milk
  powder *(generic or bulk)*
1/2 cup (120 ml) granulated sugar
Pinch of table salt

In an **electric blender**, blend at a high speed all ingredients *(plus additional ingredient(s) for a pudding variation)* for at least 30 seconds. In a **heavy-bottomed saucepan**, over a medium-high heat add blender's content; stir until it thickens and becomes bubbly. Cook another minute or two. Place in 4 small shallow bowls and serve after chilling about an hour. *See **Tips & Hints** page 149.* **Makes 2 cups (480 ml) or 4 small servings**
***LITE!* VERSION** *Simply exclude the oil!*

PUDDING VARIATIONS

Chocolate Pudding

5-6 minutes + chilling

2 tbsp (30 ml) *bulk pre-bagged* cocoa
  powder

1/2 tsp (2 ml) artificial vanilla
  extract

Add the above to *Basic Pudding* recipe.

Lemon Pudding

5-6 minutes + chilling

2 tbsp (30 ml) lemon juice from
  concentrate

Add the above to *Basic Pudding* recipe.

## Caramel Pudding					*5-6 minutes + chilling*

1/2 cup (120 ml) dark brown sugar		**1/2 tsp (2 ml) artificial vanilla extract**

Substitute granulated sugar with dark brown sugar and add vanilla in *Basic Pudding* recipe.

## Vanilla Pudding					*5-6 minutes + chilling*

1 tsp (15 ml) artificial vanilla extract
Add the above to *Basic Pudding* recipe.

## Chocolate/Caramel Swirl		*6-7 minutes + chilling*

1 cup (240 ml) chocolate pudding		**1 cup (240 ml) caramel pudding**
Using *Basic Pudding* recipe, make half a batch of each and swirl a few seconds.

## Rice Pudding					*7-17 minutes + chilling*

1 cup (240 ml) *refrigerated* precooked long grain rice		**1/2 tsp (2 ml) artificial vanilla extract**

Add the above to half the amount of the *Basic pudding* recipe. Chill as is or bake in a preheated oven set at 350°F (180°C) for about 10 minutes and then chill.

## Tapioca Pudding					*17 minutes + chilling*

1/4 cup (60 ml) small tapioca seeds		**1 tsp (5 ml) artificial vanilla extract**

Add the above to *Basic Pudding* recipe, but when mixture has thickened, lower heat to medium-low and stir for at least another 10 minutes. Add some water if required. Seeds must swell and become invisible or almost.

## Cheesecake Pudding				*7 minutes + chilling*

2 cups (480 ml) *Homemade Yogurt* or *Yogurt/Sour Cream Whey* (replaces the water, pg. 232-3, 234)
1/2-1 tsp (2-5 ml) lemon juice from concentrate
2 tbsp (30 ml) low-cost margarine
1/2 tsp (2 ml) artificial vanilla
1 extra large or 2 small egg(s)
1/4 tsp (1 ml) baking powder or baking soda
Add the above to the ingredients in *Basic Pudding* recipe.

CHOCOLATE SNACK BARS

You'll find that most chocolate bars on the market are made from a combination of a few ingredients or items like chocolate (coating), crispy ice wafers, chopped peanuts, shredded coconut, caramel, fudge, nougat, crisped rice, and peanut butter. Most of these ingredients can be made or bought cheaply. Why not make your own candy bars for about a fifth or less of the supermarket price? When you get the knack of it, we recommend that you double or quadruple the recipe yield and turn it into in a small kitchen production line.

Basic Chocolate Snack Bar   *30-40 minutes*

At least 1 cup (240 ml) *Chocolaty Coating Dip (see pages 210-11)*
3/4-1½ cup(s) (180-360 ml) *Mock Nougat (optional, see page 211)*
1-4 tbsp (15-60 ml) generic-brand caramel spread

1/4-3/4 cup (60-180 ml) fillers like chopped peanuts, crisped rice, peanut butter, shredded coconut, crispy ice wafers, etc. (pick one or two or use those from one of the following recipe variations)!

For simplicity's sake we're going to make all chocolate snack bars about 1" wide x 3/4" high x 4" long (2.5 x 2 x 10 cm). Start by melting the chocolate as outlined in the *Chocolaty Coating Dip* recipe *(see pages 210-11).* Meanwhile, for chocolate bars made from layers of ingredients, use a **small** or a portion of a **large baking sheet** or **plastic tray** *(lightly greased with margarine)* and spread a 3/8 to 1/2-inch (9-12 mm) layer of nougat with a **rubber spatula.** *Alternately, line the baking sheet or tray with wax paper instead of grease.* Nougat may have other ingredients mixed with it like peanuts, crisped rice, raisins, etc. Usually the nougat will be covered with a thin layer of caramel spread. Sometimes its better to place the nougat spread tray in freezer for 10 minutes before spreading the caramel over it. No matter what, the caramel must be placed in freezer at least 15 minutes to harden before being dipped. With a **pastry cutter** *(pizza cutting wheel)* cut the nougat into pieces about the size of commercial bars. For some chocolate bars, the nougat mixture is separated into a dozen pieces that are shaped by hand accordingly. For other bars, two ice wafers are glued together by an icing-style paste before being coated. Still others may have no nougat at all and instead have a mixture based on peanut butter. When you're ready to chocolate coat them, line a small tray or baking sheet with a sheet of wax paper and set it aside on counter close to your dipper setup. *Alternately, place the wax paper lined tray in the freezer for immediate hardening of the chocolate coating.* When chocolate dip is ready, stick a **metal skewer** partially in one of the nougat pieces, and dip it complete in melted chocolate. Maneuver as required to obtain a uniform coating and set them aside to harden on the tray. Use a **fork** to remove the **skewer** as you're placing them on the wax paper *(see page 212). Refer to the recipe variations for more specific directions.* Because our nougat contains raw egg whites, store the snack bars refrigerated wrapped in wax paper or placed in sandwich bags. **Makes about a dozen chocolate snack bars**

CHOCOLATE SNACK BAR VARIATIONS

Peanut-Caramel-Nougat Bar   *30-40 minutes*

1 1/2 cup (360 ml) *Mock Nougat!*
3/4 cup (180 ml) *bulk* toasted (unsalted) whole peanuts
2 tbsp (30 ml) of caramel spread

Use the above in *Basic Chocolate Snack Bar* recipe. Shape nougat into 12 rods by hand, then press about 1 tbsp (15 ml) of the peanuts onto its exterior surface. Place them all on a tray, pour a strip of caramel *(1/2 tsp/2 ml)* on each and freeze about 10 minutes. Remove from freezer, coat with chocolate and freeze to harden.

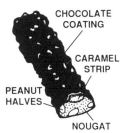

CHOCOLATE COATING

CARAMEL STRIP

PEANUT HALVES

NOUGAT

Nougat-Caramel Bar   30-40 minutes

2 1/4 cups (540 ml) *Mock Nougat*
1/4 cup (60 ml) of caramel spread
No fillers here!

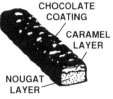

Use the above in *Basic Chocolate Snack Bar* recipe.
These bars are cutted and not hand shaped. Each bar
should have two layers, caramel over nougat *(see*
illustration). Each has about 1 tsp (5 ml) of caramel and
3 tbsp (45 ml) of nougat. Place in freezer about 10
minutes. Remove from freezer, coat with chocolate and freeze to harden again.

Crisped Rice-Peanut Butter Bar   35 minutes

1/2 cup (120 ml) generic-brand smooth
peanut butter
1/4 cup (60 ml) *bulk* **toasted (unsalted)**
peanuts, blender chopped

3/4 cup (180 ml) crisped rice
(Rice Krispies)
2 tbsp (30 ml) caramel spread

Use the above in *Basic Chocolate Snack Bar*
recipe. In a **mixing bowl**, combine peanut butter,
crisped rice, and chopped peanuts. Use hands if
necessary, and divide in twelve. Shape into bars and
pour a strip of caramel *(1/2 tsp/2 ml)* on each. Freeze
on a tray as indicated in basic recipe to harden
peanut butter mixture and caramel. Coat with
chocolate and freeze again 10-15 minutes.

Crispy Wafer-Coffee Bar   35 minutes

24 chocolate flavored crispy ice wafers
3-4 tbsp (45-60 ml) *Instant Coffee*
    Icing (see page 200)

Use the above in *Basic Chocolate Snack Bar* recipe.
Spread the instant coffee icing or paste on some of the
wafers, press a second one against it; remove excess with a
dull knife. Repeat until all done; freeze 10 minutes to
harden paste. Coat with chocolate and freeze again 10
minutes.

SUB-VARIATION *Substitute coffee paste between wafers with peanut butter!*

Chocolaty Coating Dip   15-20 minutes

This simple dip can be made with either chocolate flavored chips or semi-sweet
chocolate chips (generic or even brand names) for baking which are very
inexpensive compared to many other types of chocolate.

2 cups (480 ml) generic-brand
    chocolate flavored chips or
    semi-sweet chocolate chips

4 tsp (20 ml) generic-brand
    vegetable shortening or
    low-cost margarine

In a **double boiler**, a floating **metal bowl** in a **saucepan**, or preferably an **improvised dipper** *(see 'Improvised Dipper' illustration),* place enough hot tap water in a suitable pan depending which one of the three chocolate heating option you picked. Bring the water to a simmer and then remove heat. Place both ingredients *(use more chocolate if necessary for more dipping depth)* and the

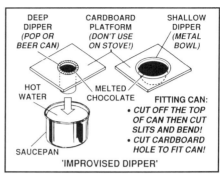

thermometer in upper metal bowl, or can. Wait 5-10 minutes before stirring the mixture; when ready chocolate mixture should be a semi-liquid that flows well, not to thick or thin. If using a metal floating bowl, remove it from hot water bath before stirring and make sure no water gets into chocolate. The best dipping 0temperature for this dip is 110-120°F (43-49°C), verify using a **floating** or **candy thermometer**. Stir occasionally. Reheat, or wait and cool to adjust temperature. For a thicker coating, use a lower temperature. A **large bowl** of cold tap water will lower the temperature quickly. Some brands of chocolate do work better, and if you find one that works well, stick to it. Some *(especially chocolate flavored chips)* continually seize and turn lumpy even if you add more shortening, avoid those. Low-cost margarine instead of shortening works also but makes a slightly messy chocolate coating. Save the leftover chocolate for the next batch. *For further instructions, see snack bars and chocolate coated ice cream treats recipes (pages 209, 212-5).* **Makes about 1 1/8 cups (270 ml)**

Mock Nougat   *35 minutes + chilling*

1 2/3 cups granulated sugar
3/8 cup (90 ml) light corn syrup
3/8 cup (90 ml) cold tap water

1/2 tbsp (7 ml) *Caramelized Sugar
    Coloring (see page 243)*
3 small egg whites

In a **heavy-bottomed saucepan**, combine all ingredients except the egg whites. Bring to a boil over a medium heat setting while stirring with a **whisk**. Lower heat slightly and continue to cook until temperature and gauge the temperature with a **candy thermometer**; continue to cook until temperature reaches 270°F (133°C) *(soft-crack stage).* Meanwhile, beat the egg whites with an **electric mixer**, till soft peaks form and set aside. When sugar mixture reaches the soft-crack stage, remove it from heat and pour it into the beaten egg whites in a thin stream while beating on a low speed. Beat about 10-15 minutes till the mixture has thickened sufficiently. Press or roll-out to 3/8- inch (1 cm) thickness *(see illustration on page 250)* on **wax paper** or a **baking sheet** and cool to harden. *Refer to specify recipes.* **Nougat is commercially available!**
Makes about 1 1/2 cups (360ml)

FROZEN TREATS

Most of our frozen treats are made with low-cost generic-brand ice cream and/or low-cost generic sweetened flavored drink crystals. Practice making one or two frozen treats at first, then turn them into productions of a dozen or more.

Caramel-Peanut Ice Cream Bar   2 hours
This recipe is the most temperamental and difficult to make of the frozen treats. The results and savings though, are well worth the effort. It costs about a quarter of the supermarket price to make.

Enough melted chocolate to coat!   2 cups (480 ml) *bargain* generic-
(see pages 210-11, or 250)   brand ice cream or ice milk,
1/3 cup (80 ml) *bulk* toasted peanuts,   vanilla or other flavor
     frozen   1/8 cup (60 ml) caramel spread

CHOCOLATE COATING / CARAMEL STRIP / PEANUT HALVES / ICE CREAM

In a **mixing bowl**, quickly combine the cold peanuts (halved) and the scooped-out pieces of hard ice cream. Very quickly separate into six parts and shape *(wearing new rubber gloves)* as illustrated. *Don't make them too frail.* Place a **metal skewer** about 3/4 way through each and place them on a wax paper lined cold **baking sheet**. Return to freezer *(set on the highest setting)* at once and freeze till hard again, at least 30 minutes. Alternately, don't use a bowl, just place the ice cream *(plus an extra amount)* on the wax paper lined baking sheet and roll it down to an appropriate thickness. Cut out bars with a **pastry/pizza cutter**, and sprinkle the peanuts on surface and press them in with a flat surfaced object. Again, freeze at once. Meanwhile, using a **saucepan**, three quarters filled with hot tap water, bring it to a temperature of about 120°F (49°C) on the highest setting. Remove from heat and place it on kitchen counter covered with **improvised can dipper (see page 211)** containing the chocolate coating ingredients. Wait about a quarter of an hour for the chocolate coating ingredients to get hot *(100-105°F/38-40°C)*; stir well. While waiting, prepare the caramel by pouring the caramel spread *(at room temperature)* into a medium-size **funnel** which has a paper towel plug at the bottom and place it in a tall glass for support. Alternately, use a **plastic bag** with a perforation at one end to line the ice cream bars with a clean stripe of caramel *(see ill. page 200)*. Remove the frozen ice cream/peanut pieces from the freezer and again very quickly pour a caramel strip *(1 tsp/5 ml)* on each. Refreeze only a quarter of an hour this time. Now they're ready to coat. Holding each one by the ring portion of the skewer dip them in the fluid chocolate in a rather fast motion and immediately return them to the wax

paper lined baking sheet. For this operation, you may leave the baking sheet in freezer or have it on the kitchen counter. When you're all done with your very small ice cream bar production, return them to the freezer for at least an hour or till the ice cream is hard again. Now you can pull out the skewers using a **fork** to hold back the coated bars *(see illustration)*. Store them frozen in plastic container, or folded in plastic sandwich bags, wax paper, or aluminum foil. **Makes 6 ice cream bars**
VARIATIONS *Apart from using different ice cream flavors, try mixing chopped or whole peanuts (or chocolate chips) with the ice cream, or add 1 tsp (5 ml) cherry, blueberry, etc. of pie filling stretcher or jelly filling instead of caramel!*

Chocolate-Coated Ice Cream Cones   30 minutes

Enough chocolate to coat (pg.210-11)! 3 cups (720 ml) *bargain* generic-
6 sugar cones *(or wafer cones*   brand ice cream or ice milk,
2 tbsp (30 ml) chopped peanuts   vanilla or other flavor

Using a **saucepan**, three quarters filled with hot tap water, bring it to
a temperature of about 120°F (49°C) on the highest setting.
Remove from heat and place it on kitchen counter covered
with **improvised** *bowl* **dipper** *(see page 211)* containing the
chocolate coating ingredients. Wait about a quarter of an
hour for the chocolate coating ingredients to get hot *(100-
105°F/38-40°C)*; stir well. Only when the chocolate *(or
shortening)* has melted and is uniformly mixed with the other
ingredients should you prepare the ice cream and sugar cones. It's
very important that the ice cream be very cold and hard. Using any type
of **ice cream scooper** *(see ill.)*, quickly place about 1/2 cup (120 ml) of ice cream
on each sugar cone *(be sure to gently jam as much ice cream as
possible into the cones)* and place them standing up in a **frozen
pop maker set** or **6 glasses** for support *(placed on kitchen counter)*. Quickly
again, holding the ice cream cones upside down, dip them one by one in the
liquid chocolate mixture in one rather fast motion, and immediately sprinkle
about 1 tsp (5 ml) of chopped *(toasted)* peanuts on each *(while chocolate is still
soft)*. If there's an open spot in the chocolate forget about it, it's too late. (If
dipping them upside down proves disastrous, just coat them with hot chocolate
using a ladle.) Immediately place the frozen pop maker set holding the cones in
freezer and wait at least an hour before wrapping or placing them in a container.
Freezer should be set on high. Store frozen in plastic container, plastic sandwich
bags, or folded in wax paper or even aluminum foil. **Makes 6 cream cones**

Chocolate-Coated Ice Cream Cookies   1½ hours

Enough melted chocolate to coat!   2 cups (480 ml) *bargain* generic-
   (see page 210-11, 250)   brand ice cream or ice milk,
16 flat cookies, 2 1/2-inch/6 cm round   vanilla or other flavor
   (any type, see pages 200-3)

Using a **saucepan**, three quarters filled with hot tap water,   CHOCOLATE
bring it to a temperature of about 120°F (49°C) on the   COATING
highest setting. Remove from heat and place it on kitchen
counter covered with **improvised** *bowl* **dipper** *(see page
211)* containing the chocolate coating ingredients. While
waiting line up the cookies on a wax paper-lined **baking
sheet** and place in freezer. Wait about a quarter of an hour   ICE CREAM
for the chocolate coating ingredients to get hot *(100-*   TWO MEDIUM
105°F/38-40°C); stir well. Only when the chocolate *(or*   COOKIES
shortening) has melted and is uniformly mixed with the other ingredients should
you prepare the cookie/ice cream sandwiches. It's very important that the ice
cream be very cold and hard. Using a **spoon**, quickly place about 1/4 cup (60 ml)
of ice cream on one cold cookie and slightly press the second cold cookie against
it. Place it on the wax paper-lined baking sheet *(on kitchen counter)* and quickly
do the second and so on. Quickly again, holding the cookie/ice cream sandwich

sideways, dip half of it in the liquid chocolate mixture in one rather fast motion. If there's an open spot forget about it its too late. Place it on baking sheet and quickly do the remainder before ice cream melts. Immediately place the baking sheet in freezer and wait at least 30 minutes before coating the second half of the cookie/ice cream sandwiches. *Freezer should be set on high.* Freeze again when done another half hour and store frozen in plastic container, plastic sandwich bags, or folded in wax paper or even aluminum foil. **Makes 8 frozen cookie/ice cream sandwiches**

VARIATIONS *Apart from using different ice cream flavors or cookie styles, try mixing chopped or whole peanuts (or chocolate chips) with the ice cream, or add 1 tsp (5 ml) of caramel spread (pie filling or jam stretchers) to each sandwich!*

Chocolate-Coated Ice Cream Pop *8-12 hours*

Enough melted chocolate to coat!   2 1/2 cups (600 ml) *bargain* **generic-**
   (see pages 210-11, 250)   **brand ice cream or ice milk,**
                                                vanilla or other flavor

Using **frozen pop maker set** *(see ill.)*, quickly spray the inside surfaces with generic-brand cooking spray. Pack semi-hard ice cream in the 6 molds. Push the plastic holders or wooden *(also called coffee stirrers or craft sticks)* into the ice cream and immediately remove them. Now pour in a little cold tap water in each of these holes. Replace the plastic holders or wooden sticks back in ice cream and place the *frozen pop maker set* in freezer. Wait at least an hour for the water in holes to harden. Meanwhile, using a **saucepan**, three quarters filled with hot tap water, bring it to a temperature of about 120°F (49°C) on the highest setting. Remove from heat and place it on kitchen counter with **improvised** **can** **dipper** *(see page 211)* containing the chocolate coating ingredients in it. Wait about a quarter of an hour for the chocolate coating ingredients to get warm *(100-105°F/38-40°C)*, stir well. Only when the chocolate *(or shortening)* has melted and is uniformly blended should you remove the ice cream pops from the freezer. It's very important that the ice cream be very cold and hard. Run cold tap water against the outside of *frozen pop maker set* to help free the frozen ice cream pops. Dip them one by one in the fluid chocolate in a rather fast motion and immediately plant them in a **styro-foam block or pad**. For this operation, you may leave the foam block in freezer or have it on the kitchen counter. When you're all done with you very small ice cream bar production, return or leave them in the freezer for about an hour till the ice cream is hard again. Store them frozen in plastic container, or wrapped in small plastic bags, in wax paper, or aluminum foil. **Makes 6 revel-style pops**

VARIATION *Mix some chopped peanuts or chocolate chips with the ice cream!*

Chocolate-Coated Soft Ice Cream Cups   *20-25 minutes*

Enough melted chocolate to coat!   4 cups (960 ml) *bargain* **generic-**
   (see pages 210-11, 250)   **brand ice cream or ice milk,**
4 wafer cups for ice cream   **vanilla or other flavor**

The first thing to do is to place a **saucepan** three quarters filled with hot tap water on stove. Bring it to a temperature of about 120°F (49°C) on the highest heat setting. Remove from heat and place it on kitchen counter with **improvised *can* dipper** *(see page 211)* containing the chocolate coating ingredients in it. Wait about a quarter of an hour for the chocolate to get warm *(100-105°F/38-40°C)*; stir well. May sure the chocolate *(or shortening)* has melted

and has been well stir before dipping the cones. To prepare the ice cream cups, line up the flat-bottomed wafer cups on the counter. In a **plastic bag**, place about half of the cold ice cream and knead it for several seconds. Then cut off one of the corner tips and force out softened ice cream using your hands in a spiral motion *(the idea is similar to the icing ill. on page 200, but with a larger opening)*. Alternately, if you think this idea is a bit **dumb** simply make conventional hard ice cream cones and dip in chocolate. At any rate, make sure each wafer cup *(or wafer cone)* is full to the bottom with ice cream. This helps prevent that the ice cream doesn't drop from the wafer cups when placed upside down. Tap each one lightly against the kitchen to force down the ice cream even more into the cup. Dip them one by one upside down in the fluid chocolate in a rather fast motion. Enjoy at once. **Makes 4 ice cream cups**
VARIATIONS *Forget the chocolate coating and serve **Plain Soft Ice Cream Cones** or **Plain Hard Ice Cream Cones**!*

Frozen Flavored Crystals Pops   3-5 hours

5 cups (1200 ml) *Flavor Crystals Drink*
(see page 230)

Pour into **two frozen pop maker set**, and freeze till solid *(several hours)*. Run tap water against the outside of *frozen pop maker set* to free the frozen pops.
Makes a dozen frozen pops
VARIATIONS *Try the numerous flavors or combining 2 or 3 flavors in one!*

Costume-Made Sundae   2-3 minutes

About 2/3 cup (160 ml) generic-brand
   vanilla ice cream
2 tbsp (30 ml) *Sugar Syrup*, flavored
   with jam or spread *(see page 217)*

1/2 tbsp (7 ml) blender chopped
   toasted unsalted peanuts
   (optional)

In a **tulip sundae dish**, **short glass**, or **small bowl**, place ice cream and pour syrup. Top with chopped peanuts. *Sorry no maraschino cherry here, they're too expensive!*
Makes one serving
VARIATIONS *Try different ice cream and syrup flavors!*

Banana-Split Delight   3-4 minutes

Half banana, split length-wise in 4
   pieces
1 cup (240 ml) generic-brand vanilla
   ice cream *(divide into 3 scoops)*

1 tbsp (15 ml) strawberry *Sugar
   Syrup (see page 217, typical)*
1 tbsp (15 ml) caramel *Sugar Syrup*
1 tbsp (15 ml) chocolate or fudge
   Sugar Syrup

In a **banana split dish, long dish**, or **dessert bowl**, place the three ice cream scoops in line *(about 1/3 cup/80 ml each)*. Top each scoop with a different type of syrup. The four banana portions are placed on each side of the dish. Things go much smoother if the syrups are ready ahead of time. **Makes one serving**

DESSERT FILLINGS, SAUCES, & SYRUPS

Creme Filling   *6-7 minutes*

1 extra-large or 2 small egg white(s)
2 tbsp (30 ml) light corn syrup
1 cup (240 ml) granulated sugar

1 1/2 tbsp (22 ml) cold tap water
Pinch of salt

In the top of a **double boiler** or in a **metal bowl** in a **saucepan** containing hot water, combine the egg white, corn syrup, sugar, water, and salt. Get the water simmering or set over a pan of simmering water. Using an **electric mixer** beat a medium speed until the mixture forms stiff peaks. Remove from the pan of water and beat another minute till smooth. Use as cake filling. **Makes 1 cup (240 ml)**

Custard Filling

1 small egg
3/4 cup (180 ml) *Reconstituted Skim Milk (see page 231)*

2 tbsp (30 ml) granulated sugar
1 tbsp (15 ml) *bulk* cornstarch
Pinch of sugar

In a **small bowl**, beat the egg with an **electric mixer**. In a **small saucepan**, combine the milk, sugar, cornstarch, and salt over a medium heat. With a **whisk**, stir constantly until thickened and bubbly. Remove from heat and set aside. Beat on a medium speed 2 tbsp (30 ml) of the hot milk mixture into the beaten egg. Add the egg mixture to the saucepan and whisk constantly. Place over a medium-low heat another 2 minutes to cook the egg. Stir constantly. Use at once or place contents in a bowl, cover and let cool to room temperature before chilling. Chill at least 30 minutes or till needed. **Makes about 1 cup (240 ml)**

Flavored Crystals Filling   *7-8 minutes*

Make cherry, strawberry, raspberry, cherry, flavored fillings with this recipe.

2 1/4 cups (560 ml) water
1/4 cup (60 ml) corn starch
    (or all-purpose flour)
1 tbsp (15 ml) margarine

1/2 cup (120 ml) granulated
    sugar
2 tbsp (30 ml) sweetened flavored
    drink crystals *(generic-brand)*

In a **heavy saucepan or skillet**, pour the water and dissolve the cornstarch *(or flour)*. Heat over a medium setting and add margarine; dissolve sugar and flavored crystals while stirring. Within 5 minutes, the mixture should thicken. Remove from heat and stir about 30 second. Use to fill doughnuts, line cakes, top Danish-style pastries, desserts, and more. **Makes about 2 1/4 cups (540 ml)**

Chocolate Sauce   *5 minutes*

A good dessert sauce to be used sparingly on sundaes, ice cream, cakes, etc. It doesn't harden when spooned on ice cream.

2/3 cup (160 ml) water	1/2 cup (120 ml) granulated sugar
1/4 cup (60 ml) instant skim milk powder	1/2 cup (120 ml) *bulk* cocoa powder
	1/4 cup (60 ml) low-cost margarine or vegetable oil

In a **small saucepan** or **metal bowl**, place water, milk powder, and sugar. Heat and stir over a medium heat a few minutes until sugar has dissolved and is no longer granular. Stir in cocoa and fat until smooth. Use hot or cold. *Turn it into chocolate syrup by combining it with sugar syrup.* **Makes over 1 cup (240 ml)**

Quick Applesauce   *8-10 minutes*

This applesauce is uncooked. The citric and ascorbic acid prevent darkening.

2 tbsp (30 ml) cold tap water	1 1/2 tbsp (22 ml) granulated sugar
1/2 tsp (2 ml) lemon juice from concentrate	1/8 tsp (1/2 ml) cinnamon
	Dash of salt
2 or 3 apples, peeled and wedged	1/8 tsp (1/2 ml) ascorbic acid

In a **blender**, place water, lemon juice and a few apple wedges, blend at low speed until smooth. Add remaining apple wedges a few at a time. Finally, add remaining ingredients and blend till smooth. Serve a once, or refrigerate up to 12 hours. *Likewise, heat applesauce in a skillet a few minutes and serve hot, or refrigerate up to 2 days.* **Makes about 1 cup (240 ml)**

Old-Fashioned Applesauce   *15-17 minutes*

This old-fashioned applesauce, or if you prefer apple compote, is cooked, spiced, and is unadulterated old-fashioned goodness.

3-4 baking apples, peeled and sliced	2 tbsp (30 ml) cornstarch or all-purpose flour
1 cup (240 ml) hot tap water	3 tbsp (45 ml) granulated sugar
1 tsp (5 ml) lemon juice from concentrate	1/8 tsp (1/2 ml) nutmeg
1/4 tsp (1 ml) ascorbic acid *(optional)*	1/8 tsp (1/2 ml) cinnamon

In a **heavy saucepan**, cook apple slices in water and lemon juice over a medium-high heat for about 10 minutes. Mash apples with a **potato masher** and add remaining ingredients. Cook, and stir *continuously* another few minutes. Pour in a **recycled jar**, cover and refrigerate. Keeps about 2 days. **Makes about 2 cups (480 ml)**

Sugar Syrup(s)   *3-4 minutes*

*These syrups are identical to those used by soda fountains and the likes. The flavored syrups are used to top **ice cream**, sundaes, desserts, and use them diluted to make frozen pops, cold drinks and as the liquid portion in floats. You get professional quality for next to nothing. The plain syrup (made from sugar only) has to be mixed with jams, jellies, sweet spreads, or sweet sauces. The syrup made from flavored drink crystals is used as it is over desserts or diluted for drinks.*

1/2 cup (120 ml) hot tap water   1 cup (240 ml) granulated sugar
                                        OR flavored drink crystals
                                           containing sugar *(generic)*

In a **small saucepan**, over a medium heat, dissolve the sugar or flavored crystals in water. Use a **whisk** to stir till solution is clear and no longer granular. Simmer a few more minutes for a thicker syrup. **Makes one cup (240 ml) of syrup**
VARIATIONS *To make **Fudge, Chocolate,** or **Caramel Syrup** mix two parts of plain sugar syrup with one part of fudge, chocolate, or caramel spread (generic-brand). To make **Strawberry, Raspberry,** (etc.) **Syrups** mix two parts of plain sugar syrup with one part of jam or jam-jelly (generic-brand)!*

Table Syrup   *1 minute*
Costs about 1/3ʳᵈ the store price to make. Time assumes the ingredients are ready.

2 cups (480 ml) *Sugar Syrup*   1/4 cup (60 ml) *Caramelized Sugar*
   (see pages 217-18)   *Coloring (see page 243)*

In a **recycled syrup bottle**, pour above; shake. Serve with cereals, pancakes, etc. *For thicker syrup, simmer a few more minutes.* **Makes 2 1/4 cups (540 ml)**

OTHER DESSERT RECIPES

Mock Cheesecake   *15-20 minutes + chill*

Most cheesecake recipes of comparable size cost between 10 and 15 dollars to make. This one will set you back barely two dollars and isn't worst than many of the no-bake cheesecake filling mixes on the market.

FILLING:
1/2 cup (120 ml) low-cost margarine   1/4 tsp (1 ml) *Caramelized Sugar*
1/2 cup (120 ml) all-purpose flour   *Coloring (see page 243)*
1/2 cup (120 ml) *Yogurt Cheese*   1/2 tsp (2 ml) artificial vanilla
   (see page 236)   extract
3 cups (720 ml) *Homemade Yogurt*   1 tsp (5 ml) lemon juice from
   (see pages 232-3)   concentrate
1 1/4 cups (300 ml) granulated sugar   4 small or 2 extra-large eggs
2 tbsp (30 ml) *bulk* corn starch   1/2 tsp (2 ml) baking soda

CRUST: TOPPING:
Half *Crumb Crust* recipe *(see page 147)* 1 cup (240 ml) *Pie Filling Stretcher*
                                              (see page 148)

In a **heavy bottomed saucepan**, melt margarine over a medium-low heat. Mix the flour with it as in making a *roux (see page 149)*. Keep stirring a minute or two and set aside. Meanwhile, in a **large mixing bowl**, combine all remaining filling ingredients except eggs and optional margarine. Beat the filling ingredients at least one minute on high with a hand-held **electric mixer**. Add eggs; beat until blended only. Pour contents of bowl into saucepan and heat over a medium-low heat until bubbly. Cook two more minutes and remove from heat. Using a **spring-foam pan** with removable bottom *(or*

SPRINGFORM PAN

round cake pan), line the bottom portion with the crumb crust mixture. Use the bottom of a glass to compress it. Do not line the side wall, it's too difficult and time consuming. Pour the warm filling in assembled spring-form pan and let cool at room temperature one hour. Cover and refrigerate at least 3 hours or overnight and top with the topping. To serve, remove the spring-form portion of pan and slice in twelve. **Makes one large cheesecake (8"/20 cm round x 1½"/3¾ cm thick) or eight cheesecake slices**

LITE! VERSION *Reduce the margarine in margarine/flour mixture to 1-2 tbsp (15-30 ml), and use low-fat cream cheese!*

VARIATIONS *For a **Cheese-less Cheesecake** replace yogurt cheese or cream cheese with same quantity of yogurt. For **Cheese-less & Yogurt-less Cheesecake** replace them with same amount of fresh whey plus 2/3 cup (160 ml) milk powder!*

Tofu Cheesecake   40 minutes + chilling

Unlike many bean-tasting tofu cheesecake recipes, this one contains much less tofu and is far better tasting.

FILLING:

1/4 cup (120 ml) low-cost margarine
1/2 cup (120 ml) all-purpose flour
1 1/2 cups (360 ml) *Homemade Firm Tofu*, mashed *(see pages 239-40)*
2 cups (480 ml) *Homemade Yogurt (see pages 232-3)*
1 1/4 cups (300 ml) granulated sugar

1 tbsp (15 ml) *bulk* cornstarch
1 tsp (5 ml) artificial vanilla extract
1 tbsp (15 ml) lemon juice from concentrate
2 small or 1 extra-large egg(s)
Pinch of salt

CRUST:
Half *Crumb Crust* recipe *(pg. 147)*

TOPPING:
1 cup (240 ml) *Pie Filling Stretcher (see page 148)*

Melt margarine and mix with flour. In a **blender** or **food processor**, combine all filling ingredients and process till smooth. Meanwhile, preheat oven to 375°F (190°C) and line the bottom only of a **spring-form** or **round cake pan** with the crumb mixture. Pour the filling into prepared crust and bake for 30 minutes, until firm. Cool one hour on counter and three hours in refrigerator. Top with pie filling stretcher or flavored crystals filling before serving. **Makes a dozen slices**

LITE! VERSION *Reduce the margarine to 1-2 tbsp (15-30 ml)!*

Single-Serving Cheesecake   7-10 minutes

2 tbsp (30 ml) crumbled *Homemade Graham Crackers (see page 201-2)*
1 tsp (5 ml) granulated sugar
2 tsp (10 ml) melted margarine
1/2 cup (120 ml) *Cheesecake Pudding (pg. 208)*
2 tbsp (30 ml) *Pie Filling Stretcher, Fruit Pie Filling (see pages 148, 147-8)*

CHEESECAKE   TOPPING
PUDDING

COOKIE
CRUMBS

Mix crumbled crackers (or cookies), sugar and melted margarine together. Assemble in a dessert bowl as illustrated. **Makes an average single serving**

LITE! VERSION *Omit margarine altogether and use the lite pudding version!*

Apple-Raisin Bread Pudding *35 minutes*

Preheat oven to 400°F (200°C).

8 slices white bread
4 small or 2 extra-large eggs
1/2 cup (120 ml) granulate sugar
1 cup (240 ml) diced cooking apples
1/4 cup (60 ml) seedless raisins
1/4 tsp (1 ml) ground cinnamon
1/8 tsp (1/2 ml) ground nutmeg

2 tbsp (30 ml) margarine, melted
1/2 cup (120 ml) instant skim milk
   powder
2 cups (480 ml) hot tap water
1 tsp (5 ml) artificial vanilla
   extract
1 tbsp (15 ml) all-purpose flour

Cut off the crust from the bread, and cut slices length-wise in 3 or 4 pieces each. In a greased **two-quart/liter baking dish or casserole**, combine bread, apples and raisins; set aside. In a **bowl**, beat the eggs slightly, then combine water, milk powder, sugar, margarine, vanilla, spices and flour; pour over bread mixture. Bake for 25-30 minutes or until knife inserted in center comes out clean and the top is well browned. Serve warm or chilled for later. **Makes 8 small servings**

Chocolate-Coated Cake with Filling   1 hour

Basic Plain Cake recipe *(see page 197)*   1-2 cup(s) (240-480 ml) *Chocolaty*
1/2 cup (120 ml) of *Creme Filling*   *Coating Dip (see page 210-11)*
   (see page 216)

CHOCOLATE   FLATCAKES
COATING

FILLING(S)

CUPCAKES   CAKE
            CRUMB

Prepare the cake batter as described in *Basic plain Cake* recipe. Using non-stick **baking sheets** or, **medium or large muffin trays**, bake numerous small cakes till golden. If using baking sheets spread the batter to 3 1/2-inch (9 cm) circles and at least 1/4-inch (.64 cm) thick. If using muffin trays, fill cups to half only to obtain cupcakes and not muffins. Cool the cakes on wire racks. Spread from 1-2 tsp (5-10 ml) of filling on each cake and line them up closely of baking sheets or plastic trays. Place in freezer for up to half an hour to harden the filling. Meanwhile, prepare the chocolate dip as described in *Chocolaty Coating Dip* recipe. Remove filling topped cakes from refrigeration; now they're ready for dipping. Use the **improvised bowl dipper** to coat the cakes. Dip half of each cake only and place on baking sheets. For cupcakes, dip the bottom half, first. For flat-cakes dip them sideways and place them flat on baking sheets. When the chocolate coating has hardened at room temperature enough to be handled with rubber gloves, coat the other half. When coatings are solid, store them refrigerated in sandwich bags or wax paper. Alternately, store them in plastic containers or small boxes with the bag or wrapping. **Makes 12 to 24 chocolate-coated cakes with filling**

VARIATIONS *Substitute the filling with caramel spread, Pie Filling Stretcher, or Flavored Crystals Filling recipe (see pages 148, 216). Try the Chocolate-Flavored Cake (see page 198), or an angel or sponge cake recipe!*

For more desserts, see chapters on dessert pies, muffins, cake, cookies, cereal bars, doughnuts, etc.!

Beverages

About Pitcher Filtered Tap Water!

For fresh, better tasting tap water, it's the best solution. It is very inexpensive, convenient, and safe. It reduces or eliminates the harmful metals and minerals; its only limitation is that it doesn't disinfect water that is microbiologically unsafe. Many of the beverage recipes call for pitcher filtered tap water.

FRUIT BEVERAGES

Our fruit beverages are very inexpensive to make, more diluted and less sweetened than those found in typical cookbooks. This doesn't mean that they're not very refreshing and great tasting. Any type of beverage that costs well under a dime a glass to make is certainly fit to be in this book. All the fruit beverages, raw vegetable juices, and shakes were made with the least expensive blender on the market.

Basic Fruit Beverage   *4-5 minutes*

3 cups (720 ml) cold tap water   1/3 cup (80 ml) *Sugar Syrup (pg 217)*
    (preferably pitcher filtered)   **1 1/2 tbsp (22 ml) lemon juice from**
1 cup (240 ml) small ice cubes   **concentrate**

In a **blender,** place above ingredients *and ingredients for any of the variations.* Blend at a high speed for 30 seconds. Quickly pass through **sieve** onto **pitcher**. Serve at once. Refrigerated most up to 8 hours; re-blend a few seconds if serving later. *All ginger ales are from 2Q/L pop bottles or homemade.* **Makes 4 cups (960 ml) or 4 servings**

FRUIT BEVERAGE VARIATIONS

Orange Cooler   *4-5 minutes*

An orange, peeled and quartered
Add above ingredient to *Basic Fruit Beverage* ingredients.

Smoothy Orange Drink   *4-5 minutes*

An orange, peeled and quartered   3 tbsp (45 ml) skim milk powder
Add above ingredients to *Basic Fruit Beverage* ingredients.

Copacabana Drink   *4-5 minutes*

1 tsp (5 ml) artificial vanilla   Half banana, sliced
   extract   1 cup (240 ml) *Homemade Yogurt*
1/2 cup (120 ml) canned pineapple   *(replaces same amount of water,*
   juice *(replaces same amount*   *see pages 232-3)*
   of water)*   2 tbsp (30 ml) skim milk powder
Add above ingredients to those in *Basic Fruit Beverage*.

Mixed Fruit Drink   *5-6 minutes*

2 tbsp (30 ml) fresh or canned   1/3 banana, chopped
   pineapple, diced   1/4 apple, diced with skin
1/3 orange, peeled and quartered
Add above ingredients to those in *Basic Fruit Beverage* recipe.

Creamy Yogurt Fruit Drink   *5-6 minutes*

Half orange, including white pulp   1/2 cup (120 ml) *Homemade Yogurt*
   under peel, chopped   *(see pages 232-3)*
Half banana, chopped   1 1/2 tbsp (22 ml) instant skim milk
                                          powder
Add above in *Basic Fruit Beverage* recipe. *Use a potato peeler for the orange.*

Fruit Delight   *5-6 minutes*

Half an apple, peeled and   1/2 cup (120 ml) red or blue
   diced   grapes *(inexpensively in season)*
Half an orange, peeled and quartered   OR 2 tbsp (30 ml) *Sugar Syrup*
                                          made with grape flavored crystals
Add above ingredients to those in *Basic Fruit Beverage* recipe.

Citrus Fruit Fizz   *4-5 minutes*

An orange, peeled and quartered
1 1/2 cups (360 ml) chilled ginger ale
   (replaces same amount of water)
Add above to the *Basic Fruit Beverage* recipe.

Mixed Fruit Fizz   *5-6 minutes*

Half an orange, peeled and   1/2 cup (120 ml) any fruit, diced
   quartered   *(inexpensively in season)*
Half an apple, not peeled and   1 1/2 cups (360 ml) chilled ginger ale
   diced   *(replaces same amount of water)*
Add above ingredients to those in *Basic Fruit Beverage* recipe.

Sangria Punch 5-6 minutes

Half an orange, peeled and quartered
1/4 cup (60 ml) canned pineapple juice
3 tbsp (45 ml) grape flavored crystals
1 1/2 cups (360 ml) generic or home ginger ale
 (replaces same amount of water)
Add above ingredients to *Basic Fruit Beverage* recipe.

Grapefruit Fizz 6 minutes

Half grapefruit, peeled and chopped 1 cup (240 ml) chilled generic ginger ale
 (replaces same amount of water)
Add above ingredients to those of *Basic Fruit Beverage.*

RAW VEGETABLE JUICES

A blender can actually derive more from fresh vegetables than a centrifugal juicer (we think!). For low-cost energizingly refreshing raw vegetable juices, try these a la **CookMISER***. They're more diluted but much cheaper than those made in juicers.*

Basic Raw Vegetable Juice 6-7 minutes

1 1/2 cups (360 ml) cold tap water   *One or more raw vegetable(s),*
1/3 cup (80 ml) small ice cubes   *coarsely chopped!*

Place water *and chopped vegetable(s) for a variation (with or without ice)* in an **electric blender** and place cover on container. Blend at a high speed for 60 seconds. Quickly pass through **sieve** onto a pitcher, add ice. Stir and serve at once. Refrigerated up to 4 hours, re-blender.**Makes about 16 fl oz/480 ml or 2 medium servings**

RAW VEGETABLE JUICE VARIATIONS

Raw Carrot Juice 6 minutes

2 medium carrots, coarse chopped
Add the above to *Basic Raw Vegetable Juice* recipe.

Fresh Celery-Carrot Juice 7 minutes

1 large carrot, chopped   1/8 tsp (1/2 ml) celery salt
1 celery stalk, chopped
Add the above to *Basic Raw Vegetable Juice* recipe.

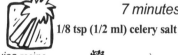

Garden Vegetable Cocktail 7-9 minutes

1 thin slice of yellow onion, chopped   1/2 cup (120 ml) cold canned
1 medium carrot, chopped   tomato juice *(replaces*
1/2 celery stalk, chopped   *same amount of water)*
A few slices of peeled or not peeled   1/2 tsp (2 ml) dried parsley
 cucumber *(optional)*   1/8 tsp (1/2 ml) celery salt
1 tsp (5 ml) lemon juice from conc.   Salt and pepper to taste
Add the above to *Basic Raw Vegetable Juice* recipe.

Raw Vegetable Tonic   7-8 minutes

1 medium carrot, coarse chopped   Quarter celery stalk, chopped
1 small beet, skinned and chopped   1/2 tbsp (7 ml) minced yellow onion
Add the above to *Basic Raw Vegetable Juice* recipe. Serve on ice.
SUB-VARIATION *Try this and other raw vegetable juice recipes using the juice from the 'Blender Grating' of cabbage when making cole slaws, see page 60!*

Spiced Carrot Drink   7 minutes

1 medium carrot, coarse chopped   Dash of *Worcestershire-Style*
1/3 cup (90 ml) canned tomato juice   *Sauce (see page 243)*
Half a celery stalk ,coarsely chopped   1/8 tsp (1/2 ml) celery salt
Add the above to *Basic Raw Vegetable Juice* recipe.

HOMEMADE SOFT DRINKS

These homemade soft drink recipes, or if you prefer pop, yield about 24 recycled 11.3 fl oz/341 ml pop filled beer bottles. Use clear, brown, or green bottles with reusable twist-off caps. The nice thing about these bottles is that they don't explode they just leak instead. These soft drinks will cost you a bit more than half the cost of the cheapest generic pops you can buy. It comes out to a few cents a glass. We recommend at first, that you try new pop recipes with a few bottles only.

Basic Homemade Soft Drink   5-7 days

Flavoring for one of the following   7 quarts/liters boiled water cooled
  homemade soft drink recipe   to lukewarm (about 115°F/46°C)
  variations!   1/4 tsp (1 ml) any active dry yeast
4 cups (960 ml) *Sugar Syrup (made*   *(use half that amount in very hot*
  from sugar only, see pages 217-18)   *weather)*

In a **stock pot**, bring the cold tap water to a boil and set aside. Let cool to lukewarm. In a very **large bowl** using a **plastic mixing spoon**, mix all ingredients together except yeast. *In cases where fresh and perishable ingredients are used, or flavor must be extracted from ingredients, simmer all ingredients except yeast together in a large saucepan or a stockpot for 10-15 minutes. Remove from heat and allow to steep for 30 minutes. It is cooled and strained.* Meanwhile, in a **small bowl**, mix yeast and 1 tsp (5 ml) of sugar with 1/4 cup (60 ml) of lukewarm

POUR *OR* SIPHON

BOTTLING

water. After 5 minutes *(if yeast is good),* add this yeast mixture to the sweetened flavored solution. Stir well and bottle immediately, fill to within one-half inch/1¼ cm of the top. More air space in bottles may cause spoilage. *Clean reused bottles and twist-off caps very carefully before bottling. Caps with nicks and bumps should be discarded, as well as damaged bottle mouths and cap seals. Start by soaking them in very hot water (a little household liquid bleach in it won't hurt) for at least 8 hours. Then wash them in hot water and soap. Remove the labels and rinse well.* Fill the bottles using a **small pitcher,** or

USE TOWEL TO TIGHTEN CAPS!

large spouted measuring cup, or a **siphoning hose.** The reused or recycled twist-off caps threads are started by hand and are tightened using a few layers of towel cloth or a kitchen mitten in the top hand. Place the bottles on their sides at room temperature away from draughts, until effervescent. This will take place at least 4-5 days after bottling. It may take longer in colder weather. At this point bottles must be removed from room temperature and set in a cool place of even temperature, like a basement closet or small room. The lower temperature puts an end to the yeast's action. You may test one of the bottles after 4 days, if carbonation is right, immediately place all bottles in the refrigerator or a place that's cold but above the freezing point. *Leaving the bottles at room temperature too many days may result in leaking or exploding bottles.* Concerning clarification, leaving pop bottles standing in refrigerator for one or two weeks will make them almost crystal clear. Don't shake them before pouring, and pour their content unto a glass slowly and gently. Soft drinks with lemon juice or citric acid may take longer to develop proper carbonation. Reused twist-off caps may be cleaned and reused many times before leaking. *Certain beer-brand twist-off caps tend to leak when reused, avoid those!* Bottles with weak carbonation if not due to leakage may be left at room temperature several weeks and will usually develop strong carbonation. *Remember that it's always better to use less yeast than too much, to avoid an undesirable yeast taste and excessive pressure. For more on* **sanitizing bottles & equipment,** *see cleaning & sterilizing equipment on page 238.* **Makes about 8 quarts/liters or 24 reused 11.3 fl oz/341 ml bottles**

SOFT DRINK VARIATIONS

Old-Fashioned Ginger Ale   *5-7 days*

1/2 cup (120 ml) lemon juice
   from concentrate
1/4 tsp (1 ml) citric acid crystals

1/2 tbsp (7 ml) ground ginger
2 tbsp (30 ml) *Caramelized Sugar Coloring (see page 243)*

Add the above as flavoring in *Basic Soft Drink* recipe. *It is better but not necessary for this recipe to simmer and steep the above ingredients.*

Mock Root Beer   *5-7 days*

1/2 tsp (7 ml) artificial vanilla
   extract
1/2 tbsp (7 ml) ground anise seed

1 cup (240 ml) *Caramelized Sugar Coloring (see page 243)*
1/2 cup (120 ml) molasses

Add the above as flavoring in *Basic Soft Drink* recipe. *It is necessary for this recipe to simmer and steep the above ingredients.*

Flavored Drink Crystals Pop   *5-7 days*

4 cups (960 ml) *Sugar Syrup* **made**
   from sweetened flavored drink crystals
   (replaces the sugar syrup, see pages 217-18)
Add the preceding ingredients to *Basic Soft Drink* recipe.
SUB-VARIATIONS *Try numerous crystal flavors or combinations*
like orange, cherry, grape, mango-berry, etc.!

Coffee-Cola Pop   *5-7 days*

1 1/2 cups (360 ml) *Caramelized*   **2 quarts/liters** *Regular Coffee*
   Sugar Coloring (pg. 243)   *(replaces same amount of*
1/4 (1 ml) citric acid crystals   *water, see page 229)*
Add the above to *Basic Soft Drink* recipe. Dissolve the instant coffee in one cup
(240 ml) of boiling water before adding to the sugar mixture.

Cream Soda Pop   *5-7 days*

1 tbsp (15 ml) artificial vanilla extract   **1/2 tsp (2 ml) cream of tartar**
Add the above to *Basic Soft Drink* recipe.

Uncola Soft Drink   *5-7 days*

1 cup (240 ml) lemon juice from   **1/2 tsp (2 ml) cream of tartar**
   concentrate   **1/2 tsp (2 ml) citric acid crystals**
Add the above to *Basic Soft Drink* recipe.

Rebottled Generic Pop   *15-20 minutes*

This is our strangest idea yet, but it works well. No need to be in such a hurry to
finish the big bottle anymore. The small glass bottles have a better feel and are
far more convenient. This way your pop will cost about half the cheapest generic-
brand pop in a can. Try it out (& test it out), at first, with a few small bottles only!

Four 2 quarts/liters generic-brand or
   Brand-Name pop bottles *(any flavor)*
Soak, clean, and rinse the beer bottles and used twisted-off caps as described in
Basic Soft Drink recipe. After you've purchased the large pop

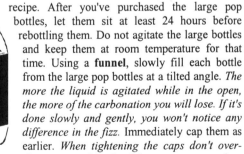

bottles, let them sit at least 24 hours before
rebottling them. Do not agitate the large bottles
and keep them at room temperature for that
time. Using a **funnel**, slowly fill each bottle
from the large pop bottles at a tilted angle. *The*
more the liquid is agitated while in the open,
the more of the carbonation you will lose. If it's
done slowly and gently, you won't notice any
difference in the fizz. Immediately cap them as
described   earlier. *When tightening the caps don't over-*
tighten nor under-   tighten to avoid leaks. When using a towel or*
kitchen mitt not very much muscle power is required. Fill to within 1-inch (2.5

cm) of the top. Serve cold as you would ordinary pop from the bottle. *Rinsing the beer bottles immediately after use makes cleaning easier!* **Makes 23 bottles**

MILK SHAKES

Basic Milk Shake *3-5 minutes*

1/2 cup (120 ml) cold water
About 3/4 cup (180 ml) small ice cubes
1/4 cup (60 ml) instant skim milk
    powder
1/4 cup (60 ml) generic-brand vanilla
    ice cream *(optional)*

1 tbsp (15 ml) vegetable oil
1 1/2 tbsp (22 ml) granulated
    sugar
*Flavoring for one of the
    recipe variations!*

In a **blender**, place all the basic *and a variation* ingredients except ice cream and blend on a low speed for about 2 minutes. The ice should be completely ground and the mixture should have the consistency of a thick milk shake. If it's too thin, add more ice and if it's too thick, add a little water. Add ice cream and blend several seconds only. Pour in a tall glass and serve at once. **Makes about 12 fl oz/360 ml or 1 large serving**

LITE! VERSION *Simply omit using the vegetable oil and ice cream!*

MILK SHAKE VARIATIONS

Chocolate Milk Shake *3-4 minutes*

1 tsp (5 ml) *bulk* unsweetened
    cocoa powder

OR 1 tbsp (15 ml) generic-brand
    instant chocolate drink mix

Add the above to *Basic Milk Shake* recipe *and reduce the sugar by half if using instant chocolate drink mix.*

Vanilla Milk Shake *3-4 minutes*

3/4 tsp (3 ml) artificial vanilla extract
Add the above to *Basic Milk Shake* recipe.

Strawberry Milk Shake *4-5 minutes*

1 tbsp (15 ml) strawberry jam stretcher
    or *Pie-Filling Stretcher (pg. 248, 148)*
Add the above to *Basic Milk Shake* recipe.
SUB-VARIATION *For more economy, use 1 tsp (5 ml) of Sugar Syrup made from sweetened strawberry flavored drink crystals. Experiment with all flavors!*

Banana Yogurt/Milk Shake *4-5 minutes*

1/2 cup (120 ml) *Homemade Yogurt*
    (replaces same amount of water)

Half a small banana, sliced
1/8 tsp (1/2 ml) generic vanilla

Add the above to *Basic Milk Shake* recipe and reduce the ice by half.

Silken Tofu/Milk Shake   4-5 minutes

1/4 cup (80 ml) *Silken-Style Tofu*   1 tsp (5 ml) artificial vanilla
(replaces half of water, see page 240)   extract
Add preceding ingredients to *Basic Milk Shake* recipe and use less ice.

SUB-VARIATIONS *Substitute vanilla with chocolate, banana, instant coffee, or other flavors. See the 'Sub-variation' option below the* Strawberry Milk Shake *recipe (page 228). Also try it with 1 tbsp (15 ml) of stretched jam or pie filling, see pages 248, 148!*

OTHER SHAKES

Soymilk Shake   4-5 minutes

3/4 cup (180 ml) *Homemade Soymilk*   1 tbsp (15 ml) vegetable oil
(see page 231)   1 tsp (5 ml) artificial vanilla
3/4 cup (180 ml) small ice cubes   extract
2 tbsp (30 ml) granulated sugar
In a **blender**, place all ingredients and process at low speed until ice is well grind.
Serve at once. **Makes 12 fl-oz/360 ml or one large serving**
VARIATIONS *Try with other flavors, see previous milk shake recipes!*

Silken Tofu Shake   4-5 minutes

1/4 cup (60 ml) soymilk or water   1 tbsp (15 ml) vegetable oil
3/4 cup (180 ml) small ice cubes   1 tsp (5 ml) artificial vanilla
2 tbsp (30 ml) granulated sugar   extract
1/2 cup (120 ml) *Silken-Style Tofu*
(see page 240)
In a **blender**, place all ingredients and process at low speed until ice is well grind.
Serve at once. **Makes 12 fl-oz/360 ml or one large serving**
VARIATIONS *Try with other flavors, see previous milk shake recipes!*

OTHER BEVERAGES

Hot Tea   8-10 minutes

1 generic-brand tea bag   2 cups (480 ml) *pitcher filtered*
                                                   boiling water

In an **earthenware, porcelain,** or **metal teapot** *(or cup),* pour the boiling water, and submerge the tea bag. The hot water and tea bag should steep in the pot or cup for close to 5 minutes, and no more. We want to get the full flavor but not the tannic acid from the tealeaves. Pour it from pot unto two drinking cups or simply remove tea bag. Tea is better if consumed clear, without sweetener or additional ingredients.

Makes 2 drinking cup portions
VARIATIONS *Try with a dash of lemon juice from concentrate, or a little honey or sugar and reconstituted skim milk to taste!*

Iced Tea 8-10 minutes

2 generic-brand tea bag
1 quart/liter *pitcher filtered*
    cold water

1/4 cup (60 ml) sugar
4 tsp (20 ml) lemon juice from
    concentrate

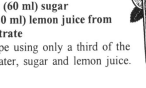

Make tea as outlined in the *Hot Tea* recipe using only a third of the water. Pour it a pitcher; add remaining water, sugar and lemon juice. Serve with ice. **Makes 4 glasses**

Regular Coffee 5-7 minutes

By regular coffee, we mean, drip, percolator, boiled and steeped coffee. All of which can be very inexpensively made when you purchase large format coffee grounds from generic brands or even bargain name brands. Use coffee grounds made for all coffee makers. The coffee instructions yield **2-8 cups (480-1920 ml)**.

1 1/2-2 tbsp (22-30 ml) regular grind coffee
    per cup of pitcher filtered tap water

ELECTRIC DRIP METHOD: Simply place corresponding amount of coffee grounds in paper or metal filter and water in the top compartment and wait. *Some people reuse the coffee grounds a second time by pouring more water in it or reheat the coffee by re-pouring it in water compartment or re-pour half-and-half for further economy. Some folks re-pour the coffee in the water compartment and through the coffee grounds again to make it stronger and even hotter. Such practices may result in a slightly harsher, bitter tasting coffee.*
Makes several drinking cups

Instant Coffee 3-4 minutes

1 tsp (5 ml) generic-brand
    instant coffee granules
1 cup (240 ml) *pitcher filtered*
    boiling water

1 tsp (5 ml) instant skim milk
    powder *(optional)*
1-2 tsp (5-10 ml) granulated
    sugar *(optional)*

Using an **electric kettle**, boil the water and pour over the instant coffee granules in a **cup**. Steep for a minute or two before serving. **Makes one coffee**

Hot Cocoa 3-4 minutes

At a dime each, a cold glass of milk (not even warmed) is 3 times more expensive.

7/8 cup (210 ml) boiling water
1 tbsp (15 ml) cold tap water
1 1/2 tbsp (22 ml) instant skim milk
    powder

1 1/2 tbsp (22 ml) granulated sugar
1 tsp (5 ml) *bulk* cocoa powder
1 tsp (5 ml) vegetable oil

Get some water boiling in an **electric kettle**; dissolve milk powder in the cold tap water and place in a **blender**. When water boils, place it and remaining ingredients in it and blend on high at least 15 seconds. Serve hot in cup. **Makes one cup (240 ml)**
VARIATION *For **Hot Mocha**, pour into blender* Instant Coffee *to make 2 cups!*

Flavor Crystals Drink 2 minutes

This is the right way to make a flavored crystals drink that's smooth and velvety, yet you don't find these instructions anywhere. Always use the generic sweetened crystals for this.

1 quart/liter cold tap *(filtered)* water
1 cup (240 ml) ice cubes *(optional)*

3/8 cup (90 ml) *Sugar Syrup* **made from flavored drink crystals** *(see pages 217-18)*

Combine all of the above in a **pitcher** and stir. Serve or refrigerate for later servings. The sugar syrup makes a smoother drink. Use this same recipe for *Frozen Flavor Crystals Pops (see page 215).* **Makes 4 cups (960 ml), or 4 servings**

VARIATIONS *For **Jelly Desserts** add 1 tsp (5 ml) of bulk neutral gelatin per cup (240 ml) of boiling water to dissolve, (soften the gelatin in a little cold water for five minutes beforehand). Add flavored sugar syrup after the boiling water; refrigerate!*

Flavor Crystals Slush Drinks 3-4 minutes

Slush drinks at about 1/8th the soda fountain price! Similar concoctions may also called 'Slurpies'. Its amazing how many inexpensive treats you can make at home!

1 1/4 cups (300 ml) cold tap *(filtered)* water
About 4 cups (960 ml) ice cubes, crushed

1/3 cup (80 ml) *Sugar Syrup* **made from flavored drink crystals** *(see pages 217-18)*

Place the cold water and flavored sugar syrup in the container of a **blender**, set aside. Meanwhile, place half of the ice in a **plastic storage bag** and give it a twist to prevent ice from coming out. Using the other side of a **meat pounder**, quickly strike the ice till crushed. Add to blender contents and process till it is of a slushy consistency. Don't overdo it. **Makes two large slush drinks**

VARIATIONS *For a **Float Slush Drink** simply add about 1/3 cup (80 ml) of generic-brand vanilla ice cream, and that's at about a very low 1/14th the price at soda shops!*

HOMEMADE DAIRY PRODUCTS

Reconstituted Skim Milk   *1 minute*

*These are the exact proportions for **one cup of reconstituted** skim milk.*

7/8 cup (210 ml) water   **1/3 cup (80 ml) generic-brand or *bulk* instant skim milk powder**

In a **small bowl**, mix the above together and use as directed in recipes.
Makes 1 cup (240 ml)

Homemade Soymilk   *25-30 minutes*

This soymilk can replace regular milk for drinking and cooking, or making tofu.

2 cups (480 ml) presoaked, frozen pre-soaked, or frozen precooked soybeans *(almost 1 cup/240 ml of dried soybeans)*   **9 cups (2160 ml) very hot water or hot tap water**

If using dried soybeans, soak soybeans overnight in cold water. If using frozen presoaked soybeans (see page 25), thaw them in hot tap water for a few minutes. In a **blender**, pour 1 1/2 cups (360 ml) of water and place half of the presoaked beans. Puree them for about 2 minutes. Repeat a second time. In a **large saucepan**, combine pureed beans with 4 cups (1 liter) of hot water; bring the soybean/water mixture to a boil over medium-high heat setting. Stir frequently using a **whisk**. Reduce heat to a low setting and simmer for 10 to 15 minutes. Be careful not to let soymilk foam up and boil over. Using a cheesecloth-lined **sieve or colander** let drain the soymilk 5 minutes. Fold in the cheesecloth over soy pulp and press out as much soymilk as possible. Pour another 2 cups (480 ml) of very hot or boiling water through the soy pulp and try to squeeze out as much soymilk as possible. Use the soymilk immediately to make tofu or refrigerate up to 5 days for later use in recipes. Save the soy-pulp for recipes *(called Okara)* refrigerated up to 1 week for recipes. *Soymilk cannot be made from frozen precooked soybeans (unlike presoaked beans) cannot be used to make tofu.* **Makes about 1 1/2 quarts/liters**

Mock Light Cream   *1-2 minute(s)*

This low cost cream may serve as coffee cream, in recipes, or on cake or dessert. Contains the equivalent of about 12% fat from vegetable oil..

7/8 cup (210 ml) cold tap water   **2 tbsp (30 ml) vegetable oil**
1/3 cup (80 ml) instant skim milk
   powder

In a **blender**, place above ingredients; blend at highest speed about 15 seconds. Use immediately. *Replace some of the water with a little ice for an immediate colder cream.* Use this cream where such a light cream is called for in recipes. Re-blend before using unused portions.
Makes 1 cup (240 ml)

Mock Heavy Cream   *1-2 minute(s)*

This table-style and recipe-grade heavy cream contains about 35% vegetable fat and should be used immediately. Unfortunately, you can't whip this cream.

2/3 cup (160 ml) cold tap water   **1/3 cup (8 ml) vegetable oil**
1/3 cup (80 ml) instant skim milk
   powder

In a **blender**, place above ingredients; blend at highest speed about 20 seconds. Serve immediately in small quantities as a heavy cream over cake, etc. *Replace some of the water with a little ice for an immediate colder cream.* Use this cream where a heavy cream is called for in recipes. **Makes 1 cup (240 ml)**

Homemade Yogurt   *8-12 hours*

Yogurt is used mostly for cooking throughout this book and can be made inexpensively at home for use mostly in recipes. It will cost from 1/3rd to half of the supermarket price to make. The following is probably the easiest way to make homemade yogurt. It's easy and requires no special equipment except perhaps a candy thermometer.

1 quart/liter fresh whole milk   **1/4 cup (60 ml) fresh plain firm-style**
   OR *Reconstituted Skim Milk*   *store-bought* **yogurt or fresh**
   (see page 231)   **homemade yogurt**

Heat the milk slowly until it is hot till scalding point 170-180ºF (77-82ºC), but do not boil *(stop short of the boiling point)*. Cool to lukewarm and gently remove the thin top floating layer. Pour the warm milk in a plastic container that has a lid *(like a recycled plastic yogurt container with lid)*. Stir the yogurt starter well before mixing it with the lukewarm milk. Add starter to milk and stir both well to avoid lumps and place lid. Turn on oven at any low temperasture setting for up to 30 seconds to bring it from room temperature to warm. Turn off oven at once. Switch on oven light and place mixture in oven for 8 hours but preferably overnight when oven is not in demand. To get your oven even warmer place a large saucepan lid *(or pie pan)* upside down over the oven vent hole located in one of the rear stovetop elements. ***Remove this lid or pie pan when using oven for baking!*** An oven used in this fashion *(heated by the oven light bulb)* makes a convenient incubator *(see*

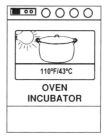

illustration) and should maintain a temperature of about 115°F (46°C). Make sure it doesn't exceed 125°F (52°C) and doesn't get lower than 105°F (40°C). *A 100 watts bulb usually does the trick!* If the temperature is too low, use a higher wattage bulb. If the temperature gets too high, remove the pan over vent. Place a fork or spoon in such a way to keep the oven door slightly open. If the oven light socket is not accessible, place a small lamp in the oven and carefully lead the electric wire to a plug outside the oven. The next morning when the yogurt has set, place container in refrigerator and don't forget to turn oven light off. *You can refrigerate the yogurt as soon as it turns firm, which could be as little as 4-5 hours. This would result in a lighter tasting yogurt good if eaten with brown sugar for example. Alternately, for a more flavorful yogurt, good for cooking or especially to make cheesecake, make a stronger tasting yogurt, we need much more lactic acid, which is made by the cultured bacteria. For this you must double the amount of starter and incubate the milk/starter mixture for as long as 12 hours.* Save 1/2 cup (120 ml) of the new yogurt as starter and refrigerated up to 10 days for the next batch. Use or consume the yogurt too within 10 days. Repeat process until it ceases to yield results, then start again with supermarket bought yogurt. The starter can last for months if continually used to make fresh yogurt batches. **Makes 1 quart/liter**

Homemade Buttermilk   *24 hours*

Here's a method of preparing buttermilk that's simple and doesn't require any special equipment. It yields cultured buttermilk very low in fat just like the one you buy but at a quarter the cost.

1 quart/liter fresh *Reconstituted Skim Milk (see page 231)*

1/4 cup (60 ml) fresh *store-bought* buttermilk or fresh homemade buttermilk starter

Pour the fresh supermarket bought buttermilk in a bottle containing one quart/liter of warm skim milk *(not hot)* made from powdered instant skim milk *(see page 231)*. Place cap on bottle but don't tighten and let stand overnight at room temperature. When milk has thicken, shake bottle and place in refrigerator to chill. Save 1/2 cup (120 ml) up to 10 days refrigerated for the next batch. Repeat process until it ceases to yield results, then start over again with supermarket-bought buttermilk. **Makes 1 quart/liter**

Recipe-Grade Sour Milk   *1-5 minute(s)*

1 cup (240 ml) water
1/3 cup (80 ml) instant skim milk powder

1 tbsp (15 ml) white vinegar
(*5% acetic acid*)

In a **small bowl**, mix all ingredients. Let it sit and thicken a few minutes and you almost instantly get recipe-grade sour milk. It is meant to be used in recipes *and not for drinking*. **Makes 1 cup (240 ml) plus**

Instant Garlic Margarine 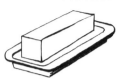   *1 minute*

2 tbsp (30 ml) margarine
1/4 tsp (1 ml) garlic powder
In a **small bowl**, mix both ingredients. You instantly get garlic margarine. Great with oven baked bread serve with soup or salad. **Makes 2 tbsp (30 ml)**

Homemade Sour Milk   *8-12 hours*

1 quart/liter fresh whole milk
   OR *Reconstituted Skim*
   Milk (see page 231)

1/4 cup (60 ml) fresh plain 14% BF
   store-bought **sour cream or fresh**
   Homemade Sour Cream **or**
   Homemade Sour Milk

Substitute the above ingredients for those in *Homemade Yogurt recipe (see page 232)*. The instructions remain the same. **Makes 1 quart/liter**

Homemade Sour Cream   *8-12 hours*

1 quart/liter fresh light cream

1/4 cup (60 ml) fresh plain 14% BF
   store-bought **sour cream or fresh**
   Homemade Sour Cream **or**
   Homemade Sour Milk

Substitute the above ingredients for those in *Homemade Yogurt* recipe *(see pages 232-3)*. The instructions remain the same. **Makes 1 quart/liter**

Yogurt/Sour Cream Whey   *8-12 hours*

Save the whey obtained from the draining of either yogurt or sour cream when making cream cheeses (see pages 236-7) for recipes like cheesecakes where you want the cream cheese taste without the cost and calories. Refrigerate it up to 2 days or freeze. **Makes at least 2 cups (480 ml)**

Mock Whole Milk 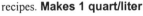   *1-2 minutes*

This milk costs a little more than half the price of fresh whole milk to make. It's healthier because it contains no animal fat, just $3\frac{1}{4}\%$ vegetable oil fat.

3 1/2 cup (840 ml) cold tap water
1 1/3 cup (320 ml) instant skim
   milk powder *(bulk or generic)*

2 tbsp (30 ml) vegetable oil
   (generic-brand)

In a **blender,** place above ingredients; blend at highest speed about 15 seconds. *Replace some of the water with a little ice for an immediate colder milk.* Use immediately and refrigerate remainder in a **recycled milk bottle.** Re-blender before using unused portions. Use this mock milk chilled where whole milk is required like cereal recipes. **Makes 1 quart/liter**

HOMEMADE CHEESE & TOFU

The cheeses we selected are those that can be made quickly and for a small fraction of the supermarket price. For the same reasons cheeses like cottage or hard cheeses (Cheddar, Swiss, Romano, Gouda) were not included since they cost almost as much to make than to purchase. There are two major methods of curd formation in cheese making. The first relies solely on acid curdling either by direct use of acid or acid production cause by the starter bacteria. The second is not exploited in this book and is the use of rennet (or rennet-like chemicals).

CULTURED CHEESES

Cultured cheeses are composed of curds obtained by the action of one of usually two common bacterial cultures. Namely, mesophilic starter cultures for sour cream and thermophilic starter cultures for yogurt. Store-bought cultured cheeses are expensive so the savings when making your own are substantial. The costs to make our cheeses will vary from $1/10^{th}$ to $1/3^{rd}$ of supermarket prices.

Basic Cultured Cheese 🐷
8-12 hours+ draining

1 quart/liter *Homemade Yogurt,* **or** *Sour Cream* **or** *Sour Milk* **(pages 232-4)**
May contain up to 33% of Soft White Cheese Curds **(to add texture to the cheese, see pages 237-8)**

Using a **large sieve** or a **colander** lined with two layers of **cheesecloth** (placed oven a deep-bowl) pour the appropriate cultured milk starter for a given cultured cheese variation. Let drain (covered with plastic wrap) refrigerated or at room temperature no hotter than 72°F (24°C) from 8 to 48 hours. *1/4 tsp (1 ml) of table salt per quart will accelerate draining.* A shorter draining period will produce a cheese spread while a longer period will give a firmer cream cheese consistency. If you intend to use store-bought yogurt to make your cheese, avoid those containing gelatin, they just won't drain. *Add flavoring ingredients according to a recipe variation before or after draining.* After draining *(and flavoring)*, water content can be further lowered by wrapping drained cheese in cheesecloth and pressed under a weight. *Alternately, bring up the corners of cheesecloth or muslin, and tie them together with kitchen twine. Hand this bag in the kitchen with a bowl beneath, for at least 2 days.* Place resulting cheese in a plastic container with lid *(like a recycled plastic cream cheese container)* and keep refrigerated up to 14 days. **Makes 8-12 ounces (240-360 ml)**

CULTURED CHEESE VARIATIONS

Yogurt Cheese   *8-12 hours+ draining*
Its similar to low-fat cream cheese with about 14% B.F. and may be served plain or seasoned in various ways.

Use Homemade Yogurt (pages 232-3)	**1/8 tsp (1/2 ml) garlic powder**
Garlic clove, finely minced *(optional)*	**1/8 tsp (1/2 ml) ground pepper**
1/4 tsp (1 ml) dried fine herbs	**Salt to taste**

Use the above in *Basic Cultured Cheese* recipe. Season after draining. Drain at least 24 hours refrigerated.

SUB-VARIATIONS *Replace any of the above seasonings with one or more of the following, dried parsley, ground cumin, paprika, thyme, basil, oregano, sage, minced olives, onions, sweet pepper, pickles, etc. The possibilities and combinations are almost endless. Convert it to a dessert cheese by adding a little granulated sugar, vanilla, and a dash of cinnamon, nutmeg or allspice. For a textured instead of smooth cheese* similar to French Neufchatel cheese, add some soft white cheese curd to yogurt before draining. For differently tasting cheeses, incubate your milk using sour cream starter instead of yogurt!*

LITE! **VERSION** *Use Reconstituted Skim Milk instead of fresh whole milk, (see page 231)!*

Fake 'Neufchatel' Cheese   *8-12 hours+ draining*
This is the Cadillac of spiced and herbed cream cheeses close to 20% BF. This concoction is made without any rennet unlike the real French cheese.

Use Homemade Yogurt	**1/4 tsp (1 ml) white pepper**
(made from fresh whole milk)!	**1/4 tsp (1 ml) dried parsley**
1/3 cup (90 ml) *Soft White Cheese*	**1/4 tsp (1 ml) garlic powder**
curds *(optional, see page 237-8)*	**1/4-1/2 tsp (1-2 ml) salt**
1 tbsp (15 ml) vegetable oil	**1/4 tsp (1 ml) fine herbs**
1 tbsp (15 ml) white vinegar	**1/8 tsp (1/2 ml)** *Caramelized Sugar Coloring (pg. 243)*

Use the above in *Basic Cultured Cheese* recipe. Mix yogurt, soft cheese curds, and all other ingredients before draining. Drain about 48 hours. Optionally, for an even firmer cheese, press in cheesecloth under a weight after draining.

SOFT WHITE CHEESES

These cheeses are the quickest to make because they instantly curd by acid coagulation. They must be drained from a few minutes to a few hours before use.

Basic Soft White Cheese   25-30 minutes + draining

1 quart/liter cold water
1 1/3 cups (320 ml) instant skim
   milk powder

1/4 cup (60 ml) vegetable oil
   (optional)
1 tbsp (15 ml) vinegar
   OR 2 tbsp (30 ml) lemon
   juice from concentrate

OR *use one quart/liter of fresh whole milk instead of cold water, milk powder and optional vegetable oil*

In a **blender**, place cold water, milk powder and vegetable oil. In **a large heavy bottom saucepan**, place the milk mixture or fresh whole milk. Bring the milk to a temperature of 170-180°F (77-82°C) over a medium heat. Stir frequently. Add the acid precipitator and stir gently; set aside 15 minutes. If milk does not curdle, add more precipitator. Using a **sieve** placed over a large **bowl**, strain the curds away from whey. *The whey is the yellow liquid* *that separates from curds. If the liquid looks milky you're curd yield is incomplete, reheat and stir solution. If that doesn't work, add a bit more precipitator.* Let drain (covered with plastic wrap) while refrigerated 15 minutes to 3 hours. *Add flavoring ingredients according to one of the following variations.* Place resulting cheese in a plastic bag or plastic wrap and keep refrigerated up to 10 days. *Alternately, bring up the corners of cheesecloth or muslin, and tie them together. Hang this bag in the kitchen with a bowl beneath for 1 to 2 days.* The liquid whey may be saved for use in certain recipes. **Makes about 8 ounces (240 ml)**

LITE! VERSION *Use reconstituted skim milk only instead of whole milk, no oil!*

SOFT WHITE CHEESE VARIATIONS

Panir (Lemon Cheese)   25-30 minutes + draining
This cheese is from India, crumbly or solid, it can be used for salads, sandwiches, or cooking.

In *Basic Soft White Cheese* recipe use lemon juice as precipitator, drain 15 minutes.

Queso Blanco   25-30 minutes + draining
This Latin American cheese is rubbery with a sweet flavor and is meant for cooking. It doesn't melt easily and is used on soups, sauces, pastas, or even pizza.

In *Basic Soft White Cheese* recipe use white vinegar as precipitator, drain a couple of hours.

PRESSING CHEESES

This method is a very simple way of pressing cheese or tofu. You will need the following items:

1. **A perforated plastic cylinder**
2. **A plastic disk**
3. **A plastic or metal plate or tray**

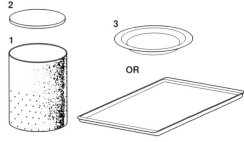

The cylinder should be made of a food-grade plastic and have straight walls. It can be made from a discarded plastic gallon like a large prepared mustard jar and should be between 3½-5½ inches (9-14 cm) in diameter. The top and bottom portions must be cut off with a pair of scissors. The bottom half of the cylinder should have a few dozen perforations punched through from the inside using a sharp nail or thumbtack. If using a thicker wall cylinder, drill tiny holes and sand the edges clean. The follower disk should be rigid if possible, but a thin one trimmed with scissors also works. A plastic jar cover of a slightly smaller diameter than the inside of cylinder placed upside-down makes a good follower. Use a pan, or table plate turned upside-down as a spacer to keep bottom of curds away from liquid. A tray serves well to collect the liquid. Assemble the four pieces as illustrated and use a jar of water as a weight.

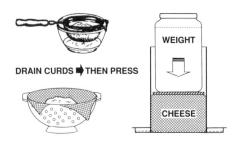

DRAIN CURDS ➡ THEN PRESS

WEIGHT

CHEESE

As mentioned before, the cheese and tofu curds must be drained in a cheesecloth-lined sieve or colander. After one or two hour(s), wrap contents of sieve in a double thickness of cheesecloth. If using a cheesecloth-lined colander, fold in the four-corners and place in press. Cover with the follower disk and add the weight. Most cheeses or tofu are pressed from a few minutes up to one day according to firmness desired.

CLEANING EQUIPMENT

Whether you're making cultured milk or cheese, cleanliness is very important. You must clean the equipment after as well as *before* use. When you're done with a utensil, immediately rinse thoroughly with *cold water.* Rinsing it in hot water will cook the milk into the pan or utensil. After rinsing, wash and scrub in very hot water using a dishwashing liquid or washing soda. Rinse well in hot water.

STERILIZING EQUIPMENT

Most of the time it isn't necessary to sterilize your equipment and utensils, but if you wish to do so here's how. *Sterilize only before use.* Non-plastic equipment can be sterilized by immersion in rapid boiling water for 3 to 5 minutes. Plastic items should be sterilized with a solution of household bleach *(sodium hypochlorite).* Dilute 2 tablespoons (30 ml) of it in a gallon (4 liters) of warm water. Afterwards, rinse thoroughly in cold water and drain. *Avoid cross-contamination by sterilizing all counters and surfaces that are exposed to the equipment. Dampen a clean cloth in bleach solution the same as above and wipe all areas clean.*

Cheese-making can be fun... *Its beyond the scope of this book to cover cheeses thoroughly. Nevertheless, apart from the few cheese covered there might be several more worth making for economy as well as other reasons. For example, when making hard cheeses, additional steps might include cooking the curd, molding or pressing the cheese, even drying, aging, and covering the finished cheese with wax. All of which makes for a modest economy and an interesting way to pass time.*

MAIL-ORDER SOURCE OF CHEESE-MAKING SUPPLIES

New England Cheese-making Supply Co.
85 Main Street
Ashfield, MA 01330

They sell books, starters, rennet, and cheese making supplies.

SOYBEAN (TOFU) CHEESES

Although supermarket bought tofu is not very expensive, you can make your own for a very small fraction of the cost. Tofu is used quite extensively in this book. Time given assumes soymilk has just been made and is ready.

Basic Tofu   *5-15 minutes*

1 1/2 quarts/liters *Homemade Soymilk (see page 231)*

1 cup (240 ml) warm water mixed with <u>one</u> of the following: *(as precipitator)*
    2 1/2 tsp (12 ml) epsom salts
      OR 3/8 cup (90 ml) white vinegar
      OR 3/8 cup (90 ml) lemon juice
        from concentrate

In a **large heavy saucepan**, bring or reheat soymilk to the boiling point and remove from heat. Pour in about a third of one of the above precipitators. Slowly and gently stir and set aside away from heat a few minutes. When soymilk has settled, sprinkle in the second half of precipitator solution over it, and stir gently. Cover and let stand up to 5 minutes. Gently sprinkle remainder of precipitator, cover and let stand another 5 minutes. *Do not stir this time.* Gently stir top portion of soymilk, and watch the soft white curds form and separate from the yellow liquid, which is the whey. *Please keep in mind curds must form very* *slowly, over a long time-period, for a higher yield of larger curds.* Using a **cheesecloth-lined** (double thickness) **sieve** or **colander** placed in a receiver **plastic bowl**, drain about 10 minutes, then press out any additional whey using the back of a **spoon**. For storage, place tofu in a plastic bag or container with lid, refrigerate up to 6 days or freeze. Alternately, press the cheesecloth wrapped tofu up to 2 hours *(depending on weight used)*, see 'Pressing cheeses' on page 238. Pressed tofu must be carefully unwrapped from cheesecloth and let to set while cooled in refrigerator. Only after it has set, can it be placed in a plastic container, covered with cold water for storage up to one week in refrigerator. *Use soymilk made from freshly presoaked soybeans and not made from frozen presoaked or precooked soybeans, it doesn't work* **Makes about 2 cups (480 ml) of tofu**

TOFU VARIATIONS

Homemade Firm Tofu   *15 minutes + pressing*

The difference between homemade firm tofu and silken tofu is that one is very firm and the other is soft and creamy.

 Using the *Basic Tofu* recipe, select the Epsom salts solution as precipitator. For even firmer curds, when the curds have formed, reheat the curd/whey mixture on a medium heat in the same saucepan until boiling and maintain a few minutes. Drain and press as earlier described. *Use soymilk made from unfrozen presoaked soybeans only*

SUB-VARIATIONS *For **Herbed & Spiced Tofu**, add about 1/4 tsp (1 ml) of dried herbs like oregano, basil, Italian herbs, thyme leaves, marjoram, and/or fine herbs with about 1/8 tsp (1 ml) of ground spices like cumin, sage, rosemary, cloves, allspice, coriander, anise seed (ground), thyme, turmeric, pepper, or even celery salt, chili powder, garlic/onion powder, or powdered salt, per cup of tofu. For **Marinated Tofu**, soak it (un-pressed) in a marinating solution as outlined on page 247. For **Brown Tofu**, add* Caramelized Sugar Coloring *as needed directly to mashed tofu and mix, and **do not** add it to the soymilk, see page 243!*

Silken-Style Tofu   *15 minutes*

Using the *Basic Tofu* recipe select the white vinegar or lemon juice from concentrate solution as precipitator. Before adding any precipitator, heat soymilk to 175-185°F (80-85°C) instead of going to boiling point. When forming the curds try to do so even more gently and slowly. Drain as outlined. After draining if an even smoother tofu is desired, blend it in **blender** and add a little soymilk *(and some vegetable oil)* to it.

High-Yield Pulp Tofu   *5 minutes*

Using the *Basic Tofu* and *Homemade Soymilk* recipes, the only difference is that the soymilk is not strain *(the pulp is left in it)*. Drain only, or drain and pressed. *The curds will contain the pulp and be bulkier...it's much less work too.*

SUB-VARIATION *The variations for the above* Homemade firm Tofu *recipe apply as well for the high-yield pulp tofu recipe!*

Homegrown Sprouts

Why Sprout Seeds?

Growing your own sprouts is like growing your own vitamins, particularly vitamin C. Dried legume, seed and grain sprouts when eaten regularly, greatly enhance the vitamin content of any diet or food regime. Due to their delicate vitamin content, they are best eaten raw whether in salads or in sandwiches. They are also useful in chop suey or stir-fried as with or with any other fresh vegetable, and even on soups.

Alfalfa seeds and mung beans are the best in their category for sprouting. Onion, mustard, radish and red clover seeds are also great for sprouting. In principle, all dried legumes and certain seeds and grains are good to sprout, though some better than others. Large dried legumes like red kidney beans (or soybeans) should have their root portion cut off before using for the sake of esthetics.

SPROUTING SEEDS

We recommend that you use store-bought sprouting trays or equipment *(see ill.)* for ease of operation. Alternately, grow your own sprouts by simply covering the bottom of a large shallow plastic container or tray(at least 2 inches in depth) *(see ill.)* with a layer of seeds or dried legumes. Cover with cold water and let soak overnight. The next morning, pour off water and place lid or make one with

STORE-BOUGHT SPROUTER

plastic wrap. The following day, cover seeds or beans with water. Discard after 5 minutes and repeat procedure the following days. Alternately, seeds may be sprouted using one or more one-quart/liter mason jar(s), the most available containers for sprouting. It's the easiest and least expensive method. Take some cheesecloth, or silk cloth and use the canning ring to hold the cloth in place *(see ill.)*. You may also purchase special sprouting lids that fit standard mason jars or make a rather thin plastic disk with small holes drilled in it to fit a mason jar. Rinse seeds or beans in a sieve or colander twice. Place seeds or beans in jar and fill it with at least 3 times as much water. Allow them to soak overnight at room temperature. Drain the next morning, then every morning for the next few days fill jar with water and drain immediately until sprouts are ready. In general, sprouted seeds should grow 3 to 5 days before being consumed. The maximum growing period is 7 days. Sprouts can grow in darkness or in some light. Keep them away from direct sunlight when growing. When they are ready to eat, you may place them in direct sunlight for a few hours so they may acquire a green color as chlorophyll develops. Please keep in mind not all sprouts are edible, for example: tomato and potato sprouts are toxic. Seeds, grains and dried legumes for eventual sprouting or consummation should be bought at health food stores or supermarkets. *Do not use seeds intended for planting because they are usually treated with poisons.* Ready sprouts should be refrigerated in perforated, breathable plastic bags and keep 3 to 6 days.

JAR SPROUTER

SPROUTING CHART

SEED/LEGUME/GRAIN	QUANTITY	GROWING TIME
Alfalfa seeds	2 tbsp (30 ml)	3-5 days
Barley	1/2 cup (120 ml)	3-4 days
Beans (most)	1 cup (240 ml)	3-5 days
Chick-peas	1 cup (240 ml)	3 days
Flax seeds	2 tbsp (30 ml)	4 days
Lentils	1/2 cup (120 ml)	3-4 days
Millet	1 cup (240 ml)	3-4 days
Mung beans	1 cup (240 ml)	4 days
Oats (unhulled)	1 cup (240 ml)	3-4 days
Onion seeds	1/4 cup (60 ml)	3-4 days
Peas (dried)	1 cup (240 ml)	3 days
Radish seeds	1/4 cup (60 ml)	3-4 days
Rice (whole grain brown only)	1 cup (240 ml)	3-4 days
Rye	1 cup (240 ml)	3-4 days
Sesame seeds (unhulled)	1 cup (240 ml)	3 days
Soybeans	1/2 cup (120 ml)	3-5 days
Sunflower seeds	1/4 cup (60 ml)	2 days
Wheat	1/2 cup (120 ml)	2-4 days

MISCELLANEOUS

Caramelized Sugar Coloring   12-15 minutes

1 cup (240 ml) granulated sugar   1 cup (240 ml) boiling water

In a **heavy-bottomed saucepan**, melt the sugar over a medium heat. Stir often continuing the heat until sugar liquefies and the mass of melted sugar has taken a dark-brown color. Remove the pan a moment from heat if it froths up excessively and starts to smoke up. At this point, it will lose its sweetness and take on a new flavor. *Be careful that the sugar doesn't burn.* Add the boiling water and stir. Eventually all of the tacky mass will dissolve and melt again. Cool the clear brown syrup-like coloring and store at room temperature in a covered container, keeps almost indefinitely. It can be filtered using a **funnel** and **paper coffee filter**. Use this non-sweet syrup to color and flavor pop drinks, desserts, gravy, cakes, rice, homemade cheese and sauces. *1 tsp (5 ml) will darken 1/2 cup (120 ml) of water or liquid.* **Makes about 3/4 cup (180 ml)**

Homemade Curry Powder   2-3 minutes

This recipe is a sort of emergency curry.

2 tbsp (30 ml) ground coriander   1/2 tbsp (7 ml) ground cumin
2 tbsp (30 ml) turmeric   1/2 tbsp (7 ml) dried mustard
1 tbsp (15 ml) black ground pepper   1 tsp (5 ml) ground ginger
1 tbsp (15 ml) ground cinnamon   1/2 tsp (2 ml) ground cloves
                                        Cayenne to taste

Place the above in a jar and close the lid tightly. Shake well. *Other versions of this recipe may include small quantities of ground cardamom, poppy seeds, allspice, chilies and even garlic. Some exclude cumin, mustard, ginger or cayenne.* **Makes about 1/2 cup (120 ml)**

Worcestershire-Style Sauce   4-5 minutes

1/4 cup (60 ml) malt vinegar   1/2 tbsp (7 ml) brown sugar
1/4 cup (60 ml) white vinegar   1/4 tsp (1 ml) table salt

1 tbsp (15 ml) molasses
1 tbsp (15 ml) soy sauce
2 tsp (10 ml) lemon juice from
   concentrate

1/4 tsp (1 ml) ground ginger
1/4 tsp (1 ml) ground cloves
1/8 tsp (1/2 ml) onion powder
Dash of garlic powder
Dash of cayenne

Place all ingredients in a jar with lid; shake until all dry ingredients have dissolved. Refrigerate and shake well before using. *If difficult to mix, use electric blender.* **Makes about 3/4 cup (180 ml)**
VARIATIONS *Substitute malt vinegar with wine or cider vinegar. If you don't have any, substitute malt vinegar with more white vinegar. Stay true to the original recipe by using blackstrap molasses, and add 1/4-1/2 tsp (1-2 ml) of tamarind concentrate (if available).*

Batter Mix   3-4 minutes

This batter mix (or premix) is for coating certain foods that are fried in a fryer or frying pan. It costs about a quarter of the supermarket price to make the mix. Use it for corn-dogs, onion rings, or wrap thin fish fillets, poultry fillets, burger patties, small meatballs, or make small plain dumplings with it.

1 cup (240 ml) all-pupose flour
   (generic-brand & bleached)
1/2 cup (120 ml) fine or medium
   cornmeal
3 tbsp (45 ml) corn flour
1 tbsp (15 ml) *bulk* corn starch
1 tbsp (15 ml) instant skim milk
   powder
1/4 tsp (1 ml) dry mustard

1 tbsp (15 ml) *bulk* soy flour
   (optional)
1 tbsp (15 ml) granulated sugar
1/2 tsp (2 ml) table salt
1 tbsp (15 ml) baking powder
1 small egg, beaten *(optional)*
2 tbsp (30 ml) low-cost margarine,
   melted *(optional)*

In a **plain** or **zipper plastic bag**, place the above ingredients except egg and margarine, and shake till well mixed. Seal bag and store in a dry place. To use, combine one leveled cupful (240 ml) of batter mix with **5/8 cup (150 ml)** of **cold tap water** *(plus optional egg and fat)*. Stir until smooth. *If too thick add more water and if too thin add more batter mix.* Heat the oil in deep fryer or frying pan to about 375°F (190°C). Meanwhile, prepare items to be battered and fried. *Items must not be wet, pat dry them if they are.* Dip and rotate items in batter until evenly coated. *For corn dogs, it might be more convenient to place batter in a tall glass!* Remove from batter and drain off excess. Immerse gradually one at a time into hot oil. Fry a few for about 3 minutes or till golden brown. **Makes about 2 cups (480 ml) or enough for at least 12 corn dogs**
LITE! **VERSION** *Do not use the optional margarine!*

Dumplings   15-20 minutes

These somewhat lean and low-cost dumplings will further lower the cost of stews, casseroles, chilies, stovetop meals, some side dishes, and even soups.

3/4 cup (180 ml) all-purpose flour
   (generic-brand & bleached)
1 tsp (5 ml) baking powder
2 tsp (10 ml) instant skim milk
   powder *(optional)*

1/2 tsp (2 ml) dried parsley
1/8 tsp (1/2 ml) dried oregano,
   basil, or thyme
1/3 cup (80 ml) cold tap water
2 tbsp (30 ml) vegetable oil

In a **bowl**, mix the dry ingredients. Add water and oil to flour mixture; stir till combined. Drop mixture from a teaspoon atop bubbling stew, casserole, or other dish. *Don't place them in the hot liquid.* Cover and simmer up to 10 minutes or till a **skewer** comes out clean. **Makes about a dozen small dumplings** **VARIATIONS** *Try substituting up to half of the flour with cornmeal or use the Batter Mix recipe for dumplings (see previous recipe)!*

Soybean Nuts   *1 hour + presoaking*
Soybeans nuts at less than 1/5th the health food store price.

2 cups (480 ml) dried soybean, pre-   *Non-stick cooking spray or vegetable*
    soaked overnight refrigerated   *oil spray for coating!*
                     Powdered Salt **to taste** *(pg. 247)*

 Scatter the presoaked beans on **1** or **2 baking sheets**, and toast in a preheated oven set at 275°F (135°C) for 45 to 55 minutes. When soybean nuts have cooled to room temperature or till warm, lightly spray them with cooking spray or vegetable oil in a **spray bottle** made for that purpose *(ill.)*. Toss in a **plastic bag** with some powdered salt and shake.

Tri-Snack   *1 minute*
A satisfying and fast to prepare snack reminiscent of the chocolate-coated peanut and raisin snacks. Though not so cheap, its far less expensive than store-bought snacks. If properly purchased, all three ingredients should cost about the same.

1/3 cup (80 ml) *bulk* unsalted peanuts   1/3 cup (80 ml) generic-brand
1/3 cup (80 ml) *bulk* or generic-brand   chocolate flavored chips or
    low-cost raisins   semi-sweet chocolate chips
Place the above in a **small zipper-type plastic bag** and shake. **Makes 4 snacks**

Popcorn   *5-6 minutes*
Popping corn is a wondrous food that expands twenty-five times its original volume. Comes out to a few cents a cup (240 ml), melted margarine and electricity included.

2 tbsp (30-45 ml) vegetable oil   2 tbsp (30 ml) hot melted margarine
1/3 cup (80 ml) *bulk* popping corn   1/16 tsp (1/4 ml) table salt
Heat a **large heavy-bottomed saucepan** over a medium setting. After a minute or so, when pan is hot, add the oil and popping corn. Stir well and cover. Meanwhile, in a **small metal bowl**, place the chilled margarine and salt. Sit bowl on an element set on medium for a couple of minutes till melted and very hot. As soon as the first few kernels pop, gently move the pan back and forth until all have popped. Transfer to a **large bowl** and drizzle with the hot melted margarine/salt mixture. Serve while hot. To reheat leftover popcorn, heat and stir in an oiled **frying pan** a couple of minutes, or use a **microwave**. **Makes about 2-2 1/2 quarts/liters, or 4 to 5 servings** **VARIATIONS** *For Caramel-Coated Popcorn, or Fruit-Flavored Popcorn, melt 1/2 cup (120 ml) of sugar or flavored drink crystals and 2 tbsp (30 ml) of margarine in a pan on medium-low heat; stir-in popcorn to glaze. Cool scattered on baking sheets!*

Fine Breadcrumbs   *35-40 minutes*

8 slices of bread   **1/4 tsp (1 ml) onion powder**
1 tsp (5 ml) table salt   **1/8 tsp (1/2 ml) garlic powder**
Preheat oven to 250°F (120°C). Meanwhile, using a **few wire racks** placed on oven racks, lay out the slices of bread. Oven-dry the bread about 30 minutes until all moisture is out. Let cool then crush till fine using a **rolling pin**. Alternately, grind chunks of bread using **blender** or between the palm of your hands. Using a **plastic bag** of appropriate size, combine all ingredients. Close bag with a **twist-tie** and shake. Store until needed. **Makes about 2 cups (480 ml)**

VARIATIONS *For **Italian Flavored Breadcrumbs** add 1 tsp (5 ml) of dried Italian seasonings or same amount of dried fine herbs for **Fine Herbs Flavored Breadcrumbs**. For **Super Fast Fine Breadcrumbs** use 2 cups (480 ml) of pre-toasted wheat germ instead of the slices of bread!*

MUSTARDS

All of the following mustard recipes are quick to make and preparing them in these small quantities ensure freshness. The mustards are all made from very inexpensive prepared mustard sold by the gallon. **Makes about 1/2 cup (120 ml)**

Hot Mustard   *2 minutes*

1/2 cup (120 ml) prepared mustard   **1/4 tsp (1 ml) red cayenne**
1/2 tsp (2 ml) mild paprika
Add the above to a **small jar** and stir. Cover at once with lid for storage.

Honey-Garlic Mustard   *2 minutes*

1/2 cup (120 ml) prepared mustard   **1/2 tsp (2 ml) garlic powder**
1/2 tbsp (7 ml) dark liquid honey
Add the above to a **small jar** and stir. Cover at once with lid for storage.

Oriental-Style mustard   *2 minutes*

6 tbsp (90 ml) prepared mustard   **1 tsp (5 ml) tamari or soy**
2 tbsp (30 ml) vegetable oil   **sauce** *(optional)*
Add the above to a **small jar** and stir. Cover at once with lid for storage.

Herbed Mustard   *2 minutes*

1/2 cup (120 ml) prepared mustard   **1/2 tsp (2 ml) ground thyme**
1 tsp (5 ml) dried parsley   **1 tsp (5 ml) onion powder**
1/2 tsp (2 ml) dried chervil   **1/2 tsp (2 ml) garlic powder**
Add the above to a **small jar** and stir. Cover at once with lid for storage.

VARIATIONS *Try replacing parsley and thyme with same amount of tarragon and ground cloves!*

For ketchup & relish, see pages 20,22

MARINADES

*There are several ways to tenderize tough cuts of meat, among them are marinating, stewing, braising, grinding, pounding, scoring, and chemical tenderizers. A few of them are used in this book. By definition, a marinade is a seasoned liquid containing an edible acid like vinegar, wine, or lemon juice, to tenderize and/or add flavor to food. They not only tenderize and flavor meat, fish, and raw vegetables but also cut down on the cooking time. Our marinades all use vinegar, contain some water, and are inherently low cost. We compensate by doubling marinate time for the water content. Beef, pork, fish, raw or blanched, or lightly steamed vegetables may be marinated with the above marinates. Adjust recipe yield to accommodate the size of cut. Use a **bowl** or **plastic bag** (tightly sealed) of appropriate size to marinate. Turn or stir foods being marinades every half-hour or hour, or by turning plastic bag on its other side. Always marinade under refrigeration. Use the marinades to tenderize the diced or thinly sliced stewing beef or pork cubes in steak subs, vegetable (and meat) pies, stews, meal-in-one-pan, casseroles, soups, or in sandwich filling recipes.*

Marinade for Vegetables   *4 hours*

1/2 cup (120 ml) cold tap water   1/2 tsp (2 ml) granulated sugar
1/3 cup (80 ml) white vinegar   1/2 tsp (2 ml) dried oregano
3 tbsp (45 ml) vegetable oil   1/4 tsp (1 ml) dried tarragon
2 tsp (10 ml) prepared mustard   1/8 tsp (1/2 ml) garlic powder
1 garlic clove, pressed or minced   1/8 tsp (1/2 ml) cayenne pepper
Mix all ingredients well. Marinate foods chilled 4 hours. **Makes 1 cup/240 ml**

Marinade for Meat or Fish   *½-8 hours*

1/2 cup (120 ml) water *(optional)*   1/8 tsp (1/2 ml) garlic powder
1/3 cup (80 ml) white vinegar   1/2 tsp (2 ml) dried parsley
3 tbsp (45 ml) vegetable oil   1 tsp (5 ml) dried Italian or fine
1 garlic clove, pressed *(optional)*   herbs
1 tsp (5 ml) worcestershire sauce   Salt and pepper to taste
Mix all ingredients well. Marinate meat cut or pieces chilled from 1/2 to 8 hours to accommodate thin slices or thick sections. **Makes 1 cup/240 ml**

VARIATIONS *For **Barbecue-Style Marinade**, add 1 tbsp (15 ml) minced yellow onions, 2 tbsp (30 ml) soy sauce, 2 tbsp (30 ml) generic catsup, plus some optional mustard, brown sugar, and chili powder. For a **Hot Marinade**, add 1/4 tsp (1 ml) red cayenne pepper or 1 tsp (5 ml) crushed chillies. Other marinade ingredients may include marjoram, rosemary, thyme, oregano, or lemon juice !*

Powdered Salt   *2-3 minutes*

Use your blender to turn granular salt in powder. Serves mostly to salt snacks.

1/4 cup (60 ml) table salt
Using **blender** grind on high 1 to 2 minutes till powdered. Store in a **plastic bag**.

Powdered Sugar   *2-3 minutes*

Same idea as previous *Powdered Salt* recipe, grind on high till powdered.

JAM STRETCHERS

We will stretch generic-brand jams using sugar syrup, cornstarch, pectin, and gelatin for economy. The two first jam stretchers must be refrigerated and keep for up to a month. Test the techniques with smaller amounts at first before doing jars. They all triple jam.

Cornstarch Jam Stretcher   5-7 minutes + chilling

This jam stretcher is the least expensive and fastest to make of jam stretchers. It actually reduces the cost of jams by almost two-thirds. Can double as pie-filling.

2/3 cup (240 ml) generic (pectin) jam   1/2 cup (120 ml) granulated sugar
1 cup (240 ml) cold tap water   2 tbsp (30 ml) sweetened flavored
2 tbsp (30 ml) cornstarch   drink crystals
1/2 tsp (2 ml) margarine *(optional)*   *(flavor and color to match jam)*

Follow the *Pie Filling Stretcher* recipe *(page 148)*, it's the same idea. Store refrigerated. *Try quadrupling your jams!* **Makes about 2 cups (480 ml)**

Gelatin Jam Stretcher   8-10 minutes + chilling

Reduces the cost of jam by a bit more than half. Gives jams an odd consistency.

2/3 cup (240 ml) generic (pectin) jam   5/8 cup (150 ml) granulated sugar
1 cup (240 ml) cold tap water   2 tbsp (30 ml) sweetened flavored
2 tsp (10 ml) *bulk pre-bagged* gelatin   drink crystals
1 tsp (5 ml) lemon juice from   *(flavor and color to match jam)*
   concentrate

In a **small bowl**, combine 1/8 cup (30 ml) of the cold tap water and add the gelatin to soften it; let it sit for 5 minutes. Meanwhile, in a **saucepan**, add all remaining ingredients except the jam and dissolve while strring before heating. Heat over a medium-high heat while stirring occasionally with a **whisk** till thickened and bubbly. Turn off the heat and immediately add the gelatin/water mixture while stirring. Add jam and stir to dissolve. **Makes 2 cups (480 ml)**

Pectin Jam Stretcher   6-8 minutes + chilling

Reduces the cost of jam by at least 40 percent. It's the most expensive of the lot but is by far the best jam stretcher.

2/3 cup (240 ml) generic (pectin) jam   7/8 cup (210 ml) granulated sugar
1 cup (240 ml) cold tap water   2 tbsp (30 ml) sweetened generic
1 tbsp (15 ml) *bulk* pectin crystals   flavored drink crystals
2 tsp (10 ml) lemon juice from   *(flavor and color to match jam)*
   concentrate

In a saucepan, combine water and lemon juice; bring to a boil over a medium-high heat. Add pectin crystals and stir. Then add sugar and sweetenened flavored drink crystals; stir. Bring to a boil again and maintain another minute. Turn off heat; add jam and stir to dissolve. Store in jars. **Makes about 2 cups (480 ml)**

Sugar Syrup Jam Stretcher   1-2 minute

Use the *Sugar Syrup* recipe variation make with sweetened flavored drink crystals to match the flavor of jam , see page 217-18 for this. Try 2 parts syrup and 1 part generic jam; stir. Store jar in pantry. **Makes about 2 cups (480 ml)**

NOTE ON JAMS: *Although* **CookMISER** *does not contain any jam recipes that doesn't mean we don't recommend that you make your own jams. Actually, we're all for it, especially during peak fruit harvest season when fruits are very inexpensive. Since many good cookbooks on the market include jam recipes and because of the limited space in this book, we didn't include any.*

Mock Hot Pepper Sauce   *2 minutes*

It's a decent low-cost pepper sauce though not quite of the superior quality as those aged in white oak barrels for years. At about 1/20th the supermarket prices, use it, be merry, and above all don't complain about its inferior quality. Think of it as sort of an emergency replacement sauce.

4 1/2 tsp (22 ml) white vinegar	1/8 tsp (1/4 ml) table salt
1 tsp (5 ml) canned ground tomatoes	1 tsp (5 ml) red cayenne pepper
OR 1/2 tsp (2 ml) tomato paste	

In a **small jar**, combine ingredients; tighten cap and shake. It's better to let it gain strength for a day or two before using it in recipes. **Makes 1/8 cup (30 ml)**

Tofu & Cheese Sauce   *10 minutes*

Starting with the *Cheese (Stretcher) Sauce* (and basic) recipe *(see page 142),* use only 1/4 cup (60 ml) of grated 'old' Cheddar, and replace the 1/4 cup (60 ml) of instant skim milk powder with 1/3-1/2 cup (80-120 ml) of mashed or unpressed tofu. Blender all ingredients except margarine and cook as outlined. **Makes at least 1 1/2 cups (360 ml)**

Mozzarella Cheese Stretcher   *6-7 minutes*

Try this cheese stretcher on pizza instead of the real thing, or top it with grated Mozzarella or any other cheeses. It's much lower in saturated fats and cost to make about 1/3rd the price of the cheese it replaces. This recipe is usable but not fantastic.

1 1/2 cups (360 ml) cold tap water	1/8 tsp (1/2 ml) table salt
3/8 cup (90 ml) *Homemade Yogurt*	1/8 tsp (1/2 ml) *Caramelized*
(see pages 232-3)	*Sugar Coloring (see pg. 243)*
2 tbsp (30 ml) *bulk* instant skim milk	1/4 cup (60 ml) vegetable oil
powder	2 tbsp (30 ml) margarine
3/8 cup (90 ml) all-purpose flour	1/2 cup (120 ml) Mozzarella
2 tbsp (30 ml) *Homemade Tofu*, mashed	cheese, crumbled or grated
(optional, see page 239-40)	1 tbsp (15 ml) lightly sautéed
	grated yellow onion *(optional)*

Better try this recipe without tofu, its was added to the recipe for nutrition. Place all ingredients except fat and cheese in a **blender**, and process on high 15-20 seconds or at least one minute if using tofu. In a large **saucepan** or **skillet**, quickly whisk together and heat on a medium-high setting till thickened. Cook another minute and remove from heat. Whisk in the oil, margarine, and grated or crumbled cheese until melted. Do not over-whisk *(no more than 30 seconds).* Save in a covered bowl chilled or pour it while hot over pizza or over a thin layer of real grated fresh Mozzarella cheese before adding final toppings. **Makes 2 cups (480 ml)**

LITE! **VERSION** *Reduce the oil and margarine content to a minimum but don't exclude them entirely. Use a low-fat cheese to begin with!*

Uniform Thickness Rolling

Try this rolling method with nougat, paste, and non-resilient dough. Use low-cost jointed pine wood sticks of appropriate thickness (eg. 3/8 square/1 cm square) for this.

Instant Mock Toffee   *4-5 minutes + chill*
1 cup (240 ml) granulated sugar   2 tbsp (30 ml) all-purpose flour
1/4 cup (60 ml) low-cost margarine

In a **heavy-bottomed saucepan**, melt the sugar over a medium-high heat. Stir continously until sugar liquefies and the mass of melted sugar has taken a golden light-brown color. Quickly add margarine and flour while stirring. Pour unto a frozen **non-stick pan**, score surface and place in freezer a few minutes. Break into pieces when hardened. **Makes 3/4 cup (180 ml) or a dozen pieces**

Aerated Crunchie-Style Candy

Same idea as previous *Instant Mock Toffee* recipe, except that you stir in **1/2 tbsp (7 ml) of baking powder** after the margarine and flour.
VARIATION *Make **Crunchie-Style Chocolate-Coated Bars** by cutting the pieces about the size of chocolate bars and coating with chocolate, see pages 210-11!*

Chocolaty Coating for Frozen Treats   *15-20 minutes*
This thin low-cost chocolate dip was designed especially for our ice cream bars and cones. Use it at a low temperature (100°F/38°C) to minimize ice cream melt.
1 cup (240ml) generic-brand semi-   1 cup (240ml) low-cost margarine
   sweet or chocolate flavored chips   2 tbsp (30 ml) vegetable oil
3 tbsp (45ml) *bulk* cocoa powder   *(optional)*

Follow the instructions on page 211. When enjoying frozen treats coated by it, don't touch the treat directly with your hand, instead keep the treat partially wrapped in its plastic bag or wrapper. **Makes almost 2 cups (480 ml)**

Super-Fast Cakes   *10-12 minutes*

Using the *Basic Cake* recipe or one of its variations *(pages 197-8)*, bake batter in **two greased medium-size baking sheets** (jelly-roll pans) at the recipe temperature but for about five minutes only till golden brown. *Use a rubber spatula to quickly spread a thin batter in pans.*

PLEASE KEEP IN MIND *that* **CookMISER** *is a book of ideas, if you don't like one, joyfully move on to the next. It doesn't matter that they're not necessarily all winners. The important thing is that the book or its contents averages well. Moreover, always test new, complex or bizarre recipes by yourself before subjecting your family, friends, or guests to them.*

INDEX

Order Form

 BOOKS ☐ Paperback (CAN. $14.95) $9.95 U.S.

☐ Spiral Binding (CAN. $17.95) $11.95 U.S.

Mail to:
Scrypt publishing
P.O.B. 624 Snowdon Station
Montreal Quebec H3X 3X8

QTY	PAPERBACK OR SPIRAL BINDING	PRICE
	SUBTOTAL_____	

Send check or money order__Subtotal plus $3.00 CAN/ $2.00 U.S. for postage and handling (Canadian orders add 7% GST) (Quebec orders add 7.5% PST too)__No cash or COD's please__**Please allow six to eight weeks for delivery**

Name_____

Address_____

City_____State/Prov._____

Zip/Postal code_____

✂ —

Order Form

 BOOKS ☐ Paperback (CAN. $14.95) $9.95 U.S.

☐ Spiral Binding (CAN. $17.95) $11.95 U.S.

Mail to:
Scrypt publishing
P.O.B. 624 Snowdon Station
Montreal Quebec H3X 3X8

QTY	PAPERBACK OR SPIRAL BINDING	PRICE
	SUBTOTAL_____	

Send check or money order__Subtotal plus $3.00 CAN/ $2.00 U.S. for postage and handling (Canadian orders add 7% GST) (Quebec orders add 7.5% PST too)__No cash or COD's please__**Please allow six to eight weeks for delivery**

Name_____

Address_____

City_____State/Prov._____

Zip/Postal code_____